Responsible Innovation

T0338210

Responsible Innovation

Managing the responsible emergence of science and innovation in society

Edited by

RICHARD OWEN
University of Exeter, Exeter, UK

JOHN BESSANT
University of Exeter, Exeter, UK

and

MAGGY HEINTZ
French Embassy, London, UK

A John Wiley & Sons, Ltd., Publication

This edition first published 2013
© 2013 John Wiley & Sons, Ltd

Registered office
John Wiley & Sons Ltd, The Atrium, Southern Gate, Chichester, West Sussex, PO19 8SQ, United Kingdom

For details of our global editorial offices, for customer services and for information about how to apply for permission to reuse the copyright material in this book please see our website at www.wiley.com.

The right of the author to be identified as the author of this work has been asserted in accordance with the Copyright, Designs and Patents Act 1988.

All rights reserved. No part of this publication may be reproduced, stored in a retrieval system, or transmitted, in any form or by any means, electronic, mechanical, photocopying, recording or otherwise, except as permitted by the UK Copyright, Designs and Patents Act 1988, without the prior permission of the publisher.

Wiley also publishes its books in a variety of electronic formats. Some content that appears in print may not be available in electronic books.

Designations used by companies to distinguish their products are often claimed as trademarks. All brand names and product names used in this book are trade names, service marks, trademarks or registered trademarks of their respective owners. The publisher is not associated with any product or vendor mentioned in this book. This publication is designed to provide accurate and authoritative information in regard to the subject matter covered. It is sold on the understanding that the publisher is not engaged in rendering professional services. If professional advice or other expert assistance is required, the services of a competent professional should be sought.

The publisher and the author make no representations or warranties with respect to the accuracy or completeness of the contents of this work and specifically disclaim all warranties, including without limitation any implied warranties of fitness for a particular purpose. This work is sold with the understanding that the publisher is not engaged in rendering professional services. The advice and strategies contained herein may not be suitable for every situation. In view of ongoing research, equipment modifications, changes in governmental regulations, and the constant flow of information relating to the use of experimental reagents, equipment, and devices, the reader is urged to review and evaluate the information provided in the package insert or instructions for each chemical, piece of equipment, reagent, or device for, among other things, any changes in the instructions or indication of usage and for added warnings and precautions. The fact that an organization or Website is referred to in this work as a citation and/or a potential source of further information does not mean that the author or the publisher endorses the information the organization or Website may provide or recommendations it may make. Further, readers should be aware that Internet Websites listed in this work may have changed or disappeared between when this work was written and when it is read. No warranty may be created or extended by any promotional statements for this work. Neither the publisher nor the author shall be liable for any damages arising herefrom.

Library of Congress Cataloging-in-Publication Data

Responsible innovation / edited by Professor Richard Owen, Professor John Bessant, Dr. Maggy Heintz.
   pages cm
   Includes index.
   ISBN 978-1-119-96636-4 (cloth)
   1. Technological innovations–Environmental aspects. 2. New products–Environmental aspects. 3. Research, Industrial–Moral and ethical aspects. I. Owen, Richard (Richard J.) II. Bessant, J. R. III. Heintz, Maggy.
   HD45.R394 2013
   338′.064–dc23

                                                                                          2013002826

A catalogue record for this book is available from the British Library.

ISBN (HB): 9781119966364
ISBN (PB): 9781119966357

Set in 10/12pt Times by Laserwords Private Limited, Chennai, India
Printed and bound in Malaysia by Vivar Printing Sdn Bhd

Contents

Foreword: Why Responsible Innovation?   **xi**
   Jack Stilgoe
Preface   **xvii**
List of Contributors   **xxiii**

1. Innovation in the Twenty-First Century   **1**
   John Bessant

   1.1   Introduction   1
   1.2   How Can We Innovate? – Innovation as a Process   3
   1.3   Where Could We Innovate? – Innovation Strategy   4
   1.4   Reframing Innovation   5
   1.5   Reframing Challenges for Twenty-First Century Innovation   9
       1.5.1   The Spaghetti Challenge   9
       1.5.2   The Sappho Challenge – Bringing Stakeholders into the Frame   14
       1.5.3   The Sustainability Challenge – Innovation for Sustainable
              Development   17
   1.6   Emergent Properties of the New Innovation Environment   21

2. A Framework for Responsible Innovation   **27**
   Richard Owen, Jack Stilgoe, Phil Macnaghten, Mike Gorman, Erik Fisher,
   and Dave Guston

   2.1   Introduction   27
   2.2   Context: the Imperative for Responsible Innovation   30
       2.2.1   Re-evaluating the Social Contract for Science and Innovation   30
       2.2.2   The Responsibility Gap   31
       2.2.3   The Dilemma of Control   33
       2.2.4   Products and Purposes: the Democratic Governance of Intent   34
   2.3   Locating Responsible Innovation within Prospective Dimensions of
       Responsibility   35
   2.4   Four Dimensions of Responsible Innovation   38
   2.5   Responsible Innovation: from Principles to Practice   39
       2.5.1   Some Experiments in Responsible Innovation   40
   2.6   Toward the Future: Building Capacity for Responsible Innovation   44

3. A Vision of Responsible Research and Innovation   **51**
René von Schomberg

3.1 Introduction: Technical Inventions, Innovation, and Responsibility   52
3.2 Responsible Research and Innovation and the Quest for the Right
     Impacts of Research   54
3.3 Defining the Right Impacts and Outcomes of Research   56
3.4 From Normative Anchor Points Toward the Defining of "Grand
     Challenges" and the Direction of Innovation   58
3.5 Responsible Research and Innovation: Organizing Collective
     Responsibility   59
     3.5.1 Some Examples of Irresponsible Innovation   60
3.6 A Framework for Responsible Research and Innovation   63
     3.6.1 Use of Technology Assessment and Technology Foresight   65
     3.6.2 Application of Precautionary Principle   67
     3.6.3 Innovation Governance   67
3.7 Outlook   71

4. Value Sensitive Design and Responsible Innovation   **75**
Jeroen van den Hoven

4.1 Introduction   75
4.2 Innovation and Moral Overload   77
4.3 Values and Design   78
4.4 Responsible Innovation   80

5. Responsible Innovation – Opening Up Dialogue and Debate   **85**
Kathy Sykes and Phil Macnaghten

5.1 A Short History of Controversies about Science and Technology   85
5.2 The Evolution of Public Engagement   87
5.3 The Case of Genetically Modified Foods in the UK   90
5.4 Sciencewise and the Institutional Embedding of Public Engagement in
     the UK   92
5.5 Motivations for Public Dialogue   94
5.6 The Claims for Public Dialogue   97
5.7 How (and When) Can Debate and Dialogue Be Opened Up?   99
5.8 The Substance of Public Concerns and Their Implications for
     Governance   102
5.9 Concluding Remarks   104

**6. "Daddy, Can I Have a Puddle Gator?": Creativity, Anticipation,
     and Responsible Innovation**   **109**
David H. Guston

6.1 Introduction   109
6.2 Understanding Anticipation   111

6.3   The Politics of Novelty   112
6.4   The Challenge of Speculative Ethics   114
6.5   Conclusion   116

7. **What Is "Responsible" about Responsible Innovation? Understanding the Ethical Issues**   **119**
    Alexei Grinbaum and Christopher Groves

    7.1   Introduction   119
    7.2   The Changing Meaning of Responsibility   120
            7.2.1   From the Divine Corporation to the Sovereign Individual   120
            7.2.2   Knowledge, Uncertainty, and Human Finitude   123
            7.2.3   Reciprocal and Non-Reciprocal Responsibility   126
    7.3   Beyond the Sovereign Individual: Collective Responsibility, Desire, and Cultural Narratives   128
            7.3.1   Passion Sits Alongside Reason   128
            7.3.2   Non-Consequentialist Individual Responsibility   130
            7.3.3   Collective Political Responsibility   132
            7.3.4   The Virtues of Responsible Innovation   134
            7.3.5   Narratives Take over Where Cost–Benefit Analysis Fails   135
    7.4   Conclusion: Responsibility and Meaning   139

8. **Adaptive Governance for Responsible Innovation**   **143**
    Robert G. Lee and JudithPetts

    8.1   Introduction   143
    8.2   Risk and Adaptive Governance   145
    8.3   Responsibility and Accountability   147
    8.4   The Rationale for Regulation   150
    8.5   Risk Regulation and Accountability for Product Safety   151
    8.6   The Adaptation of Risk Regulation   154
    8.7   Adaptive Innovation Governance: Limits and Needs   158
    8.8   Conclusion   160

9. **Responsible Innovation: Multi-Level Dynamics and Soft Intervention Practices**   **165**
    Erik Fisher and Arie Rip

    9.1   Introduction   165
    9.2   Discourse and Activities at Different Levels of Governance   166
            9.2.1   International and Bi-Lateral Meetings   167
            9.2.2   Legislative Initiatives   168
            9.2.3   Research Funding Agencies   169
            9.2.4   Intermediary Organizations and Consortia   171
            9.2.5   Concrete Activities   172
    9.3   Two Cases of "Soft" Intervention   173
            9.3.1   STIRing the Capacities of Science and Innovation Practitioners   173

9.3.2   Constructive Technology Assessment (CTA) of Newly
Emerging Science and Technology   175
9.4   Concluding Observations on Governance   177

10. Responsible Innovation in Finance: Directions and Implications   185
Fabian Muniesa and Marc Lenglet

10.1   Introduction   185
10.2   Perspectives on Responsible Innovation in Finance   187
10.2.1   Perspective on Function   187
10.2.2   Perspective on Moral Rules   188
10.2.3   Perspective on Internalized Values   188
10.2.4   Perspective on Aggregate Consequences   189
10.2.5   Perspective on Accountability   189
10.2.6   Perspective on Precaution   190
10.2.7   Perspective on Democracy   191
10.3   Some Directions for Further Reflection   191
10.4   Conclusion   194

**11. Responsible Research and Innovation in Information and
Communication Technology: Identifying and Engaging with the Ethical
Implications of ICTs   199**
Bernd Carsten Stahl, Grace Eden, and Marina Jirotka

11.1   Introduction   199
11.2   Conceptualizing Responsibility and Responsible Research and
Innovation in ICT   200
11.2.1   Responsibility as a Social Ascription   200
11.2.2   Responsible Research and Innovation as Meta-Responsibility 201
11.2.3   Responsible Research and Innovation: the Four "P"s   202
11.3   Building a Framework for RRI in ICT   203
11.3.1   Product: ICTs and Their Ethical Implications   203
11.3.2   People: Landscape of ICT Ethics   208
11.3.3   Process: Governance of RRI in ICT   212
11.4   Critical Reflections   214
11.4.1   The Meta-Responsibilities of RRI   214
11.4.2   Further Research   215

12. Deliberation and Responsible Innovation: a Geoengineering Case Study   219
Karen Parkhill, Nick Pidgeon, Adam Corner, and Naomi Vaughan

12.1   Introduction   219
12.2   Public Perceptions of Geoengineering   222
12.3   Exploring Public Perceptions of Geoengineering: an Empirical Study   223
12.3.1   Context   223
12.3.2   Method: Deliberating SPICE   224
12.3.3   Analysis   225

12.4 Public Perceptions of Geoengineering through the Lens of Responsible
     Innovation   226
     12.4.1 Intentions   226
     12.4.2 Responsibility   229
     12.4.3 Impacts   231
     12.4.4 The Role of the Public   232
12.5 Conclusion: Geoengineering – Responsible Innovation?   234

13. Visions, Hype, and Expectations: a Place for Responsibility   **241**
Elena Simakova and Christopher Coenen

13.1 Introduction   241
13.2 The Repertoires of Nano Futures   243
13.3 Narratives of Responsibility   253
     13.3.1 Narrative 1: Nanofutures, Boundary Work and Technology
           Assessment Activities in the US and Germany   253
     13.3.2 Narrative 2: Responsibility as Knowledge and Technology
           Transfer in the United States   256
13.4 Narratives, Visions and Conflicts: Lessons for RRI?   259

Endnotes: Building Capacity for Responsible Innovation   **269**
Jonny Hankins

     Building Capacity for Responsible Innovation: Awareness
     and Engagement   271
     Less Stick and More Carrot: Building Capacity through Education   272

Index   **275**

Foreword: Why Responsible Innovation?

Jack Stilgoe

This disparity between rich and poor has been noticed... Whatever else survives to the year 2000, that won't. CP Snow, The Two Cultures *(1959)*

CP Snow's 1959 Rede lecture is most famous for the dichotomy that it diagnosed (and so exacerbated) between the sciences and the arts. Snow's feeling was that, if science was to realize its almost limitless potential, it needed to better connect with the cultures around it. In going on to make a prediction that science would alleviate global poverty within four decades, Snow was not the first clever man to be let down by his foresight. Quotes from leading innovators (almost certainly apocryphal) that reveal a laughable pessimism are readily Googleable: "I think there is a world market for maybe five computers" (Thomas Watson, founder of IBM); "Some day, every town in America will have one of these" (Alexander Graham Bell, talking about the telephone). Snow's prediction fell the other way. So optimistic was he about the power of science that he imagined even the toughest social problems would succumb to a technological fix soon enough.

Here we are, five decades later and twelve years after Snow's deadline. The gap between the global rich and global poor has got larger, while the productivity of science has exponentially increased. Science, as Francis Bacon described it, is about both "intellectual enlightenment" and "the relief of man's estate." One could be forgiven for thinking there had been rather more emphasis on the former than the latter.

It is clearly unfair to focus on the unmet promises that others have made for science while ignoring its vast, often unpredictable, often serendipitous benefits. At least in rich countries, the products of scientific research and technological innovation are visibly woven into our everyday lives. And even in those countries where people do not see the same share of benefits, there is unarguable evidence of science-led progress in medicine, agriculture and other areas. But if we let science and innovation take credit for these transformative advantages, we should not be afraid of also asking where responsibility lies for the unrealized promises and unintended consequences of innovation. The broad aim of responsible innovation is to connect the practice of research and innovation in the present to the futures that it promises and helps bring about.

Discussions of responsibility in science often zoom in on individuals. We point to heroes such as Jonas Salk, who gave away the Polio vaccine that he invented, or Joseph Rotblat, the physicist-turned-nuclear disarmament campaigner. And we have our caricatured antiheroes – Drs Frankenstein, Strangelove and co. This emphasis on individual morality gives us codes of conduct or Hippocratic Oaths, but it gets us no closer to understanding why Snow made his grand prediction, nor why the world has failed to live up to it. We must instead find ways to analyze, describe and change how systems of innovation engage, not just with their intended or envisaged futures, but with a full range of implications. The connection between scientific discovery and innovation is not as straightforward as many scientists would like to claim. This linear model is less fiercely defended when things go wrong. The pattern in the past has been that, in matters of innovation, science takes the credit while society gets the blame. Innovation is rarely so heroic.

With a systemic view, we can see the problems clearly enough. According to one analysis, 90% of the world's pharmaceutical research is targeted at the common diseases of the richest 10% of the world's population (the so-called "90/10" gap). This sort of imbalance is not inevitable. There are reasons why the world's combined innovative capacity has spewed forth iPhones and space shuttles but not yet managed to produce clean energy or universal access to clean water. If such inequities trouble us, we might explain them away as an artifact of conventional market and political mechanisms. Or we might choose to interrogate science and innovation themselves.

Once we lift the lid on innovation to reveal its politics, we can start to see that, for all of the good intentions of individual researchers, innovation can be a form of what Ulrich Beck calls "organized irresponsibility." Scientists may insist that efficient science demands autonomy – "let us get on with the research; society can worry about the implications." This division of moral labor follows a perennial science policy debate, played out in another era between Michael Polanyi and J.D. Bernal, about the desirability of controlling the direction of scientific research. A university research scientist, facing growing administrative burdens and shrinking research budgets, might argue that Bernal has won the day. But, when it comes to questions of responsibility, Polanyi's maxim that "you can kill or mutilate the advance of science, [but] you cannot shape it," still echoes.

This book is a response to a problem – innovation's systemic irresponsibility – as well as a progress report on a range of activities that have, from different directions, tried to improve the situation. As David Guston describes in Chapter 6, emerging technologies have become a testing ground for new approaches to governance. Fisher and Rip (Chapter 9) take nanotechnology as an example, Stahl and colleagues (Chapter 11) focus on information and communication technologies (ICT), Parkhill and colleagues (Chapter 12) consider geoengineering and Guston himself points to the debate about synthetic biology. The hope is that, before these technologies are fully formed, we might be able to nudge their trajectories in various ways toward responsible, desirable futures. These radically innovative areas are the sites of both scientific and governance experiments. Scientists and research funders in Europe, the United States and elsewhere, have recognized the need for new forms of public engagement (see the Chapters 5 and 12) and interdisciplinary collaboration (Chapters 6 and 9). There is a growing recognition that the questions brought to the surface by each Next Big Thing (Who benefits? Who decides? What are the risks? Who's in control? What if we're wrong? What are the alternatives? Who's responsible? etc.) are not unique to a particular technology and they will only get louder as research presents ever more disruptive possibilities for intervention, be it in our genes, our natural environments, our economies or our private lives. The alternative ways of governing described in this book should be taken as an antidote to the narrative of inevitability that often accompanies new technologies. As befits an approach that is sceptical of technological fixes, tools such as public dialogue, constructive technology assessment, foresight or codes of conduct should not be taken as panaceas. The tools that are used should follow from the strategies that are adopted. Responsible innovation knits together activities that previously seemed sporadic or piecemeal.

The idea of Responsible Innovation, if it takes off, will be buffeted by political and economic headwinds. Those rich western economies that have historically oligopolized science and innovation now face economic crises of varying depths. These have narrowed the minds of policymakers, pushing environmental, global and intergenerational responsibilities down the agenda. De facto policies of hoping for the best and letting the future take care of itself appear to be taking hold. Public funding for science, at least in Europe and the United States, is static or waning, and researchers are expected to demonstrate that they are having ever-greater economic impact. The scientists' response, that it is foolhardy to predict and pick winners given the vagaries of research, is understandable. They might extend the same reasoning to responsible innovation, arguing that responsibility demands foresight, which, as CP Snow and others have discovered, is notoriously unreliable (see Chapter 7). Prediction is impossible, but anticipation of possible, plural futures is vital. The flipside of Polanyi's call for scientific autonomy is a rejection of the possibility of anticipation, which Guston argues is so vital, and so of responsibility.

The emerging thinking on Responsible Innovation contained in this book should help scientists assert their public value. Alongside governmental diktats to squeeze economic growth from science and innovation we see a growing policy interest in science tackling so-called "Grand Challenges" of sustainability, global health and food, water and energy security (see Chapter 3). Responsible innovation should help provide the foundation for policies that take grand challenges seriously. Responsible innovation seeks to avoid the problems of new technologies, but it also points to new opportunities. Cautionary tales of irresponsible innovation should be accompanied by stories of new innovation possibilities created through closer attention to particular responsibilities, such as the emergence of the world-beating Danish wind energy industry, following concerted Government policies that combined environmental and economic priorities.

If Responsible Innovation is to be viewed as a constructive endeavor, it must escape a predominant perception that is about regulation – saying "no" to things. Indeed, if Responsible Innovation is to make a difference, it will be through questioning the separation between innovation and regulation.

There's a game played at British village fetes called "splat the rat." The equipment is no more complicated than a piece of pipe, three or four feet long, nailed to a board. An over-confident child waits at the bottom of the pipe with some sort of whacking device – old cricket bat, grandfather's shoe, that sort of thing. The stallholder – let's say it's the vicar's wife – holds the toy rat in the top of the pipe. She lets the rat go. The child can either wait until the rat shoots out of the bottom or swing wildly at the plank beneath the pipe, anticipating the rat's arrival. Either way, the odds are against the child leaving with a prize. Nine times out of ten, the rat shoots out of the end of the pipe, unsplatted. The vicar's wife tries to hide her smile as another child walks away disappointed.

In pharmaceutical companies, innovation is often referred to as a "pipeline." Money and brainpower go in one end and useful technologies come out of the other. The governance of innovation, in such a model, happens at the end of the pipe. The regulator is the child with the splatting device, waiting for innovations to emerge. The regulator has to anticipate the arrival of the innovation and react accordingly, although the timing, size and shape of the particular technologies that emerge may all be unknown. Whether or not these innovations are controlled in the public interest is largely a question of luck.

We have become familiar with the limits of this regulatory duel. As Petts and Lee describe in Chapter 8, attempts to rationalize regulation, to make it more "risk-based", fail to acknowledge how little we know about the risks of new technologies. There is a litany of regulatory failure, from asbestos, through Thalidomide, to Mad Cow Disease and beyond. These cases strengthen arguments in favor of the precautionary principle, giving the child a bigger thing to whack with, asking the vicar's wife to tip back her pipe to slow down the rat, or demanding a transparent pipe. But there are those who argue that precaution has gone too far, stifling innovation. Transhumanists and others have started to talk about a "proactionary principle" that tips the balance of regulation back in favor of innovators. These arguments, which imagine innovation as a runaway train that can only be sped up or slowed down, are a reflection of failures further upstream. They presuppose a clear division of responsibility between innovator and regulator. If we are to imagine innovation being steered in more responsible directions, we need to bring these two imagined sets of interests together.

As Fisher and Rip describe in Chapter 9, a Responsible Innovation perspective distributes responsibility more evenly. The chapters in this book do not presume that the world can be divided into those who would promote technologies and those who would control them. There needs instead to be collective conversations, not just about the products of innovation, but also the purposes of innovation, the directions in which innovation appears to be pointing. Fisher and Rip refer back to earlier developments (pioneered by Rip and colleagues) in "constructive technology assessment" to make the point that, because technologies "co-evolve" from the interactions of many different interests, so we should see responsibility for their direction as a collective one.

This book tries to bring intellectual coherence to a diverse set of practices. But it also strives to be useful. Responsible Innovation is necessarily responsive, in two senses of that word. First, asking the questions is not enough. We need to start demanding answers, particularly from those institutions involved in the governance of innovation. And second, we need to make our innovation systems more flexible, more resilient and more resistant to various technological lock-ins.

In the UK, the Engineering and Physical Sciences Research Council have recognized the need for a systematic approach to Responsible Innovation and have been open-minded enough to involve me and others in their thinking. The framework that we outline in this book (Chapter 2) is, we hope, both coherent and practically applicable.

As with any new idea that attracts the attention of policymakers, there is a need for researchers to maintain a critical awareness of the ways in which Responsible Innovation is publicly invoked. There is a danger that the term becomes a polite label for the status quo. After all, who would argue against it? Who would wave a flag for Irresponsible Stagnation? If Responsible Innovation is to make a difference, there needs to be clarity about what it is and, crucially, what it isn't. Two chapters in this book explore the reality of "responsibility" (Chapter 7) and "innovation" (Chapter 1). Both notions are multi-dimensional. Responsibility is not synonymous with liability, and innovation looks less and less like a pipeline, if indeed it ever resembled one. Again, the picture that emerges should reassure innovators. Responsible innovation starts from an understanding of innovation as a system, a web of myriad actors, rather than a pipe. As Bessant describes, users are becoming increasingly assertive in innovation processes, so we must include them in the web along with scientists, entrepreneurs, governments and others. This complexity gives innovation the unpredictability that flummoxes Snow and others, but it suggests opportunities for previously closed conversations about innovation to include new perspectives and new questions. In computing, we see the rapid growth of particular innovations such as Facebook, driven by users, force new questions about privacy as the volume of available personal data explodes. If we turn, as Muniesa and Lenglet do in Chapter 10, to the world of finance, we can see that Responsible Innovation is made more complicated by the hybrid nature of financial innovations. But if the credit crisis has taught us anything, it is that efforts to govern complex systems should not be deterred by complexity.

There is a danger that any discussion of science and innovation policy gets bogged down in the technical intricacies of a particular area, be it finance, computing, geoengineering or nanotechnology. The chapters in this book suggest that, if we take a step back, to ask what responsible innovation might look like in general, the view we get can form the basis of a new approach to governance.

Preface

On April 1st 1956 the science fiction film Forbidden Planet went on general release. With echoes of Shakespeare's The Tempest, and featuring an innovative electronic music score and award-winning special effects, it is considered to be one of the greatest science fiction films of its time. The creative arts have always provided engaging ways to think about the promise and perils of science, technology and innovation, from Shelley's Frankenstein to Ridley Scott's Bladerunner. Forbidden Planet is no exception.

Set in the early twenty-third century, it opens with a United Planets cruiser approaching a distant planet called Altair IV, some 16 light years from Earth. The cruiser and its crew, captained by a young-looking Leslie Nielsen, have been dispatched to find out what has happened to a scientific expedition sent to Altair IV 20 years earlier. On approaching the planet the crackly voice of Dr Edward Morbius radios to warn them away and to turn back. He and his daughter are the lone survivors of the expedition, the others of which had been mysteriously killed by a dark and terrible planetary force, and he cannot guarantee the crew's safety. The crew land anyway, where they are astonished to be met by a highly advanced robot called Robby, 'tinkered together' by Morbius, which whisks them away to Morbius' residence, a home filled with a staggering array of technology the like of which they have never seen before. How did such wonders come about?

Morbius provides an explanation for this world of technological wonder. Taking them on a voyage deep within the planet he shows them a vast, intact citadel with 92 thermonuclear reactors, constructed by a long gone civilisation – the Krell. They had invented a machine – the "plastic educator"– which allowed the Krell to advance their intellectual capacity to unbelievable heights, to create 3D thought projections, materializing any object they could imagine: creation by mere thought. But all was not well on Altair IV. In advancing their intellect the Krell had also unwittingly heightened the dark forces of their subconscious – "monsters from the Id!", and on one night 200 000 years ago these forces overcame their civilisation, which was destroyed in a finale of brutal self-destruction. Morbius' use of the plastic educator had allowed him to create Robby, but now his own monsters were also being awoken, threatening the crew whom he feared would intrude on his world, taking him back to Earth....

Well of course Forbidden Planet is science fiction: we are not the Krell and we do not inhabit a planet 16 light years from Earth. But even so, this story, the ending of which you will need to find out for yourself, illustrates some important features of science and innovation that are very real on our own planet. First, while science and innovation produce knowledge and value of many different kinds – in ways that can be radical and transformative – they also produce unanticipated impacts and unintended consequences. Our history is littered with the unintended consequences of innovations past, from destruction of stratospheric ozone by chlorofluorocarbons, to birth defects associated with thalidomide and mesothelioma associated with asbestos inhalation, to the near collapse of the global financial system in 2008, in which the innovation of complex financial products, such as the 'toxic' collateralized debt obligations based on 'subprime' asset-backed securities, played no small part. These unplanned impacts can cut across borders, and across generations, reflecting what Hans Jonas called the 'altered nature of human action'[1] of late modernity. Science and innovation, as Ulrich Beck noted, co-produce risks with value, and such risks must be expected to occur, to varying degrees. Unexpected impacts might not have led us to the same fate as the Krell, but sometimes it feels as if we may be sailing rather close to the wind.

The impacts of science and innovation are often unpredictable, and always uncertain. How on earth (or rather Altair IV) could the Krell have predicted that an innovation like the plastic educator would conjure up "monsters from the Id" so powerful they would bring about the extinction of their race? Clearly this was not an intended outcome. Innovation, and the science this is sometimes based on, cannot be thought of as a simple, linear process where a brilliant idea translates into a set of predictable, and manageable, outcomes. It is messy, often involving many, where interactions, uses, and applications may or may not come about, with dead-ends and with impacts that can be diverse and complex in nature. Techno-science and innovation are as much social as technical phenomena. The impacts of the plastic educator on the Krell were a complex interplay of technology and psychology, involving what some might describe as the 'naturalization' of technology as it makes its uncertain and unpredictable way in society, Krell or our own.

Here, on our own planet, our penchant for liberal market economies (at least in recent times) initially allowed us to hope that an Adam Smith-like "Invisible Hand" would be sufficient to govern the 'products' of innovation and their impacts – which could be best managed by market forces. The progressive introduction of regulation in many spheres (notably after Rachel Carson's bleak description of the "Silent Spring" that widespread use of pesticides was causing on wildlife post World War II and the environmental protection regulation that subsequently evolved) have reflected our awareness of the limits of Hayekian thinking, and the need for governance beyond the market. Such regulation, which is sometimes required before authorization, marketing, and use in areas of innovation, such as pharmaceuticals and industrial chemicals, is a powerful and important codification of responsibility that accords with the norms and values of society – the values of a clean environment, protection of health, and so on.

But the decades since the 1950s have also shown the limits of regulation itself in the face of the unpredictability, uncertainty and ignorance associated with science and innovation. Put simply, regulation can be partially sighted, or blind, to that which it has not encountered before, to new things that inhabit its margins, or lie beyond. Things like geoengineering, or nanotechnology, or synthetic biology. Innovation is about creativity, often about doing things differently, in instances where there may be no rules, or the rules are fuzzy and partial. It was David Collingridge who alerted us to the dilemma this presents, one that surfaces often in debates concerning precaution: we can either wait for sufficient evidence to make the case for control (for example by bringing in new regulation or amending it) but risking what he described as 'technological lock-in' that

---

[1] For this and other references cited refer to Chapter 2, in which a full bibliography is given

is, that the innovation is so embedded in society that control may come at huge cost, and be resisted by vested interests. Or we can act earlier on, when there is far greater scope for control – but where evidence of undesirable impacts is poor, the case for control weaker, and the risk of lost benefits in the future great. In this case we may decide not to act, and hope not to be subjected to what Bernard Williams described as moral luck – that in the fullness of time we may still be held morally accountable for our actions. We can hope not to be subjected to the same fate as Frankenstein, facing the demon of our creativity as it approaches us across the glacier. Or we can try to do something else. But what might that be?

These issues get to the very heart of this book. At its core is a set of perspectives that addresses a couple of difficult, but important challenges. The first of these is how we can proceed (innovate, conduct science) responsibly under such conditions of unpredictability, uncertainty, and ignorance. It was the physical chemist, economist and philosopher, Michael Polanyi, 60 years ago, who asserted that '*you can kill or mutilate the advance of science, you cannot shape it*'. In his independent "Republic of Science" scientists had role responsibilities – to produce knowledge, to adhere to norms of professional conduct associated with data falsification, with plagiarism and so on. As Heather Douglas has so eloquently written, to reflect on wider moral considerations has had limited place in such role responsibilities, establishing a clear moral division of labour. Douglas herself acknowledges the generalization inherent in this statement, quoting notable instances, such as the angst and actions of early nuclear physicists, who were concerned as much with the dangers as the wonders of their science. Indeed, most scientists and innovators would not wish to neglect their wider moral responsibilities, and many wish to see a better world as a result of their creativity. Many will understand the problems inherent within the independent Republic of Science, the Invisible Hand and regulation, and find the alternative position of succumbing to time, the risks of lock-in and moral luck unsettling and ethically problematic.

But this understanding is of only limited use if we cannot present a way forward, making clear (or at least beginning a conversation about) what "innovating responsibly" means, what it might involve, and how it might differ from what has come before. This is the aim of this book. It seeks to describe how we might conduct science and innovation responsibly under conditions of uncertainty and ignorance, collectively enlarging our role responsibilities to include a greater moral dimension, to those living now, those yet to be born, and those beyond our own species. This is not an easy feat. We cannot predict the future, but we can do our best to anticipate, to reflect, and deliberate on the future we are creating as this unfolds, to collectively steward this to acceptable and desirable ends in a way that is democratic, equitable and sustainable. The emphasis here is on the word 'we': this is a collective responsibility, reflecting the collective nature of science and innovation itself, where irresponsibility is a product not of the individual, but the system.

In order to tackle this there is a requirement to understand what responsibility means, particularly in the context of science and innovation as future-oriented activities with uncertain impacts. There is a need to consider the responsible in responsible innovation. Various chapters in the book, and notably the contribution by Chris Groves and Alexei Grinbaum, tackle the ambiguous term 'responsibility'. Here, you will be reminded of responsibility as accountability, answerability and liability, as consequentialism – and the problems these present for innovation, for reasons we have described above. Other framings of responsibility that are future-oriented in nature, and that accommodate uncertainty and values – dimensions of care and responsiveness – then become important. As Henry Richardson has written, those of us who are parents, or who have responsibilities for others in similar ways, will be very familiar with these dimensions. We understand that when acting responsibly, we cannot predetermine the lives, lovers, careers and crimes of our children, but we can instil in them values on which we hope they will conduct their lives, and then respond as they grow and change in the face of uncertainty and a changing world. When we think about responsibility in these sorts of ways, it starts to become easier to understand how to innovate responsibly.

This introduces an equally important challenge for responsible innovation, one that goes beyond understanding and managing unintended consequences. This challenge is about what we *do* want science and innovation to do, as much as what we want them *not to do*. What values do we want science and innovation to be anchored in, how can these values be democratically defined, and how can the inevitable tensions and dilemmas (e.g. between innovation for economic growth and environmental sustainability) be negotiated, and resolved. This is no longer just a question of the governance of unintended consequences, but one of the governance of intent, one that is about the very purposes, motivations and visions of scientists, innovators and those who fund them. These have been key considerations for ethically-problematic areas such as genetic modification and geoengineering, where the framing of intent and motivation becomes key. And yet current modes of research and innovation governance allow little scope for reflection on purposes and motivations, beyond narrowly configured ethical approval for research involving animals and people. The reader will find chapters in the book that discuss concepts of values-sensitive design, of the quest for the 'right impacts' of research and innovation. This is an important departure point for responsible innovation, challenging us to ask what kind of future we want from science and innovation, and the values this is based on. It will highlight an essentially political dimension to responsible innovation. And it will present responsible innovation not as a burden in which loss of freedom and the inhibition of creativity is a casualty, but as an opportunity to identify targets for science and innovation to create value in ways that are socially desirable. It would be easy for responsible innovation to become another form of ethical review, or a bureaucratic hurdle that is required but not valued. This is not the ambition of the authors of the chapters of this book. A broader reconfiguration, one that creates opportunity for innovation toward socially desirable ends, as well as opportunities for timely management, is needed. A reconfiguration that is values- and not rules-based, that is flexible in the face of uncertainty, and that allows us to take collective responsibility for a future which science and innovation play such critical roles in shaping.

The book is laid out in the following way: after setting the scene regarding the contemporary innovation landscape and its management in the first chapter, subsequent chapters in the book present a vision and framework for responsible innovation, including the call to embed integrated and iterative processes of individual and collective reflection, anticipation and broad deliberation in and around the science and innovation process itself, to include both its products (intended or otherwise) and purposes. This, as Andy Stirling has described, is a process of opening up, of inviting in, of encouraging debate and even contestation, understanding that the wider social context of science and innovation cannot be understood by personal reflection alone. Various elements of a proposed responsible innovation approach are then outlined in more detail, around, for example, the dimensions of anticipation, and opening up dialogue and debate; and the concept of responsibility itself is presented for philosophical analysis. Such dimensions have a rich history in the literature, including anticipatory governance, technology assessment in its various forms, upstream engagement and socio-technical integration. It is the further dimension of responsiveness that becomes important here – how we develop ways to respond at various scales (personally, institutionally, politically) to ensure innovation itself can look different in response. Chapters on dynamics of responsible innovation, governance and regulation develop further thinking on these themes. The book concludes with an important set of chapters that consider the emerging concepts of responsible innovation in important areas of contemporary science and innovation; in finance, in geoengineering, information technologies and nanotechnology.

Scholars will recognise important parallels and cognates, from the work of von Hippel to Callon, Jonas and many others, extending perhaps as far back as Francis Bacon. These provide important foundations for responsible innovation that should not be ignored, and from which the concept rightly will evolve. It is very important to note that this book does not purport to be a definitive guide to responsible innovation. Such hubris is both premature and may serve to lock-in the term itself at a time when study and open debate are what is needed. The book instead offers a set of perspectives in an evolving field that many are trying to make sense of and to understand in terms of motivation. It was Heraclitus who reminded us that we never step in the same river twice. Let us hope that many will have the opportunity to dip their toes.

The impetus for this book was an international workshop on Responsible Innovation[2] held at the Residence of the French Ambassador in London in May 2011, and funded by the Science and Technology department of the Embassy: many of the contributing authors attended this event. We are indebted to the French Embassy, without which this workshop, and consequently this book, would not have been possible. Our particular thanks go to Serge Plattard and intern Pauline Gandré. We would also like to thank the UK Engineering and Physical Sciences Research Council (and in particular Peter Ferris, Atti Emecz, Alison Wall, Nicola Goldberg and Nick Cook), and the Economic and Social Research Council (and in particular Andy Gibbs) and the UK Foreign and Commonwealth Office (and in particular Fabien Deswartes and Mark Sinclair of the Science and Innovation team) for their support. R.O. would also like to thank Michael Depledge, Geoff Petts and members of the sadly missed Royal Commission on Environmental Pollution for their support.

We dedicate this book to future generations who will, we hope, most benefit from it.

Richard Owen
John Bessant
Maggy Heintz
December 2012

[2] http://www.ambafrance-uk.org/Franco-British-workshop-on,18791

List of Contributors

Adam Corner, Cardiff University, School of Psychology, UK

Alexei Grinbaum, CEA-Saclay/LARSIM, France

Arie Rip, University of Twente, The Netherlands

Bernd Stahl, Centre for Computing and Social Responsibility, De Montfort University, UK

Christopher Coenen, Karlsruhe Institute of Technology (KIT), Germany

Christopher Groves, Cardiff University, ESRC Centre for the Economic and Social Aspects of Genomics, UK

David H. Guston, Arizona State University, USA

Elena Simakova, University of Exeter Business School, UK

Erik Fisher, Arizona State University, Consortium for Science, Policy and Outcomes, USA

Fabian Muniesa, Centre de Sociologie de l'Innovation, Mines ParisTech, France

Grace Eden, Oxford e-Research Centre, Oxford University, UK

Jack Stilgoe, University of Exeter Business School, UK

Jeroen van den Hoven, Delft University of Technology, The Netherlands

John Bessant, University of Exeter Business School, UK

Jonny Hankins, The Bassetti Foundation, Italy

Judith Petts, University of Southampton, Faculty of Social and Human Sciences, UK

Kathy Sykes, University of Bristol, UK

Karen Parkhill, Cardiff University, School of Psychology, UK

Marc Lenglet, European Business School, France

Marina Jirotka, Oxford e-Research Centre, Oxford University, UK

Mike Gorman, University of Virginia, USA

Naomi Vaughan, University of East Anglia, Norwich Research Park, UK

Nick Pidgeon, Cardiff University, School of Psychology, UK

Phil Macnaghten, Durham University, UK and State University of Campinas, Brazil

René von Schomberg, European Commission, Directorate General for Research and Innovation, Belgium

Richard Owen, University of Exeter Business School, UK

Robert G Lee, University of Exeter, Law School, UK

1

Innovation in the Twenty-First Century

John Bessant
University of Exeter Business School, UK

1.1 Introduction

It is not the strongest of the species that survives, nor the most intelligent that survives. It is the one that is the most adaptable to change

(Charles Darwin)

Darwin was right. His famous comment underlines one of the key challenges facing organizations – unless they are prepared to change what they offer the world and the ways they create and deliver those offerings they could be in trouble. The challenge is not whether or not to innovate, but *how?* This makes building the capability to deliver a steady stream of innovation a strategic imperative, not just for commercial organizations, but for any enterprise dealing with the turbulent conditions of the early twenty-first century. Public services struggling to balance rising demand and expectations of high quality delivery against the rising costs of provision need to seek new ways of meeting social needs. Third sector organizations concerned with improving social conditions recognize the importance of thinking and working in new directions if they are to gain attention and acquire the resources they need to carry through their agenda.

Innovation is about change and this can take place along a spectrum of increasing novelty, from simple incremental improvements – "doing what we do, but better" – through to radical, new to the world changes. The risks involved vary, as do the benefits,but it is clear that even sustaining growth through incremental innovation is not going to happen by accident. Any organization might get lucky once but in order to be

Responsible Innovation, First Edition. Edited by Richard Owen, John Bessant and Maggy Heintz.
© 2013 John Wiley & Sons, Ltd. Published 2013 by John Wiley & Sons, Ltd.

able to repeat the trick there is a need for some kind of organized, structured approach to managing the process. This needs to find answers to two key questions:

- *Where* can we innovate?

and

- *How* can we innovate?

The trouble is that innovation involves trying to hit a moving target. Environments constantly shift and pose new threats – new technologies appear, new markets emerge, the regulatory framework changes – and unless organizations have the capacity to innovate their approaches to innovation they may not survive in the long term. History is clear about this – very few organizations are long-term survivors and those which have managed to stick around for over 100 years have made some major changes to what they do and how they do it (Francis *et al.*, 2003).

Sometimes the changes are pretty dramatic, challenging the roots of where the company began and overturning a lot in the process. TUI, for example, is the largest European travel and tourism services company, owning (amongst others) Thomson Holidays, Britannia Airways, and Lunn Poly travel agents. Its origins, however, go back to 1917 where it began as the Prussian state-owned lead mining and smelting company! Nokia's key role as a leader in mobile telephony hides its origins as a diverse timber products conglomerate with interests as wide as rubber boots and toilet paper! One of the oldest companies in the world is the Stora company in Sweden, which was founded in the twelfth century as a timber cutting and processing operation. It is still thriving today – albeit in the very different areas of food processing and electronics.

A key dimension when exploring innovation lies in the concept of responsibility. Clearly, not all innovations are necessarily good things. Others may start out offering positive benefits, but later turn out to have unintended negative consequences. The famous example of DDT is a case in point – originally hailed as a breakthrough innovation in the field of pesticides it later turned out to have significant negative impacts. Other examples include the pharmaceutical thalidomide, nuclear power, and chlorofluorocarbons (CFCs) used as refrigerants and propellants.

The key issue is around how far we explore and consider innovation in its early stages in terms of the potential impacts it might have, and how far we are able and prepared to modify, ameliorate, or possibly abandon, projects which have the potential for negative effects – what Owen *et al.* (Chapter 2) describe as the dimension of responsiveness. It is this dimension and others (anticipation, reflection, and deliberation) which together underpin the concept of responsible innovation. The ways in which this can be conceptualized and operationalized in the face of uncertainty form the core theme of this book. Interestingly, much of the academic and policy-oriented innovation research tradition evolved around such concerns, riding on the back of the science and society movement in the 1970s. This led to key institutes (like the Science Policy Research unit at Sussex University) being established (Cole *et al.*, 1973). While a sophisticated toolkit of approaches and resources emerged from much of this pioneering work, its use has often been limited and considerations of "responsible innovation" have often been marginalized in strategic management thinking (although there have been some high profile exceptions, such as the long-running debate around genetically modified food – see Von Schomberg (Chapter 3).

The key themes and content of responsible innovation will be explored in detail in later chapters in this book. The purpose of this chapter is to look at how the twenty-first century environment is changing and the challenges this poses for innovating organizations: important context for the discussions of responsible innovation that follow. In the face of some radical technological, market, social, and political shifts, how should they be thinking in terms of adapting and configuring their innovation processes? What are the strategic options open to them and how could they best explore the innovation space? Of the bundle of learned behavior patterns which they make use of, which ones should they be doing more of, reinforcing and strengthening? Which ones should they be doing less of, or even stopping – things which worked in the past but may no longer be suitable approaches? And which new behaviors are they going to need to learn and practice to take advantage of the newly – emerging context in which they are operating?

Before we move to the challenges it is worth spending a little time looking at two core questions around where and how organizations could innovate.

1.2   How Can We Innovate? – Innovation as a Process

Unlike the cartoon image, innovation requires a little more than just a light-bulb moment as an idea flashes above someone's head. In reality it involves a journey, growing and shaping the original trigger idea into something which can spread across a population and create value. As Figure 1.1 shows, traveling along this road means finding answers to some key questions:

No organization starts with a perfect model of the innovation process. Instead it is something they build up through a learning process, trying out new behaviors and hanging on to those which work. Eventually these patterns of repeated and learned behaviors – "routines" – become embedded in "the way we do things around here" and take shape in the form of policies, procedures, and rules (Nelson and Winter, 1982; Zollo and Winter, 2002). They will vary between organizations – everyone finds their

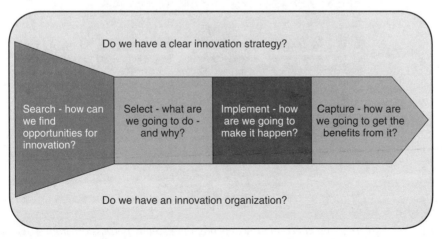

Figure 1.1   *Simple model of the innovation process (Reprinted with permission from [Tidd and Bessant, 2009] Copyright (2009) John Wiley & Sons Ltd)*

own particular way of answering the basic questions and some recipes work better than others. This is useful, since it allows us to learn not only through experience but also by watching how others manage the innovation task and grafting on useful new approaches and ideas.

However, we should also recognize that learning to manage innovation is not just a matter of building capability to deal with the questions of searching, selecting, implementing, and so on. Environments are unpredictable and complex, so we don't know what will emerge in the way of new threats or opportunities. So the key to long-term innovation management success is to build "dynamic capability" – to be able to step back and review our innovation process and reconfigure it on a continuing basis (Teece *et al.*, 1997). This is as much about letting go of old routines as it is about developing new ones.

1.3   Where Could We Innovate? – Innovation Strategy

Innovation can take many different forms – as Figure 1.2 suggests, there is plenty of space to explore (Francis and Bessant, 2005). We can think of four core dimensions:

- "product innovation" – changes in the things (products/services) which an organization offers;

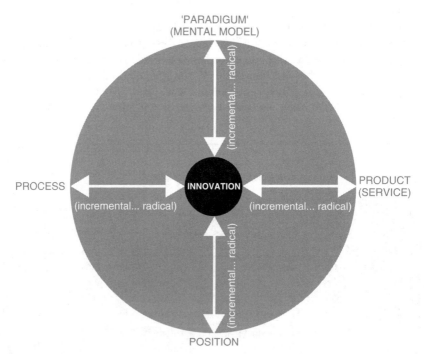

Figure 1.2 *Exploring the innovation space (Reprinted with permission from [Tidd and Bessant, 2009] Copyright (2009) John Wiley & Sons Ltd)*

- "process innovation" – changes in the ways in which products and services are created and delivered;
- "position innovation" – changes in the context in which the products/services are introduced;
- "paradigm innovation" – changes in the underlying mental models which frame what the organization does.

Table 1.1 gives some examples of these. In reality, of course, various combinations of incremental and radical innovation across these fields are possible. The key issue for any organization is to ensure that it explores its options thoroughly – it may choose not to pursue every idea but it is important to avoid being surprised!

1.4 Reframing Innovation

As I have discussed above, organizations create routines for managing the basic challenges of search (for innovation trigger signals), selection (resource allocation) and implementation. However, no organization can look at and respond to all the signals, and so it defines a search and selection space within which it innovates – and this selection environment shapes what it pays attention to and what it decides to do about it. It is of course not the only way of looking at the environment – reframing brings new challenges and opportunities to light and opens up new options for solving problems. This is what entrepreneurs do – seeing new or different elements within a different frame and exploiting innovation opportunities for this. This sets up the competitive dynamics which characterize innovation.

Established players are typically strong within their framed environment and have developed well-rehearsed and effective routines for dealing with it (March, 1991). But this can also mean that they lack the ability to search and explore in different ways or directions – often expressed as an inability to "think outside the box." At the limit – as Dorothy Leonard argues – their core competencies may become core rigidities, limiting the organization's ability to deal with changing conditions (Leonard, 1992).

We can map this challenge as in Figure 1.3, which provides a simple model of the innovation space. The vertical axis refers to the core activity of innovation – search, select, and implement – carried out in incremental steps or big leaps. The horizontal axis relates to environmental complexity – the number of different elements and the ways in which they interact. As we move to the right, new elements are brought into the frame and new challenges and opportunities emerge.

Using this space we can see four "zones" which have different implications for innovation management. Zones 1 and 2 are essentially the familiar territory of innovation, where established players dominate. They have well-developed routines for handling the search and selection problem and can not only exploit their well-defined space but also push its frontiers along key trajectories.

It is in zones 3 and 4 that the problems emerge for them since, by definition, these spaces involve bringing new elements into the frame and exploring new combinations. The old rules of the game don't apply here, and it is in this space that the entrepreneur's skills come to the fore. Being open and flexible and being able to reframe and reconfigure are key strengths and it is here that dynamic capability

Table 1.1   *Potential directions for innovation strategy*

Innovation type	Incremental – do what we do but better	Radical – do something different
Product – what we offer the world	Windows 7® and Windows 8® replacing Vista® and XP® – essentially improving on an existing software idea	New to the world software – for example, the first speech recognition program
	New versions of established car models – for example, the VW Golf essentially improving on established car design	Toyota Prius – bringing a new concept – hybrid engines. Tesla – high performance electric car.
	Improved performance incandescent light bulbs	LED-based lighting, using completely different and more energy efficient principles
	CDs replacing vinyl records essentially improving on the storage technology	Spotify® and other music streaming services – changing the pattern from owning your own collection to renting a vast library of music
Process – how we create and deliver that offering	Improved fixed line telephone services	Skype® and similar systems
	Extended range of stock broking services	On-line share trading
	Improved auction house operations	eBay®
	Improved factory operations efficiency through upgraded equipment	Toyota Production System® and other "lean" approaches
	Improved range of banking services delivered at branch banks	Online banking and now mobile banking in Kenya, Philippines – using phones as an alternative to banking systems
	Improved retailing logistics	On line shopping
Position – where we target that offering and the story we tell about it	Häagen-Daz® changing the target market for ice cream, from children to consenting adults	Addressing underserved markets – for example, the Tata Nano aimed at the emerging but relatively poor Indian market with cars priced around $2000
	Airlines segmenting service offering for different passenger groups – Virgin Upper Class, BA Premium Economy, and so on	Low cost airlines opening up air travel to those previously unable to afford it – create new markets and also disrupt existing ones
	Dell® and others segmenting and customizing computer configuration for individual users	Variations on the "One laptop per child" project – for example, Indian government $20 computer for schools

Table 1.1   (continued)

Innovation type	Incremental – do what we do but better	Radical – do something different
	On line support for traditional higher education courses	University of Phoenix and others, building large education businesses via online approaches to reach different markets
	Banking services targeted at key segments – students, retired people, and so on	"Bottom of the pyramid" (Prahalad, 2006) approaches using a similar principle but tapping into huge and very different high volume/low margin markets – Aravind eye care, Cemex® construction products
Paradigm – how we frame what we do	Bausch and Lomb – moved from "eye wear" to "eye care" as their business model, effectively letting go of the old business of spectacles, sunglasses (Raybans®), and contact lenses all of which were becoming commodity businesses. Instead they moved into newer high tech fields like laser surgery equipment, specialist optical devices, and research into artificial eyesight	Grameen Bank and other microfinance models – rethinking the assumptions about credit and the poor iTunes® platform – a complete system of personalized entertainment Cirque du Soleil – redefining the circus experience
	Dyson® redefining the home appliance market in terms of high performance engineered products	Amazon, Google, Skype – redefining industries like retailing, advertizing, and telecoms through online models
	Rolls Royce – from high quality aero engines to becoming a service company offering "power by the hour"	Linux®, Mozilla®, Apache® – moving from passive users to active communities of users co-creating new products and services
	IBM®, from being a machine maker to a service and solution company – selling off its computer-making operations and building up its consultancy and service side.	

*Reprinted with permission from [Tidd and Bessant, 2009] Copyright (2009) John Wiley & Sons Ltd

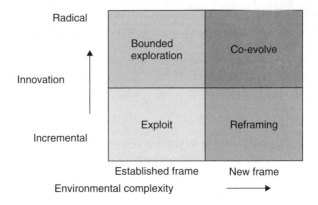

Figure 1.3   *Framing innovation space*

is an essential requirement. The problem for established players is that they cannot simply abandon their old approaches and adopt new ones – they face the challenge of overcoming well-established mindsets which see the world in particular ways – and they often have significant investments in the old spaces which they are unable or unwilling to relinquish. For them the challenge is exploring new spaces whilst simultaneously maintaining a "mainstream" approach to innovation; many writers talk about the problem of "ambidexterity" in this connection (Tushman and O'Reilly, 1996; Benner and Tushman, 2003; Birkinshaw and Gibson, 2004).

In particular, the reframing problem is difficult because it requires *rewiring* the knowledge systems which organizations use. As long as they stay within the frame, knowledge flows support a virtuous circle of *sustaining* innovation (Christensen, 1997). Smart firms are often radical innovators, pushing the frontiers of knowledge through extensive exploration, and they become adept at working closely with customers, suppliers, and other players to help them run a successful innovation system in which regular and well-managed searching leads to the kinds of innovations which that group of players value. Building strong ties generates a healthy flow of innovation and everyone wins.

However, when there is a need to look through a different frame, this set of assets becomes a liability. Knowledge flows along different channels and between different points, and new and different connections must be made. For a newcomer firm that is not a problem – its knowledge networks are laid down from scratch and the new opportunities offered by the emerging new model can start to be exploited. The trouble is that for established players there is a natural tendency to reinforce the existing systems since they used to work so well. This risks compounding the problem – the old networks can get in the way, overriding or clashing with the emerging new ones (Henderson and Clark, 1990).

This is at the heart of Christensen's observations about disruptive innovation. For example, when the computer disk drive industry began to change with the emergence of new players, the response of the incumbent players was not to sit still and do nothing. The problem was not that they did not listen to customers – they listened really well – but they were listening to the *wrong* customers and the organizational systems for reward and reinforcement supported the old wiring and made the emergence of new connections very difficult (Christensen, 1997).

1.5   Reframing Challenges for Twenty-First Century Innovation

It follows from the above model that moving into new innovation space involves being able to reframe in order to see and exploit new opportunities. Standing still may not be an option – staying on the left-hand side of the model risks something emerging on the right-hand side which disrupts the game – a pattern we have increasingly seen across sectors and even whole industries. For example, the role of the internet in opening up innovation space to new elements and players has radically transformed industries as diverse as bookselling, music creation and distribution, share dealing, banking, insurance, and travel.

In the following section we will look at three megatrends which are opening up the frame of innovation management, pushing us into the right-hand zones. They offer significant opportunity to those able to reframe, but may also pose threats to existing players unless they are able to deploy dynamic capability in reconfiguring their approaches. These challenges – which I call "spaghetti," "Sappho," and "sustainability" – are examples of a much broader range of issues which are emerging along the innovation frontier and which require us to rethink our approaches to innovation management.

1.5.1   The Spaghetti Challenge

At the heart of the innovation process is an engine which runs on knowledge. The fuel for innovation is different kinds of knowledge – about technological possibilities, market needs, legal options, financial issues, political enablers and constraints, and a host of other diverse knowledge sets. The innovation process works by weaving the various strands of this "knowledge spaghetti" into something which creates value (Bessant and Venables, 2008).

As I have noted earlier, we have learned a lot about effective ways to manage this knowledge spaghetti, bringing different knowledge sets together in various forms to build organizations which can deliver a steady stream of innovation. We recognize that innovation is a multi-player game; successful innovators work with a network of knowledge sources to create value. They understand and work with customers, drawing their knowledge into the process. They collaborate with key suppliers, bringing their expertise to bear. They may link to specialist institutions – universities, banks, technical centers – to pull in external knowledge, and they recruit new staff to bring knowledge into the organization. Within the organization they configure for knowledge flows between functions, units, and departments to allow for optimum combination, and they invest in creating their own knowledge – through R&D, market research, forecasting the future, and so on (Griffin *et al.*, 1996; Dodgson *et al.*, 2008; Goffin and Mitchell, 2010).

The idea of innovation as a knowledge-based, multi-player game is, of course, not new. Carter and Williams, for example, carried out a pioneering study in 1957 of "technically progressive" firms in the UK and found that the degree of "cosmopolitan" orientation (as opposed to "parochial") was a significant determinant of innovation success (Carter and Williams, 1957). In other words, those organizations with rich networks of connections were more likely to be successful innovators. This theme emerged in the many major studies of innovation throughout the 1960s and 1970s, – for example, Project SAPPHO stressed linkages as a critical factor while the Manchester "Wealth from knowledge" research provided extensive case examples of award-winning innovators who shared a common external orientation (Langrish *et al.*, 1972; Rothwell, 1992).

But we are working at a moving frontier, along which an increasing number of people are brought into the innovation game through a growing number of channels. Powerful technological shifts around information and communication, coupled with major social changes (in particular the rise of social networking) means that *the context in which innovation takes place is significantly different to even a decade ago.* A problem emerges when the amount of knowledge and its distribution outstrips the models we have been using to weave knowledge spaghetti to create value.

In his pioneering work on innovation management, Roy Rothwell drew attention to models of innovation which policy agents and practitioners make use of – how they think the innovation process works – and the limitations of these (Dodgson and Rothwell, 1995). Such mental models are important because they shape what decision-makers pay attention to, what they commit resources to, and how they manage the process. He suggested five generations of thinking about innovation management, moving from the simplistic linear push or pull models of the 1960s, through increasingly sophisticated coupling models which recognize the need for intra- and inter-organizational links. His 1992 paper predicted a fifth generation which would involve extensive use of ICT(information and communications technology), rich and diverse networking, which was globally-distributed (Rothwell, 1992). Within such a highly networked, multi-actor environment he foresaw that the emergent properties of the innovation system would be likely to require different approaches.

Table 1.2 gives some examples of the massive acceleration of change along several knowledge-linked trajectories which has changed the global landscape, and with it the innovation agenda. The issue for new and established organizations is increasingly one of finding new models to work in this "fifth generation" innovation world.

Under these conditions – an explosion of knowledge – the innovation emphasis moves from knowledge creation to knowledge *flow*. It is a much more fluid, open game with a constant swirl of knowledge around organizations, moving into and out from them. The term open innovation was coined by US professor Henry Chesbrough in 2003 and it neatly encapsulates the challenge. In a world which is so rich in knowledge, the message for even the largest, most research-active organization is clear – "*not all the smart guys work for us.*"

This has huge implications for the ways in which organizations work on innovation – as we can see in the well-documented case of the giant Procter and Gamble corporation (Huston and Sakkab, 2006). In the late 1990s they faced a number of innovation challenges; as CEO Alan Lafley explained: "*Our R&D productivity had levelled off, and our innovation success rate – the percentage of new products that met financial objectives – had stagnated at about 35%.*" Their response was to implement Connect + Develop[(SM)] – an innovation process based on open innovation principles (Lafley and Charan, 2008). The original target was to get 50% of innovations coming from outside the company. At the time only 35% of new products had elements which originated from outside. R&D productivity has since increased by nearly 60% and the innovation

Table 1.2   *Changing context for innovation*

Context change	Indicative examples
Acceleration of knowledge production	OECD estimates that around $750 billion is spent each year (public and private sector) in creating new knowledge – and hence extending the frontier along which breakthrough technological developments may happen.
Global distribution of knowledge production	Knowledge production is increasingly involving new players, especially in emerging market fields like the BRIC (Brazil, Russia, India, and China) nations – so there is need to search for innovation opportunities across a much wider space. One consequence of this is that "knowledge workers" are now much more widely distributed and concentrated in new locations – for example, Microsoft® third largest R&D Centre employing thousands of scientists and engineers is now in Shanghai, China.
Market expansion	Traditionally much of the world of business has focused on the needs of around 1 billion people since they represent wealthy enough consumers. But the world's population has just passed the 7 billion mark and population – and by extension market – growth is increasingly concentrated in non-traditional areas like rural Asia, Latin America, and Africa. Understanding the needs and constraints of this "new" population represents a significant challenge in terms of market knowledge.
Market fragmentation	Globalization has massively increased the range of markets and segments so that these are now widely dispersed and locally varied – putting pressure on innovation search activity to cover much more territory, often far from traditional experiences – such as the bottom of the pyramid conditions in many emerging markets (Prahalad, 2006) or along the so-called long tail – the large number of individuals or small target markets with highly differentiated needs and expectations.
Market virtualization	The emergence of large-scale social networks in cyberspace poses challenges in market research approaches – for example, Facebook® with 800 million members is technically the third largest country in the world by population. Further challenges arise in the emergence of parallel world communities – for example, Second Life® now has over 6 million "residents," while World of Warcraft® has over 10 million players.
Rise of active users	Although users have long been recognized as a source of innovation there has been an acceleration in the ways in which this is now taking place – for example, the growth of Linux has been a user-led open community development (Von Hippel, 2005). In sectors like media, the line between consumers and creators is increasingly blurred – for example, You Tube® has around 100 million videos viewed each day but also has over 70 000 new videos uploaded every day from its user base.
Development of technological and social infrastructure	Increasing linkages enabled by information and communications technologies around the internet and broadband have enabled and reinforced alternative social networking possibilities. At the same time the increasing availability of simulation and prototyping tools has reduced the separation between users and producers (Schrage, 2000; Gann, 2004).

Reprinted with permission from [Bessant and Venables, 2008] Copyright (2008) Edward Elgar Publishing.

success rate more than doubled – yet their R&D spend reduced from 4.8% of turnover in 2000 to 3.4% in 2007.

Successful open innovation strategies require new ways of accessing a wide and diverse set of ideas (NESTA, 2010) and connecting these to sites within the organization which can make effective use of them. In turn, this raises questions of networking and knowledge management, issues identified by Allen back in the 1970s but which are now coming to the fore in an era of social networking and enabling technologies (Allen, 1977; Dahlander and Gann, 2008). Much of the new challenge is about combining and creating communities of practice around key themes which transcend traditional organizational boundaries (Wenger, 1999; Brown and Duguid, 2000; Lafley and Charan, 2008).

Many organizations are using open innovation approaches – organizations such as the BBC®, LEGO®, and Ordnance Survey® are, for example, increasingly extending their networks to engage communities of software developers, sharing source code and inviting them to *"use our stuff to build your stuff."* This is the highly successful open model behind the Apple® Developer® Connection, an online community allowing thousands of developers to create applications which make the core product more attractive.

"Crowdsourcing" is another variant of open innovation, whereby companies open up their innovation challenges to the outside world, often in the form of a web-enabled competition. Swarovski®, the crystal company, has, for example, deployed crowdsourcing approaches to expand its design capacity, while Audi and BMW use it to prototype and explore new features. Other examples include:

- OSRAM, a leading lighting manufacturer which initiated a user idea generation platform. Designers and interested persons worldwide were invited to join the "LED-Emotionalize your light" community to create innovative light solutions with the latest LED (light emitting diode) technology. The goal of the contest was to involve interested users, developers, designers, and engineers in the innovation process in a new and exciting manner. Within only 11 weeks, 909 participants from nearly 100 countries joined the lighting community to showcase their talent and submit their ideas, including designs, technical solutions, and application scenarios of LED solutions. In total, they created 568 LED ideas and concepts in different segments, such as furniture, bathroom, outdoor locations, toys and children's play locations.
- The business model of Netflix®, the online and mail-order film rental business, depends on having a good understanding of what people want and tailoring advertising and offers to their preferences. In 2006, in an effort to improve the algorithm it used to develop these recommendations, it offered a $1 million reward – the Netflix Prize – to anyone who could improve the performance of its algorithm by 10% or better. Over 18 000 contestants from 125 countries registered within three months; within three years, there were 51 000 contestants from 186 countries, with 44 000 valid entries. Netflix's huge, global, if temporary, R&D laboratory that it created from the competition, produced over 7000 better algorithms.
- As the year 2000 approached, the mining company Goldcorp® was wrestling with the challenge of finding new sources of gold. In a radical departure from conventional surveying approaches the firm opened up its geological database and asked for ideas

about where it should prospect. Tapping into the combined insights of 1200 people from 50 countries helped the company locate 110 new sites, 80% of which produced gold. The business has grown from $100 million in 1999 to over $4 billion today.

The crowdsourcing model has also been applied in a variety of settings, including public sector and social enterprise. For example, the Bavarian government runs an innovation contest, encouraging its citizens to suggest ideas for new public services and how to improve the existing ones. In 2006 the Seoul Metropolitan Government launched an "ideas bank," inviting citizens to suggest ways of improving public services; by 2007 it was receiving around 140 ideas per day (74 000 over the year) and 1300 were implemented.

Researchers at the University of Erlangen-Nuremberg and the Center for Leading Innovation and Cooperation (CLIC) have identified and classified more than 360 innovation contests (www.innovation-contest.org). This database shows how widely the approach is being used and also the different forms in which such an open model can be deployed.

Another development has been the rise of innovation markets – essentially using the e-Bay® principle to link communities around innovation themes. A good example is InnoCentive® (www.innocentive.com) – an online marketplace where innovation seekers and solution providers meet. The company was launched in 2001 by former employees of Eli Lilly & Co and offers a broad range of open innovation services to companies to leverage their internal R&D with external innovators. R&D problems are framed as challenges and offered on the online marketplace to a large community of more than 200 000 innovators (so-called solvers) worldwide. Successful solvers are offered a cash award for their submissions. From an organizational perspective, InnoCentive acts as an intermediary between companies seeking solutions to innovation challenges and innovators worldwide interested in proposing solutions to these challenges.

Recombinant innovation is another variant of open innovation, using ideas developed in one world to good effect in another. Cross-sector learning throws some unlikely partners together and opens up new ways of looking at old problems. For example, low cost airlines like Ryanair® and Easyjet® learned about rapid turnaround in airports by watching pit stop teams in Formula1®, while the UK National Health Service is learning powerful lessons about patient safety from oil rigs, chemical plants, and aircraft cockpits.

Open innovation is not simply about casting a wide net. It may also involve a more intimate exchange of ideas, requiring a high degree of trust, between new partners who may be able to share ideas and intellectual property but who would not normally have made such a connection. Third party agencies, innovation brokers, often act as intermediaries that bring parties together and enable the sharing of ideas in a controlled and high trust environment. Models used range from online dating agencies through to more people-based approaches, such as the trusted intermediary model used by the Innovation Exchange®, which places skilled individuals within companies and then enables those individuals to regularly share information under high trust conditions.

Opening up the innovation search activity and reframing from closed to open models is clearly a rich source of new opportunity but exploiting it will depend on building new innovation management capabilities – and letting go of some well-established ones. Amongst the challenges which moving to open innovation poses are:

- **Intellectual property management** – in an open innovation world how do creators of knowledge appropriate the gains from their investments in creating knowledge?
- **Connectivity** – how are the rich new linkages which social and technological change make possible enabled? Who/what are the mechanisms for broking and bridging between different knowledge worlds, and how can the skills for doing this be developed?
- **Network-building** – research has shown that an effective team is not simply a collection of individuals but the result of complex dynamics around *"forming, storming, norming, and performing"* (Tuckman and Jensen, 1977). In the same way, new knowledge networks need to be constructed but this raises challenges of "finding, forming, and performing" (Birkinshaw *et al.*, 2007).

1.5.2   The Sappho Challenge – Bringing Stakeholders into the Frame

A significant strand of research concerns the concept of user-led innovation (Von Hippel, 1988, 2005; Herstatt and von Hippel, 1992). We know that users are rarely passive in the innovation process – they are often frustrated with the available solutions and sometimes that frustration drives them to create their own alternative solutions. They may do this on their own, producing sketches and prototypes, or they may work with others to help them realize their ideas. Without doubt user-led innovation is a powerful force – especially when it engages a community of such frustrated innovators. That, of course, is the story behind Linux – now a vibrant community of software developers and users supporting and continuously extending a powerful operating system in widespread use. But there is no Linux Corporation with formal R&D, marketing, and other facilities – instead it is a community which grew out of the dissatisfaction with proprietary systems felt by Linus Torvald and other early users who began to develop and share their ideas about an alternative.

While already a well-documented and important source of innovation, the emergence of powerful communication technologies which enable active co-operation of user communities in co-creation and diffusion has accelerated the trend toward more active engagement of users (Von Hippel, 2005; Dahlander and Gann, 2008, 2010).

A good illustration comes from Daimler-Benz who initiated the *"style your Smart"* design contest as a user-linked crowdsourcing project (www.smart-design-contest.com/). The aim was not just to attract interesting design ideas but also to try to establish a relationship with a community of active users. Participants from all over the world were invited online to style the skin of the Smart car, vote for the designs of others and comment on them. The online platform combined an innovation contest with the full functionality of a state-of-the art community platform, including a Facebook-connect® feature and a Twitter® channel. Besides the highly interactive and attractive community-based innovation contest, several prizes for the best designs, as well as the most active members, were offered as additional incentives to fuel motivation and the level of engagement of the participants. A five-star community evaluation and a smart internal expert round helped to pre-select the most attractive designs and the best designs were selected by an expert jury. Within a period of only six weeks, the contest attracted 8864 participants from 110 nations worldwide. In total, the participants contributed 52 170 designs and spent 12 723 hours on the platform.

Increasingly companies like LEGO®, Threadless®, Adidas®, and Muji are engaging with users as front-end co-creators of new products and services.[1] In the public sector too there is growing use of these approaches to create innovative and more successful public services. Hospitals increasingly focus on patients as a source of experience-based design input, while innovative partnerships, like Nokia's Living Lab, work closely with users, co-developing services for long-term care.

Innovation of this form often takes place entirely within the user community as a co-operative enterprise – the examples of Linux®, Mozilla®, and Apache® software projects underline the potential of such emergent properties as an alternative to R&D centered on the firm. At its limit, this involves communities creating innovation amongst and for themselves, with the resulting innovations only then being appropriated by the traditional corporate agents in public and private sectors – a significant reversal of the traditional innovation model. Much public sector innovation is driven by the needs of particular groups in society and finding ways of engaging their creativity and entrepreneurial drive to co-create new approaches to delivering those services offers a powerful alternative innovation model (Murray *et al.*, 2010; Bason, 2011).

As Eric von Hippel points out, there is a class of user whose needs require particular solutions which lie far ahead of the mainstream. Examining the ways in which they approach the problem may identify very different solution pathways which could have much wider relevance if they could be scaled and developed. He gives the example of anti-lock braking systems, which were originally developed for the extreme conditions of stopping aircraft safely and without skidding. The learning from such extreme conditions eventually transferred to the much bigger market for general automobiles.

The significant point about learning from extreme conditions is that the starting point may be different and the class of solutions and their direction of development may open up alternative trajectories along which innovation can take place. For example, in the development of medical devices to assist in infection control, ideas from extreme conditions far from the mainstream of general hospital use might be captured. Studying battlefield operating theaters, veterinary practices, and even advanced clean room technology in semiconductor manufacture offers new insights which can lead to the development of new approaches within the medical world. The principle is that today's extreme users may provide clues for tomorrow's mainstream innovations.

An example of this comes from the "bottom of the pyramid" identified by Prahalad – the 5 billion or so members of the world population with very limited resources (Prahalad, 2006). Opening up to the challenges posed by this market is leading to radical innovation in the field of healthcare, which offers significant new insights into how established economies can deal with the rising costs and demands for "good enough" quality healthcare. For example, the Aravind eye clinics in India originally targeted the 9 million cataract sufferers in India, but the resulting model has profound implications for low cost surgical care across a much broader frontier.

---

[1] Example case studies of these and other organizations can be found on the web site www.managing-innovation.com

While cataract treatment itself – diagnosis, operation, and after-care – is well-developed in the eye hospitals of the world, it comes at a price. In the USA, for example, treating cataracts costs around $3000 and even in an Indian hospital it is $300. The innovation challenge was to reduce this cost to the point where care became accessible to the bottom of the pyramid market and this required a reduction in average cost to closer to $30 per operation. The Aravind® Eye Care System is now the largest and most productive eye care facility in the world – for example, in the year 2007–2008, about 2.4 million persons received outpatient eye care and over 285 000 underwent eye surgeries.[2] The extreme conditions posed by this market forced the search for new approaches and involved the transfer of concepts originating in the fast food industry, which in turn came from the mass production ideas of Henry Ford (Tidd and Bessant, 2009).

Extreme conditions are also found in crisis situations where humanitarian agencies are forced to solve problems quickly and creatively. Increasingly such experience is being seen not only as something to be shared across the community, but also as a source of radical new insights into key problems like logistics and communications (Ramalingam *et al.*, 2010).

Another aspect of *opening up the involvement space* is the considerable untapped potential of employees within the organization. It is not a new concept – attempts to utilize this approach in a formal way can be traced back to the eighteenth century, when the 8th shogun Yoshimune Tokugawa introduced the suggestion box in Japan. In 1871, Denny's shipyard in Dumbarton, Scotland, employed a program of incentives to encourage suggestions about productivity-improving techniques; they sought to draw out "*any change by which work is rendered either superior in quality or more economical in cost.*" In 1894, the National Cash Register (NCR®) company made considerable efforts to mobilize the "hundred–headed brain" which their staff represented. Eastman Kodak introduced one of the first documented systems of employee involvement in 1909, while the Lincoln Electric Company started implementing an incentive management system in 1915. NCR®'s ideas, especially around suggestion schemes, found their way to Japan, where the textile firm of Kanebuchi Boseki introduced them in 1905.

But it was particularly in the post-war period that these ideas were exploited on a large scale; much of the momentum came from Japanese experience, taking forward ideas about employee involvement in innovation which were originally introduced as part of the US "Training within industry" (TWI) initiative (Schroeder and Robinson, 2004). Over the next 60 years, the system – largely involving incremental innovation or *kaizen* – has evolved and developed and represents a potent force for improving various aspects of organizational performance. For example, much early innovation was in the domain of quality, where a reputation for poor and shoddy products was turned into one in which world standards, measured in defective parts of one per million or less, were set. *Kaizen* has been applied with equal effect in other areas, such as increasing flexibility (through set-up time reduction), increasing plant availability (through total productive maintenance), and cost reduction (in particular, keeping pace with a highly valued Yen) (Bessant, 2003).

---

[2] Example case studies of these and other organizations can be found on the web site www.managing-innovation.com

These days, employee involvement is widely recognized as a key source of innovation. For example, an Ideas UK (www.ideasuk.com) survey of around 160 organizations highlighted cost savings of over £100 million, with the average implemented idea being worth £1400, giving a return on investment of around 5 to 1. Participation rates across the workforce were around 28%. Similar data can be found in other countries – for example, a study conducted by the Employee Involvement Association in the USA suggested that companies can expect to save close to £200 annually per employee by implementing a suggestion system. Ideas America reports around 6000 schemes operating. In Germany, specific company savings reported by Zentrums Ideenmanagement include (2010 figures) Deutsche Post DHL €220 million, Siemens €189 million, Volkswagen €94 million. Importantly, the benefits are not confined to large firms – amongst small and medium enterprises were Takata Petri (€6.3 million), Herbier Antriebstechnik (€3.1 million), and Mitsubishi Polyester Film (€1.8 million). In a survey of 164 German and Austrian firms, representing 1.5 million workers, they found around 20% (326 000) workers were involved, contributing just under 1 million ideas (955 701). Of these, two thirds (621 109) were implemented, producing savings of €1.086 billion. The investment needed to generate these was of the order of €109 million, giving an impressive rate of return.

But in many ways this is just scratching the surface; the real potential of high involvement innovation comes when employees can begin to act as internal entrepreneurs, not just contributing to "do better" incremental innovation but also suggesting ways of moving in more radical directions. Considerable acceleration of this trend has happened, with an increasing number of on-line schemes which allow high levels of participation. For example, France Telecom have been running a program called "Idee Cliq" for the past three years, generating savings of close to €1 billion across its workforce, and also creating a parallel innovation system with employees commenting and building upon suggested ideas, voting for the best and committing themselves to implementing the emerging ideas.

Opening up innovation to users, employees, and other stakeholders is then an important and established theme. This is explored in far more detail in the context of responsible innovation in the chapter by Sykes and Macnaghten in Chapter 5 and should not be perceived as something that is alien to, or indeed unwelcome in, innovative organizations.

1.5.3   The Sustainability Challenge – Innovation for Sustainable Development

The evidence underpinning concern about sustainability is extensive and there is a sense of urgency about much of the discussion it provokes (MEA, 2005; UNEP, 2007; Rockstrom, 2009). The World Wildlife Fund (WWF), for example, suggests that lifestyles in the developed world at present require the resources of around two planets, and that if emerging economies follow the same trajectory this will rise to 2.5 by 2050 (WWF, 2010). Others draw attention to the implications of reaching "peak" availability of key strategic energy and physical resources (Heinberg, 2007; Adams and Jeanrenaud, 2008; Brown, 2011). However, it is also important to reflect a more optimistic view, which sees significant *opportunities* emerging. The provision of alternative goods and services, more efficient approaches to resource and energy management, new partnerships and ways of working can help unleash a new era of economic development. A recent Pricewaterhouse Coopers (PWC) report suggests significant market potential in the provision of green goods and services; their estimate was as high as 3% of global GDP (gross domestic product). UNEP's (2011) report illustrates how "greening the economy" is already becoming a powerful new engine of growth in the twenty-first century (UNEP, 2011). The World Business Council for Sustainable Development's (WBCSD) Vision 2050 sets out new opportunities for businesses in responding to sustainability challenges, promoting whole system perspectives (WBCSD, 2010).

The scale on which change is required is also leading some commentators to talk about a systems level shift and to argue that what is emerging – as a consequence of socio-economic pressures and enabling technologies – is another "long wave" of innovation (Freeman and Perez, 1989; Perez, 2002).

Growing concern of the kind described above is driving a combination of increasingly strong legislation, international environmental management standards, new sustainability metrics, and reporting standards that will force business to adopt greener approaches if they are to retain a social license to operate. At the same time the opportunities opened up for "doing what we do better" (through lean, green investments in improving efficiencies around resources, energy, logistics, etc.) and "doing different" (radical new moves toward systems change) make it an increasingly significant item in strategic planning amongst progressive organizations of all sizes. Evidence for this can be seen in their participation and active engagement with United Nations and NGO business initiatives (such as the UN Global Compact and The Climate Group) and in networks like the Global Sustainability Forum.

Innovation for sustainable development (ISD) highlights the problem of dynamic capability in that it forces firms to learn new approaches and let go of old ones around the core search, select and implement questions. By its nature, ISD involves working with different knowledge components – new technologies, new markets, new environmental or regulatory conditions, and so on, – and firms need to develop enhanced absorptive capacity for handling this (Zahra and George, 2002). In particular they need capability (and enabling tools and methods) to acquire, assimilate, and exploit new knowledge and to work at a systems level.

Reconfiguration can take place at an incremental level (zone 3) – essentially finding new ways of doing what we already do. The case of "lean" thinking provides an example; the extreme conditions of post-war Japan brought new elements into the frame as far as manufacturing was concerned. Faced with shortages of skilled labor, reliable energy sources, or key raw materials, firms like Toyota were unable to follow the established mass production trajectories which dominated innovation thinking at the time. Instead, they developed an alternative approach to process innovation based around minimizing waste. This led to radically different performance in terms of key productivity indicators. It also involved a suite of new innovation management routines (for example, the development of effective employee involvement, concurrent engineering, *kaizen* tools and methods, and so on, some of which I have discussed above).

Similarly the "eco-efficiency" concept (WBCSD, 2000) involves finding new and more efficient ways of "doing more with less"; its famous 3Rs – reduce, re-use, and recycle – has its roots in early industrialization, but is now being widely adopted by companies. Reducing carbon footprint through supply chain improvements or switching to less energy or resource intensive products and services which deliver equivalent value can generate significant savings. 3M, for example, saved nearly $1.4 billion over a

34 year period and prevented billions of pounds of pollutants entering the environment through their Pollution-Prevention-Pays (3P) programs (3M, 2011). GE Industrial saved $12.8 million per year by using high-efficiency lights in their plants. One of Alcoa's facilities in France achieved an 85% reduction in water consumption, leading to a $40 000 per year reduction in operating costs (Senge *et al.*, 2008).

Significantly, some of the approaches around crowdsourcing mentioned in Section 1.5.1 are also being deployed. For example, the energy company EON is sponsoring a TV series in the UK in which people are asked to contribute ideas for energy saving and management innovations. As well as showcasing user ideas in the program itself, the company has set up an innovation platform where the watching public will be invited to contribute and further develop their ideas.

Sony launched an "Ideas challenge" in 2010 in partnership with WWF aimed at drawing in ideas for sustainability solutions which might take advantage of Sony technologies. As their web site explained: "*Sony and WWF want to hear your smart ideas about using technology to make the most of our planet's resources. And to get you started, we've pulled together a showcase of technologies that are ripe for re-purposing. Now it's up to you to put them together in radical new ways ... and shape a cleaner, more sustainable future for our planet. How can we make better use of our scarce natural resources? How can we actively change people's behaviour and encourage more sustainable lifestyles?*"

Zone 4 ISD will involve significant *systems* level thinking, representing a shift from eco-efficiency to eco-effectiveness (McDonough and Braungart, 2002). According to Porter and Kramer the focus on creating shared value, which builds connections between social, environmental, and economic progress, has the power to unleash the next wave of global growth (Porter and Kramer, 2011).

One aspect of this is the involvement of multiple players, who have traditionally not worked together, in co-creating system level change. For instance, Grameen Shakti, a rural renewable energy initiative in Bangladesh, fosters collaboration between the microfinance sector, suppliers of solar energy equipment, and consumers, enabling millions of poor households to leapfrog to new energy systems. It is generating new employment opportunities, increasing rural incomes, empowering women, and reducing the use of environmentally polluting kerosene. Grameen Shakti is the world's largest and fastest growing rural renewable energy company in the world (Shakti, 2011).

Reconfiguring an established organization's innovation approaches and portfolio on this scale is a major strategic undertaking and requires a combination of clear and stretching vision linked to a coherent roadmap for delivering it. A number of models for such frameworks are emerging around the sustainability challenge – for example, the World Business Council for Sustainable Development involved 29 major multi-national companies and many NGOs, academics and other partners in elaborating a vision in which "*by 2050 some 9 billion people live well, and with the limits of the planet.*"

Applying such long-term models for business planning is beginning to deliver business as well as social benefits; for example, one of the success stories has been the growth of floorings business InterfaceFLOR which has made radical changes to its business and operating model and secured significant business growth. It has cut greenhouse gas emissions by 82%, fossil fuel consumption by 60%, waste by 66%, water use by 75%, and increased sales by 66%, doubling earnings and raising profit margins. Significantly, the process has involved a complete repositioning of the business model from product supply to service delivery – a major change in direction which necessitated a great deal of unlearning as well as the acquisition of new competencies. To quote Ray Anderson, founder and chairman; *"As we climb Mount Sustainability with the four sustainability principles on top, we are doing better than ever on bottom-line business. This is not at the cost of social or ecological systems, but at the cost of our competitors who still haven't got it."*

Moving into the space characterized by zones 3 and 4 requires more than exploring possible options; the new approaches need to become embedded within the innovation management processes of the organization. An example of this long-term transition can be found in the case of the giant Philips Corporation, which has been exploring innovation space since the early 1990s. Its EcoVision programs were first launched in 1998, setting corporate sustainability-related targets and the first green innovation targets were introduced in 2007. In 2003, the Philips Environmental Report (first published in 1999) was extended into a Sustainability Report, and in 2009 this was integrated into the Philips Annual Report, signaling the full embedding of sustainability in Philips' business practices.

In its ambitious five year plan launched in 2010 (Vision 2015) the company articulates a clear commitment to becoming *"a global leader in health and well-being . . . to simply make a difference to people's lives with meaningful, sustainable innovations."*

This vision is backed by specific targets for sustainable innovation which include extending the range of people in its market space, improving the energy efficiency of their overall product portfolio by 50%, doubling the amount of recycled materials in their products, and doubling the collection and recycling of their products.

To achieve this, the innovation system within the company has adapted, bringing these criteria to the center of selection and resource allocation decisions while simultaneously spreading much more widely the search net to create new knowledge networks outside the organization. One area in which this can be seen is the development of "Green Products" – those offering significant environmental improvements in one or more key areas of energy efficiency, packaging, hazardous substances, weight, recycling, disposal, and lifetime reliability.

Examples include the Performer EnergyCare vacuum cleaner, 50% made from post-industrial plastics and 25% from bio-based plastics. It is extremely energy-efficient, but it earns its designation as a Green Product primarily because it scores so highly in the focal area of recycling. Another example is the award-winning Econova LED TV. This high-performance LED TV consumes 60% less power than its predecessor. Even the remote control is efficient – powered by solar energy. In addition, the TV is completely free of PVC and brominated flame retardants, and 60% of the aluminum used in the set is recycled. Overall some €1 billion has already been invested to support this development; in 2010 Green Products accounted for 37.5% of Philips sales and the 2015 target is 50%.

We saw earlier the challenges posed to innovation management in moving into the zone 3 and 4 innovation space posed by sustainability-led innovation (SLI). In particular, there is a need for clear strategic frameworks to guide and shape project level activities over a sustained period of time. In the Philips example, we can see this pattern emerging – with a long-term commitment to sustainability taking a more concrete form in the past decade with an explicit vision providing the context for specific and targeted initiatives. As a recent report suggests, SLI is becoming a mainstream approach characterized by early adopters – termed embracers – who have an explicit strategy and roadmap to shape their activities (Boston Consulting Group, 2011).

But SLI involves challenges to their innovation management systems. For example, search strategies based on conventional R&D or market research may need to shift to take account of new signals giving early warning of newly emerging innovation trajectories (Bessant and Von Stamm, 2007). An indicator here is the growth of new functions within established organizations associated with searching and building links into the emerging sustainability communities.

Similarly, resource allocation systems will need to shift to embed SLI values and criteria into established frameworks, such as stage gate systems (Bessant *et al.*, 2011). Developing explicit criteria, and measuring performance against these, will become an important driver of behavior change within innovation systems.

1.6 Emergent Properties of the New Innovation Environment

None of the above strands are new, they all have deep historical roots, but the combination of technology and shifting social patterns has accelerated progress along each of them, and their growing convergence. The result is an explosion of new innovation opportunities and an opening up of the innovation game. Shifts to more open innovation approaches lower the entry barriers – increasingly innovation need not require the resources of a giant corporation but instead will depend on knowing where and how to access knowledge.

For example, the idea of an innovation contest is not new, but in the past it required significant resources to be able to put up a prize, publicize the challenge, filter and judge the submissions, and eventually arrive at a solution. John Harrison's chronometer, which changed the face of naval navigation by allowing accurate determination of longitude, was a result of a challenge offered by the UK government (with a prize worth the equivalent of $4 million!) while Emperor Louis Napoleon's sponsorship of a competition to find a substitute for butter led to the development of margarine. But while innovation contests were once the province of kings and emperors they are now open to anyone who wishes to organize or participate in them.

The process also works in reverse – whereas the problem for small enterprises has often been their isolation, we are now in a situation where getting connected becomes increasingly possible. Open innovation has led many large players to expand their search, and in the process discover rich potential among small enterprises which would previously not have featured on their radar screens. Tiny businesses are now able to access global markets from anywhere and to build links and partnerships which give them access to the resources they need to grow without necessarily owning all those resources.

Shifts in the innovation landscape open new options for public services. For example, GemeinsamSelten (www.gemeinsamselten.de) is an ambitious initiative that aims to mobilize innovators across German-speaking countries to help identify and solve problems related to rare diseases. Rare diseases are a real challenge for today's national healthcare systems, as they represent an example of what Anderson calls the long tail

(Anderson, 2004). Just as traditional bookstores (with restricted shelf space) have a hard time dealing with rare books, national healthcare systems cannot cope with the enormous number of rare diseases. However, while a traditional bookstore might cover 40 000–100 000 books, Amazon is able to offer about 3 million books in its online bookstore and even offers the most specialized ones. Similarly, rare diseases and the huge number of specialized problems linked to them could profit from open collective innovation and an online co-creation platform.

Another powerful consequence of opening up access to mobile communications and computing is the liberating of creativity across previously disadvantaged groups. So fishermen in Kerula, India, no longer have to work hard to catch fish and then sell them at prices fixed by local merchants – now they can use their mobile internet access to work out where to fish, what to fish for, and where to sail in order to sell at the most advantageous price. Mobile banking has emerged bottom-up in dispersed population areas like the islands of the Philippines, or across rural Africa, and the co-creation of new applications for mobile communications is opening up other rich and socially valuable possibilities.

However, while these are examples of the significant new opportunities associated with shifts in the innovation landscape, it is worth concluding with the reflection made at the start of this chapter: that innovation is not necessarily always a good thing. Even if it appears to be so in the initial stages, there may be unanticipated negative consequences which emerge downstream – examples from nuclear power to a wide range of "miracle" drugs. For this reason, we need to think carefully about innovation choices at our selection stage in the model and ensure that the approaches we take allow for "responsible innovation." That is the focus of the rest of the book.

References

Adams, W. and Jeanrenaud, S. (2008) Transition to Sustainability: Towards a Diverse and Humane World, IUCN, Gland, Switzerland.

Allen, T. (1977) *Managing the Flow of Technology*. Cambridge, MA, MIT Press.

Anderson, C. (2004) *The Long Tail*. New York, Random House.

Bason, C. (2011). *Leading Public Sector Innovation*. London, Policy Press.

Benner, M. J. and M. L. Tushman (2003). Exploitation, exploration, and process management: the productivity dilemma revisited. *The Academy of Management Review* **28**(2): 238.

Bessant, J. (2003). *High Involvement Innovation*. Chichester, John Wiley & Sons, Ltd.

Bessant, J. and T. Venables (2008). *Creating Wealth from Knowledge: Meeting the Innovation Challenge*. Cheltenham, Edward Elgar.

Bessant, J. and Von Stamm, B. (2007) Twelve Search Strategies Which Might Save Your Organization, AIM Executive Briefing, London.

Bessant, J., B. Von Stamm, and Moeslein, K. (2011). Backing outsiders: selection strategies for discontinuous innovation. *R&D Management* **40**(4): 345–356.

Birkinshaw, J., J. Bessant, and Delbridge, R. (2007). Finding, forming, and performing: creating networks for discontinuous innovation. *California Management Review* **49**(3): 67–83.

Birkinshaw, J. and C. Gibson (2004). Building ambidexterity into an organization. *Sloan Management Review* **45**(4): 47–55.

Boston_Consulting_Group (2011) Sustainability – The Embracers Seize the Advantage, BCG, Boston.

Brown, L. (2011). *World on the Edge: How to Prevent Environmental and Economic Collapse*. New York, Norton.

Brown, J. and P. Duguid (2000). *The Social Life of Information*. Boston, MA, Harvard Business School Press.

Carter, C. and B. Williams (1957). *Industry and Technical Progress*. Oxford, Oxford University Press.

Christensen, C. (1997). *The Innovator's Dilemma*. Cambridge, MA, Harvard Business School Press.

Cole, H., C. Freeman, Pavitt, K.,*et al.* (1973). *Thinking about the Future: A Critique of the Limits to Growth*. London, Chatto & Windus.

Dahlander, L. and D. Gann (2008). How open is innovation? in *Creating Wealth from Knowledge*. J. Bessant and T. Venables. Cheltenham, Edward Elgar.

Dahlander, L. and D. Gann (2010). How open is innovation? *Research Policy* **39**: 699–709.

Dodgson, M. and R. Rothwell, (eds), (1995). *The Handbook of Industrial Innovation*. London, Edward Elgar.

Dodgson, M., A. Salter, and Gann, D. (2008). *The Management of Technological Innovation*. Oxford, Oxford University Press.

Francis, D. and J. Bessant (2005). Targeting innovation and implications for capability development. *Technovation* **25**(3): 171–183.

Francis, D., J. Bessant, and M. Hobday, *et al.* (2003). Managing radical organisational transformation. *Management Decision* **41**(1): 18–31.

Freeman, C. and C. Perez (1989). Structural crises of adjustment: business cycles and investment behaviour, in *Technical Change and Economic Theory*. G. Dosi. London, Frances Pinter: 39–66.

Dodgson, M., Gann, D., and A. Salter (2005). *Think, Play, Do: Technology and Organization in the Emerging Innovation Process*. Oxford, Oxford University Press.

Goffin, K. and R. Mitchell (2010). *Innovation Management*. London, Pearson.

Griffin, A., M. Rosenau, Castellion ,G., *et al.* (1996). *The PDMA Handbook of New Product Development*. New York, John Wiley & Sons, Inc.

Heinberg, R. (2007). *Peak Everything: Waking up to the Century of Decline in Earth's Resources*. London, Clairview.

Henderson, R. and K. Clark (1990). Architectural innovation: the reconfiguration of existing product technologies and the failure of established firms. *Administrative Science Quarterly* **35**: 9–30.

Herstatt, C. and E. von Hippel (1992). Developing new product concepts via the lead user method. *The Journal of Product Innovation Management* **9**(3): 213–221.

Huston, L. and N. Sakkab (2006). Connect and develop: inside Procter & Gamble's new model for innovation. *Harvard Business Review* **84**(3), S. 58–66.

Lafley, A. and R. Charan (2008). *The Game Changer*. New York, Profile.

Langrish, J., M. Gibbons, Evans, W., *et al.* (1972). *Wealth from Knowledge*. London, Macmillan Publishing.

Leonard, D. (1992). Core capabilities and core rigidities; a paradox in new product development. *Strategic Management Journal* **13**: 111–125.

3M (2011) Pollution Prevention, http://engineering.dartmouth.edu/~cushman/courses/engs171/Pollution-Prevention.pdf (accessed 27 April 2011).

March, J. (1991). Exploration and exploitation in organizational learning. *Organization Science* **2**(1): 71–87.

McDonough, W. and M. Braungart (2002). *Cradle to Cradle: Remaking the Way We Make Things*. New York, Universe Books.

MEA (2005). *Ecosystems and Human Wellbeing*. Washington, DC, Island Press.

Murray, R., Caulier-Grice, J., and Mulgan, G. (2010) The Open Book of Social Innovation, The Young Foundation, London.

Nelson, R. and S. Winter (1982). *An Evolutionary Theory of Economic Change*. Cambridge, MA, Harvard University Press.

NESTA (2010) Open Innovation, NESTA, London.

Perez, C. (2002). *Technological Revolutions and Financial Capital*. Cheltenham, Edward Elgar.

Porter, M. and M. Kramer (2011). Creating shared value. *Harvard Business Review* **89**(1/2), 62–77.

Prahalad, C. K. (2006). *The Fortune at the Bottom of the Pyramid*, Wharton School Publishing.

Ramalingam, B., Scriven, K. and Foley, C. (2010) Innovations in International Humanitarian Action, ALNAP, London.

Rockstrom, J. (2009). Planetary boundaries: exploring the safe operating space for humanity. *Nature* **461**: 472–475.

Rothwell, R. (1992). Successful industrial innovation: critical success factors for the 1990s. *R&D Management* **22**(3): 221–239.

Schrage, M. (2000). *Serious Play: How the World's Best Companies Simulate to Innovate*. Boston, MA, Harvard Business School Press.

Schroeder, A. and D. Robinson (2004). *Ideas Are Free: How the Idea Revolution Is Liberating People and Transforming Organizations*. New York, Berrett Koehler.

Senge, P.M., B. Smith, Kruschwitz, N. *et al.* (2008). *The Necessary Revolution: How Individuals and Organizations are Working Together to Create a Sustainable World*. New York, Doubleday.

Shakti, G. (2011) Grameen Shakti, http://www.gshakti.org/ (accessed 27 April 2011).

Teece, D., G. Pisano, and A. Shuen (1997). Dynamic capabilities and strategic management. *Strategic Management Journal* **18**(7): 509–533.

Tidd, J. and J. Bessant (2009). *Managing Innovation: Integrating Technological, Market and Organizational Change*. Chichester, John Wiley & Sons, Ltd.

Tuckman, B. and N. Jensen (1977). Stages of small group development revisited. *Group and Organizational Studies* **2**: 419–427.

Tushman, M. and C. O'Reilly (1996). Ambidextrous organizations: managing evolutionary and revolutionary change. *California Management Review* **38**(4): 8–30.

UNEP (2007) Global Environmental Outlook GE04, United Nations Environment Programme, Nairobi.

UNEP (2011) Towards a Green Economy: Pathways to Sustainable Development and Poverty Eradication, United Nations Environment Programme, Online version http://hqweb.unep.org/greeneconomy/Portals/88/documents/ger/GER_synthesis_en.pdf.

Von Hippel, E. (1988). *The Sources of Innovation*. Cambridge, MA, MIT Press.

Von Hippel, E. (2005). *The Democratization of Innovation*. Cambridge, MA, MIT Press.

WBCSD (2000) Eco-Efficiency: Doing More with Less, World Business Council for Sustainable Development, Geneva.

WBCSD (2010) Vision 2050, World Business Council for Sustainable Development, Geneva.

Wenger, E. (1999). *Communities of Practice: Learning, Meaning, and Identity*. Cambridge, Cambridge University Press.

WWF (2010) Living Planet Report 2010: Biodiversity, Biocapacity and Development, WWF International, Gland, Switzerland.

Zahra, S. A. and G. George (2002). Absorptive capacity: a review, reconceptualization and extension. *The Academy of Management Review*, **27**: 185–194.

Zollo, M. and S. G. Winter (2002). Deliberate learning and the evolution of dynamic capabilities. *Organization Science* **13**(3): 339–351.

2

A Framework for Responsible Innovation

Richard Owen,[1] *Jack Stilgoe,*[1] *Phil Macnaghten,*[2] *Mike Gorman,*[3]
Erik Fisher,[4] *and Dave Guston*[4]

[1]*University of Exeter Business School, UK*
[2]*Durham University, UK*
[3]*University of Virginia, USA*
[4]*Arizona State University, USA*

2.1 Introduction

Few would disagree that science and innovation should be undertaken responsibly. "Responsible innovation" intuitively feels right in sentiment, as an ideal or aspiration. It has positive, constructive overtones, where science and innovation are directed at, and undertaken towards, socially desirable and socially acceptable ends, with connotations of trust and integrity. However, in reality, it lacks definition and clarity, both in concept and practice: What might it involve? Who might it involve? When might it be applied? In this chapter we explore these questions, proposing a framework for responsible innovation and highlighting some examples of its translation into practice.

Before doing this we first need to provide some context. Why is there a need for a framework for responsible innovation, and what are the deficits of our current approach to innovation governance? In this chapter we will begin by emphasizing that science and innovation have not only produced understanding, knowledge, and value (economic, social, or otherwise), but also questions, dilemmas, and unintended (and sometimes undesirable) impacts. This is well understood. Some impacts, such as those associated with the financial crisis of 2008, have been both profound and global in nature, see Muniesa and Lenglet, Chapter 10. They have highlighted inefficiencies, and even failures, in the principle of regulation by market choice in liberal economies, which struggles,

Responsible Innovation, First Edition. Edited by Richard Owen, John Bessant and Maggy Heintz.
© 2013 John Wiley & Sons, Ltd. Published 2013 by John Wiley & Sons, Ltd.

sometimes spectacularly, with "externalities" associated with innovation, see Lee and Petts, Chapter 8. We will describe how, historically, the response to this has been one of governing the products of innovation (we mean products in their widest sense, to include impacts that are co-produced and unintended), usually after these have emerged in society. In this approach, where impacts (e.g., to society, health, or the environment) are found to be undesirable or harmful we may then decide to manage and control these, commonly through regulatory instruments. Such retrospective regulation can also look forward: we may introduce or amend regulation to protect society from such impacts occurring again. Precautionary "data before market" legislation, for example, seeks to ensure that the mistakes of history are not repeated.

But for impacts that are poorly characterized or highly uncertain (including those that emerge as a result of the complex, dynamic, and globalized nature of contemporary innovation and its naturalization process in modern society (see Chapter 1)), this knowledge – and often risk-based – model of regulation fares less well. In these circumstances the current approach consigns scientists, innovators, and users to moral luck (Williams, 1981). By this we mean that in hindsight, and in the fullness of time, the consequences and impacts of innovation may well be judged to be undesirable, even harmful. But, burdened with imperfect foresight, we take a chance, hoping to be excused from moral blame if it can be demonstrated we did not have sufficient knowledge of the future consequences of our actions at the time: that these could not have been "reasonably foreseen" (see Grinbaum and Groves, Chapters 7 and Lee and Petts, Chapter 8). In the absence of certainty, of evidence and understanding, what other option is there? How should we proceed responsibly under such conditions of ignorance and uncertainty (Collingridge, 1980; RCEP, 2008)?

The appropriate (and proportionate) oversight and stewardship of the processes of science and innovation under such conditions then become a central challenge for responsible innovation. Codes of conduct (e.g., European Commission, 2008) and formal processes of ethical review for research and innovation do exist, but only in rather narrow contexts. We will argue the need for a far wider, systemic reconfiguration, and indeed a significant culture change in this regard. Importantly, we will argue that stewardship of science and innovation must not only include broad reflection and deliberation on their products, however uncertain these may be, but also (and critically) the very *purposes* of science or innovation: why do it, what are the intentions and motivations, who might benefit and who might not? What should the targets for innovation be – what Von Schomberg (Chapter 3) describes as the "right impacts" (see also Von Schomberg, 2011a) – and how can these be democratically defined? What values should these based on (see Van den Hoven, Chapter 4)? Despite being important sources of controversy in many areas of science and technology, from genetic modification (GM) to geoengineering, early, ethical reflection and inclusive deliberation on purposes and underlying motivations is currently limited: by the time such deliberation does occur positions may be entrenched and vested interests significant. Here we concern ourselves with the democratic governance of intent (Stilgoe, 2011) and the principle of science *for* society (Owen, Macnaghten, and Stilgoe, (2012)). There is an obvious tension between this and the principle of scientific freedom, one that is far from new (Polanyi, 1962). While this may not be as keenly felt for innovation, for science this is a tension that any formulation of responsible innovation ignores at its peril.

Reflection on purposes implies that any framework for responsible innovation needs to accommodate not only what we do not want science and innovation to do – the identification, assessment, and where necessary control of their wider impacts and associated risks – but what we *do* want them to do. "What are the risks?" – important question though this is to consider within any framework – is not the departure point for responsible innovation. As we go on to describe, this frames responsible innovation as, at least in the first instance, a discussion concerning what sorts of futures we want science and innovation to bring into the World. This opens up new opportunities for creating value in society through science and technology. But such a conversation requires a new vocabulary. This needs to go beyond narrower preoccupations with, on the one hand, risks and regulation (Owen and Goldberg, 2010) and, on the other, maximizing the economic and social benefits (or "impact") of science and innovation (Kearnes and Weinroth, 2011). It will need to consist of more than a simplistic prescription to, on the one hand "do no harm" and on the other contribute to economic competitiveness and social wellbeing (Guston, 2004, 2007).

Having provided some important context we then develop the framework itself. We first provide a philosophical anchoring for this, looking to those prospective, forward-looking dimensions of responsibility, (notably *care* and *responsiveness*) which allow consideration of purposes and accommodate uncertainty, a defining feature of innovation (Jonas, 1984; Richardson, 1999; Pellizzoni, 2004; Groves, 2006; Adam and Groves, 2011; and Grinbaum and Groves in Chapter 7). We then transcribe this in terms of four dimensions of responsible innovation. These suggest that to innovate responsibly entails a continuous commitment to be *anticipatory, reflective, inclusively deliberative*, and *responsive*. For each there is much we can learn from decades of thought and study in science and technology studies and beyond. These dimensions will require some elaboration in order to impart meaning to them, but they are not in themselves new. Familiar concepts that include technology assessment, "upstream" engagement and anticipatory governance are foundations for responsible innovation that should not be discarded or ignored.

We then consider how such integrated dimensions might be applied in the real world, how they can be translated into practice. We will emphasize that this translation must not be rules-based and that it must be flexible in the face of uncertainty (Richardson, 1999). There are in fact numerous examples, some of which we highlight, where one or more of these dimensions has been applied, to varying degrees. These serve to signpost specific methods and approaches that can allow the dimensions we describe to be translated into practice. We observe that, however, there are currently few, if any, examples of a systematic and institutionally-embedded framework that integrates and iteratively applies all four dimensions together in and around the processes of science and innovation, supporting what Wynne (1993) describes as "institutional reflexivity." Important here is the dimension of responsiveness, that is, the coupling of reflection and deliberation to action that has a material influence on the direction and trajectory of innovation itself. We conclude the chapter with some reflections regarding implementation and how this might be supported, drawn from our own experiences.

In this chapter we will refer to both science and innovation. We will ask how we can embed responsibility within innovation as a complex, multi-actor phenomenon that involves the translation of ideas into some sort of value in the future. But we extend this ambition to the practice of science. Much science is curiosity-driven, producing knowledge and understanding that is not intentionally directed at value creation in a narrower sense. It could be argued that there is less justification for applying such a framework in such circumstances, at least initially. However, we must also remember that many areas of science (e.g., in the fields of quantum mechanics and molecular biology) have been, and continue to be, an important catalyst for innovation. Recognizing this, the potential (beneficial) impact – economic and social – of even curiosity-driven research is now an increasingly important funding consideration. Such visions of application and impact are important locations for considerations of responsibility (Simakova and Coenen, Chapter 13). Some areas of science are also purposefully funded with the promise of creating economic or social value, for example, to meet societal challenges (Lund Declaration, 2009; Kearnes and Weinroth, 2011). Many areas of science, directed or otherwise, can have unanticipated impacts. As such, we argue the framework we propose should be extended to include both science and innovation, but it is important to note that we make no assumption that it should be applied in every case.

What our following discussion also does not imply is that what has come before has necessarily been "irresponsible innovation" or "irresponsible science." Von Schomberg, in Chapter 3, certainly describes some examples where, in his view, this may have been the case, but these rarely if ever result from the actions of an individual scientist or innovator (Von Schomberg, 2007). Irresponsibility, we (and others) argue, is often the product of a globalized and complex ecosystem of innovation, involving the creation by many (separated across space and time) of what Bessant in Chapter 1 describes as "knowledge spaghetti." It is within such an ecosystem that responsible innovation must be located. The emergent nature of irresponsibility in this context (Beck's "organized irresponsibility" (Beck, 1995)) requires a new way of thinking about responsibility. Responsibility is a social ascription that has changed and evolved over time, in part reflecting the changing nature and norms of society. What we (and others (e.g., Jonas, 1984; Adam and Groves, 2011; and Grinbaum and Groves, Chapter 7) argue is that how we think about responsibility in the context of science and innovation now needs to change again, reflecting the modern context in which innovation occurs. This requires a redrawing of the contours of responsibility, including, but going beyond evidence-based regulation and established codes of responsible conduct in science. This redrawing will need to be done in a way that allows the constructive and democratic stewardship of science and innovation in the face of uncertainty toward futures we agree are both acceptable and desirable: this is *a collective responsibility*. It in turn will require reflection on the societal values in which innovation is anchored (Von Schomberg, 2011a, 2011b; and Von Schomberg in Chapter 3) and the conflicts and dilemmas that inevitably arise when these are considered in combination: for example, the tensions between the goals of innovation for economic growth or environmental sustainability. It will also challenge us to ask how we can and should respond as the future materializes in often complex, unpredictable ways, including ways not initially intended. Some of these challenges we will only be able to touch on here, but they serve to warnus that redrawing the contours of responsibility will be far from easy. Our contribution provides just one input into a broader discussion concerning how this might be achieved.

2.2   Context: the Imperative for Responsible Innovation

2.2.1   Re-evaluating the Social Contract for Science and Innovation

Our capacity, and appetite, for invention and innovation has profoundly shaped human societies and the world we live in since the dawn of civilization. We are an incredibly inquisitive, imaginative, and innovative species. Science and innovation are an integral part of the structure of nearly all modern societies and their place remains assured. We look to them to meet the myriad societal challenges we currently face – future sources of economic growth, wealth, environmental sustainability, health and the security of food, water, and energy (e.g., BIS, 2011). At least since the Enlightenment in the seventeenth century, and in particular since the middle of the twentieth century, an informal social contract has come to exist between scientists and innovators, and wider society (Guston, 2004; Pielke, 2007). Freedom, social licence, and funding to invent, innovate, and pursue scientific endeavors have been exchanged for the promise, and sometimes expectation, of knowledge, understanding, and value (economic, social, or otherwise). Certain responsibilities are implicit within this contract, including the expectations that existing norms, laws, and standards of conduct are adhered to: there is a long history of responsibility in the context of research integrity in this regard. This includes scientists' responsibilities relating, for example, to fraud, the falsification of data, or plagiarism. Going further, some have argued that within this contract the production of knowledge and its translation into economic and social impact has been (and continues to be) a key responsibility of institutions of science and innovation (see Guston, 2004; and Simakova and Coenen in Chapter 13 for more discussion). Here a desire to demonstrate the public value of science and innovation translates into a responsibility to drive knowledge and technology transfer (Chapter 13).

The last half a century has forced a re-evaluation of this contract. As well as new knowledge and value, science and innovation have time and again been shown to simultaneously co-produce often unintended and unforeseen impacts (Beck, 2000) and to have complex interactions with, and transformative consequences for society. From the environmental effects of chemicals first brought to widespread public attention by Rachel Carson in the 1960s (Carson, 1962), to the profound consequences of complex financial products in the last decade (Mackenzie, 2010; and Muniesa and Lenglet in Chapter 10), we have come to realize that, uncertain though they may be, such impacts *must be expected to occur* (Hoffman-Riem and Wynne, 2002; and Grinbaum and Groves in Chapter 7), sometimes at global and intergenerational scales. This is a symptom of what Hans Jonas described as the "altered nature of human action," mediated through technology and innovation (Jonas, 1984).

2.2.2   The Responsibility Gap

Historically, where free markets have failed to manage so-called externalities of innovation, our response has been one based largely on governance through mechanisms of regulation, that is, legal instruments of authorization and control, which are often underpinned by methods of probabilistic risk assessment and evaluation. Here, the products of innovation may be retrospectively subjected to regulation once they have been developed, marketed, and introduced into society (Lee, 2012; and Lee and Petts in Chapter 8), if and when there is evidence of undesirable or harmful impacts. Governance of this kind can also have a prospective dimension, through a process of adaptive learning. It may be introduced or amended to safeguard society and the environment from known impacts, with the aim of preventing these from occurring again. This has led to stringent regulatory governance in certain areas of innovation, such as medicines, where the harmful consequences of some medicines, such as thalidomide and diethylstilbestrol, (which had intergenerational effects on health) were important catalysts for regulatory development (EEA, 2001). In addition to general liability regimes (e.g., product liability – see Chapter 8), sector – specific regulation in areas such as pharmaceuticals and novel foods includes precautionary legislation that has evolved over the last half century, and which now requires "data before market" prior to authorization and use, specifically to safeguard health. Safety is considered as important as efficacy in this regard. Prospective legal concepts, such as duty of care in tort law, which are aimed at protecting people and property, have also been developed over the last century.

These forms of legal responsibility have a foundation in knowledge, and specifically, evidence (notably of causality) (Groves, 2006). Knowledge of several kinds is required: first, knowledge of the nature of impacts, knowledge that these are undesirable or harmful, and knowledge of the sorts of behaviors that will have a strong probability of leading to these (what in law can be "reasonably foreseen" given the status of knowledge at the time of acting); secondly, knowledge of the legal, or moral, norms that exist in society and which aim to ensure these impacts and behaviors are avoided or prevented; and thirdly, evidential and causal knowledge that such norms have been transgressed. Transgression of such legal or moral responsibilities may render one accountable (legally in a court of law and/or morally to society), when one is then judged retrospectively in the context of such knowledge, and on the basis of the consequences of one's actions.[1] A pre-requisite for this is that one had the *capacity* to understand these norms at the time and, as autonomous individuals who exert free will, one then transgressed these (intentionally or otherwise i.e., by being reckless or negligent). For this there is a requirement for evidence, often independently verified. One can already envisage the problems this formulation of responsibility poses for science and innovation, with their attendant uncertainties, complexities, and areas of ignorance, and where the limits to knowledge are often great. We will speak more about this presently.

For now we note that responsibility of this kind, manifested, for example, through instruments of regulation, is an important part of responsible innovation, but that it has severe limitations. It is poorly equipped to govern areas of novel science and technology which are highly uncertain in terms of their current and future impacts, or which, by virtue of their novelty, have no historical precedent. Regulation, put simply, struggles with innovations that it has not encountered before, where it has no immune response. And innovation is a process of imagination, invention, and development that *actively seeks* novelty, with the creation of value as its goal. Here, by definition, regulatory forms of governance and control may not exist, or are unclear in terms of their coverage (Lee and Petts, Chapter 8): knowledge of the social norms against which transgression can be judged may also be poorly defined, unclear, or contested. There may in these cases be no requirement for "data before market," because we may not know what data to ask for or we may lack the technical ability to procure it. Such data requirements that do exist may also be limited in context, covering, for example, certain aspects of environment, health, and safety, but not impacts on, or interactions with, society. Areas such as nanotechnology, synthetic biology, geoengineering, and information technologies, which can occur at the interface of disciplines and for which there is often no established regulatory regime, are current examples of these (see Chapters 11–13).

---

[1] The root of the word responsibility is "respondere," whereby one is held to account and asked to respond in a court of law or some other higher authority (Grinbaum and Groves, Chapter 7).

The requirement for knowledge before regulatory action is, at face value, both rational and logical. It entails the procurement of evidence of impacts, which must be understood with a degree of certainty, which then becomes a key requirement for the establishment or amendment of legal or moral norms, and for the amendment or development of regulation. In many emerging areas of science and technology, programs of research in the fields of safety, environment, and health have often been commissioned that follow in the wake of innovation, and which are directed to support policy and regulatory development, to establish the forms of knowledge we describe above. The limitations of this approach are well known (EEA, 2001; RCEP, 2008; Owen *et al.*, 2009a, 2009b). There have been many cases where it did not identify in advance, or in good time, a number of very serious impacts on society, environment, and health (EEA, 2001), serving to remind us of the limits of knowledge, risk assessment, and foresight (Hoffman-Riem and Wynne, 2002), and in turn the limits of evidence-based regulation.

We know from experience that the reach of innovators will always exceed the grasp of regulators, and that it is often many decades before understanding of the wider impacts, implications, and consequences of innovations become clear enough for a case for a regulatory response to be made (EEA, 2001; RCEP, 2008; Pacces, 2010). Long time lags between innovations, understanding of their impacts and the evolution of policies to govern them result (Owen *et al.*, 2009a, 2009b). Callon, Lascoumes, and Barthe (2010) use a metaphor of science and technology "overflowing" the boundaries of existing regulatory frameworks. Groves describes this as "a fundamental gap between the technologically-enhanced power of industrialized societies to create futures, and our ability as agents within these societies to take responsibility for the kinds of futures we create" (Groves, 2006). This is compounded by the complex, messy, and often globalized nature of contemporary innovation itself. Innovation is not a simple, linear model with clear lines of sight from invention to impact, and where accountability for such impacts can be traced. It is an undulating path, sometimes with dead ends, involving many, often loosely-connected actors. It is a *complex, collective, and dynamic* phenomenon. We will emphasize later the importance of co-responsibility in this context (Mitcham, 2003; Von Schomberg, 2007). As a consequence, it may not be so much individual scientists or innovators as the *ecosystem of innovation* that supports the emergence of what Beck (1995) called "organized irresponsibility" and which permits an easy discounting of the future. This emergent, ecosystem-level behavior is a product of uncertainty, complexity, and distance, both spatial and temporal. Governing such an ecosystem is, some might argue, an almost impossible challenge.

2.2.3   The Dilemma of Control

The responsibility gap we have described has several important implications. It was David Collingridge who alerted us to the first of these, the risks of technological "lock in" and path dependence (Collingridge, 1980; Arthur, 1989; David, 2001). In essence, by the time we have procured knowledge that leads to a better understanding of the impacts of innovation (notwithstanding the fact that knowledge itself is a source of further uncertainty) the innovation may be so "locked in" to society that we may have little appetite, or power, to do anything about it. The costs (financial or otherwise) of control may be too great, and vested interests may fight this. Lock in and path dependence, sometimes fueled by incentives (as was the case for some notable recent financial innovations), serve to close down options to modulate, shape, or control innovation (Stirling, 2007, 2008), even in the face of impacts which are profound, but which may be too costly to control (Owen and Jobling, 2012). This is one horn of the "dilemma of control" that Collingridge presents us with when considering how we might govern innovation. The other horn is equally problematic. At the earlier stages of innovation we may have most opportunity to shape and control innovation, with far fewer costs and vested interests; but it is precisely at these early stages that we have little or no evidence to make the case for control. If the dangers of lock in are the price of waiting for the accumulation of knowledge before action, then the risks of missed opportunity are the price of acting too early, of being too precautionary. Given this, promissory statements of benefit can predominate over calls for precaution, which may be seen to slow down, or impede our insatiable appetite for progress.

Under such circumstances we may prefer to take our chances. This subjects scientists, innovators, and users of innovation to "moral luck" (Williams, 1981; and Grinbaum and Groves, Chapter 7). In time such innovations may, with the benefit of hindsight and accumulation of knowledge, be found to have undesirable or harmful impacts. Critically, whether one is held to account for the consequences of one's actions in this context depends, as we have already noted, on what one knew at the time (i.e., the status of the types of knowledge we have described) and what could have been reasonably foreseen. As Grinbaum and Groves argue in Chapter 7, this consequentialist view of responsibility is wholly unsatisfactory in the context of innovation as an uncertain, often knowledge-poor phenomenon. Not only that, but as the results of public dialogues around emerging areas of science and technology (such as synthetic biology[2]) have shown, public desire for scientists (and those that fund them) to actively take more responsibility for the wider implications of their research is strong (TNS-BMRB, 2010; and Sykes and Macnaghten, Chapter 5. Allowing the future to take care of itself in the face of uncertainty is neither a satisfactory, or acceptable approach.

2.2.4   Products and Purposes: the Democratic Governance of Intent

We have so far considered problems associated with the identification and management of impacts under conditions of ignorance and uncertainty: the products of innovation. There is, however, a deeper, but equally important deficit to our current approach to governing science and innovation, one that is also evident from public dialogues concerning new technologies. This is related to products, but is primarily concerned with the *purposes* and *motivations* for the innovation itself. Why do it? Who might benefit and how? Will such benefits be equitable? Will it confer burdens to some or many? In whose interests is it being undertaken and what are the motivations of those involved? Do we (as a society) want it? Our current approach to governing science and innovation rarely, if ever, allows reflection on purposes, underlying intentions and motivations (Stilgoe, 2011).

A framework for responsible innovation must then not just include consideration of products, but also purposes, not just what we do not want science and innovation to do, but what we do want them to do. This is the departure point for responsible innovation. It compels us to reflect on what sort of future(s) we want science and technology to bring into the world, what futures we care about, what challenges we want these to meet,

---

[2] www.bbsrc.ac.uk/web/FILES/Reviews/synbio_summary-report.pdf.

what values these are anchored in, and whether the negotiations of such technologically-enabled futures are democratic. It asks how the targets for innovation can be identified in an ethical, inclusive, and equitable manner. This takes us beyond the "closing down" framing of conventional ethical review in research, which may be seen as a hurdle for researchers (e.g., where their research involves people, animals, and genetic material). Rather, its primary purpose is to inclusively and democratically define and realize new areas of public value for innovation (Wilsdon, Wynne, and Stilgoe, 2005). Here responsible innovation should be viewed as creating opportunity. Having set the initial direction of travel, responsible innovation then asks how we can change the trajectories of innovation as new information and new perspectives emerge: how we should respond in the face of uncertainty and how innovation might look different in response. It is these dimensions of care and responsiveness that form the philosophical cornerstones of the framework we now describe.

2.3 Locating Responsible Innovation within Prospective Dimensions of Responsibility

How can we address the deficits of our current approach to governing science and innovation in contemporary society? What might a framework for responsible innovation look like, and will it be different to what has come before? To begin we need first to provide a philosophical foundation for the framework, one that locates it within a prospective conceptualization of responsibility that both allows for reflection on purposes, i.e., is ethical and values-based (van den Hoven, Lokhorst, and van de Poel, 2012; and van den Hoven in Chapter 4), and also allows for and accommodates uncertainty, i.e., is responsive to the changing nature of innovation as it makes its uncertain and unpredictable way in the world.

Care and responsiveness are two dimensions of prospective responsibility (Richardson, 1999; Pellizzoni, 2004; Groves, 2006; Adam and Groves, 2011; and Grinbaum and Groves, Chapter 7) that are relevant here. They allow us to reflect on the purposes of science and innovation, to articulate what we want science and innovation to do, and not to do (the dimension of care) and to be responsive to views and knowledge (of many different kinds) both in terms of defining the targets for innovation and how its trajectory then evolves.

Responsiveness is a key dimension that allows options to be kept open (Stirling, 2007, 2008); it is the antidote to lock in and path dependence. It is linked to what Collingridge described as the continuous goal to discover, and act on, those decisions that one has made in error: corrigibility (Collingridge, 1980). Importantly, it not only embeds the concept of responding to a changing information environment, that is, being *adaptive*, but also to responding to the views, perspectives, and framings of others – publics, stakeholders – , that is, being *deliberative*. This introduces the principle of deliberative democracy into the dimension of responsiveness. It is important that such deliberation is widely configured, that it seeks not simply to understand views on the purposes and intended products of science and innovation and their acceptability, but that such engagement pro-actively helps establish and shape new agendas which set the direction of science and innovation themselves. The Altzheimers's Society in the UK, for example, has a research network of some 200 carers and people with dementia who help set research priorities, prioritize grant applications and sit on grant selection panels[3] (Wilsdon, Wynne, and Stilgoe, 2005).

If care and responsiveness are two dimensions of responsibility that are helpful to underpin a framework for responsible innovation, they are dimensions that will be less familiar in comparison with those of liability, accountability, even blame, which are knowledge based (as we have discussed above), and which are retrospectively applied after the fact. These dimensions of responsibility have a long and rich history. As a social ascription they defined for many generations the contours of acceptable and desirable behavior in societies. Both moral and legal in nature, they have been particularly important since the emergence of liberalism and individualism in the sixteenth century, which is by no coincidence where the modern ascent of science, and the emergence of capitalism from mercantile economies, began in earnest. Although the specifics (e.g., nature of norms and laws) have evolved as our societies have evolved, these dimensions of responsibility have predominated over history, to varying degrees, with ever more sophisticated frameworks that guide, bound, and limit behavior, helping to maintain social order. They are important to maintain the rights of individuals in a "free," democratic society (e.g., in the modern era the right to own property and the right to free speech). Reciprocal forms of responsibility such as these (Groves, 2006), in which we respect each others' rights and are accountable under the law if these are transgressed, can be traced back to classical times (Jonas, 1984) and were, arguably, sufficient for societies where responsibilities were framed predominately in the context of contemporaries who lived close to one another, and whose actions rarely had irreversible effects on the world at large. As a deterrent, responsibility had a future orientation only in as much as one would be judged retrospectively (and evidentially) in the future according to the consequence of one's past actions.

But as we have already noted, and as Jonas so eloquently described, our world is no longer one of close contemporaries. Our actions, mediated through technology, affect others across continents and across generations: from the stratospheric ozone depletion caused by chlorofluorocarbons (CFCs) used in refrigerators and aerosol can propellants, to the collapse of investment banks in the wake of the innovation of collateralized debt obligations based on "toxic," asset-backed securities. While innovation may be a collective, future-oriented activity steeped in uncertainty, what is certain is that it has made our world a far smaller, interdependent, and uncertain place. Jonas and others since (see Chapter 7) argue that, in this context, the predominant reciprocal and consequentialist view of responsibility is inadequate, requiring what Jonas went on to argue should be a new conceptualization, one that goes beyond the "ethics of the neighborhood." When considering matters of science and innovation, this must include dimensions that are non-reciprocal and future-oriented in nature (Adam and Groves, 2011; Groves, 2006). It is within this conceptualization of responsibility that we find dimensions such as care and responsiveness, and which form the cornerstones of a framework for responsible innovation. These allow us to develop an intentionally broad definition for responsible innovation:

> Responsible innovation is a collective commitment of care for the future through responsive stewardship of science and innovation in the present.

---

[3] http://alzheimers.org.uk/site/scripts/document_pdf.php?documentID=1109.

This definition provides a general framing for responsible innovation, under which we will shortly propose four dimensions, which when integrated together may allow such a commitment of care and stewardship to be enacted.

In fact, we have already implicitly introduced these four dimensions: we have, for example, advocated the need for innovation to be responsive and deliberative. We have also spoken of the need for reflection on the purposes of innovation and the values these are anchored in, and on the need to anticipate the impacts innovation might have. But before explicitly describing these dimensions, we must say one last, important thing about care. We care about what is of constitutive value to us, mediated through our attachments, identities, beliefs, and the various roles we play, and the influences which bear, and which have had bearing upon our lives. The first and foremost task for responsible innovation is then to ask what futures do we collectively want science and innovation to bring about, and on what values are these based? This is reflected in discussions concerning values-sensitive design (see Chapter 4), the need to articulate the "right impacts" of research and innovation (Von Schomberg, 2011a, 2011b) and the focusing of these on societal challenges (e.g., Lund Declaration, 2009), that is, science for society (see Owen, Macnaghten, and Stilgoe, 2012) for a more detailed discussion in a European context). Von Schomberg argues that we cannot aspire to the abstract ideals of the Aristotelian "good life," however contested this may be, and takes a more pragmatic view that, at least in a European context, the "right impacts" are those constitutionally enshrined in the European Treaty, such as a competitive social market economy, sustainable development, and quality of life. Meeting these, he asserts, should be achieved in a way that is ethically acceptable, socially desirable, safe, and sustainable (Chapter 3).

In combination, such targets for innovation of course embed tensions, complex dilemmas, as well as areas of contestation and outright conflict. Two challenges then emerge from this: the first is which if any of these targets should be prioritized as the "right impacts," and whether some of these targets should in fact be excluded? This question had both political and ethical dimensions. The World Wildlife Fund (WWF, 2012), for example, considers the right impacts for innovation as being *dematerialization* (i.e., products, services, or processes that dramatically cut the use of natural resources), *restorative* (i.e., innovations that contribute to net positive environmental impacts and the restoration of biodiversity and the environment), *open loop* (where waste from products is turned back into resource), and *renewable energy and low carbon*. Are these the "right impacts"?

One might extend this to argue that any process of responsible innovation that serves to target innovation at those "right impacts" which support the increasingly unsustainable grand Capitalist project of modernity might, in the longer (or even medium) term, be viewed as an irresponsible innovation in itself. Should responsible innovation as an innovation simply serve to promote the status quo, propagating and expediting the sustainability crisis facing society in the twenty-first century (Thomson, 2011 and references within)? These are inherently political discussions, involving considerations of power, democracy, and equity, and suggest that responsible innovation cannot, and should not, be decoupled from its political and economic context.

The second challenge then is how a framework for responsible innovation can accommodate plurality of political and ethical considerations as these relate to social desirability and acceptability, allowing the inevitable tensions, dilemmas, and conflicts to be identified and navigated, with a view to a democratic, equitable, and legitimate resolution. These challenges make the case for broad, inclusive deliberation concerning the purposes of, and motivations for, innovation essential.

2.4   Four Dimensions of Responsible Innovation

We suggest that to innovate responsibly entails a collective and continuous commitment to be:

Anticipatory – describing and analyzing those intended and potentially unintended impacts that might arise, be these economic, social, environmental, or otherwise. Supported by methodologies that include those of foresight, technology assessment, and scenario development,[4] these not only serve to articulate promissory narratives of expectation but to explore other pathways to other impacts, to prompt scientists and innovators to ask "what if..." and "what else might it do?" questions. Tempered by the need for plausibility, such methods do not aim to predict, but are useful as a space to surface issues and explore possible impacts and implications that may otherwise remain uncovered and little discussed. They serve as a useful entry point for reflection on the purposes, promises, and possible impacts of innovation. Guston in Chapter 6 provides further discussion on this dimension.

Reflective – reflecting on underlying purposes, motivations, and potential impacts, what is known (including those areas of regulation, ethical review, or other forms of governance that may exist – see Chapter 8) and what is not known; associated uncertainties, risks, areas of ignorance, assumptions, questions, and dilemmas.

Deliberative – inclusively *opening up* visions, purposes, questions, and dilemmas to broad, collective deliberation through processes of dialogue, engagement, and debate, inviting and listening to wider perspectives from publics and diverse stakeholders. This allows the introduction of a broad range of perspectives to reframe issues and the identification of areas of potential contestation. Sykes and Macnaghten in Chapter 5 describe a number of specific methods that can be employed, emphasizing the goals of such deliberation should be normative (i.e., that dialogue is the right thing to do for reasons of democracy, equity, and justice) and substantive (i.e., that choices concerning the nature and trajectory of innovation can be co-produced with publics in ways that authentically embody diverse sources of social knowledge, values, and meanings (Stirling, 2005; Stirling, 2008; Marris and Rose, 2010)).

Responsive – using this collective process of reflexivity to both set the direction and influence the subsequent trajectory and pace of innovation, through effective mechanisms of participatory and anticipatory governance.[5] This should be an iterative, inclusive, and open process of adaptive learning, with dynamic capability.

In total we see these combined dimensions as meeting two goals; first, they collectively serve to build what we might rather grandiosely term "reflexive capital" concerning the purposes, processes, and products of science and innovation in an iterative, inclusive, and deliberative way. Secondly, they couple this reflexive capital to decisions about the

---

[4] See Chapter 9 for more details.

[5] Anticipatory governance is a broad-based capacity extended through society that can act on a variety of inputs to manage emerging knowledge-based technologies while such management is still possible (Chapter 6).

specific goals for innovation, and how the trajectory of innovation can be modulated as it progresses in uncertain and unpredictable ways: that is, how we can collectively respond. Reflection and deliberation are, in themselves, important, but they are of real value and impact if they can inform how innovation should look different in response.

These dimensions align well with a definition of responsible (research and) innovation offered by Von Schomberg (2011a,b), which reflects a vision in which science and society are "mutually responsive to each other with a view to the (ethical) acceptability, sustainability, and societal desirability" of innovation:

> Responsible Research and Innovation is a transparent, interactive process by which societal actors and innovators become mutually responsive to each other with a view on the (ethical) acceptability, sustainability and societal desirability of the innovation process and its marketable products (in order to allow a proper embedding of scientific and technological advances in our society).

To be effective such dimensions must be institutionally embedded in and around science and innovation: they must be far more than principles. This is a significant challenge that may require a reconfiguration of how science and innovation are funded, and undertaken. But this should not be viewed as a restrictive approach that will stifle creativity and curiosity. We make no *a priori* assumptions regarding the nature, trajectory, and pace of any particular area of innovation. Rather, this should necessarily be a product of the reflexive process itself, which may speed innovation up, slow it down, or change its direction accordingly. In this way responsible innovation not only offers space for precaution, but for opportunity.

2.5   Responsible Innovation: from Principles to Practice

Although the term responsible innovation has become increasingly fashionable in recent years (and notably in European policy circles, (Owen, Macnaghten, and Stilgoe, (2012))), as a term it has a history stretching back at least a decade (Hellstrom, 2003; Guston, 2004; Barben *et al.*, 2008; Owen *et al.*, 2009a; Owen and Goldberg, 2010; Von Schomberg, 2011a,2011b; Lee, 2012; Armstrong *et al.*, 2012: see Fisher and Rip, Chapter 9 for a brief discourse analysis). It also has a number of broader synonyms, including "responsible development" (which is, for example, one of four strategic goals of the US National Nanotechnology Initiative (NNI, 2004)). While discussions focused on responsible innovation are relatively recent, they are heirs to earlier ones over the ethical, legal, and social implications of (e.g., genomic) research, human research subjects, technology assessment, socio-technical integration, research integrity, social responsibility and the function of science, intellectual property, and the economic productivity of research (Fisher and Rip review some of these in Chapter 9). Elements of responsible innovation are also visible in science and technology policy discourse, including, for example, calls for collaborations between social scientists, natural scientists, engineers, and publics evident within the EU Framework Programme (in particular since FP5[6]; Rodriguez, Fisher,

---

[6] For example, "More must be done ... to find ways of actively engaging with civil society, stakeholder groups and the public at large in the preparation and execution of research" (Stančič, 2007, p. 1).

and Schuurbiers, 2013), moving toward what Guston describes as "collaborative assurance," which attempts to take the societal and scientific elements of co-production more self-consciously in hand.

Arguably, the language of responsible innovation began to emerge alongside large-scale programs of nanosciences and nanotechnology research, in some jurisdictions (e.g., in the UK) heuristically framed by previous science and technology policy traumas (such as GM) and the desire to ensure that the "mistakes of GM were not repeated again." In the US, the National Nanotechnology Initiative adopted a strategic goal of "responsible development," and in Europe the European Commission developed a Code for Responsible Nanosciences and Nanotechnologies Research (European Commission, 2008). This trend has since accelerated in the emerging fields of synthetic biology and geoengineering.

If the term responsible innovation is an emergent one with a history that can be traced back many decades, then the dimensions of responsible innovation that we have described above have an equally rich history in thought, study, and practice in a number of fields, including science and technology studies, philosophy of science, science policy, and strategic innovation management. In this regard responsible innovation is evolutionary in nature.

The framework we describe brings together a number of established approaches that, in various ways, have contributed significantly to one or more of the dimensions. These recognize the need to stimulate the reflexivity of scientists, broaden the scope of strategic choices, "open up" and embed more reflective capacity into the practice of science (Rip, Misa, and Schot, 1995; Stirling, 2005; 2008; Wilsdon *et al.*, 2005). Approaches such as anticipatory governance (Barben *et al.*, 2008; Karinen and Guston, 2010), technology assessment in all its various formulations (constructive[7] and real time, for example; Schot and Rip, 1996; Guston and Sarewitz, 2002), upstream engagement (Wilsdon *et al.*, 2005), socio-technical integration, and midstream modulation (Fisher *et al.*, 2006; Fisher, 2007; Schuurbiers and Fisher, 2009) and values-sensitive design (see van den Hoven, Chapter 4) are all important foundations for, and have significant contributions to make to the concept of responsible innovation. These variously re-affirm the value of concepts of, for example, foresight, engagement, and integration (Barben *et al.*, 2008). In some sense responsible innovation blatantly plagiarizes and builds on these foundations, with good justification. More applied approaches from the fields of strategic innovation management (Tidd and Bessant, 2009) and innovation studies (including concepts such as the democratization of innovation (von Hippel, 2005)) and open innovation (Chesborough, 2003) make an equally important contribution, for example, by emphasizing the role of users in innovation and the use of innovation governance mechanisms, such as stage gating, in new product development and beyond.

2.5.1   Some Experiments in Responsible Innovation

Fisher and Rip (Chapter 9) provide several examples of integrated approaches that support the concept of responsible innovation proposed above. We can also highlight one or two specific examples of experiments in responsible innovation that serve as illustrations. Each focuses on one or more responsible innovation dimensions, providing useful insights into how these could be practically taken forward.

---

[7] Constructive technology assessment aims to broaden technological design, development and embedding in society by including more actors, and to use insights from such actors to modulate technological dynamics (for more details see Chapter 9).

These include one experiment which, through a process of public deliberation, reflected on the purposes of research and used this reflection to frame a research funding call in the area of nanotechnology for medicine and healthcare (Jones, 2008). The public dialogues provided a clear steer about the relative priorities of six potential application areas of nanotechnology for healthcare, informing and shaping the nature of the funding call itself, such that it could respond better to social values (for more detail see Chapter 5). This example illustrates how dimensions of reflection, deliberation, and responsiveness were embedded within the process of science funding.

Another experiment asked applicants responding to a call on nanosciences for carbon capture to reflect on the wider implications of their proposed research and the applications this might lead to (Owen and Goldberg, 2010). In this case scientists were required to submit a risk register identifying the wider risks and levels of uncertainty associated with the project's activities and future impacts (be these social, environmental, health, or otherwise), who would manage these and how. This provided a useful entry point for them to consider some of the wider risks associated with their proposed research. At the same time it clearly showed the limits of an approach based solely on risk assessment, with identified risks being confined largely to health and safety associated with handling and disposal of nanomaterials in the lab, and with little considerations of the wider potential impacts on society or the environment, either for the research itself or what it might lead to. Unlike the first example, in this experiment there was little explicit reflection on the purposes of the research, but some reflection on its wider potential (if only proximal) products. This process exhibited strong, formal mechanisms of responsiveness, notably in that risk registers were evaluated as a secondary criterion by a funding panel which made recommendations as to which projects should be funded. What it also demonstrated was the imaginative capacity of some scientists and researchers to rise to the challenge of responsible innovation. While some were content with the *de minimus* requirement to submit a risk register, others embedded supplementary methods of public engagement, technology assessment, and life cycle analysis that began to explore other dimensions we have proposed.

The Socio-Technical Integration Research (STIR) program is a third example of an experiment in responsible innovation (Fisher *et al.*, 2006; Fisher, 2007; Schuurbiers and Fisher, 2009; and Fisher and Rip, Chapter 9). This program has embedded social scientists and humanities scholars into over 25 laboratories on three continents with the aim of testing the viability of "midstream modulation" as an integral part of science and engineering research. Midstream modulation embeds a process which allows for the incremental adjustment of science and innovation to address social norms and values, as science and innovation actually occur. These norms and values Fisher and Rip argue are typically only addressed downstream in the process of innovation (e.g., through regulation as we have discussed), or upstream, during policy and priority setting.

The STIR program uses a protocol that unpacks social and ethical values midstream, that is, as decisions by scientists and innovators are being made, in real-time. The protocol introduces social scientists and humanities scholars into laboratory settings and takes the interdisciplinary collaborators (i.e., natural and physical scientists) through an iterative set of questions designed to probe capacities for responsible innovation (Table 2.1).

As a result of using the protocol on a regular basis during routine laboratory decision-making, STIR laboratory engagements have documented "productive research disruptions" that have led to changes in research direction, experimental design, safety and

Table 2.1   STIR protocol decision components for "midstream modulation"

Decision component	Critical question	Capacity built
Opportunity	*What* are you working on?	Reflexive
Considerations	*Why* are you working on it?	Reflexive, deliberative
Alternatives	*How* could you approach it differently?	Responsive
Outcomes	*Who* might be affected in the future?	Anticipatory

environmental practices, and public outreach, that is, the dimension of responsiveness. These changes are voluntary, since the lab researchers choose whether or not to make them, integrative, since they expand the perception of both social values and technical options that are considered, and collaborative.

By way of one final example, Macnaghten and Owen (2011) describe an experiment in the controversial and emerging field of climate engineering research, whereby the dimensions of responsible innovation were embedded within a "stage gating" model of innovation governance, originally drawn from strategic innovation management, but applied in a novel way in this context. Climate engineering embodies a range of potential approaches that are broadly aimed at either carbon dioxide removal from the atmosphere or solar radiation management (SRM) (reflecting incoming solar radiation to reduce air temperature) Royal Society (2009). Research in this area is now being undertaken, and one such project (the SPICE – or Stratospheric Particle Injection for Climate Engineering project) aimed to evaluate candidate particles for SRM, identify feasible ways of delivering particles into the stratosphere, and undertake modeling to understand efficacy and effects, noting that volcanic eruptions of sulfate particles (e.g., Mount Pinatubu in 1991) have been associated with significant, if transitory, decreases in global air temperature.

The project embedded a proposed field trial of a potential particle delivery technology, in which the project team would investigate the dynamics of a 1 km balloon-tethered hose that would spray only water. This would inform the design of a future 20 km high delivery system. The test bed would not undertake any climate engineering itself, but was highly symbolic and attracted significant media interest and a broad range of opinions, including widespread resistance from civil society groups. Before making a decision on whether to allow the field trial to go ahead, the UK Research Councils who funded the project employed a stage gate model of innovation governance, in which we embedded the dimensions of responsible innovation discussed above (Macnaghten and Owen, 2011). Stage gating is a well-established mechanism of innovation management (originally designed for new product development) whereby decision points are periodically introduced into the R&D process, which is thus phased in terms of investment. Traditionally, inputs into each decision gate are technical and market-based considerations of feasibility, market potential, and so on. The stage gate approach was broadened to include the dimensions of responsible innovation described above (Figure 2.1).

The SPICE team were asked to anticipate, reflect, and deliberate (with publics and stakeholders) on the purposes and possible impacts of both the research, and what it could lead to. An independent stage gate panel evaluated their responses and in turn advised the funders on whether, and if so, how to proceed. This evaluation was made in terms of five criteria into which the dimensions of responsible innovation were translated. These were that the test-bed deployment was safe and principal risks had been

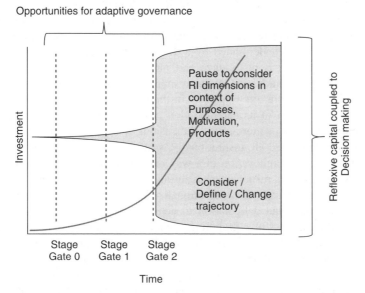

Figure 2.1 *Embedding dimensions of responsible innovation within a stage gating innovation governance model*

identified, managed, and deemed acceptable (Criterion 1); the test-bed deployment was compliant with relevant regulations (Criterion 2); the nature and purpose of SPICE would be clearly communicated to all relevant parties to inform and promote balanced discussion (Criterion 3); future applications and impacts had been described, and mechanisms put in place to review these in the light of new information (Criterion 4); and mechanisms had been identified to understand public and stakeholder views regarding the potential applications and impacts (Criterion 5).

The last three of these criteria were not met fully and the panel advised the Research Councils to delay the test bed to allow these to be addressed, notably to allow a full package of stakeholder engagement to be undertaken and the wider social and ethical issues to be explored. As a result of deeper questioning that followed, and in particular as this related to the purposes and motivations of the research, issues of patenting and commercialization surfaced and the SPICE project team chose to abandon the test bed, concentrating instead on the laboratory and modeling aspects of the research, and (critically) stakeholder engagement.

What these examples demonstrate is that there are in fact numerous ways of implementing the dimensions of responsible innovation, and that as an approach it should not be strongly prescriptive, or rules based in its implementation (Richardson, 1999). Beneath the general framework researchers, innovators, and those who fund them should have flexibility in the details of how its dimensions are taken forward, in creative and imaginative ways that suit its context of application best and that they themselves value.

In summary, responsible innovation coalesces and integrates a number of complementary approaches under a coherent framework. But can it be really any more than a carefully – sewn quilt made up of a patchwork of such previous incarnations?

Owen, Macnaghten, and Stilgoe (2012) distinguish three distinct, emergent features of responsible innovation, the first two of which are strongly evolutionary in nature. The first, as we have discussed, is an emphasis on science and innovation for society – a focus on purposes, where research and innovation are targeted at societal challenges and the "right impacts," underpinned by a deliberative democracy. The second, linked to the first, is an emphasis on science and innovation with society – a focus on the need for research and innovation to be responsive to society in terms of setting its direction, and in modulating its trajectory in the face of the uncertain ways innovation invariably unfolds as part of its naturalization in the world. While many approaches to date have embedded one or more of the dimensions of responsible innovation described above, few have embedded all, institutionally, systematically and iteratively, around the processes of science and innovation in a way that supports reflection on their purposes and products, and enables responsiveness through effective mechanisms of governance. Responsible innovation calls for institutionalized responsiveness, for the coupling of anticipation, reflection, and deliberation to action. Or as Guston and Sarewitz (2002) put it "the key to successfully grappling with unpredictability is to build a decision process that is continuously reflexive, so that the attributes of and relations between co-evolving components of the system become apparent, and informed incremental response is feasible." The strength of a framework for responsible innovation lies in the integration and application of such approaches as an institutionally embedded culture, one in which the total becomes far greater than the sum of its parts.[8]

These two features, as we have already noted, build on trends toward challenge-led research (Lund Declaration, 2009), and socio-technical integration (Fisher *et al.*, 2006; Barben *et al.*, 2008). The third feature is perhaps more novel, being encapsulated in the explicit linking of research and innovation to responsibility, the "responsible" in responsible innovation (Grinbaum and Groves, Chapter 7). This is currently lacking from both theoretical approaches, and more applied ones such as strategic innovation management (Tidd and Bessant, 2009). It is prompting a re-evaluation of the concept of responsibility as a moral and philosophical social ascription, in the context of innovation as a future-oriented, deeply uncertain, often complex and always collective phenomenon. This in turn is challenging scientists, innovators, business partners, research funders, policy makers and (not least) those who use, benefit from, and are burdened by innovation to reflect on their own roles and responsibilities.

2.6   Toward the Future: Building Capacity for Responsible Innovation

In this chapter we have developed a framework for responsible innovation, based on four dimensions, and grounded in a prospective model of responsibility that emphasizes dimensions of care and responsiveness. We have emphasized that this must be able to reflect on both the products and purposes of science and innovation. We have been reminded of the rich history in a number of fields of study, both theoretical and applied, which make a significant and important contribution both to the framing and definition

---

[8] The move toward more integrative projects has been catalyzed by some research councils, for example, in Norway (Research Council of Norway) and The Netherlands (Maatschappelijk Verantwoord Innoveren (Responsible Innovation) program: www.nwo.nl/responsible-innovation.

of responsible innovation, and to how this is translated through the dimensions into practice. The chapters that follow in the book provide further perspectives on, and specific details regarding, individual dimensions and attendant methodologies (e.g., Sykes and Macnaghten, Chapter 5).

We now conclude with some closing thoughts on implementation, on how the embedding of responsible innovation as a genuinely transformative and constructive[9] approach can be supported. First of these is the important question concerning which areas and kinds of science and innovation such an approach should be targeted at. We have already alluded to this in the introduction, but it is worth laboring here as it is a question that frequently surfaces. There is clearly a wide spectrum between curiosity–driven science and applied research and development, between Francis Crick and James Watson developing models of DNA at the Cavendish Laboratory in Cambridge in the 1950s, and the development of genetically modified "Round Up–ready" seeds by Monsanto decades later.

Ultimately, the decision of when to employ such a framework will be a judgment call, and it is clear that for some areas of, for example, purely descriptive science there may be little impetus to do so, at least until more specific areas of application become envisioned. But once such visions become plausible (and fundable) our experiences demonstrate the need for such a framework to be considered early on, such that it is embedded from the outset, rather than bolted on, or retro-fitted at a later stage. Von Schomberg (this volume) provides some cautionary examples of technologies that have been pushed in the absence of such an approach and the consequences that have resulted. In the case of the SPICE project described above, for example, this should have been initiated before the launch of the geoengineering funding call, at the time when research funders were considering whether to put resource into this area of science. Efforts to engage publics and stakeholders in areas of controversial and contested science and innovation are likely to be viewed at best as being disingenuous if these are perceived as being simply a way to smooth the pathway of technologies into society in an instrumental way, and they will rightly be suspicious of the motivations. Such deliberation must be extended to decisions as to whether such areas should be commissioned at all.

The expectations of responsible innovation should also be clear to all (Lee and Petts, Chapter 8), and the ability to rise to such expectations supported and resourced accordingly. Our second observation then relates to the concept of capacity. Responsibility is a learned behavior: our children are not born with the capacity to be responsible, or to take responsibility. It is a social ascription that is learned, and we go to some lengths to teach them responsible behavior, to understand the norms and contours of responsibility, before we let them make their independent way in the world. Capacity for responsible innovation must be nurtured, across and within our institutions of science and innovation. Education and training are key to this, supporting the development of the necessary multi- and inter-disciplinary competencies that allow and support the responsible innovation approach we have described (McGregor and Wetmore, 2009). This must be sensitive to cultural differences that exist within and beyond higher education institutions, research institutes, and companies, and that in turn reflect the globalized nature of modern society, and of science and innovation itself (Lee and Petts, Chapter 8).

---

[9] Note that by the term constructive we do not mean instrumental.

This leads us to our third observation, one which we have already touched on in this chapter. Responsible innovation is ultimately about being responsible, taking responsibility, and innovating responsibly: but this is a collective endeavor. Scientists and innovators play an important role, but responsible innovation must be a holistic approach across the innovation ecosystem, with an important role for universities, institutes, and research funders to play. This stresses the need for co-responsibility (Mitcham, 2003; Von Schomberg, 2007). In this complex landscape where governance is a seemingly insurmountable challenge, those who fund and manage research in our places of learning and in our innovative companies are uniquely placed to help define, and implement, the contours of responsible innovation, to institutionally embed the framework we have proposed.

Fourthly, responsible innovation must be a continuous, iterative process of learning, one that is embedded in and around science and innovation, one which integrates expertise and understanding and invites in perspectives from stakeholders and publics. But as an innovation itself, responsible innovation must abide by its own framework in this regard, and be anticipatory, reflective, deliberative, and responsive in its constitution and implementation. Its own purposes, intentions, and motivations must be clear. We have argued elsewhere that it should be undertaken for substantive and normative, rather than purely instrumental reasons (Owen, Macnaghten, and Stilgoe, 2012). It must also be able to respond to the inevitable resistance such a framework will encounter if it is perceived as posing threats to scientific freedom or national interests – from economic growth to scientific competitiveness. These are not insurmountable challenges. If such challenges can be responded to, and if a framework for responsible innovation can be developed inclusively in a way that supports genuine culture change, perhaps then it might open up new possibilities for science and innovation and support their democratic, and responsible, emergence in society.

References

Adam, B. and Groves, G., (2011) Futures tended: care and future-oriented responsibility. *Bulletin of Science Technology Society,* **31**(1) 17–27.

Armstrong, M., G. Cornut, S. Delacôte, M. Lenglet, Y. Millo, F. Muniesa, A. Pointier and Y. Tadjeddine (2012). Towards a practical approach to responsible innovation in finance: new product committees revisited. *Journal of Financial Regulation and Compliance,* **20**(2), 147–168.

Arthur,W. (1989). Competing technologies, increasing returns, and lock-in by historical events. *The Economic Journal* **99**:116–131.

Barben, D., Fisher, E., Selin, C., and Guston, D. H. (2008). Anticipatory governance of nanotechnology: foresight, engagement, and integration. in *The Handbook of Science and Technology Studies* (eds O. A. Edward, J. Hackett, M. Lynch and J. Wajcman. (3rd edn, pp. 979–1000). Cambridge, MA: MIT Press.

Beck, U. (1995) *Ecological Politics in an Age of Risk*. Polity Press. p. 224.

Beck, U., (2000). Risk society revisited: theory, politics and research programmes. in *The Risk Society and Beyond: Critical Issues for Social Theory* (eds Adam, B., Beck, U. and Van Loon, J.). Sage Publications, London.

BIS (2011) www.bis.gov.uk/assets/biscore/innovation/docs/i/11-1387-innovation-and -research-strategy-for-growth.pdf. Accessed 20/1/2013.

Callon M., Lascoumes P., Barthe Y. (2010) *On Acting in an Uncertain World: An Essay on Technological Democracy*. Boston, MA: MIT Press.

Carson R. (1962) *Silent Spring*. Penguin Classics p. 336.

Chesborough, H. (2003) *Open Innovation: The New Imperative for Creating and Profiting from Technology*. Harvard Business School Publishing Corporation.

Collingridge D. (1980) *The Social Control of Technology*. Francis Pinter Ltd, London.

David, P. A., (2001) Path dependence, its critics and the quest for 'historical economics', in *Evolution and Path Dependence in Economic Ideas: Past and Present* (eds Garrouste, P., and Ioannides, S.). Edward Elgar Publishing, Cheltenham.

EEA (European Environment Agency) (2001) *Late Lessons from Early Warnings: The Precautionary Principle 1896–2000*. Luxemburg: Office for Official Publications of the European Communities.

European Commission (2008) European Commissions Code of Conduct for Responsible Nanotechnologies Research, http://.ec.europa.eu/nanotechnology/pdf/nanocode -rec pe0894c-en.pdf (accessed 27 September 2010).

Fisher, E., (2007). Ethnographic invention: probing the capacity of laboratory decisions. *NanoEthics* **1**(2): 155–165.

Fisher, E., Mahajan, R. & Mitcham, C. (2006). Midstream modulation of technology: governance from within. *Bulletin of Science Technology Society* **26**(6), 485–496.

Groves, C. (2006) Technological futures and Non-reciprocal responsibility. *The International Journal of the Humanities,* **4** (2), pp. 57–61.

Guston D.H. (2004) Responsible innovation in the commercialised university. in *Buying in or Selling Out: The Commercialisation of the American Research University* (ed D.G. Stein), New Brunswick: Rutgers University Press pp. 161–174.

Guston, D. H. (2007) Toward centres for responsible innovation in the commercialized university. in *Public Science in Liberal Democracy: The Challenge to Science and Democracy* (eds. P.W.B. Phillips and J. Porter), Toronto: University of Toronto Press, pp. 295-312.

Guston, D. H. and Sarewitz, D., 2002. Real-time technology assessment. *Technology in Society* **24** (1), 93–109.

Hellstrom T. (2003) Systemic innovation and risk: technology assessment and the challenge of responsible innovation, *Technology in Society* **25** 369–384.

von Hippel, E. (2005) Democratizing Innovation, Available online at http://web.mit.edu /evhippel/www/democ1.htm. Accessed 20/1/2013.

Hoffman-Riem, H., & Wynne, B. (2002). In risk assessment, one has to admit ignorance. *Nature,* 416, 123.

van den Hoven, M. J., Lokhorst, G.J.C. and van de Poel, I., (2012) Engineering and the problem of moral overload. *Science and Engineering Ethics* **18**(1), 1–13.

Jonas H. (1984). *The Imperative of Responsibility*. University of Chicago Press, Chicago p. 255.

Jones R. (2008).When it pays to ask the public. *Nature Nanotechnology* **3**, 578–579.

Karinen R., Guston D.H. (2010). Towards anticipatory governance. The experience with nanotechnology. in *Governing Future Technologies. Nanotechnology and the Rise of an Assessment Regime* (ed M. Kaiser), Springer: Dordrecht, Heidelberg, London, and New York.

Kearnes, M and Weinroth, M (2011) A New Mandate? Research Policy in a Technological Society. Research Report RES-061-25-0208, Durham University, Durham.

Lee, R.G. Look at mother nature on the Run in the 21st century: responsibility, research and innovation. *Transnational Environmental Law,* **1**:1 (2012), pp. 105–117.

Lund Declaration (2009) Conference: New Worlds – New Solutions. Research and Innovation as a Basis for Developing Europe in a Global Context, Lund, Sweden, 7–8 July 2009, Online Available at, http://www.se2009.eu/polopoly_fs/1.8460!menu/standard/file/lund_declaration_final_version_9_july.pdf. Accessed 20/1/2013.

McGregor J, Wetmore JM. (2009) Researching and teaching the ethics and social implications of emerging technologies in the laboratory. *NanoEthics* **3**: 17–30.

Mackenzie D. (2010) Unlocking the Language of Structured Securities. Financial Times (Aug. 19, 2010), www.sps.ed.ac.uk/__data/assets/pdf_file/0007/53998/ftaug10.pdf (accessed 26 July 2012).

Macnaghten, P., Owen, R., (2011). Good governance for geoengineering. *Nature* **479**, 293.

Marris, C. and Rose, N. (2010). Open engagement: exploring public participation in the biosciences. *PLoS Biology,* **8**(11): e1000549.

Mitcham, C., (2003). Co-responsibility for research integrity. *Science and Engineering Ethics* **9**, 273–290.

NNI (2004) The National Nanotechnology Initiative Strategic Plan, December 2004, U.S.A.

Owen, R. and Goldberg, N., (2010) Responsible innovation: a pilot study with the U.K. Engineering and physical sciences research council. *Risk Analysis,* **30**: 1699–1707.

Owen R. and Jobling S. (2012) The hidden costs of flexible fertility. *Nature* **485**: 441.

Owen R, Baxter D, Maynard T, Depledge MH. (2009a) Beyond regulation: risk pricing and responsible innovation. *Environmental Science and Technology,* **43**(14):5171–5175.

Owen R., Crane M., Deanne K., Handy R.D., Linkov I., Depledge M.H. (2009b) Strategic approaches for the management of environmental risk uncertainties posed by nanomaterials. in *Nanotechnologies: Risks and Benefits* (eds. I. Linkov and J. Steevens) NATO Science for Peace and Security Series C: Environmental Security, Springer, pp. 369–384.

Owen R., Macnaghten P., Stilgoe J. (2012) Responsible research and innovation: from science in society to science for society, with society. *Science and Public Policy,* 6: 751–760.

Pacces A.(2010). Consequences of uncertainty for regulation: Law and economics of the financial crisis. *European Company & Financial Law Review,* **7**, 479–511.

Pellizzoni, L., (2004). Responsibility and environmental governance. *Environmental Politics,* **13**(3), 541–565.

Pielke R. (2007) *The Honest Broker, Making Sense of Science in Policy and Politics.* Cambridge University Press, Cambridge.

Polanyi, M. (1962). The Republic of Science: Its Political and Economic Theory. Minerva 1, 54–74.

RCEP, Royal Commission on Environmental Pollution (2008) Novel Materials in the Environment: The Case of Nanotechnology, www.official-documents.gov.uk /document/cm74/7468/7468.pdf (accessed 26 July 2012).

Richardson, H. S., (1999). Institutionally divided moral responsibility, in Paul, E. F., Miller, F. D., Paul, J., (eds.) *Responsibility*. Cambridge University Press, Cambridge, pp. 218–249.

Rip, A., Misa, T. and Schot, J. (eds), 1995. *Managing Technology in Society: The Approach of Constructive Technology Assessment*. Thomson, London.

Rodriguez, H., Fisher, E., Schuurbiers D. 2013 Integrating science and society in European framework programmes: trends in project-level solicitations. in press, Research Policy.

Royal Society (2009) Geoengineering the Climate: Science, Governance and Uncertainty, http://royalsociety.org/uploadedFiles/Royal_Society_Content/policy/publications/2009 /8693.pdf (accessed 26 July 2012).

Schot J, Rip A. (1996) The past and future of constructive technology assessment. *Technological Forecasting and Social Change* **54**:251–268.

Schuurbiers D., and Fisher E., (2009). Lab-scale intervention. Science and society series on convergence research. *EMBO Reports,* **10**(5), 424–427.

Stančič, Z., (2007). Foreword, in Integrating Science in Society Issues in Scientific Research: Main Findings of the Study on the Integration of Science and Society Issues in the Sixth Framework Programme Report to the European Commission EUR 22976 (eds Braithwaite, M., Fries, R., Zadrozny, T., Wuiame, N., Anasagasti-Corta, M., Ings, N.), Office for Official Publications of the European Communities, Luxembourg, p. 1.

Stilgoe, J. (2011) A question of intent. *Nature Climate Change* **1**, 325–326.

Stirling, A. (2005) Opening up or closing down? Analysis, participation and power in the social appraisal of technology, in *Science and Citizens: Globalization and the Challenge of Engagement (Claiming citizenship)*, (eds M Leach, M., I. Scoones, I. and B. Wynne, B.) London: Zed pp. 218–31.

Stirling, A. (2007). A general framework for analysing diversity in science, technology and society. *Journal of the Royal Society, Interface* **4**, 707–719.

Stirling, A. (2008) "Opening up" and "closing down": power, participation, and pluralism in the social appraisal of technology. *Science Technology and Human Values* **33**, 262–294.

Thomson B. (2011) Pachakuti: indigenous perspectives, buen vivir, sumaq kawsay and degrowth. *Development,* **54**(4), (448–454).

Tidd, J. and J. Bessant (2009). *Managing Innovation: Integrating Technological, Market and Organizational Change*. Chichester, John Wiley & Sons, Ltd.

TNS-BMRB (2010) *Synthetic Biology Dialogue*. London: Sciencewise.

Von Schomberg, R. (2007) From the Ethics of Technology Towards and Ethics of Knowledge Policy and Knowledge Assessment, http://ec.europa.eu/research/science-society /pdf/ethicsofknowledgepolicy_en.pdf (accessed 26 July 2012).

Von Schomberg (2011a) The quest for the "right" impacts of science and technology. An outlook towards a framework for responsible research and innovation. in *Technikfolgen Abschätzen Lehren. Bildungspotenziale Transdisziplinärer Methoden* (eds M. Dusseldorp, R. Beecroft). Springer-Verlag p. 394.

Von Schomberg, R. (2011b). Towards Responsible Research and Innovation in the Information and Communication Technologies and Security *Technologies Fields*, European Commission, Brussels, http://ec.europa.eu/research/science-society/document_library/pdf_06/mep-rapport-2011_en.pdf. Accessed 20/1/2013.

Williams, B. (1981) *Moral Luck*. Cambridge: Cambridge University Press, pp. 20–39.

Wilsdon, J., Wynne, B. and Stilgoe, J., (2005) *The PublicValue of Science*. Demos, London.

WWF (World Wildlife Fund) (2011) Green Game-Changers: 50 Innovations to Inspire Business Transformation, http://assets.wwf.org.uk/downloads/green_game_changersx50.pdf (accessed 26 July 2012).

Wynne, B, (1993) Public uptake of science: a case for institutional reflexivity, *Public Understanding of Science,* **2** (4) 321–337.

3

A Vision of Responsible Research and Innovation

René von Schomberg[1]
European Commission, Directorate General for Research
and Innovation, Belgium

Responsible research and innovation (RRI) has become an increasingly important phrase within policy narratives, in particular in Europe, where it will be a cross-cutting issue under the prospective European Union (EU) Framework Programme for Research and Innovation "Horizon 2020." In EU member states there are also various initiatives supporting RRI, notably under schemes of national research councils (e.g., the United Kingdom, Norway, and the Netherlands). However, there is as yet no agreed definition of the concept, and thoughts on how it should be implemented vary.

This chapter outlines a vision behind RRI, taking a largely European policy perspective. It provides a definition of the concept and proposes a broad framework for its implementation under research and innovation schemes around the world.

I will make the case that RRI should be understood as a strategy of stakeholders to become mutually responsive to each other, anticipating research and innovation outcomes aimed at the "grand challenges" of our time, for which they share responsibility.

Research and innovation processes need to become more responsive and adaptive to these grand challenges. This implies, among others, the introduction of broader foresight and impact assessments for new technologies, beyond their anticipated market-benefits and risks.

---

[1] Dr. Dr.phil. René von Schomberg (email: Rene.vonschomberg@ec.europa.eu) is at the European Commission, Directorate General for Research and Innovation. The views expressed here are those of the author and may not in any circumstances be regarded as stating an official position of the European Commission.

Responsible Innovation, First Edition. Edited by Richard Owen, John Bessant and Maggy Heintz.
© 2013 John Wiley & Sons, Ltd. Published 2013 by John Wiley & Sons, Ltd.

3.1   Introduction: Technical Inventions, Innovation, and Responsibility

In order to be able to specify the "responsibility" in RRI, I contrast the process of modern innovations with mere technical inventions. In order to be able to understand the responsibility concept solely with regard to technical inventions, I give a historical example of pre-modern times, so that I can "isolate" the role of responsibility in this context. This allows me to rule out such connotations of "responsibility" in the light of the modern innovation context with which we are so familiar.

At the very beginning of the eighteenth century, the Portuguese priest Bartolomeu Lourenço de Gusmão claimed to have developed a "machine for sailing through the air." His invention was called Passarola (meaning "ugly bird" in Portuguese – because of its resemblance to a bird) and the "ship" was filled with numerous tubes through which the wind was supposed to flow and fill out bulges (see design of the prototype, Figure 3.1).

Bartolomeu informed the Portuguese King John V about his inventions in a letter[2]: "Father Bartolomeu Lourenço dares to inform Your Majesty that he has discovered an implement by which he can travel through air.... With it, he will manage 200 leagues

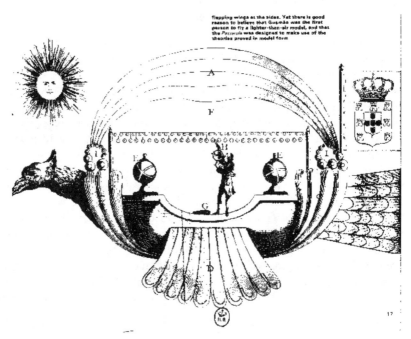

Figure 3.1 *Prototype of the Passarola. (Reprinted from http://en.wikipedia.org/wiki /File:Passarola.png Last accessed 12/11/12)*

---

[2] The quotes comes from the original letter Bartolomeu wrote to King John V. It was displayed at the exhibition "*Lux in Arcana. The Vatican secret archives reveals itself*" (Capitoline Museum, Rome, March 2012 to September 2012). The Museum display gave the following further information: Gusmão presented a demonstration of his inventions, but we do not know for sure if the passarola itself was used, or simply a hot-air balloon. Neither do we know how big the prototype was: it seemed to be triggered by a strange combination of sails, wings and electromagnetism.

a day: thus, he will be able to bring armies and far away countries news and orders.... The furthermost regions will be discovered, at the world's poles, and the Portuguese nation will benefit from such discovery...."

Bartolomeu pointed not only to the potential benefit of his invention but also to its negative side-effects: "Many crimes will be committed, as it allows to easily flee from one country to the other: its use will have to be limited."

On 17 April 1707, John V decreed the exclusive right for Bartolomeu to perfect his machine and assigned him a lifelong appointment at Coimbra University. In the same decree John V made it clear that anyone trying to copy his work would receive the death penalty.

This example shows that historically "responsible" use and control of technical inventions was limited to those who were deemed able to act responsibly: in this case the King (see Chapter 7 for discussions concerning deontological responsibility). Right up to modern times technical inventions were still considered with a view on "who is in control" and "who can make use of it." Negative consequences of the technology were notably associated with who could use/misuse the technology, rather than with the properties of the technology itself. The politics of non-proliferation of nuclear weapons still echoes this tradition: only a few "responsible" governments are supposed to control the production of these weapons. All others should keep moral constraint and trust the "responsible" governors of this technology.

Whereas technological inventions were, historically, controlled by a central agent to avoid abuse, modern innovations are, in contrast, distributed through market mechanisms whereby property rights allow, in principle, the further improvements of the innovations by other market operators over time. Economic exploitation of innovations implies a loss of a sole control agent; yet the state demands from industrial operators that they address the so-called "three market hurdles" of efficacy, quality, and safety before they can legally market their products or processes. Responsible marketing is thus ensured by conditions required by state regulations, and (product) law specifies the legal requirements prior to marketing (see Chapter 8 for further discussion). In the area of pharmaceuticals, even a fourth hurdle of clinical effectiveness and cost-efficiency became operational to some extent under modern legislation, not least in order to be more responsible for the outcomes of innovation processes. For modern innovations, responsibility for the consequences of implementation is then primarily related to the properties and characteristics of the products or the technology and less to the privileged owners and creators of the technology. On the contrary, all informed citizens should be able to make (safe and responsible) use of it and the "benefits" of new technologies are determined by their success in the market rather than the glory of a nation or of the King (national space and defense programs, however, still echo the pre-modern pride associated with the mere ability to do things others cannot do).

Modern technological innovation therefore receives its specific form through *technology which has been democratized in its use and privatized in its production.* Competition in the market should ensure product improvement for the benefit of all, rather than a demonstration of the capabilities of a single actor (e.g., the King or the state) and its establishment of superiority. Technology from now on can be discussed in terms of benefits and risks for all citizens. Competition in the market is fostered by openness and access to knowledge.[3] Innovation becomes a goal itself, with improvements of existing products and services through innovation being achieved via the free market.

However, this "evaluation" scheme of benefits and risks of technology is now put in question by the call for RRI. I will elaborate this claim in the following section.

3.2   Responsible Research and Innovation and the Quest for the Right Impacts of Research

In modern societies we do not have a specific forum or policy for evaluating particular technologies within a legislative context. We only have at our disposal formal safety, quality, and efficacy assessment procedures that evaluate the properties of products in the course of passing the three market hurdles described above. Different technologies are often combined in single products. Thus, eventually the benefits of technologies are "demonstrated" by market success and the potential negative consequences are evaluated under formal risk assessment schemes. This gives a peculiar division of responsibilities among the stakeholders concerned. The state is responsible for defining the risks of technologies under product authorization procedures and product liability law, and ensuring market operators compliance, whereas we lack a particular responsibility for what could count as a positive impact of the technology. The assumption here is that these "benefits" cannot be universalized and that, through a plurality of the market, consumers are offered a variety of choices and thus the diverging preferences of consumers can be satisfied. Competitors can improve their products through innovation, driven by market demand. Thus, the normative dimension of what counts as an "improvement" *is decided by market mechanisms.* On top of that, technological innovations are unpredictable and positive impacts of innovations under public research and innovation policy schemes are solely justified in purely economic terms. For instance, one assessment is that achieving the EU target of 3% of EU GDP through research and development could create 3.7 million jobs and increase annual GDP by close to €800 billion by 2025 (Zagamé, 2010). This assessment is completely neutral to which specific technologies (and their accompanying benefits and risks) will eventually hit the market and which technologies are specifically associated with the increase in jobs.[4] The positive impacts of research and innovation are only generally couched in terms of fostering the prosperity and wealth of nations: the availability of finance for research and innovation in general is seen as a condition for achieving such prosperity.

The Flagship Innovation Union is a central part of the EU 2020 strategy, and within this innovation is seen as a means for "smart growth," defined as "developing an economy based on knowledge and innovation" (European Commission, 2010). The Innovation Union aims "to improve framework conditions and access to finance for research and

---

[3] In the time of Bartolomeu, it was important to keep your knowledge to yourself rather than sharing the knowledge with a view to scientific progress or innovation. The curators of the museum explain: Nowadays the Passarola seems to have been conceived by Gusmão to trick the many snoopers who wanted to know the results of his experiments. It seems that the scientist also contributed to the spread of false news in the press about one of his flights from Portugal to Vienna aboard the Passarola.

[4] Paradoxically, although the positive impacts of research and innovation cannot be specified for particular technologies (as their development is unpredictable) this unpredictability is sharply contrasted with rather precise economic figures in terms of GDP increase and job production (Would we require less investment in research and development if the figure of 3.6 million jobs turns out to be far less, or call for more investment, if the figure is much higher?).

innovation so as to ensure that innovative ideas can be turned into products and services that create growth and jobs."

Discussions of particular technologies in terms of benefits or risks within this frame are *informal*: there is no formal weighing under public policies of the benefits of particular technologies versus their risks. While there is a clearly defined responsibility for operators and the state to address the risks in formal procedures, there is no equivalent for a formal evaluation of the benefits. The responsibility for the positive outcomes of the use of technologies evaporates once they are marketed (whereas responsibility for the negative outcomes remains). More importantly, there seems to be no normative baseline on which we could judge the positive impacts and benefits of technologies. The responsibility for the positive impacts is left to market operators who look for economically exploitable products. Public investment in research and innovation policy, and thus the positive outcomes of science and technology, are primarily justified in macro-economic terms.

This implies that a discussion on the benefits and risks of a particular technology is not only necessarily informal, but is also *artificial*. Formalizing an evaluation of the positive outcomes (other than in macro-economic terms) is not possible: the success of innovation on the market is unpredictable and reflects a continuous shift of needs and preferences of consumers. Innovation is not fully in the hands of the producers of technology, with the users of the technology dramatically shifting the context of its use and thereby triggering new innovations. For example, the Kinect interactive games made for home computers by Microsoft have been recently used by surgeons to carry out delicate keyhole surgery. This shift of context of use by the users/consumers of this technology was completely unforeseen by Microsoft, yet experts now believe that this technology, further adapted to the surgery context, will be the norm over the next 10–15 years (Adam Brimelow, health correspondent, BBC news, 31 May 2012). German researchers have also transformed the Kinect technology into an interactive, augmented reality X-ray machine. These new applications are enabled by the availability of open source framework software. It is likely that many more contexts of use will trigger innovations whose course cannot be foreseen.

This brings us to the (apparently impossible) question: can we justify our public investments in research and innovation beyond uncertain and unpredictable macro-economic benefits?

Eric Santor, Majority leader in the US senate, not only thinks we can, but that we should. He launched a web site "You cut," allowing citizens to vote on cutting particular research funding programs. Santor, at the launch of his web site three years ago, complained that federal funds had been used, among other things, for supporting researchers to improve video gaming technology. Santor wants to change the "culture of spending" and invites citizens to vote on cutting wasteful federal programs. Currently, Eric Santor's web site allows citizens to vote, for example, on the termination of the Christopher Columbus Fellowship foundation, which was designed to produce new discoveries in all fields of endeavor for the benefit of mankind but allegedly does not "demonstrate clear outcomes."[5]

The web site is biased toward negative voting (i.e., "you cut") rather than what people *do* wish to support. The following question may arise: would people have complained

---

[5] Majorityleader.gov/You Cut, 112th Congress, week 27.

about (or voted to cut) financial support to develop video gaming technology, if they could have known the potential for other contexts of use, such as the surgery described above? How are citizens to evaluate whether the Christopher Columbus Fellowship program does or does not deliver? It seems tricky enough to vote "negatively" on programs such as public support for video-gaming technology. Is it then virtually impossible to decide upon positive outcomes, which we all wish to achieve? More complicated still: is it possible to direct innovation and its funding mechanisms to the "right impacts"?

Following this discussion, responsible research innovation can then be related to two issues:

- Can we define the right outcomes and impacts of research and innovation?
- Can we subsequently be successful in directing innovation toward these outcomes, if we agree upon these?

I will deal with these questions in the following sections.

3.3   Defining the Right Impacts and Outcomes of Research

Some philosophers of technology have recently argued that science should move beyond a contractual relationship with society and join in the quest for the common good. In their view, the "good in science, just as in medicine, is integral to, and finds its proper place in that overarching common good about which both scientists and citizens deliberate" (Mitcham and Frodeman, 2000). This view may sound attractive, but it fails to show how various communities with competing concepts of the "good life" within modern societies could arrive at a consensus, and how this could drive public (research) policy. Moreover, an Aristotelian concept of the good life is difficult to marry with a modern rights approach whereby, for instance, in the case of the EU, the European Charter of Fundamental Rights provides a legitimate and actual basis for European Public Policy. Nonetheless, their point of departure remains challenging: "We philosophers believe that publicly funded scientists have a moral and political obligation to consider the broader effects of their research; to paraphrase Socrates, unexamined research is not worth funding" (Frodeman and Holbrook, 2007).

European policy, however, is also increasingly legitimized in terms of public values, driving public policies toward positive impacts. The following citations of prominent European policy makers illustrate the case:

- "The defence of human rights and a justice system based on the full respect of human dignity is a key part of our shared European values." Jerzy Buzek, European Parliament President (10 October 2009).
- "Europe is a community of values." Van Rompuy, First European Council President, 19 November 2009.
- "My political guidelines for the Commission's next mandate stress the idea that Europe's actions must be based on its values." President Barroso, European values in the new global governance, 14 October 2009.

Indeed, European public policies are, arguably, driven toward positive impacts, underpinned by common European values. European environmental policies, for example, highlight the European value of maintaining a high level of protection for the environment. Research and innovation policy seems, however, to have been an exception to the rule. Although research and innovation policy are articulated more and more in terms of public values, research and innovation program assessments are typically limited to economic considerations that "imperfectly take into account these values" (Fisher *et al.*, 2010).

The US National Science Foundation assesses proposals in terms of "broader impacts" when considering research proposals for funding. Under the European Framework Programmes for Research, there is also a long tradition of awarding research grants on the basis of anticipated impacts. Indeed, even at the stage of evaluating research proposals particular impacts are sought. Currently, expected impacts of research topics which are the subject of public calls for proposals are listed in the work programmes of the 7th Framework Programme. But are there legitimate, normative assumptions which support these expected impacts? Do these allow an articulation of the "right impacts" that allow us to steer public research agendas?

In this regard we cannot make an appeal to concepts of the good life, but we can make an appeal to the normative targets which we can find in the Treaty on the EU. These normative targets have been democratically agreed and provide the legitimate basis for a publicly-funded framework programme for research at the European Level. From Article 3 of the Treaty on the EU (European Union, 2010) we can derive the following:

- The Union shall (...) work for the sustainable development of Europe based on balanced economic growth and price stability, a highly competitive social market economy, aiming at full employment and social progress, and a high level of protection and improvement of the quality of the environment. It shall promote scientific and technological advance.
- It shall combat social exclusion and discrimination, and shall promote social justice and protection, equality between women and men, solidarity between generations and protection of the rights of the child.
- To promote (...) harmonious, balanced, and sustainable development of economic activities, a high level of employment and of social protection, equality between men and women, sustainable and non-inflationary growth, a high degree of competitiveness and convergence of economic performance, a high level of protection and improvement of the quality of the environment, the raising of the standard of living and quality of life, and economic and social cohesion and solidarity among Member States.

Rather than pre-empting views and concepts of the "good life," the European Treaty on the EU provides us then with some normative anchor points. These normative anchor points and their mutual relationship thus provide a legitimate basis for defining the type of impacts, or the "right" impacts that research and innovation should pursue (see Figure 3.2). These are of course normative anchor points which also have impacts beyond the EU. The EU's commitment to promote Human Rights and demonstrate solidarity with the poorest on Earth, is, for example, reflected in its international policies. If applied to international research and innovation policies, this could invite us to address issues such as technology divides, ethics free zones, and broad benefit-sharing from scientific and technological advance (see Ozolina *et al.*, 2012). Research and innovation policy can also be a form of development policy.

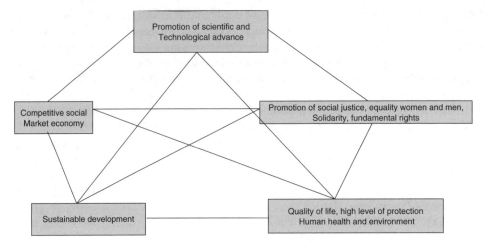

Figure 3.2   *Normative anchor points derived from the Treaty on the European Union*

3.4   From Normative Anchor Points Toward the Defining of "Grand Challenges" and the Direction of Innovation

Under the prospective framework programme Horizon 2020, a number of Grand Challenges have been defined, which follow the call in the Lund Declaration for a Europe that "must focus on the grand challenges of our time" (Lund Declaration, 2009). Sustainable solutions are sought in areas such as "global warming, tightening supplies of energy, water and food, ageing societies, public health, pandemics, and security" (Lund Declaration, 2009, p. 1).

Arguably, the "Grand Challenges" of our time reflect a number of normative anchor points of the Treaty and thus can be seen as legitimate. The Lund Declaration states that, in order to be responsive, the European Research Area must develop processes for the identification of Grand Challenges, which gain political support and gradually move away from the current thematic approaches toward a structure where research priorities are based on these "Grand challenges." It hopes to give direction to research and innovation in the form of "broad areas of issue-oriented research in relevant fields." It calls for (amongst other things), broad stakeholder involvement and the establishment of public–private partnerships.

The current macro-economic justification of investment in research and innovation emphasizes that innovation is the "only answer" to tackle societal challenges, "returning to growth and higher levels of employment, combating climate change and moving towards a low carbon society" (EC, 2011). This approach implicitly assumes that access to and availability of finance for research and innovation will automatically lead to the creation of jobs and economic growth, thereby tackling societal challenges along the way. The more innovation, the better. The faster it becomes available, the better. In this macro-economic model, innovation is assumed to be *steerless but inherently good* as it produces prosperity and jobs and meets societal challenges, addressed, as I have already discussed, through market-demand.

The Lund Declaration gives, however, an alternative justification for investing in research and innovation, primarily framing this in terms of responding to societal Grand Challenges, and further stating that "meeting the grand challenges will be a prerequisite for continued economic growth and for improved changes to tackle key issues." Here, the assumption is that sustainable economic growth is only possible when particular societal objectives are met, in the form of responses to Grand Challenges. Innovation is seen neither as steerless nor as inherently good. Economic prosperity and the anticipation that innovation yields positive anticipated impacts (such as the creation of jobs and growth) crucially become *dependent upon the social context*. The Lund Declaration points out that measures are "needed to maximize the economic and *societal* impact of knowledge" (italics by the author). The idea is clear; to steer the innovation process toward societally-beneficial objectives. Additional measures that go beyond the removal of barriers to research and innovation and the availability of and access to finance for research and innovation then become necessary. The Lund Declaration defines a type of justification for investment in research and innovation toward *particular* positive outcomes and underlines a justification for research and innovation beyond purely economic terms. This reflects comments made recently by European Commissioner for Research, Innovation and Science, Geoghegan-Quinn, who stated that "Research and innovation must respond to the needs and ambitions of society, reflect its values and be responsible."[6]

3.5   Responsible Research and Innovation: Organizing Collective Responsibility

The impacts of technological innovations are difficult to predict. Social scientists have given up the idea of ever being able to foresee technological innovations and the field of science and technology studies has, since the 1970s, abandoned ideas of "technological forecasting." Recent forms of technology assessment (among other "real time technology assessment," Guston and Sarewitz (2002)) generally focus their attention on monitoring of research and innovation processes and making them more dynamic and inclusive (Schot and Rip, 1997). RRI has to reflect these circumstances. Pre-modern technical inventions, as I have already discussed, were judged by the moral intentions of their designers or privileged users. Modern innovations, in contrast, hardly ever have a single "author" who can be held responsible for their use (by others). Moreover, the negative consequences are often neither foreseeable nor intentional. The fear of a mad scientist creating a Frankenstein is not appropriate in the context of modern innovation – where knowledge is co-produced by many "authors." Modern "Frankensteins" are not intentionally created by a single actor, but (if they arise), are more likely to result from the unforeseen side effects of *collective action*. Indeed, techno-scientific applications can remain ethically problematic, even in cases where scientists and engineers have the best possible intentions and users have no conscious intention to misuse or abuse. This situation constitutes the major ethical challenge we face today. An ethics focused on the intentions and/or consequence of actions of individuals is not appropriate for

---

[6] "Science in Dialogue" conference: Towards a European Model for Responsible Research and Innovation. Odense, Denmark 23–25 April 2012.

innovation[7] (see Chapter 7, for further discussion). There is a collective responsibility both for the right impacts and negative consequences, whether these impacts are intentional or not. This is why I have previously argued for the necessity of knowledge assessment procedures (Von Schomberg, 2007).

In order to specify a scheme which effectively organizes collective responsibility, we might first consider what counts as irresponsible innovation in the modern context.

3.5.1   Some Examples of Irresponsible Innovation

As many actors are involved in the innovation process, "irresponsible" outcomes are seldom the result of one single, irresponsible actor. More typically, irresponsible innovation is reflected in practices where stakeholders were unaware of the importance of the innovation's societal context, or where stakeholder interactions were unproductive in the resolutions of conflicts.

I categorize here four types of irresponsible innovation: (i) *technology push*, (ii) *neglect of fundamental ethical principles*, (iii) *policy pull, and* (iv) *lack of precautionary measures and technology foresight*. One seldom finds examples which reflect only one of these four dimensions of "irresponsible" innovation, as more often than not a mix of these is at play. Nonetheless, in particular examples, one particular dimension may play a more dominant role than another.

3.5.1.1   Technology Push

An example of technology push occurred in the EU when the company Monsanto tried to accomplish a *fait accompli* with the market introduction of genetically modified soya in the mid 1990s. Environmental groups (notably Greenpeace, which had not reacted to Genetically Modified Organisms (GMOs) as an environmental concern prior to their introduction on the market) responded with outright rejection to the first shipment of genetically modified soya entering the Dutch port of Rotterdam in 1996. The subsequent process of innovation (or lack of it) was framed by an often bitter fight among a very few industrial actors and a growing group of NGOs opposing the introduction of the "technology." This occurred while indecisive and reluctant European national governments devised contradictory measures, some of which had to be challenged at the European Court of Justice by the European Commission. During the subsequent years after the first marketed GMO, NGOs and European governments overbid each other with calls for increasingly stricter regulations of GMOs, eventually resulting in a revised set of GMO regulations and directives (e.g., EU Directive 2001/18, European Communities, 2001), which to date have never been applied consistently. Currently, the European Council is considering a response from the European Parliament to an EU Commission proposal to give Member States somewhat greater flexibility in banning cultivation of GMOs on their own territory.

The general public became deeply sceptical about future GMO applications, and public perception largely was that this type of innovation does not deliver sufficient

---

[7] I have previously outlined the concept of collective co-responsibility in response to the actual shortcomings of professional role-responsibility in science and engineering in: *From the ethics of technology, towards an ethics of knowledge policy & knowledge assessment*, A working document for the services of the European Commission, Publication Office of the European Union, 2007. Free pdf available at http://bookshop.europa.eu/en/home.

benefit.[8] A major European company, BASF, made an announcement in January 2012, after lengthy consultations with NGOs, that it would not market a genetically modified potato, withdrawing from the European market even though it had received an authorization to cultivate the potato in 2010. This second authorization was remarkable as virtually all previous procedures were inconclusive, and this particular "authorization" success seemed to have triggered a further collapse of the system, mobilizing EU Member States unwilling to grant approval for cultivation.[9]

What was the irresponsible dimension in this case? This example shows how substantial dissent among major stakeholders can frustrate responsible technological development. NGOs felt that they had little influence on the direction in which this technology would lead us. Regulations were exclusively focused on safety aspects, and the broader environmental, social, and agricultural contexts were not brought into the equation. The need for European harmonization of market introduction sharply contrasted with a variety of national cultures and led to a *de facto* moratorium in 1998. The outcome should be seen as irresponsible because one company took the lead with a technology push, some NGOs then entered the discussion with a radical view at the moment the technology hit the market stage: the result was that the rest of the industrial sector had to pay a price. A cumbersome, slow political process on adopting ever new measures under the already comprehensive framework sealed the sector's fate.

The example shows the requirement for stakeholders to share co-responsibility for innovation trajectories. Technology push is a self-defeating strategy. Unlike Monsanto, BASF operated clearly more in line with the requirements of RRI. It had to take a painful decision but has gained from this by promoting a good company image, whereas Monsanto is still often perceived as the "bad guy." It is interesting to note that in the Netherlands discussions among stakeholders (including NGOs) on the course agricultural biotechnology should take (i.e., prior to the marketing of any product) were reopened after the actions of Greenpeace and delays concerning implementation of proper labeling schemes at a national level as a consequence of delays and persisting disagreements at the EU level (Von Schomberg, 1999). This shows that EU legislation which frustrates stakeholder agreement can in fact make things worse.

3.5.1.2   Neglect of Fundamental Ethical Principles

In 2011 the Dutch government had to abandon an electronic patient record system (EPRS) project, after the Senate voted down the project due to unresolved privacy issues. The decision is, in economic terms, disastrous: €300 million had been invested over the previous 15 years. EPRS projects elsewhere in the EU face similar problems.

The reason for the failure is that privacy issues were only dealt with at a very late stage of the project, which was initially fully technology-driven. Issues such as "who owns the data?" and "who is responsible for mistakes?" (and their consequences!) became difficult to deal with once the project was technically mature. In addition, the technology evolved over a long period (as ICT technology became significantly more powerful), and lack

---

[8] The Eurobarometer survey of October 2010 mentions that 61% of Europeans feel uneasy about GM food, and 53% believe that GMOs harm the environment. In not a single European Member State is there a majority that believe GM food is good for the national economy.

[9] See the instructive article of Vesco Paskalev (2012).

of proper technology foresight precluded proper implementation. Economic loss for a project which in itself carries a legitimate public purpose should be seen as irresponsible. The costs of acting "irresponsibly" are always substantial. A top-manager of Nokia stated: "Typically, the costs of corrective actions are a 1000 times more costly when a service is in the operational phase compared to the design phase" (Bräutigam, 2012).

Earlier stakeholder involvement, earlier and better public engagement, notably taking into account the implications of a right to privacy (with the associated "right to be forgotten" as proposed by Commissioner Reding for Justice, Fundamental rights and Citizenship) would have made the project more successful. A similar problem has occurred with the introduction of smart-meters, to be installed in private homes, which allow actual monitoring of energy use. As it became clear that third parties (e.g., potential thieves) would be able to identify the absence of people in their homes, the authorities had to give up the idea of mandatory introduction.

3.5.1.3   Policy Pull

A strong policy pull has catalyzed the introduction of security technologies, such as the use of biometrics for passports, asylum applications, and whole body image technology ("body scanners") at airports. Politicians and policy makers have been eager to accept and promote the implementation of these technologies, sometimes beyond their technical feasibility.

The introduction of the body scanner was discussed fully and consensually within technical advisory committees and within European policy. There seemed to have been no doubt about the reasonableness of its introduction until the German Supreme Court of Justice ruled the introduction as being disproportional to its ends. The European Parliament, which had already ordered the body scanner for use on its premises, canceled its implementation (Mordini, 2011). The introduction of the body scanner seemed to be incident-driven, after a terrorist managed to board a flight to Chicago from Amsterdam airport in late 2009. More recently, after the widespread introduction of the body scanner at airports in the US, the device has come under attack, as it apparently does not deliver substantial security gains, or worse, can in fact introduce new security threats. The introduction of body scanners at airports in Europe was eventually approved by the European Parliament in 2011, however, with substantial requirements: there is no mandatory use for passengers, the body scanner does not make pictures, but rather representations of the body, and the representations are not stored. Such requirements could have been anticipated much earlier, if the technology had been guided by proper technology assessments and public scrutiny.

The general assessment problem in this case was how to judge the proportionality of the introduction of this type of technology. The European Commission must deliver general impact assessments on all its major legislative proposals within the framework for better regulation (European Communities, 2006). This follows an integrated approach which was introduced in 2002. These impact assessments include, among others, social, environmental, and economic impacts. Thus directives and regulations related to the introduction of security technologies such as biometrics have been subject to such an assessment. Such an analysis should identify whether particular measures, or potential infringement of privacy and data protection, are proportional, and constitute legitimate objection against implementing security technologies. However, the determination of proportionality *cannot be fully left to legal experts*. One would need to assume normative baselines for acceptable risks or acceptable infringements of privacy rights. These baselines are essentially political and not defined in legislation. Therefore, the baseline should be subject to public debate. As a consequence we find in the EU diverging practices concerning security technologies: biometrics, for example, is allowed in the Netherlands, for people to enter into public swimming pools, whereas in France it is prohibited. In the Netherlands, biometric passports have been introduced whereby the data are stored in a central data base (but this is found to be disproportional in most other Member States of the EU). But the risk of failure of biometrics estimated by technicians (1 in many millions) has translated in practice into one out of five passports not being read correctly.

3.5.1.4   *Lack of Precautionary Measures and Technology Foresight*

The report "Late lessons from early warning" (EEA, 2002) gives an impressive account of 12 cases, such as benzene, PCBs, hormones as growth promoters, and asbestos, the latter for which the European death toll alone is estimated to become 400 000. I will not here elaborate in too much detail on the negative (anticipated or not) consequences of innovation, as these are well described by many others, including authors in that particular report. Nonetheless, a framework for RRI needs to address these consequences, as well as build on the work of these authors. The lessons learned from these 12 cases mainly relate to decision making under scientific uncertainty and scientific ignorance. However, they also relate to the benefits of innovation by making an appeal to "promote more robust, diverse, and adaptable technologies, so as to minimize the costs of surprises and maximize the benefits of innovation" (EEA, 2002). The authors of the report make the case for channeling innovation into alternative routes, for which the cases of asbestos and halocarbons provide forceful illustrations. Rather than a constraint, the precautionary principle can thus provide an incentive to open up alternative research and development trajectories.

3.6   A Framework for Responsible Research and Innovation

The following definition for RRI is proposed:

> *Responsible Research and Innovation is a transparent, interactive process by which societal actors and innovators become mutually responsive to each other with a view to the (ethical) acceptability, sustainability and societal desirability of the innovation process and its marketable products (in order to allow a proper embedding of scientific and technological advances in our society).*

There is a significant time lag (this can be several decades) between the occurrence of technical inventions (or planned promising research) and the eventual marketing of products resulting from research and innovation processes. The societal impacts of scientific and technological advances are difficult to predict. Even major technological advances, such as the use of the internet and the partial failure of the introduction of GMOs in Europe (see above), have not been anticipated by governing bodies. Early societal intervention in the research and innovation process can help avoid technologies failing to embed in society and/or help ensure that their positive and negative impacts are better governed and exploited at a much earlier stage. Two interrelated dimensions can be identified: the *product* dimension, capturing products in terms of overarching and specific normative anchor points (see discussion above) and a *process* dimension reflecting a deliberative democracy.

The normative anchor points should be reflected in the product dimension. They should be:

- **(Ethically) acceptable:** in an EU context this refers to a mandatory compliance with the fundamental values of the EU charter on fundamental rights (right for privacy, etc.) and the safety protection level set by the EU. This may sound obvious, but the practice of implementing ICT technologies has already demonstrated in various cases that the fundamental right for privacy and data protection can and has been neglected (see above). It also refers to the 'safety' of products in terms of *acceptable* risks. It goes without saying that ongoing risk assessments are part of the procedure toward acceptable products when safety issues are concerned. However, the issue of safety should be taken in a far broader perspective. The United Kingdom's largest public funder of basic innovation research, the Engineering and Physical Science and Research Council in 2009 asked applicants to report the wider implications and potential risk (environmental, health, societal, and ethical) associated with their proposed research in the area of nanosciences (Owen and Goldberg, 2010). This highlighted the fact that, often, the risks related to new technologies can neither be quantified nor a normative baseline of acceptability be assumed by scientists (acknowledging that any particular baseline cannot be assumed to represent *the* baseline of societal acceptance).
- **Sustainable:** contributing to the EU's objective of sustainable development. The EU follows the 1997 UN "definition" of sustainable development, consisting of economic, social, and environmental dimensions, in mutual dependence. This overarching anchor point can become further materialized under the following one:
- **Socially desirable:** "socially desirable" captures the relevant, and more specific normative anchor points of the Treaty on the EU, such as "Quality of life," "Equality among men and women," and so on (see above). It has to be noted that a systematic inclusion of these anchor points in product development and evaluation would clearly go beyond simple market profitability, although the latter could be a precondition for a product's viability in market competitive economies. However, it would be consistent with the EU treaty to promote such product development through the financing of research and development actions. In other words, at this point, RRI would not need any new policy guidelines, but would simply require a consistent application of the EU's fundamental values to the research and innovation process, as reflected in the Treaty on the EU. Perhaps it has been wrongly assumed that these values could not be considered in the context of research and innovation. Since the Lund Declaration, a process to take into account societal objectives in the form of addressing Grand Challenges has been set in motion.

RRI features both a product and process dimension:

Product dimension:

Products should be evaluated and designed with a view to these normative anchor points: with a high level of protection to the environment and human health, sustainability, and societal desirability.

Process dimension:

The challenge here is to arrive at a more responsive, adaptive, and integrated management of the innovation process. A multidisciplinary approach, with the involvement of stakeholders and other interested parties, should lead to an inclusive innovation process whereby technical innovators become responsive to societal needs and societal actors become co-responsible for the innovation process through a constructive input in terms of defining societally-desirable products. The product and process dimension are naturally interrelated. Implementation is enabled by five mechanisms: technology assessment and foresight, application of the precautionary principle, normative/ethical principles to design technology, innovation governance and stakeholder involvement and public engagement.

Table 3.1 provides a matrix which describes examples of lead questions to be answered by stakeholders, either from a product or process perspective in order to fully implement an RRI scheme.

3.6.1   Use of Technology Assessment and Technology Foresight

This is done in order to anticipate positive and negative impacts or, whenever possible, define desirable impacts of research and innovation, both in terms of impacts on consumers and communities. Setting of research priorities and their anticipated impacts needs to be subject to a societal review. This implies broadening the review of research proposals beyond scientific excellence to include societal impacts.[10] Specific Technology Assessment methods also help to identify societally desirable products by addressing normative anchor points throughout their development. Methodologies to further "script" the future expected impacts of research should be developed (see, for example, Den Boer, Rip, and Speller, 2009). A good example exists in the field of synthetic biology by Bedau *et al.* (2009). They have identified six key checkpoints in protocell development (e.g., cells produced from non-living components by means of synthetic biology) in which particular attention should be given to specific ethical, social, and regulatory issues, and made 10 recommendations for responsible protocell science that are tied to the achievement of these checkpoints.

Technology Assessment and Technology Foresight can reduce the human cost of trial and error and take advantage of a societal learning process involving stakeholders and technical innovators. It creates a possibility for anticipatory governance (see Karinen and Guston, 2010; and Chapter 6). This should ultimately lead to products which are (more) societally-robust.

---

[10] The Netherlands Organization for Scientific Research (NWO) has developed a research funding program on Responsible Innovation under which research proposals are subject to a review in terms of societal relevance. See: http://www.nwo.nl/nwohome.nsf/pages/NWOA_7E2EZG_Eng.

Table 3.1 Responsible research and innovation matrix
The matrix is composed of 10 'twin' issues, representing emphasis on either the process-dimension or the product dimension. For example, the twin issues 'the identification of nature of risks' and 'the development of procedures to cope with risks' are at the cross-roads of applying the precautionary principle and technology assessment and foresight.

Product-dimension → / Process-dimension ↓	Technology assessment and foresight	Application of the precautionary principle	Normative/ethical principles to design technology	Innovation governance and stakeholder involvement	Public engagement
Technology assessment and foresight	–	Development of procedures to cope with risks	Which design objectives to choose?	Stakeholder involvement in foresight and TA	How to engage the public?
Application of the precautionary principle	Identification of nature of risks	–	Choice and development of standards	Defining proportionality: how much precaution?	How safe is safe enough?
Normative/ethical principles to design technology	"Privacy" and "safety" by design	Setting of risk/uncertainty thresholds	–	Which principles to choose?	Which technologies for which social desirable goals?
Innovation governance models and stakeholder involvement	Defining scope and methodology for TA/foresight by stakeholders	Defining the precautionary approaches by stakeholders	Translating normative principles in technological design	–	How can innovation be geared toward social desirable objective
Public engagement and public debate	Defining/choice of methodology for public engagement	Setting of acceptable standards	Setting of social desirability of RRI outcome	Stakeholders roles in achieving social desirable outcomes	–

3.6.2   Application of Precautionary Principle

The precautionary principle is embedded in EU law and applies especially within EU product authorization procedures (e.g., REACH (registration, evaluation, authorization and restriction of chemical substances), GMO directives, etc.). The precautionary principle works as an incentive to make safe and sustainable products and allows governmental bodies to intervene with risk management decisions (such as temporary licensing, case-by-case decision making, etc.) whenever necessary, in order to avoid negative impacts.

The responsible development of new technologies must be viewed in its historical context. Some governance principles have been inherited from previous cases: this is particularly notable for the application of the precautionary principle to new fields, such as that of the nanosciences and nanotechnologies. The precautionary principle is firmly embedded in European policy, and is enshrined in the 1992 Maastricht Treaty as one of the three principles upon which all environmental policy is based. It has been progressively applied to other fields of policy, including food safety, trade, and research.

The principle runs through legislation, for example, in the "No data, no market" principle of the REACH directive for chemical substances, or the pre-market reviews required by the Novel Foods regulation as well as the directive on the deliberate release of GMOs into the environment. More generally, within the context of the general principles and requirements of European food law it is acknowledged that "scientific risk assessment alone cannot provide the full basis for risk management decisions" (Commission of the European Communities, 2002) – leaving open the possibility of risk management decisions which are made partly based on ethical principles or particular consumer interests.

In the European Commission's Recommendation on a Code of Conduct for Nanosciences and Nanotechnologies Research, the principle appears in the call for risk assessment before any public funding of research (a strategy currently applied in the 7th Framework Programme for research). Rather than stifling research and innovation, the precautionary principle acts within the Code of Conduct as a focus for action, in that it calls for funding for the development of risk methodologies, the execution of risk research, and the active identification of knowledge gaps.

3.6.3   Innovation Governance

3.6.3.1   *Multi-stakeholder Involvement*

Multi-stakeholder involvement in RRI projects should bring together actors from industry, civil society, and research to jointly define an implementation plan for the responsible development of a particular product within a specific research/innovation field, such as information and communication technology or nanotechnology. Responsible innovation should be materialized in terms of the research and innovation process as well as in terms of (product) outcomes. The advantage here is that actors cannot exclusively focus on particular aspects (for instance, civil society organizations addressing only the risk aspects) but have to take a position on all aspects of the innovation process. This allows the process to go beyond risk governance and move to innovation governance. The company BASF, for example, has established a dialogue forum with civil society organizations and also developed a code of conduct for the development of new products.[11]

3.6.3.2   Use of Codes of Conduct

Codes of Conduct, in contrast to regulatory interventions, allow a constructive steering of the innovation process (see Chapter 8). They support the establishment of a proactive scientific community which identifies and reports to public authorities on risks and benefits at an early stage. Codes of Conduct are particular useful when risks are uncertain and when there is uncertain ground for legislative action (nanotechnology, for example). Codes of Conduct also help to identify knowledge gaps and direct research funds toward societal objectives.

Policy development treads a fine line here: governments should not make the mistake of responding too early to a technology, failing to adequately address its nature, or of acting too late, and thereby missing the opportunity to intervene. A good governance approach, then, might be one which allows flexibility in response to new developments and emerging stakeholder and public perspectives (see Chapter 2). After a regulatory review in 2008, the European Commission came to the conclusion that there is no immediate need for new legislation on nanotechnology, and that adequate responses can be developed – especially with regard to risk assessment – by adapting existing legislation.

In the absence of a clear consensus on definitions, the preparation of new nano-specific measures will be difficult and although there continues to be significant scientific uncertainty on the nature of the risks involved, good governance will have to go beyond policy making that focuses only on legislative action (see Chapter 8). The power of governments is arguably limited by their dependence on the insights and cooperation of societal actors when it comes to the governance of new technologies: the development of a code of conduct, then, is one of their few options for intervening in a timely and responsible manner. The European Commission states in the second implementation report on the action plan for nanotechnologies that "its effective implementation requires an efficient structure and coordination, and regular consultation with the Member States and all stakeholders" (Commission of the European Communities, 2009). Similarly, legislators are dependent on scientists' proactive involvement in communicating possible risks of nanomaterials, and must steer clear of any legislative actions which might restrict scientific communication and reporting on risk. The ideal is a situation in which all the actors involved communicate and collaborate. The philosophy behind the European Commission's code of conduct, then, is precisely to support and promote active and inclusive governance and communication (Commission of the European Communities, 2008). It assigns responsibilities to actors beyond governments, and promotes these actors' active involvement against the backdrop of a set of basic and widely shared principles of governance and ethics. Through codes of conduct, governments can allocate tasks and roles to all actors involved in technological development, thereby organizing collective responsibility for

---

[11] In the BASF Dialogueforum Nano representatives of environmental and consumer organisations, trade unions, scientific institutes and churches (Civil Society Organisations/Non Governmental Organisations) work together with employees of the chemical company BASF SE on various issues related to the subject of nanotechnologies. See for a recent report: http://www .risiko-dialogue.ch/component/content/article/507- basf-dialogueforum-nano-final-report-2009-2010, accessed 14/12/2012.

the field (Von Schomberg, 2007). Similarly, Mantovani and Porcari (2010) propose a governance plan which both makes use of existing governance structures and suggests new ones, as well as proposing how they should relate to each other.

The European Commission's recommendation on a Code of Conduct views Member States of the European Union as responsible actors, and invites them to use the Code as an instrument to encourage dialogue amongst 'policy makers, researchers, industry, ethics committees, civil society organizations and society at large' (recommendation number 8 to Member States, cited on page 6 of the Commission's recommendation, Commission of the European Communities, 2008), as well as to share experiences and to review the Code at a European level on a biannual basis. It should be considered that such Codes of Conduct would in the future extend their scope beyond research and also address the innovation process.[12]

3.6.3.3   Adoption of Standards, Certification, and Self-Regulation

The adoption of standards and even "definitions" are fundamental requirements for responsible development. The outstanding adoption of a definition for nanoparticles, for example, makes legislation and adequate labeling practices difficult, if not impossible. Bush (2010) notes that the use of standards, certifications, and accreditations constitutes a new form of governance which has progressively replaced and transmuted positive law as a product of the state with its market equivalent. Although this form of governance is in need of improvement, we unavoidably have to make productive use of it, as the flood of products and processes coming on to the market will not be manageable through governmental bodies and agencies alone. The perception and working practice of these standards is significant. In 2005, it was claimed that the EU had forced local authorities to remove see-saws from children's playgrounds. No such EU measures were in fact taken. Some standards were set by the European Committee for Standardization (CEN), a voluntary organization made up of national standards bodies. CEN sought to limit the height from which children could fall, by specifying the maximum height for seats and stands, and by setting standards for hand supports and footrests. Manufacturers could choose to follow these standards, which carried the advantage of export potential across Europe, instead of having to apply for certification in each country (European Communities, 2006).

The area of data and privacy protection in the context of the use of ICT and security technologies (discussed above) should also be impacted by forms of self-regulation and standard setting. Data controllers based within operators need to provide accountability, which can be termed as a form of verifiable responsibility (Guagnin, Hempel, and Ilten, 2011). The involvement of third parties which can implement, even minimally, a transparent verification practice will be crucial. In other fields, the certification has been carried out by a third party. For example, in 1996, the World Wildlife Fund (WWF) and Unilever joined forces and collectively constructed a long-term program for sustainable fisheries. They founded an independent non-profit organization to foster worldwide fisheries. They also applied "standards of sustainable fishing," which is further monitored by independent certifying agencies to control those standards.

---

[12] The European Project NANOCODE makes this point concerning nanosciences and nanotechnologies, see: http://www.nanocode.eu/. An analysis of the meaning and implication of the responsible development of nanotechnologies with a view on the role of public debate has been documented in Von Schomberg and Davies, 2010.

Standards will also need to reflect particular ethical considerations and go well beyond mere technical safety issues. Currently, the development of new ISO standards for nanofoods might involve the inclusion of ethical standards (Forsberg, 2010).

3.6.3.4   Ethics as a "Design" Factor of Technology and Increasing Social-Ethical Reflexivity in Research Practices

Ethics should not be seen as being only a constraint of technological advances. Incorporating ethical principles in the design process of technology can lead to well accepted technological advances (see Chapter 4 for further discussion). As discussed above, in Europe, the employment of Body Imaging Technology at airports has, for example, raised constitutional concerns in Germany. It has been questioned whether the introduction is proportional to the objectives being pursued. The introduction of a "smart meter" at the homes of people in the Netherlands to allow for detection of and optimization of energy use, was also rejected on privacy grounds, as it might have allowed third parties to monitor whether people are actually in their homes. These concerns could have been avoided if societal actors had been involved in the design of technology early on. "Privacy by design" has become a good counter example in the field of ICT, by which technology is designed with a view to taking privacy into account as a design principle of the technology itself. Yet, practicing it is still rare. The European project ETICA[13] (see Chapter 11) has recommended the introduction of specific governance structures for emerging (ICT) technologies in this regard.

Recently, "Midstream Modulation" (Fisher, Mahajan, and Mitcham, 2006; Fisher, 2007; and Chapter 9) has emerged as a promising approach to increase social-ethical reflexivity within research practices. In the form of laboratory engagement practices, social scientists and ethicists are embedded in research teams of natural scientists. The embedded social scientist engages natural scientists in the wider impact of their work, while doing research in the laboratories. Reports from these practices could feed into schemes on RRI.

3.6.3.5   Deliberative Mechanisms for Allowing Feedback with Policymakers: Devising Models for Responsible Governance and Public Engagement/Public Debate

Continuous feedback from information generated in technology assessment, technology foresight and demonstration projects to policy makers could allow for a productive innovation cycle. Knowledge assessment procedures should be developed in order to allow assessment of the quality of information within policy process, especially in areas in which scientific assessments contradict each other, or in the case of serious knowledge gaps (the EC practices this partly with its impact assessments for legislative actions). Knowledge assessment could integrate distinct approaches of cost-benefit analysis and environmental and sustainability impact assessments. In short, models of responsible governance should be devised which allocate roles of responsibility to all actors involved in the innovation process. Ideally, this should lead to a situation in which actors can resolve conflicts and go beyond their traditional roles, for example, where companies highlight benefits and NGOs risks. Co-responsibility implies here that actors have to become *mutually responsive*, companies adopting a perspective that goes beyond immediate market competitiveness and NGOs reflecting on the constructive role of new technologies for

---

[13] See: Bernd Carsten Stahl's *et al*. chapter (11) in this volume http://www.etica-project.eu/.

sustainable product development. In this context, technology assessment, as practiced, for example, by the Dutch Rathenau Institute, can take up the function of "seducing actors to get involved and act" (Van Est, 2010).

Ongoing public debate and monitoring of public opinion is needed for the legitimacy of research funding and particular scientific and technological advances. Continuous public platforms should replace one-off public engagement activities (Chapter 5) concerning a particular technology and, ideally, a link with the policy process should be established. The function of public debate in viable democracies includes enabling policy makers to exercise agenda and priority setting. Public debate, ideally, should have a moderating impact on "technology push" and "policy pull" of new technologies, even if this sometimes unavoidably may occur.

3.7 Outlook

RRI need to be addressed by various actors and institutions. Institutionally, some progress is under way at the level of programs of individual Research Councils. As a positive counterexample to the "You cut" initiative of the American senator highlighted at the beginning of this chapter, Jones (2008) describes one noteworthy experiment where, through a process of public deliberation, there was wider reflection on the purposes of research: this reflection was used to frame a research funding call in the area of nanotechnology for medicine and healthcare. The public dialogues provided a clear steer about the relative priorities of six potential application areas of nanotechnology for healthcare, informing and shaping the nature of the funding call itself, such that it could respond better to social values (for more detail see Chapter 5). One can imagine further initiatives in which citizens shape calls for research proposals.

The most crucial advancement of RRI will be dependent on the willingness of stakeholders to work together toward socially desirable products. Until now, examples of industry–NGO cooperation have been primarily limited to addressing the risks, for example, the negative aspects of products. Under the European 7th Framework Programme for Research and Innovation, the 2013 Science in Society work program provides an opportunity for a "demonstration project" incentivizing actors from industry, civil society, and research institutions to "jointly define an implementation plan for the responsible development of a particular product to be developed within a specific research and innovation field." RRI should be shown in terms of the product development process (such as stakeholder involvement, etc.) and the quality of the final product (complying with, among other standards, those relating to sustainability and ethics).

Furthermore, further institutionalizations of technology foresight and technology assessments are necessary within the legislative process. At the European level, now that impact assessments have been made mandatory, there is an opportunity to make better and systematic use of assessments. I have argued that we have to go beyond assessing research and innovation purely in terms of their economic impacts. Bozeman and Sarewitz (2011) have proposed a framework for a new approach for assessing the capacity of research programs to achieve social goals. The further development of such frameworks is badly needed as the promises of scientists to address social objectives (regularly leading to "hype" and corresponding increased levels of research funding, see Chapter 13) while developing their research is often sharply contrasted with the actual outcomes.

Internationally, a global perspective needs to be developed. Diverging ethical standards at the international level and "ethics-free" zones pose challenges for the introduction of RRI at the global level. Ozolina *et al.* (2012) have recently addressed the challenges RRI faces at the global level and advocate an international framework for RRI, to be achieved by means of multilateral dialogue.

All these initiatives may well help us to address socio-economic concerns around research and innovation processes, without formally introducing a fourth hurdle. Instead of a "hurdle," RRI should become a research and innovation "design" strategy which drives innovation and gives some "steer" toward achieving societally desirable goals.

References

Bedau, M., Parke, E.C., Tangen U. and Hantsche-Tangen B. (2009) Social and ethical checkpoints for bottom-up synthetic biology, or protocells, *Systems and Synthetic Biology* **3**:65–75.

Bozeman, B., Sarewitz, D. (2011) Public value mapping and science policy evaluation *Minerva* **49** 1.

Bräutigam, T. (2012) PIA: cornerstone of privacy compliance at Nokia, in D. Wright and P. De Hert, *Privacy Impact Assessment*, Springer, Dordrecht, p. 263.

Bush, L. (2010) Standards, law and governance. *Journal of Rural Social Sciences* **25** (3), 56-78.

Commission of the European Communities (2002) Regulation (EC) no 178/2002 of the European Parliament and of the Council of 28 January2002 laying down the general principles and requirements of food law, establishing the European Food Safety Authority and laying down procedures in matters of food safety.

Commission of the European Communities (2008) Commission Recommendation of 7 February 2008, on a Code of Conduct for Responsible Nanosciences and Nanotechnologies Research, 7 February 2008.

Commission of the European Communities (2009) Communication from the Commission to the Council, the European Parliament and the European Economic and Social Committee. Nanosciences and Nanotechnologies: An Action Plan for Europe 2005–2009. Second Implementation Report 2007–2009, Brussels, 29.10.2009, COM(2009)607 final (citation on page 10).

Den Boer, D., Rip, A. and Speller, S. (2009) Scripting possible futures of nanotechnologies: a methodology that enhances reflexivity. *Technology in Society* **31** 295–304.

European Commission (2010) Communication from the Commission. Europe 2020. A Strategy for Smart, Sustainable and Inclusive Growth. COM(2010) 2020 final (citation on page 3).

European Commission (2011) Europe 2020 Flagship Initiative Innovation Union, Communication to the European Parliament, the Council, the European Economic Committee, and the Committee of the Regions. SEC(2010) 1161.

European Communities (2001) Directive 2001/18/EC of the European Parliament and of the Council of 12 March 2001 on the deliberate release into the environment of genetically modified organisms and repealing Council directive 90/220/ EEC-Commission Declaration, *Official Journal of the European Communities,* **L 106**.

European Communities (2006) *Better Regulation. Simply Explained*, Office for Official Publications of the European Communities, Luxembourg.

European Environmental Agency (2002) The Precautionary Principle in the Twentieth Century: Late Lessons From Early Warnings, http://www.rachel.org/lib/late_lessons _from_early_warnings.030201.pdf (accessed 14 December 2012).

European Union (2010) Consolidated version of the Treaty on European Union. *Official Journal of the European Union,* **53**(C83 of 30 March 2010), Article 3, 13.

Fisher, E. (2007) Ethnographic invention: probing the capacity of laboratory decisions. *NanoEthics* **1**(2): 155–165.

Fisher, E., Mahajan, R.L. and Mitcham, C. (2006). Midstream modulation of technology: governance from within. *Bulletin of Science Technology Society* **26**(6): 485–496.

Fisher, E. Slade, C.P., Anderson D. Bozeman B. (2010) The public value of nanotechnology? *Scientometrics* **85** (1), 29–39.

Forsberg, E.M. (2010) Safe and socially robust development of nanofood through ISO standards? in *Global Food Security: Ethical and Legal Challenges* (eds Romeo Casabona, C.M., Escajedo San Epifanio, L. and A. Emaldi Cirión). Academic Press, Wageningen, pp. 521–526.

Frodeman, R. and Holbrook J.B. (2007) Science's social effects Issues in *Science and Technology,* Spring.

Guagnin, D., Hempel L., Ilten C. (2011) Privacy practices and the claim for account- ability in: R. Von Schomberg (ed.) *Towards Responsible Research and Innovation in the Information and Communication Technologies and Security Technologies Fields*. Luxembourg: Publication Office of the European Union, pp. 99–115.

Guston, D., Sarewitz D. (2002) Real-time technology assessment *Technology in Society,* **24** (1–2), 93–109.

Jones, R. (2008) When it pays to ask the public, *Nature Nanotechnology,* **3**: 578–579.

Karinen, R., and D.H. Guston (2010) Towards anticipatory governance. The experi- ence with nanotechnology. in: *Governing Future Technologies. Nanotechnology and the Rise of an Assessment Regime*, M. Kaiser (ed.) Springer: Dordrecht, Heidelberg, London, New York, page 217ff.

Lund Declaration (2009) Conference: New Worlds – New Solutions. Research and Inno- vation as a Basis for Developing Europe in a Global Context, Lund, Sweden, July 7–8, 2009, http://www.se2009.eu/polopoly_fs/1.8460!menu/standard/file/lund_declaration _final_version_9_july.pdf.

Mantovani, E. and Porcari A. (2010). A governance platform to secure the responsi- ble development of nanotechnologies: the FramingNano Project in *Understanding Public Debate on Nanotechnologies. Options for Framing Public Policy* (eds R. Von Schomberg and S. Davies). Luxembourg: Publication Office of the European Union, pp. 39–53.

Mitcham, C. and Frodeman R. (2000) Beyond the Social Contract Myth: Science should move beyond a contractual relationship with society and join in the quest for the common good. Issues in *Science and Technology,* Summer (Online).

Mordini, E. (2011) Policy brief on whole body image technology in: R. Von Schomberg (ed.) *Towards Responsible Research and Innovation in the Information and Communication Technologies and Security Technologies Fields*. Luxembourg: Publication Office of the European Union, pp. 165–211.

Owen, R. and Goldberg N. (2010) Responsible innovation. A pilot study with the UK engineering and physical science and research council *Risk Analysis,* **30**, 11, 1699.

Ozolina, Z., Mitcham C., Schroeder D., Mordini E., McCarthy P. and Crowley J.(2012) *Ethical and Regulatory Challenges to Science and Research Policy at the Global Level. Expert Group Report, Directorate-General for Research and Innovation of the European Commission*, Luxembourg: Publication Office of the European Union.

Paskalev, V. (2012). Can science tame politics: the collapse of the new GMO Regime in the EU. *European Journal of Risk Regulation,* **2/2012**, 190 ff.

Schot, J. and Rip A. (1997), The past and future of constructive technology assessment *Technological Forecasting and Social Change* **54**, 251–268.

B. Stahl, M. Jirotka and G. Eden (forthcoming) Responsible research and innovation in information and communication technology: indentifying and engaging with the ethical implications of ICTs, *Responsible Innovation*, John Wiley & Sons, Ltd, Chichester (this volume).

Van Est, R. (2010) From techno-talk to social reflection and action. Lessons from public participation in converging technologies. International Workshop "Deliberating Converging Technologies," IÖW, Berlin, November 25–26, 2010.

Von Schomberg, R. (1999) The Netherlands: Reopening a Consensus on Agricultural Biotechnology Policy, http://technology.open.ac.uk/cts/srtc/NL-NAtReport.pdf (accessed 7 September 2012).

Von Schomberg, R. (2007) From the Ethics of Technology Towards and Ethics of Knowledge Policy. Working Document of the Service of the European Commission, http://ec.europa.eu/research/science-society/pdf/ethicsofknowledgepolicy_en.pdf (accessed 18 May 2011).

Von Schomberg R., Davies S. (eds.) (2010) *Understanding Public Debate on Nanotechnologies. Options for Framing Public Policy*. Luxembourg: Publication Office of the European Union.

Zagamé, P. (2010) The Cost of a Non-Innovative Europe (quoted in the Europe 2020 Flagship Initiative Innovation Union3 (2011)), p. 5.

4

Value Sensitive Design and Responsible Innovation

Jeroen van den Hoven
Delft University of Technology, Section of Philosophy, The Netherlands

4.1 Introduction

The Netherlands has learned interesting lessons about ethics and innovation in the first decade of the twenty-first century. A first instructive case was the attempt to introduce smart electricity meters nationwide. In order to make the electricity grids more efficient and meet the EU CO_2 reduction targets by 2020, every household in The Netherlands would have to be transformed into an intelligent node in the electricity network. Each household could thus provide detailed information about electricity consumption and help electricity companies to predict peaks and learn how to "shave off" the peaks in consumption patterns. After some years of R&D, a plan to equip every Dutch household with a smart meter was proposed to parliament. In the meantime, however, opposition to the proposal by privacy groups had gradually increased over the years (Abdulkarim, 2011). The meter was now seen as a "spying device" and a threat to the personal sphere of life, because it could take snapshots of electricity consumption every seven seconds, store data in a database of the electricity companies for data mining, and provide the most wonderful information about what was going on inside the homes of Dutch citizens. With some effort it could even help to tell which movie someone had been watching on a given night. By the time the proposal was brought to the upper house of the Dutch parliament for approval, public concern about the privacy aspects was very prominent and the upper house rejected the plan on data protection grounds. The European Commission, being devoted to the development of smart electricity grids in its member states, feared that the Dutch reaction to this type of innovation would set an example for other countries

---

Responsible Innovation, First Edition. Edited by Richard Owen, John Bessant and Maggy Heintz.
© 2013 John Wiley & Sons, Ltd. Published 2013 by John Wiley & Sons, Ltd.

and would jeopardize the EU-wide adoption of sustainable and energy saving solutions in an EU market for electricity (Al Abdulkarim and Lukszo, 2009).

Another story – not very different from that of the smart meter – is the introduction of a nationwide electronic patient record system in The Netherlands. After 10 years of R&D and preparations, lobbying, stakeholder consultation, and debates – and last but not least an estimated investment of €300 million – the proposal was rejected by the upper house of parliament on the basis of privacy and security considerations (Tange, 2008; Van Twist, 2010).

Clearly, these innovations in the electricity and health care systems could have helped The Netherlands to achieve cost reduction, greater efficiency, sustainability goals, and in the case of the electronic patient record system, higher levels of patient safety. In both cases, however, privacy considerations were not sufficiently incorporated in the plans so as to make them acceptable. If the engineers had taken privacy more seriously right from the start, and if they had made greater efforts to incorporate and express the value of privacy into the architecture at all levels of the system, transparently and demonstrably, then these problems would probably not have arisen.

The important lesson to learn from these cases is that values and moral considerations (i.e., privacy considerations) should have been taken into account as "non-functional requirements" at a very early stage of the development of the system, alongside the functional requirements, for example, storage capacity, speed, bandwidth, and compliance with technical standards and protocols. A real innovative design for an electronic patient record system or a truly smart electricity meter, would thus have *anticipated or pre-empted moral concerns and accommodated them into its design*, reconciling efficiency, privacy, sustainability, and safety. Value-focused thinking at the early stages of development at least might have helped engineers to do a better job in this respect. There is a range of fine grained design features that could have been considered and presented as choices for consumers. A smart meter is not a given, it is to a large extent what we design and make it to be. Respect for privacy can be *built in* (Garcia and Jacobs, 2011; Jawurek, Johns, and Kerschbaum, 2011). There are several objections to this suggestion. The first is that of moralism, another is that of relativism. Should values be built-in at all, and if so *which* values should be "built-in" and with what justification? There seems such a great variety of values. Empirical research seems to indicate that there is no coherent and stable set of European values, let alone global values (see Chapter 3 for a discussion of European values). Both objections I think can be addressed satisfactorily. No technology is ever value neutral (Van den Hoven, 2012a). It is always possible that a particular technology, application, or service, favors or accommodates a particular conception of the good life, at the expense of another, whether this was intended or not. There is, therefore, virtue in making particular values at play explicit, and in evaluating how their implementations work out in practice, adjusting our thinking accordingly. If we are overly impressed in the field of technology by objections of moralism and relativism, and as a result abstain from working with values in an explicit and reflective way, we run the risk that commercial forces, routine and bad intentions would reign free and impose values on technology that were not discussed and reflected upon by relevant parties.

Two European cases can serve as a contrast with the two aforementioned Dutch failures in innovation. They show that early and serious attention to moral considerations in design and R&D may not only have good *moral* outcomes, but also may lead to good *economic* outcomes. Consider the case of so-called "privacy enhancing technologies." The emphasis on data protection and the protection of the personal sphere of life is reflected in demanding EU data protection laws and regulation. The rest of the world has always considered the preoccupation with privacy as a typically European political issue. As a result of the sustained and systematic attention to data protection and privacy, Europe has become an important cradle of new products and services in the field of Privacy by Design or Privacy Enhancing Technologies. Now the Big Data society is on our doorstep and many computer users – also outside Europe – are starting to appreciate products and services that can accommodate user preferences and values concerning privacy, security, and identity, Europe has a competitive advantage and is turning out to be an important commercial player in this branch of the IT industry.

A second case concerns Germany's success in the development of sustainability technology. Germany is one of the leading countries in the world in sustainability technology. During the twentieth century, in the 1960s and 1970s, the world felt sorry for West Germany. Members of the Green Party chained themselves to every new chemical plant and seemingly frustrated economic growth by means of their disruptive protests. The conflict between economic growth and sustainability was a genuine value conflict that divided the political landscape and led to tensions in society. But in hindsight the conflict between different value orientations seems to have *stimulated* innovation rather than stifled it. The conflict and political tension formed the occasion and trigger for Germany to try to have its cake and eat it. The environmental technology that they felt the need to develop in the past has laid the foundation for commercial successes in the future.

4.2 Innovation and Moral Overload

Innovation can thus take the shape of (engineering) design solutions to situations of *moral overload* (Van den Hoven *et al.*, 2012b). One is morally overloaded when one is burdened by conflicting obligations or conflicting values, which cannot be realized at the same time. But as we saw above, conflicts of privacy and national security seem amenable to resolution by design and innovation in the form of privacy enhancing technologies. Conflicts between economic growth and sustainability were resolved by sustainability technology. Some think of these solutions as mere "technical fixes" and not as real solutions to moral problems. I do not take a stance on this issue here. I just want to point out that in such cases it seems to me that we have an obligation to bring about the required change by design or innovation (Van den Hoven *et al.*, 2012b).

> (I) If a contingent state of the world at time t1 does not allow us to satisfy two or more of our moral values or moral obligations at the same time, but we can bring about change by innovation in the world at t1 that allows us to satisfy them all together at a later time t2, then we have a moral obligation at t1 to innovate.

I consider this an important part of what responsibility implies in the context of innovation. It construes innovation as a second-order moral obligation: the obligation to bring about a change in the world that allows us to make more of our first-order moral obligations (e.g., for security *and* privacy, for economic growth *and* sustainability, safety *and* security) than we could have done without the innovation (see Chapter 2 for a discussion of how these dilemmas can be the subject of discursive strategies of reflection and deliberation). Normally, the principle that "ought" implies "can" holds, but a noteworthy feature of this second-order obligation to innovate is that it does not imply "can." This means that we may be under the obligation to come up with an innovation that solves our problem, although success is not guaranteed.

It may seem fairly obvious to claim that we have a higher order moral obligation to innovate when it leads to moral progress, but it requires a considerable shift in our thinking about innovation. We need to learn to think of ethical considerations and moral values in terms of requirements in design and research and development at an early stage. Value discourse should, therefore, not be left on an abstract level, but needs to be operationalized or "functionally decomposed," as is often done with high level and abstract requirements in engineering and design work. The process of functional decomposition leads eventually to a level of detail that points to quite specific design features of the system. This requires engineers to be value focused in their thinking and capable of articulating the values at play with different stakeholders (Pommeranz, 2012).

4.3   Values and Design

The above examples show that articulation and transparency concerning values are important to innovation processes. These allow us to detect dubious value commitments and allow us to design for shared public value commitments (see also Chapter 3). The history of technology is full of examples where values have been obfuscated or tacitly lodged in designs or products. They range from "racist overpasses," which were designed to be so low as to prevent buses from poor black neighborhoods being routed to the beaches of the white middle class near New York (Winner, 1980), to misleading biases in search engines, flaws in models in financial software – serious enough to "kill Wall Street" – and deceptive maps in the user interfaces of Geographical Information Systems (Van den Hoven, 2007).

Technical systems and innovative technology are the solidification of thousands of design decisions. Some of these were consciously taken after painstakingly precise discussion among designers and engineers with good intentions. Some, however, were inserted negligently or malevolently to serve the interests of the designer, or those commissioning him or her. What they have in common is that they may affect the lives of future or entire societies. In the twenty-first century we will have to help ourselves to the tools, methodologies, institutions, and procedures (see Chapter 2 for specific suggestions) that allow us to discuss design decisions explicitly, and see to it that our world of technology and innovation is the best possible expression of our shared and public values.

The idea of making social and moral values central to the design and development of new technology originated at Stanford in the 1970s, where it was a central subject of study in Computer Science. It has now been adopted by many research groups and is often referred to as *Value-Sensitive Design* (VSD). Various groups in the world are now working on this theme. Batya Friedman (Friedman (1997, 2004) and Friedman, Kahn, and Borning (2002)) was one of the first to formulate this idea of VSD, others have followed with similar approaches, for example, "Values in Design" at University of California (Bowker; Gregory) at Irvine and NYU (Nissenbaum, 2001) and "Values for Design" (Van den Hoven, 2007). These approaches share the following features:

- First, there is the claim that values can be expressed and embedded in technology. Values and moral considerations can, through their incorporation in technology, shape the space of action of future users, that is, they can affect the set of affordances and constraints of users. A road from A to B allows one to drive to B, but not to C. Large concrete walls without doors make it necessary to take a detour. Architects and town planners have known this for quite some time. An ancient example not very different from the low hanging overpasses example of the early twentieth century is the so-called "door of humility" in the birth church of Jesus in Nazareth. The door is exceptionally low and whoever wants to enter needs to bow his or her head, hence its name. The historical reason has been quite a different one from that of reminding people of the virtue of humility. The door was made intentionally low at the time of construction so as to make it impossible for mounted horsemen to enter the church on horseback in raiding attacks. If values can be imparted to technology and shape the space of actions of human beings, then we need to learn to incorporate and express shared values in the things we design and make.
- Secondly, there is the claim that conscious and explicit thinking about the values that are imparted to our inventions is morally significant. Churchill famously observed: "first we shape our dwellings and then our dwellings start to shape us." Technology and innovation are formidable shapers of human lives and society. It is, therefore, very important to think about what we are doing to ourselves and to each other by means of technology. Contemporary moral philosophers have started to become aware of this and want their ideas to have an impact in the real world of technology, policy, and economics. Modern applied ethics attempts to make a difference by informing the way we design things. A good example of this design trend in ethics can be found in the recent work of Cass Sunstein entitled *Nudge*, which construes the task of applied ethicists and public policy as one of *choice architecture* (Sunnstein and Thaler, 2010; Van den Hoven *et al.*, 2013). Think, for example, of the person who arranges the food in your university lunch room. By placing the deep fried stuff almost beyond reach and the healthy fruit and vegetables in front, the consumer is invited (not forced) to go for the healthy stuff (the nudge). Speed bumps and the "fly" in men's urinals are other examples of persuasion and nudging by technology.
- A third feature of the value-design approach is that moral considerations need to be articulated early on in the process, at the moment of the design and development when value considerations can still make a difference. This sounds easier that in fact it is. This desideratum runs into the Collingridge dilemma, that states that early in the process of development of a technology the degrees of freedom for design are significant, but information that could inform design is scarce, while later on in the development of the technology, as information starts to become available, the degrees of freedom in design have diminished. The world of technology is a world of probabilities, ignorance, and uncertainty. Ethics and the law have had problems with the associated epistemic insecurity of our own making. Still, ethics will have to rise to the occasion in order to be relevant to a man-made world of complex adaptive systems, chaotic phenomena, and emergence. One way to deal with this is to be honest

and explicit about what can be known about what we have created. We cannot be held responsible for not knowing what is by its very nature epistemically inaccessible. We can, however, be held responsible for not thinking about the limits of what is epistemically accessible, and for obfuscating what we know about our epistemic limits. Sometimes we have to act and choose under conditions of uncertainty or ignorance and take responsibility for what we do relative to what we know, and be held responsible relative to what we knew and what we could have known.

4.4   Responsible Innovation

Every country and every company in the world wants to be innovative. Innovation is encouraged, subsidized, and praised. Innovation is also extensively studied. Studies in innovation economics, management, and psychology are booming at nearly every university. Thousands of scholars in the last two decades have turned into "innovation experts." They study the legal, fiscal, and cultural and socio-economic conditions which are conducive to innovation, they describe best practices and make recommendations on how to be innovative. There is a panoply of definitions of innovation available (Baregheh *et al.*, 2009). I define innovation as follows:

Definition

Innovation is an activity or process which may lead to previously unknown designs pertaining either to the physical world (e.g., designs of buildings and infrastructure), the conceptual world (e.g., conceptual frameworks, mathematics, logic, theory, software), the institutional world (social and legal institutions, procedures and organization) or combinations of these, which – when implemented – expand the set of relevant feasible options for action, either physical or cognitive.

Innovation processes are well studied in the literature of the Sociology of Science and Technology and the literature on management of innovation and R&D. They can extend in time over generations, can be spread across the globe, may be either haphazard and serendipitous or carefully and meticulously planned, they may involve one person or several thousands of persons, and involve complex interactions between people, artifacts, propositional contents, in the context of rules, institutions, and organizations (see Chapter 1).

Innovations in this sense typically concern technical artifacts or technical systems – but as the definition above indicates they are not limited to the material domain – that allow us to do things we could not do before, or allow us to think about things we had not thought about before, or allow us to do familiar things in new ways, for example, do them better, faster, cheaper, and so on.

Now we can turn to the qualifier "responsible" in the expression "responsible innovation." "Responsibility" is a philosophical notion that has become prominent in the last century in ethical theory and in moral discourse. There are various ways to explicate the term and there are many different paradigms, theories, accounts, and connotations (see Chapter 7). Some argue that "responsibility" has become a central organizing concept in moral and social discourse. Others argue that its centrality is undeserved. In the world of work and the professions we speak of "professional responsibility" (or role responsibility), and in the world of international criminal and humanitarian law we speak of "the responsibility to protect." Responsibility is predicated primarily of persons and only derivatively of their actions, that is, the subject and the object (see Chapter 11). Strictly speaking, the paradigm case of responsibility is "the responsibility of a person for his or her actions – in light of his or her intentions – and their effects in the world." We say, for example, that "John is responsible for breaking the vase." Alternatively we can say that it was "John's responsibility to prevent the breaking of the vase," or that is was "his responsibility to put it in a safe place." We can also speak of "a responsible person." More recently, however, the qualification "responsible" has become attached to impersonal events and processes. We can thus also talk about "a responsible way of proceeding," "a responsible investment," "a responsible procedure," or "an irresponsible bonus structure." Similarly, with respect to technology, applied science, and engineering, we now have come to talk about "Responsible Innovation."

The use of "responsible" in the expression "responsible innovation" resembles the use of "lazy" in the expression "a lazy chair": strictly speaking the chair is not lazy. The word "lazy" in this expression refers to chairs that invite and accommodate people who can be said to be lazy, who feel lazy, are lazy, or behave as if they were lazy. Analogously, it is not the innovation itself that is responsible. "Responsible innovation" is a truncated and indirect way of referring to contexts in which people who are the appropriate subjects of responsibility claims either feel responsible, or can be held or can be made responsible. "Responsible innovation" can thus be used to refer, in the realm of innovation, to whatever invites, accommodates, stimulates, enhances, fosters, implies, or incentivizes responsible action.

If some innovative organization or process would be praised in virtue of its being "responsible" this would imply among other things that those who initiated it and were involved in it must have been accommodated as moral and responsible agents, that is, they must have been enabled:

(A) to obtain – as much as possible – the relevant knowledge on (i) the consequences of the outcomes of their actions and on (ii) the range of options open to them and

(B) to evaluate both outcomes and options effectively in terms of relevant moral values (including, but not limited to wellbeing, justice, equality, privacy, autonomy, safety, security, sustainability, accountability, democracy and efficiency).

(see Chapters 2 and 7 for further discussion of consequentialism and the status of knowledge and the problems of this in the context of innovation as an uncertain, collective and future-oriented activity.)

In the light of (A) and (B) above I suggest that another implication of the notion of Responsible Innovation is the capability of relevant moral agents

(C) to use these considerations (A and B) as requirements for design and development of new technology, products, and services leading to moral improvement

In Section 4.1, I concluded that there could be a higher order moral obligation to innovate. On the basis of this characterization of innovation and the implications (A), (B), and (C) we may characterize Responsible Innovation in summary as follows:

> Responsible Innovation is an activity or process which may give rise to previously unknown designs pertaining either to the physical world (e.g., designs of buildings and infrastructure), the conceptual world (e.g., conceptual frameworks, mathematics, logic, theory, software), the institutional world (social and legal institutions, procedures, and organization) or combinations of these, which – when implemented – *"expand the set of relevant feasible options regarding solving a set of moral problems."*

I thus suggest a core conception of responsible innovation which refers to, among other things, a transition to a new situation, and which has as its defining characteristic that it allows us to meet more obligations and honor more duties than before. A simple demonstration goes as follows. Let us consider how innovation could bring moral progress by solving a moral dilemma. The one who solves a moral dilemma, has overcome the problem of choosing between two obligations and thus escapes from a situation where one is bound to fail, because one of the two obligations cannot be met. A solution by innovation means, in this context, that one is able to discharge both obligations. Responsible innovation aims at changing the world in such a way that the pursuit of one horn of the dilemma is no longer necessarily at the expense of grabbing the other. Responsible innovation aims at grabbing the bull by both horns. Responsible innovation should, therefore, be distinguished from *mere innovation* or the adding of mere new functionality. Responsible innovation is the endeavor of attempting to add morally relevant functionality which allows us to do more good than before.

References

Al Abdulkarim, L.O. and Lukszo, Z. (2009a) Smart metering for the future energy systems in the Netherlands. *Proceedings of the Fourth International Conference on Critical Infrastructures, 2009 (CRIS 2009), Linköping University, Sweden, April 28-April 30, 2009, [s.l.]*, IEEE, pp. 1–7. ISBN: 978-1-4244-4636-0.

AlAbdulkarim, L., Lukszo, Z., "Impact of privacy concerns on consumers' acceptance of smart metering in the Netherlands," Networking, Sensing and Control (ICNSC), 2011 IEEE International Conference on , vol., no., pp. 287–292, 11–13 April 2011.

A. Baregheh, J. Rowley, S. Sambrook, (2009) Towards a multidisciplinary definition of innovation, *Management Decision*, **47**, 8, pp.1323–1339.

Friedman, B. (1997). *Human Values and the Design of Computer Technology*, CSLI Lecture Notes, Vol. **72**. New York: Cambridge University Press.

Friedman, B. (2004) Value sensitive design, in: Bainbridge, W.S. (ed.) *Berkshire Encyclopedia of Human-Computer Interaction*, Berkshire Publishing Group.

Friedman, B., Kahn, P., and Borning, A. (2002) Value sensitive design: Theory and methods. University of Washington technical report, 02-12.

Garcia, F. & Jacobs, B., (2011), Privacy friendly energy metering via homomorphic encryption. *Lecture Notes in Computer Science*, **6710**, 226–238.

Nissenbaum, H. (2001). How computer systems embody values. *IEEE Computer,* **34**(3), 118–120.

Tange, H. (2008) http://hpm.org/en/Surveys/BEOZ_Maastricht_-_Netherlands/12 /Electronic_patient_records_in_the_Netherlands.html accessed 2012.

Thaler, Richard H., Sunstein, Cass R. and Balz, John P. Choice Architecture (April 2, 2010). Available at SSRN: http://ssrn.com/abstract=1583509 or http://dx.doi.org /10.2139/ssrn.1583509.

Van den Hoven, M.J. (2007). Moral methodology and information technology, in: H. Tavani and K. Himma (eds.) *Handbook of Computer Ethics*. Hoboken, NJ: John Wiley & Sons, Inc.

Van den Hoven, M.J., (2012a). Neutrality and technology: Ortega Y Gasset on the good life. In: Brey, P., Briggle, A., Spence, E., (eds) *The Good Life in a Technological Age*. Routledge, London, pp. 327–339.

Van den Hoven, M.J., *et al.* (2012b). Engineering and the problem of moral overload. *Science and Engineering Ethics*, Volume 18, Issue 1 , pp. 143–155.

Van den Hoven, M.J., *et al.* (eds) (2013). *The Design Turn in Applied Ethics*. Cambridge University Press, Cambridge, forthcoming.

Van Twist, M. (2010) http://www.rijksoverheid.nl/bestanden/documenten-en-publicaties /rapporten/2012/02/08/rapport-het-epd-voorbij/rapport-het-epd-voorbij.pdf   accessed 2012.

Winner, L. (1980) Do artifacts have politics? *Dædalus,* **109**(1), 121–136.

5

Responsible Innovation – Opening Up Dialogue and Debate

Kathy Sykes[1] and Phil Macnaghten[2]

[1]*University of Bristol, UK*
[2]*Durham University, UK and State University of Campinas, Brazil*

5.1 A Short History of Controversies about Science and Technology

Probably, for as long as there have been technological revolutions, there have been debates, dialogue, and, at times, near warfare about them. Between 1811 and 1816 the Luddites flourished in Britain, opposing the Industrial Revolution. Bands of masked men destroyed machinery, mostly in the textile industry, and the term Luddite has now become a derogatory one, usually used to accuse people of being naively anti-technology or anti-progress.

But the modern-day meaning of "Luddite" may not be fair. Luddites resorted to violence, destroyed wool and cotton mills and threatened economic progress, but they surely had a reason, not just an irrational dislike of the new? Technological "advancements" were putting skilled workers out of jobs, and money and power into the hands of the few, the already wealthy. The Luddites could see their jobs being lost to the machines, and the prospect of greater exploitation and greater class division; they were part of a rising tide of English working-class discontent in the early nineteenth century. And the British Government's response was to send in troops and make "machine breaking" a capital crime, hanging at least 17 Luddites.

It would be nice to think that, 200 years on, we are more capable as a society of considering new technologies in a mature way, and thinking through some of the benefits, and also the potential inequities and downsides, in advance of their application; that we are now better at developing technologies in a responsible way, and talking through with the beneficiaries, and the potentially disadvantaged, how to ensure the impact of new

Responsible Innovation, First Edition. Edited by Richard Owen, John Bessant and Maggy Heintz.
© 2013 John Wiley & Sons, Ltd. Published 2013 by John Wiley & Sons, Ltd.

developments creates a better world based on shared values, rather than just giving more power and money to the already powerful. And that we might be able to do it without resorting to violence.

How far have we come since then? Some of the scenes of arrests of anti-genetic modification (GM) protestors ripping up fields of GM crops may seem somewhat reminiscent of the battles going on between the British Government and the Luddites, though admittedly with no hangings. And some would argue that the issues still hinge on equity and power and disputed visions of the future, rather than people just having an extreme dislike of the new. There is, however, a growing movement of scientists, policy-makers, science communicators, and science funders who are trying to move to a place where "business-as-usual" is to open up potentially contentious issues to dialogue and debate with members of the public and other stakeholders to explore ways to negotiate more equitable and considered impacts, more attuned to their seen and unforeseen effects.

In the 1960s there was a quite widespread optimism about technology. The contraceptive pill, television, fashion, and more access to "pleasure and leisure" activity were making changes to social relationships across the class system, at a time when the ravages of World War 2 were fading. In 1963 the Labour Prime Minister Harold Wilson's famous speech enthused about *"How the Britain that is going to be forged in the white heat of this revolution will be no place for restrictive practices or outdated methods on either side of industry."*

However, the glimmerings of an environmental movement, prepared to ask questions about the price of progress, were beginning. Just a year before Harold Wilson's speech, Rachel Carson published "Silent Spring" (Carson, 1962), which brought environmental concerns to wide portions of the US public, and called into question the paradigm of "scientific progress" that had been defining post-war American culture and technology-inspired visions of the American dream. The book charted the effects of pesticides on wildlife, notably DDT, as these "elixirs of death" worked their way through the food chain (Hynes, 1989). The book was serialized in the *New Yorker* from June 1962, and selected as Book of the Month that October by the "Book of the Month Club." Carson's work helped to inspire activism and the grassroots environmental and ecology movements. The use of DDT was phased out. The Environmental Protection Agency was created. New environmentalism was born, and, critically, the proposition that science and technology were ineluctably a force for good was thrown into doubt (Lutts, 1985).

Carson made uncomfortable observations, wrote a book that became widely publicized, helped to inspire environmental movements, and perhaps partly helped to change the mindset of the everyday American person – in the World's leading industrial nation. And ever since, there have been environmental groups and others who question the impact of technological developments, asking if the consequences of technological development are worth it.

Over the past 50 years debates and dialogue around science and its uses have increasingly taken place in the media, often between pressure groups and large companies or governments. Science is no longer indisputably a force for good. It produces unforeseen effects, increasingly global in scale and long-term in nature. It is involved both in the production of environmental harms and in their resolution. It is also part of the contemporary social and economic order, and closely tied to processes of industrialism and consumerism. Scientists have taken different sides in these debates, and sometimes felt uncomfortably stuck in the middle.

In this chapter we examine the evolution of public dialogue on science and technology. We identify its roots in public controversy and its role as an ingredient in the new scientific governance. We look, in particular, at the case of GM foods and crops in the UK, and how this provided the context for the institutional embedding of public engagement in UK policy. We then scrutinize the various ways in which dialogue is used in governance processes, and the claims for what constitutes "good dialogue," before setting out a set of suggestions on how debate and dialogue can be opened up, and the substantive issues which it should address. The chapter is centrally focused on the UK case, reflecting the practical and analytical experience of the authors. However, reference to experiences of dialogue in other contexts will be made, from other parts of Europe and beyond.

5.2 The Evolution of Public Engagement

Calls for greater public engagement in the development of new science and technology emerged as a response to four dynamics: the new politics of protest about certain technological projects and visions, visible in the growth of environmental and anti-nuclear movements from the 1960s; the requirement for governments (and parliaments) to have robust knowledge of the impacts of new science and technology in order to better anticipate their societal consequences; the perceived need to extend spaces for citizen participation, typically through the involvement of organized civil society groups, to make the governance of science and technology more accountable; and the demands from science communities to improve public understanding of science (PUS) where conflicts and tensions are presumed to stem from public ignorance and misunderstanding.

A key influence was the development of technology assessment (TA) organizations, which emerged in the United States and Europe from the 1970s. These organizations were typically linked to the legislature, aimed at providing authoritative information to US Congress and parliaments to inform decision-making, and provide early warning of future technological mishaps. The paradigm of TA reflected a model that presumed that the "problem" of technology was associated with a lack of democratic (and technical) input in technological governance, and that this could be redressed through providing elected representatives with authoritative information at an early stage (Van Eijndhoven, 1997). Thus, the US Office of Technology Assessment (OTA) was established in 1972 by Congress to provide information on the secondary effects of technology. A decade later, a parliamentary TA office was set up in France in 1983. Denmark, the Netherlands, and the European Parliament set up TA offices in 1986, while Britain and Germany followed suit in 1989. It is important to note that each office had its own distinctive model of assessment. The US OTA developed an expert-analytic and stakeholder model, involving a plural array of expertise and representatives of organized stakeholder groups as a means to counter accusations of bias or "technocracy," especially in the problem definition of issues. This stakeholder model was also an integral element of European-wide assessments, for similar reasons, which saw parliamentary TA as a form of expert policy analysis.

However, the Danish Board of Technology adopted a more inclusive approach to assessment. Seeing its role not simply as one of *informing* Parliament through formal assessments but also of *fostering* public debates, it developed a model of public deliberation around the technique of the consensus conference that became emulated throughout Europe and beyond. This was an explicitly dialogical model of public engagement; they saw the public as an important group to help to think through and make decisions about policy issues around science and technology, rather than a group of people who needed to be taught about science. Over the last decade and a half they have pioneered the use of participatory processes to assess the risks and societal impact of new technologies. The Board has established approaches to access public thinking around a series of issues every year, running Citizens' Hearings and Consensus Conferences. The Board's role has been to undertake independent technology evaluations, give accounts of technological alternatives and potential consequences, and also communicate their findings to parliament, other decision-makers, and the public. The purpose was to further public debate and knowledge of technology.

The Netherlands has also been a site for institutional innovation on public deliberation. The Rathenau Institute (originally called the Netherlands Organization for Technology Assessment, NOTA) has pioneered a host of deliberative fora, across a wide diversity of technological domains, publishing research on the social impact of new technologies and organizing debates on the issues and dilemmas they pose (see Chapter 9). Early public deliberation in the 1980s had referred to the engagement of organized civil society groups and experts to help clarify issues and identify how best to frame them at an early stage in the decision-making process (van Est, 2011). By the 1990s, however, the definition of public engagement had been expanded to embrace the wider public. This transformation had taken place partly as the result of intense debates that were taking place, both in the media and in civil society organizations, on issues surrounding the ethical use of animals and the genetic modification of plants and animals. Both issues reflected highly divergent and contested social values and perspectives that could not be resolved by expert advice, or by the deliberation of representatives of stakeholder groups. Both required, according to the Dutch Parliament, broad societal debates. Responding to this call, the Dutch Government was asked to organize dialogue on cloning (1998–2000), xeno-transplantation (2000–2001) and GM foods (2000–2001).

In the UK, the evolution of public engagement reflected its own distinctive political and administrative culture. Traditionally, scientific governance had been an avowedly expert-led activity, based on "sound science" and expert advice, with little implied role for the wider public. In 1985, the Royal Society's "The Public Understanding of Science" report marked the beginning of the "Public Understanding of Science" movement in the UK and beyond (Bodmer, 1985). The report argued that PUS was essential for the UK to make the most of its scientific potential. It adopted an "information deficit" model that presumed that scientists are knowledgeable experts; that economic prosperity requires scientific expertise; that members of the public need to make decisions that involve science and technology in their everyday lives, but that the public do not understand science well enough and are in need of education (Wynne, 1995). It asked that scientists develop an explicitly public role to help the public understand science and their work. From 1985 onwards there has been a huge growth in initiatives and supporting organizations committed to engaging the public in science. Science communication has ever since become more mainstream, with a surprising growth in hands-on science centers, popular science books, science festivals, and science television and radio. And it has become a core subject in the national curriculum. But it was not until 2000 that it became clear in the UK that scientists needed to *listen* to the public, not just talk at them.

Spurred on partly by the ferocious media debates on GM crops and bovine spongiform encephalopathy (BSE), the House of Lords Science and Technology Select Committee's report, "Science and Society," in 2000, marked a point of transition, where gradually the science communication movement, and then, more slowly, scientists themselves, realized that good communication must be two-way (House of Lords, 2000). The report observed that the public's confidence in science had been rocked by science-based controversies around GM crops, BSE and nuclear power, but that the public at the same time was generally positive about science. It said that science communication was too top-down and that scientists needed to listen to the public better. In particular, it argued that dialogue with the public needed to become embedded in policy-making and in science itself:

> direct dialogue with the public should move from being an optional add-on to science-based policy-making & to the activities of research organisations & learned institutions, and should become a normal & integral part of the process.

> (recommendation (1), paragraph 5.48)

And they made a call on individual scientists too:

> Science is conducted and applied by individuals; as individuals and as a collection of professions, scientists must have morality and values, and must be allowed and indeed expected to apply them to their work and its applications. By declaring the values which underpin their work, and by engaging with the values and attitudes of the public, they are far more likely to command public support.

> (paragraph 2.65)

After the House of Lords report in 2000, many people who had been working in "PUS" in the UK now began to wrestle with what dialogue might mean, or look like. Some of the new hands-on science centers, created with Millennium funding, tried to include exhibits and themes that opened up questions around science and how it is used, rather than assuming their role was just to promote science. The first "café scientifique," where scientists have conversations with interested members of the public in a café or bar, was run in 1998 by Duncan Dallas, and is an idea that now spans the world. Science festivals increasingly run debates and dialogues, rather than just lectures.

For some, a key part of the new way of thinking was that it was not sufficient for scientists and the public just to have conversations, but that the public's ideas, thinking, and views needed to be listened to and captured, and that scientists and policy-makers had a duty to hear what ordinary people were thinking about new developments in science.

One project that developed, arising out of a sense of frustration about conversations about dialogue with the public was "Small Talk" (Small Talk, 2005) in 2005, run by Think-lab. It was a collaboration between the British Association (now the British Science Association), the Royal Institution and the Cheltenham Science Festival. It aimed to have discussions between scientists and the public about nanotechnologies, to capture what was being said by the public and to share learning between different festivals and events, and then share what was found with scientists and policy-makers. Toward the end of the project, a high profile event was run at Thinktank, the science center in Birmingham, which hosted a young people's parliament event, with a government minister attending. Each of the different venues valued the learning from previous events. And what the public were saying about nanotechnologies echoed some of the findings from deliberative dialogue events run more formally.

A further project, funded by the UK's Economic and Social Research Council (ESRC) between 2004 and 2006, was aimed at stimulating "upstream" dialogue between scientists and the public (Kearnes, Macnaghten, and Wilsdon, 2006). Involving a collaboration between the Thinktank Demos and Lancaster University, the project sought to understand the social and scientific visions that are influencing nanotechnology research, and to subject such visions to public deliberation. Following research with scientists and policymakers – in which the implicit social assumptions were drawn out – the project carried out a series of focus groups, which explored questions of risk, responsibility, and control, and which identified possible fault lines of public controversy. At a final workshop, a group of nanoscientists and citizens shared their hopes, fears and concerns. The tone of their conversation was open and realistic, and generated a surprising degree of consensus, as members of the public developed a better sense of the laboratory, and the scientists grew to appreciate the legitimacy of public concerns.

An array of projects, with similar aims and aspirations, has been developed across Europe and beyond, many funded by the European Commission (EC). The Science and Society streams of the EC's Framework 6 and Framework 7 projects have, in particular, been important contexts for innovation and learning. These include the 2004–2006 "Meeting of Minds: European Citizen's Deliberation on Brain Science" project,[1] set up to examine the social and ethical implications of developments in brain science. Run by the King Baudouin Foundation, with support from the EC, the project involved TA bodies, science centers and museums, academic institutions, and public foundations, with 126 citizens across nine countries in eight different languages. Recommendations were made to the European Parliament.

A key finding, which is repeated again and again in dialogues between scientists and the public, was that "*contrary no doubt to many scientists' expectations – people of varied backgrounds, with no special expertise in the scientific issues, are able to hold a fruitful, intelligent dialogue with experts and to produce meaningful and useful results.*" However, a key unknown remains, concerning the *impact* of many of these kinds of initiatives on policy-makers and scientists: whether they actually listened or learned from the public. A government minister attending an event and hearing views from across the project is possibly an empowering experience for the people present, but does not mean that the minister was influenced. "Recommendations being given" does not mean that any attention was paid to those recommendations (see Chapter 2 for further discussions of the importance of the dimension of responsiveness in the context of responsible innovation).

5.3   The Case of Genetically Modified Foods in the UK

An early example of public deliberation in the UK was the National Consensus Conference on Plant Biotechnology in 1994 (Durrant, 1994). Hosted by the Science Museum

---

[1] Meeting of Minds – European Citizens' Deliberation on Brain Science, available at www.meetingmindseurope.org.

and funded by the Biotechnology and Biological Sciences Research Council (BBSRC), the conference was based on a procedural model developed by the Danish Board of Technology. A lay panel of 16 members, selected by the steering committee, became informed about plant biotechnology through written information and preliminary meetings prior to the conference itself. The panel then developed a set of questions they wanted to pose to experts, whom they had nominated to attend. The conference itself was run along judicial lines: experts were called to provide evidence and were cross-examined by the panel in front of an audience. The final phase involved the lay panel writing a report that was subsequently published and distributed to politicians, scientists, industrialists and journalists. Again, although the lay-panel report was widely circulated, the impact on policy was negligible. Perhaps this is regrettable. In retrospect, key recommendations seem worthy of being considered. These included: that products containing GM material should be labeled, and that labeling should be agreed across countries, so consumers would have a choice; that patenting laws were not ready yet to deal with the issues that GM plants would bring; that if developing countries really were to feel benefits of the new technologies, they needed "bringing to the table" to help decision-making; and that plant biotechnologies presented such opportunities and risks that a government minister should be named to keep an overview of developments.

A second example of public deliberation was a research project funded by Unilever and undertaken in association with a variety of environmental and consumer groups in 1997 (Grove-White *et al.*, 1997). Run by Lancaster University, the research aimed at understanding public responses to Genetically Modified Organisms (GMOs) in food (actual and latent), the factors shaping these responses, and whether or not the "framing" of the issue by government and industry reflected public sensibilities. Using a set of in-depth discussion groups, the research found considerable ambivalence in the UK toward GMO products in food, mixed feelings about the adequacy and integrity of present patterns of regulation and assurances of safety, and a profound sense of fatalism about the future of GMOs in foods (which were seen as likely to be pervasive irrespective of public opinion). Again, the study had little direct impact on policy (government or industry) although two years later, at the height of the GM controversy, Sir Robert May, at the time the Government's Chief Scientific Adviser, commented: *"I now have had a chance to read 'Uncertain World', which I wish I had indeed read earlier. It is in many ways a remarkably prescient document"* (R. Grove-White, personal communication, 1999).

Later, in 2004, Lord Sainsbury, the then UK Science Minister, was growing increasingly concerned about the direction public debate was taking on GM crops and the impact this was having on UK science. The debate in the media had become extremely polarized. This easily happens: the media likes to show conflicting views on an issue, and in this case the large American-based company Monsanto was aggressively trying to get GM products into use and into UK research agendas. This large multinational appeared to be driven primarily by a narrowly defined understanding of shareholders' interests, and this fueled increased public concerns about a technology that had significant potential impacts, and which was seen as being imposed. It had become a battle between pressure groups, companies, some in government (who did not want the UK to lose a research edge in these technologies), and some scientists. Funding was becoming harder to get; locations for testing GM crops were being targeted by Greenpeace and others; and suddenly some scientists' research areas were thrown into the limelight in ways they could not have predicted. Usually, media debates about science and technology had been able to run without having a material impact on the science itself. This issue was different.

The Government ran the *GM Nation?* public debate in 2002–2003, a citizen engagement exercise aimed at getting public involvement. However, many members of the public and people in pressure groups felt that decisions had already been made. A large strand of this approach was to hold open meetings across the country in different venues. These became opportunities for the people who felt most angry, on either side of the debate, to come and argue with each other some more. There was little opportunity for people who were interested in the issue, but who had not yet decided what they thought, to come and explore the nuances of the opportunities or threats. Alongside this series of meetings was a "narrow but deep" strand of public dialogue, where people from a wide demographic came together to learn about the issues, and hear from experts of different kinds, and discuss the issues over time. While the deliberations of this group were more balanced, and possibly useful for policy-makers, the shouting, media attention, and loss of goodwill resulting from the open meetings drowned out the potential insights from this other strand. Lord Sainsbury, and many others, were concerned that the kind of mistakes that had been made should not be repeated; that if dialogue were to be done with the public, it needed to be based on good practice, and needed to help get nuanced discussions about possible pros and cons of different kinds of GM crop development, not violent fights with different sides seeming to say "all GM research is necessary" or "all GM crops are wrong."

5.4   Sciencewise and the Institutional Embedding of Public Engagement in the UK

In 2005, the UK Government's top-level science advisory group, the Council for Science and Technology, published its report, "Policy through dialogue" (Council for Science and Technology, 2005). This asked for government to develop a "corporate memory" about how to do public dialogue on science and technology issues well, and that government should use dialogue on potentially contentious issues, ideally before they become polarized in the media, to help to inform and improve its decision-making.

Sciencewise was set up in 2004, to try to develop this "corporate memory" and to try to change the culture of decision-making in government, across all departments and agencies, so that when policy-makers are tackling difficult issues involving science and technology, they naturally turn to using good practice in public dialogue to help them grapple with the issues. Sciencewise was rooted in the 10 year Science and Innovation Framework: 2004–2014 (HM Treasury/DTI/DfES, 2004). In this Her Majesty's Treasury made a specific commitment to upstream public engagement,

> to enable [public] debate to take place "upstream" in the scientific and technological development process, and not "downstream" where technologies are waiting to be exploited but may be held back by public scepticism brought about through poor engagement and dialogue on issues of concern.

(p. 105)

Thus began an opportunity to have different kinds of dialogue and debates with the public, in "safe" spaces, with people from many different kinds of background, without vested interests, with time to learn about issues, to consider and reflect on them, change their minds, hear different perspectives and together give their feedback to policy-makers: with the aim of making scientific developments safer, and to have better impacts on society with more equitable outcomes. Public deliberation became an integral element of the new scientific governance. Embedded within this style of policy-making were a number of assumptions: that expert and scientific framings of risk issues can be at odds with lay ethical judgments and concerns, and that this can be remedied by giving lay people a greater voice; and that public dialogue should be promoted by government as part of the democratic process (Irwin, 2006). The framing of public dialogue evolved throughout the early 2000s. It shifted from a set of debates around the framing of regulatory science, to a wider and more inclusive set of debates about the social and ethical dimensions of science and technology, and on how these could be anticipated by techniques of public engagement (Wilsdon and Willis, 2004).

The evolution of Sciencewise itself reflects these changes. When Sciencewise first began, the issues it focused on were ones identified by the then Science Minister Lord Sainsbury: including nanotechnologies, climate change, and animal experimentation. Specific questions about these areas were not identified, and there were not any specific policy decisions to be made. Funding was distributed by an open call, so different groups were able to bid for funding for activities to frame and address one of these issues. An independent advisory group was brought together to oversee and steer Sciencewise, with social scientists, scientists, science communicators, educationalists, people from industry, and civil servants working across different departments. At its first meeting, the group questioned the approach, saying that the focus was too distant from government, and the public and policy-makers too far apart. Instead, "a light needed to be shone" into the recesses of government, to identify where people were making policies and where there were opportunities to inform policies that were actually being made.

The first round of projects did enable some good discussions between the public and scientists; the people running the processes learned how to run them better, and there were a few impacts on policy-makers. But the activities were too far away from policy makers and the actual decisions being made. Sciencewise shifted to a mode where dialogues would only be held when there was a "policy hook"; a need from policy-makers to make some decisions; time available to run a thorough process; and policy-makers prepared to commission and own the process. Funding was offered from Sciencewise, but only if the dialogue was to be run according to the guidelines[2] and as part funding to a department or agency[3]. Mentoring and support would be offered, and now dialogues would be commissioned. So the process of open calls for ideas was abandoned.

Another key reason to involve policy-makers from the start is that it was found to help to legitimize the process. If groups of the public hear directly from a policy-maker why they are being asked to consider an issue, and that their deliberations are wanted, the whole exercise is, and feels, a more genuine one. Sciencewise also asked that scientists be more directly involved in the processes, to be available to respond to questions

---

[2] Sciencewise–ERC Guiding Principles, http://www.sciencewise-erc.org.uk/cms/assets/Uploads/Project-files/Sciencewise-ERC -Guiding-Principles.pdf

[3] http://www.sciencewise-erc.org.uk/cms/assets/Uploads/Project-files/SWP01-Grant-guidance.pdf

and to discuss ideas, and thus to be an element of the learning and reflective process for participants. Sciencewise, which gained the name Expert Resource Centre (ERC) in 2008, also shifted focus onto capacity building for civil servants and other policy-makers. If a policy-maker does not know what pubic dialogue might be, or why it might be useful, or how it might be done, why would they consider doing it?

Over its first five years, Sciencewise had a budget of up to £2 million a year and by 2009 had stimulated an additional total investment of £2.7 million from other government departments. It had helped government agencies or departments to run seventeen dialogues, to work on capacity building for policy-makers, to commission research, to publish reports and to develop a web site of resources[4].

There have also been moves to embed public engagement and dialogue within universities. The "Beacons for Public Engagement" represented one of the largest funding initiatives in public engagement, where Research Councils UK (RCUK), the Higher Education Funding Councils for England, Wales, and Scotland, and the Wellcome Trust funded six "Beacons of Excellence" for public engagement, each seeking to change the culture within higher education institutions to reward, encourage, and commit to engaging the public, and listening to them. A National Coordinating Centre for Public Engagement (NCCPE), hosted by the University of Bristol and the University of the West of England, was also funded, to capture learning and share it with the rest of the sector. The Beacons ran their culture change programs and experiments between 2007 and 2011. In late 2011 there was a further funding call, from RCUK, for "Catalysts for Public Engagement," to enable more universities to embed engaging the public in their research, with the NCCPE continuing in its role of supporting, sharing and embedding learning across the sector, asking universities to sign up and commit to a Manifesto for Public Engagement[5]. Many research funding bodies and learned institutions also published a Concordat for Engaging the Public with Research[6], requiring universities to embed, support, and commit to public engagement. Research and funding councils are now also asking all researchers to try to think through and budget for "impact" – how their research might affect, or has affected, society or the economy. Public engagement is a recognized route through which such impact may be made.

So, across government departments, funding bodies, and universities in the UK, moves have been made to try to turn dialogue into the "normal and integral part of the process" that the House of Lords report asked for. These recent developments are indicative of a more general shift in institutional rhetoric and practice – from a focus on public dialogue and engagement in responding to issues of public trust in science, toward a broader appreciation of the governance of science, technology, and innovation system as a whole.

5.5   Motivations for Public Dialogue

So far, we have attempted to provide a short history of how public dialogue and debate on emerging science and technology has evolved, with particular reference to

---

[4] See Sciencewise Expert Resource Centre http://www.sciencewise-erc.org.uk/

[5] The Engaged University: A Manifesto for Public Engagement, http://www.publicengagement.ac.uk/sites/default/files/Manifesto%20for%20Public%20Engagement%20Final%20January%202010.pdf.

[6] Concordat for Engaging the Public with Research: a Set of Principles Drawn up by the Funders of Research in the UK, http://www.rcuk.ac.uk/documents/scisoc/ConcordatforEngagingthePublicwithResearch.pdf.

the institutional context of the UK. In the next two sections we untangle the competing claims and motivations for public dialogue, with some evaluation.

Andy Stirling has analyzed the various motivations for greater participation in the social appraisal of science and technology (Stirling, 2005; see also Fiorino 1989). These include: the normative (e.g., that dialogue is the right thing to do for reasons of democracy, equity, equality, and justice), the instrumental (e.g., that dialogue provides social intelligence to deliver pre-committed policy objectives, such as those of building trust or of avoiding adverse public reaction), and the substantive (e.g., that policy choices can be co-produced with publics in ways that authentically embody diverse social knowledge, values, and meanings in a substantive manner).

Using this typology it is possible to evaluate the different motivations that underpin institutional uses of public engagement. Charles Thorpe and Jane Gregory, for example, claim that the rise of participatory discourse in science policy in the UK is primarily a product of a set of neoliberal policies for investment and innovation in science and technology aimed at wealth creation. The creation of the Sciencewise-ERC is seen as explicitly and institutionally linked to an instrumental mode of governing, as part of the UK Government's desire to produce "Post-Fordist" publics in the quest for new markets, providing the State with social intelligence to ensure the smooth passage of income-generating science and technology (Thorpe and Gregory, 2010). Brian Wynne has developed a related argument, critiquing the ways in which public engagement has been used by scientific and policy institutions with the particular goal of restoring public trust in science (Wynne, 2006).

Are such claims justified? In an analysis of the Sciencewise dialogues, Chilvers and Macnaghten identified examples of dialogues that followed an instrumental logic (Chilvers and Macnaghten, 2011, see also Macnaghten and Chilvers, 2012). There is less scope in these dialogue to contest the ways in which the debate has been framed, and the options and subject areas that are deemed to be relevant. For this reason, such dialogues assume a malleable subject who is able to bend through the provision of information and argument by the sponsoring institution. Interestingly, this model of dialogue is common in dialogues on climate change, responding to the policy goal of stimulating behavior change as part of the government's commitment to a legally binding target for greenhouse gas emissions by 2050. Policy-derived questions shaping the various dialogues include: how to cut emissions at a local level and how to encourage people to change their energy behavior to reduce their carbon footprint.

However, while instrumental logics were apparent in some dialogues, these were minority cases. More commonly, dialogues employed logics that were both "substantive" and "normative." Good dialogue was embraced as not only the right thing to do in itself but also, and critically, as leading to better policy outcomes. Indeed, these substantive logics are themselves embedded in the guidance and advice streams in Sciencewise-ERC's Resource Library on what constitutes good dialogue.[7] This includes continued emphasis that dialogue is not concerned with one-way communication of policy outcomes that government already is pre-committed toward. Good dialogue is presented as involving two-way or multi-way communication between publics, scientists, and policy-makers. In its guiding principles for public dialogue there is explicit guidance that the

---

[7] Sciencewise – ERC Guiding Principles, *op. cit.* note 2.

scope of the dialogue process (i.e., the range of issues and policy options covered) must reflect the full range of aspirations and concerns held by publics, scientists, and policy makers. This appeal for inclusiveness also pertains to the ways in which the dialogue is itself framed, which should be agreed, preferably through dialogue, such that it focuses on broad questions and a range of alternatives.

To unpack further the different kinds of logics that underpinned the Sciencewise dialogues we make use of a typology developed by Roger Pielke in his book, *The Honest Broker* (Pielke, 2007). Pielke differentiates four ways in which the scientist can choose to engage in the policy process. These are: as a "pure scientist" (who only focuses on pure research with no consideration for its utility, and has no interaction with policy makers), as a "science arbiter" (who answers specific factual questions posed by decision-makers), as an "issue advocate" (who has decided for themselves on the "right" policy decision, through their understanding of science, and becomes an advocate for the "solution," often reducing the scope of choices available to decision-makers), and as an "honest broker of policy alternatives" (who expands, or at least clarifies, the scope of options and choices available to decision-makers). He argues that on issues where there exist high levels of uncertainty and/or high levels of disagreement between stakeholders on the value of pursuing particular options, there is a need to promote the "honest broker" model of science policy deliberation, to contribute both to better policy and to a healthy democracy.

In the Sciencewise dialogues, Chilvers and Macnaghten found that public participants (not scientists) were being asked to deliberate on the social and ethical issues associated with particular science and technology for various reasons. In the dialogues highlighted above, where instrumental logics prevailed, the dialogue process was used to seek to legitimate or find a pathway toward a previously established position or policy commitment. These were examples of the "issue advocate" model of public dialogue, where publics are expected to accept, rather than challenge, the vision of science and its relationship to a pre-established policy option which is being presented to them. However, other dialogues were more open-ended, aimed at helping policy-makers clarify issues, expand choices, and reflect on the implications of alternative courses of action. In this sense, publics were cast as honest brokers within a substantive model of public engagement.

However, two distinct variants of honest broker dialogue are in play. On the one hand, there is the honest broker model of dialogue, corresponding to Pielke's original formulation, where the aim is to deliberate on different policy options and to evaluate the pros and cons of different policy outcomes, with justification. On the other hand, there is the "upstream" model of dialogue, a category that extends Pielke's typology, where the aim is to develop a process through which publics can engage in conversations on the issues and questions posed by science and technology at a relatively early stage in the innovation process. In the upstream dialogues, conversations tend to be exploratory, to concern the ways in which the science and technology is being imagined by social actors, to scrutinize the views and visions of actors, to open up future possible worlds, to articulate what the social and ethical issues associated with those worlds are, and to deliberate on the factors that shape concern, hope, and possibility. Such dialogue events tend to be tied only loosely to specific policy goals and outcomes, and are more apt to offer generic advice on the governance of science and technology. In such processes participants are citizens, developing novel identities and positions in which new ideas of the common interest can emerge, and in which there is (ideally) an equality of voice amongst lay and expert groups. In the Sciencewise dialogues the projects that used the upstream model included those related to specific areas of emergent science and technology – such as synthetic biology, nanotechnology, industrial biotechnology and geoengineering – as well as projects that explored possible future directions in science in general.

Dialogues that fall under the honest broker model, in contrast with the upstream model, tend to position the role of the public as a lay, ethical arbiter in providing views on how to proceed, weighing up the pros and cons of different courses of action, articulating the conditions under which different options are acceptable or not, and thus helping inform a policy decision. The substance of the dialogues is less exploratory than in the upstream model, since the contours of the debate are known, and established positions may already be set out. Such dialogue events thus tend to be tied closely to specific policy goals and outcomes, on domains of science and technology which are relatively developed, and which are known already to pose social and ethical problems and dilemmas. In the Sciencewise dialogues, the honest broker model tended to be favored for health-related questions, where the aim is one of helping sponsors to determine whether, and under what conditions, to fund and move forward with specific and ethically-challenging research. Examples include dialogues on research on stem cells and research on embryos that contain both animal and human material.

5.6 The Claims for Public Dialogue

Numerous claims are made about what public dialogue can achieve. Of course, the different motivations for doing it, the timing of dialogues, the way they are run and the involvement and responses of policy-makers are key in determining the actual impacts and outcomes.

One set of claims is that dialogue can draw on the knowledge of the public, aiding in the exploration of different policy options (see above). Discussing an issue over time can help policy-makers to reflect on long-term impacts, benefits, harms and risks. Considering who the beneficiaries are can be helpful, widening thinking about who else might benefit or be disadvantaged as a basis for identifying actions that could make more equitable use of the technologies. Some funders claim that dialogue can help them explore how to increase the social benefit of their research. Discussing issues with the public can also help challenge the assumptions of scientists and policy-makers, providing wider perspectives than they usually hear.

For policy-makers, dialogue is often claimed to increase the legitimacy of their decisions. For others it can help them to explore the grey areas of public opinion, away from polarized discussion and media sensation, enabling more nuanced and in-depth thinking about an issue, and giving them confidence that there could be public support for policies that might immediately seem unpopular. John Hutton, then UK Secretary of State for Work and Pensions, said that public dialogue about pensions helped his team to think through the issues and write the Pensions White Paper in 2006. He said it gave them the confidence to make braver decisions, including a recommendation to increase the age of retirement.

An example of a public dialogue with a demonstrable impact on policy – in this case on science funding – is a dialogue commissioned by the Engineering and Physical Sciences Research Council (EPSRC), on how to frame a call for funding in the area of nanotechnology for medicine and healthcare. The connection to a policy decision was clear – EPSRC would be deciding on how to support one or two sub-areas of nanomedicine, and the decision on which areas to fund would be informed by the results of the public dialogue. This clearly allowed for a focused and engaged discussion. The dialogue showed that while funding for healthcare was generally supported, there was a clear preference for technologies that would permit people more control and autonomy in their lives. In relation to options for funding, the dialogue provided a clear steer about the relative priorities of six potential application areas of nanotechnology for health-care. The highest priority was for applications of nanotechnology for the prevention and early diagnosis of disease, with better-targeted drug delivery for serious diseases coming second. The biggest misgivings were reserved for "theranostics" – the idea of combin-ing diagnosis and therapy in a single, automatic device – even though this option has been favored using the EPSRC's usual approach of a "Town Meeting," where scientists prioritize areas of research to fund. Theranostics was perceived by the public as being potentially disempowering. The public were also less enthusiastic than scientists about applications such as self-cleaning surfaces for hospitals. They said that hospitals should just always follow good rules of hygiene and cleanliness.

The dialogue process thus directly informed the decision-making process and led, arguably, to more socially-robust and better decisions. It was still a small team of scien-tists and science funders who made the final decision, but their opinions seemed swayed by the findings of the public dialogue. Professor Richard Jones, the "nano-champion" who made the dialogue happen, said that being involved helped prompt scientists to *"re-examine unspoken assumptions and clarify aims and objectives,"* that scientists *"are reminded of the high standing of scientists and scientific enterprise in our society,"* and that *"there are strong arguments that public deliberation and interaction can lead to more robust science policy"* (Jones, 2008). Having been directly involved in some of the public dialogue, he was also prompted to change the direction of his own research team.

The above claims relate primarily to honest broker dialogue. For upstream dialogue the uses of dialogue can be more exploratory. For these areas of science it may be less clear what the issues are, and dialogues may be used to help define the matters of concern at a time when this can be integrated back into the R&D innovation process. Dialogue in these cases can help clarify the social and ethical issues associated with a technological development or pathway, including accounts of why certain forms of technological inno-vation may be disruptive: socially, ethically, economically, and politically. In some cases new technologies may have the potential to blur key moral and ethical distinctions. For example, in a study on the social and ethical dimensions of emerging nanotechnologies, Matthew Kearnes and colleagues[8] found that what underpinned people's ambivalence to the technology was unease with the "programmatic imaginaries" that were driving the development of the technology (see Chapter 13), including the foundational conception that nanotechnology represents a new paradigm of control and manipulation based on a style of thought that conceives of nature and humans as infinitely malleable. Public dia-logue can illuminate the stakes of the issue, at the level of politics, economy, ethics, and ontology, and bring them to the attention of policy-makers and governance processes.

Such claims relate so far to the value of "invited dialogues," typically government-sponsored and involving selected and moderated small group discussions. However,

---

[8] Matthew Kearnes, Phil Macnaghten and James Wilsdon (2006) Governing at the Nanoscale: People, policies and emerging technologies. London: Demos.

"uninvited" spaces for public engagement also exist, orchestrated by citizens themselves rather than government institutions, and involving forms of activism and protest. Historically, these have tended to be dismissed and denied by science and policy institutions as either irrational and/or irresponsible and/or counter-productive to good governance. However, an alternative and more positive view of the potential for institutional reflexivity in this regard is possible, concerning the ways in which "counter publics" can impact on the policy process (Warner, 2002). For example, even though the protests over GM crops and foods in the UK are commonly seen as having undermined the authority of science-led governance, they nevertheless contributed to some positive effects. Thus, without overt confrontation and adversity it is questionable whether a more deliberative model of scientific governance would have been developed in the UK (see Section 5.5 above), or whether the BBSRC, the key public funder of crop science in the UK, would have reoriented UK plant and crop science research strategies from a narrow vision concentrated on genetic improvements to a more holistic, diverse, and flexible portfolio configured around "public good – plant breeding" objectives (Doubleday and Wynne, 2011).

5.7   How (and When) Can Debate and Dialogue Be Opened Up?

Typically, now and in the past, debates around science and technology have taken place in the media. Different actors have been involved; whether pressure groups, scientists, governments, learned societies, or companies. Some areas, like nanotechnologies, have had a relatively smooth ride globally. Other areas, like GM crops in Europe and research involving stem cells in the US have involved quite bloody battles.

In the UK, the Science Media Centre (SMC), now based at the Wellcome Trust, has helped to make many of these media debates more mature. When a press release that may be about to sensationalize or over-state an area of science is going out, the SMC finds scientists able to speak reasonably about the issue, and lures them out, supporting them to talk with the media. The Centre has gained the trust of scientists and journalists alike. Many scientists believe that they have helped to take some unnecessary sting out of some stories, and helped to balance others.

The UK can boast of excellent science correspondents in its main newspapers and television news stations. Many have degrees or even PhDs in science, and try to report stories in a balanced manner and without too much hype. At times, issues become media battles when the news editors start to take control of the stories: the issue has become so political, that now it is out of the hands of the science correspondents. However, the framing of the science-policy interface may itself lend the science to becoming politicized, as in climate change, where getting the science right is often seen as important for determining policy. In such topics there is a need to develop the role of the honest broker in public dialogue, to open up new and complementary narratives for science-based policy making for the twenty-first century (Pielke, 2010).

Opening up expert advice and deliberation to wider actors – away from the old, sole reliance on committees of technical experts – has become a common feature of contemporary science and technology governance. An excellent example is the Nanotechnologies Report by the Royal Society and Royal Academy of Engineering (Royal Society, 2004). They were invited to write this report by the British Government, to explore the emerging area of nanotechnology. The committee, chaired by Professor Ann

Dowling in 2003, had diverse membership, including social scientists, people from pressure groups and scientists. They all had time to learn about the science and the issues, to discuss and listen to each other's perspectives. They then wrote a lengthy, thoughtful report, giving the Government advice about how to carry this area forward. And while the report may not have created a whirlwind of media attention, and while some of the recommendations have not been followed, it has informed many people involved in the area with a range of different perspectives.

Since 2004, social scientists and lay members of the public have become regular members on expert advisory groups. *Inter alia* these include, membership of Royal Society reports on geoengineering and food security, societal panels for the research councils, open and public meetings on strategy planning (ESRC), a Citizen's Advisory Forum for a major cross-council research initiative known as Living With Environmental Change and a stage-gate review process for the field test of geoengineering research (see Chapter 2). Such initiatives suggest that social and ethical reflection has, to some extent, become embedded in research governance.

More widely, since the House of Lords Report on Science and Society in 2000, there have been increasing opportunities for small-scale, informal discussions to take place between scientists and the public. As well as the science café movement, since 1998, many science festivals, science centers, museums, and universities have experimented with innovative two-way discussion formats. These small-scale discussions have provided important territory for scientists and the public alike to learn about a new way of communicating.

The range of different techniques for conducting dialogue has exploded over the last decade. Reviewing the Sciencewise-ERC dialogue projects, Chilvers and Macnaghten identified a remarkable range of group-based and bespoke deliberative methods. These include, amongst others, full day public workshops, citizens' juries, citizens' inquiries, reconvened deliberative groups, deliberative panels, national public conversations, self-managed group discussions, facilitated public events, regional workshops, outreach workshops, brainbox workshops, online consultation, blogs, and open access events, alongside non-deliberative interview, electronic voting and opinion poll survey techniques.

However, while the growth of dialogue over the past decade has undoubtedly been a good thing, questions remain. As Jason Chilvers (2010) points out, the professionalization of public engagement in recent years has led to an increased separation and polarization between academic social scientists and dialogue practitioners; a growing public engagement industry whose commercial interests can compromise democratic ideals of participation; an emphasis on a limited and homogeneous set of techniques that has tended to reinforce consensus and to homogenize views in ways that may unwittingly iron out differences and minority perspectives; the favoring of top-down institutional framings of public dialogue which may neglect other, more uninvited, alternative framings on science-related issues; and, most significantly, a host of examples of dialogue for dialogue's sake that has often only marginally influenced the governance of science organizations.

To respond to these criticisms we now set out what we suggest are good and bad ways of conducting dialogue. Ways of doing it badly include:

- When the decision is already made;
- When the sponsoring body is not prepared to listen;

- When the dialogue does not involve an appropriately diverse array of stakeholders or members of the public;
- When the issue being debated has been framed without public or stakeholder input;
- When the timeframe is not appropriate, being either too early in the R&D process (when the issues associated with the science are too provisional) or too late (when there remains little opportunity to change its trajectory).

Michel Callon and colleagues have developed a set of criteria for classifying good dialogic practices (Callon, Lascoumes, and Barthe, 2010). For Callon *et al.*, the key issue is not simply to (re)legitimize "lay knowledge" or "lay values" through deliberative processes. Such a framing itself would reinforce an unproductive separation between science and the public. Rather Callon *et al.*'s ambition is to reconfigure such relationships, through what he terms "hybrid forums" and in the spirit of collective experimentation. Such processes may take place upstream (pre-innovation) or downstream (at the point of innovation). What is more important, to Callon *et al.*, is to design a process through which publics and issues emerge (neither pre-exist each other), and which is pluralist, inclusive, and interdisciplinary. To design a good process, the following questions should be asked:

1. How early and with what level of intensity are laypersons able to be involved in research and innovation processes (criterion of intensity)?
2. How able is the deliberative forum to facilitate the shared definition of the issue and thus the composition of the collective in the exploration of future worlds (criterion of intensity)?
3. How diverse are the groups invited to participate and how open is the process to the articulation of plural views and for the redefinition of an issue or issues at stake (criterion of openness)?
4. What level of control exists for including groups who do more than represent existing interests (criterion of openness)?
5. How well supported are participants to develop their arguments and claims, to answer questions, and to develop positions (criterion of quality)?
6. How continuous are the structured engagements and to what degree can there be a continuity of voice (criterion of quality)?
7. To what extent is the funding institution obliged to listen to the concerns of the collective and to take into account the prescriptions (criterion of responsiveness)?

Of course, embedding dialogue into governance is hard. For policy institutions it can threaten the status quo and seem to take power and authority from expert groups. It can detract from the autonomy of the estate of science, which traditionally has seen itself as best placed to make decisions on science (a principle enshrined in the research councils). And it can be tough, especially when scientific issues raise potentially far-reaching social, political, and ethical issues, such as in stem cell research or genetic engineering, or in technologies that intentionally set out to manipulate the earth's climate systems, such as solar radiation management, one form of geoengineering. And finally, it can be difficult for those in authority to genuinely listen and be prepared to change taken-for-granted positions and understandings. One future challenge for public dialogue is to ask whether one-off dialogue events are sufficient or whether a more synoptic, far-reaching form of dialogue, deeply embedded in governance, is required – a key issue for nascent programs of responsible innovation.

5.8   The Substance of Public Concerns and Their Implications for Governance

So far we have said little about the substantive character of public concerns, fears and hopes for technological innovation, and their implications for governance. This is understandable. The literature to date has been preoccupied with questions of process. The stuff of what people say, and their implications for governance, has received far less attention. Yet, there remain common themes across dialogues. This section follows an analysis of themes across the 17 Sciencewise-sponsored dialogues highlighted above[9].

A common finding is that people generally express positive attitudes to science, and to the scientists involved. Almost all areas of scientific research presented to the public are seen as beneficial, and the public in general feels better informed about science than before. Across the dialogues we are presented with a picture of the public that is generally positive, upbeat, and excited about science, and about its transformative potential in delivering improvements to our everyday lives and to the environment. This includes in particular: medical research to create new cures; environmental and energy research to promote sustainability; new technologies offering novel environmental solutions; and investment that consolidates Britain's role as a leader in new science and technology. In addition, lay participants were pleased to be asked to participate in dialogue events, and even more pleased when they felt they were being listened to. Consultation was seen as a good thing and there was a latent desire to be involved more.

Notwithstanding such optimism, there remained five areas of generic concern. Firstly, people are concerned at times with the purposes of particular areas of science and the motivations of those involved. In whose interests is the science being developed? Are particular innovations necessary? Are there alternatives? Medical and health technologies are seen by and large as driven by good purposes, including the curing of diseases, improving wellbeing and prolonging life. Research is thus accorded high importance, even when there are acknowledged ethical dilemmas. In upstream dialogues where the science is at an early stage, with clear potential for good and bad, ensuring that the science is conducted for good reasons is a critical question. A clear hope was that the science could address some of the big challenges facing society today, such as global warming, serious diseases, energy problems, and food security. Curiosity-driven science, though seen as important, was not considered reason enough to pursue ideas when the known and unknown impacts may be serious and long-term.

Secondly, there is the question of trust. A pervasive feature across a number of dialogue projects was that people rarely trusted the motives or ability of Government to act in the public interest. This general mistrust is prominent in upstream dialogues, including those on synthetic biology, nanotechnology, and industrial biotechnology, where even at an early stage of innovation R&D, the direction being undertaken by science is seen as in danger of being overly directed by private rather than public interests. This distrust is apparent especially in domains where there is a perceived proximity between government and industry, most notably in agricultural and industrial biotechnology. Indeed, while the motives of scientists may be trusted, in general, the motives of government and industry are not. Trust becomes a critical dimension in issue advocate dialogues, notably on

---

[9] See: Chilvers and Macnaghten (2011).

climate change issues, which depend on the public being willing to accept the framing of the issue by the commissioning institution. The notable exception was regarding health-related honest broker dialogues where, alternatively, there appeared to be an underlying sense of trust and confidence in regulation, oversight, and in the good intentions of Government.

Thirdly, there is the perception of powerlessness. In 1995, in a project on public perceptions and sustainability, Lancaster academics observed that the pronounced fatal-ism and cynicism that people expressed toward national and local government is a key barrier to environmental behavior change (Macnaghten and Jacobs, 1997). They further argued that attempts by government to galvanize community action would depend on their ability to develop relational mechanisms through which a sense of inclusion and shared purpose could be established. Ten to 15 years later, and despite a heightened institutional rhetoric on inclusion, it is clear that many people still feel they are not included in deciding what kinds of public science and technology get funded and for whose interests: they feel they are kept in the dark.

Fourthly, there are concerns over the speed and direction of the innovation process. Examples of this kind of concern can be seen in the dialogue on stem cells (was research being pushed to deliver applications too soon?), and in the dialogue on synthetic biology (what were the dangers of speeding up natural and evolutionary processes?). As can be seen from the examples above there were two variants. In the honest broker dia-logues this concern tended to be expressed through the danger of short-term commercial pressures trumping social and ethical considerations. While in the upstream dialogues this concern was expressed more ontologically, in relation to the power of emergent science to disrupt and mess with natural orders and processes (Macnaghten, 2010). Con-cerns were also voiced concerning the direction science is taking us, and whether this has been adequately considered and deliberated upon in advance (Stirling, 2007). These concerns, chiefly manifest in the upstream dialogues, extended beyond matters of safety and technical risk to a broader set of social and ethical issues that included: concerns over unforeseen consequences, including controllability and reversibility; impacts on perceived naturalness; and impacts in terms of fairness and equity.

Fifthly, there are concerns over ethics. A primary consideration is whether there was a sense of genuine social benefit from publicly funded science. At an individual level, where the social benefit was high, the public was prepared to accept higher trade-offs. Thus, in the dialogue on stem cells, research was seen as acceptable only in cases where there existed the potential for very significant medical breakthroughs for the treatment of incurable diseases. In cases where stem cells were proposed in cosmetic applications, or for the purposes of human enhancement, where the social benefit was seen as low, the research was seen as less acceptable. This kind of trade-off was commonplace in the hon-est broker dialogues. There are further concerns over the social distribution of those costs and benefits. There was a concern across many of the dialogues that the political economy of new science and technology would disproportionately impact upon vulnerable groups, particularly the poor, the ill, the unborn and those unable to defend themselves. Concern was expressed that nanotechnologies would benefit the rich and the powerful, not the poor or the unemployed; that medical research would be biased toward western and affluent illnesses rather than those in developing countries; that the use of new national databases could be used by governments to further discriminate against ethnic minorities;

and that the development of new drug treatments in the management of mental health conditions could be seen as a cheap alternative to social and behavioral therapy. This kind of consideration was again most common in the honest broker dialogues.

To summarize, the review of public responses in public dialogue fora highlights a range of concerns surrounding the governance of science and technology: whether research is being conducted in the public interest, whether government or the institutions overseeing research are to be trusted, whether people feel included or excluded in deciding what kinds of science gets funded, whether the speed of innovation processes exceeds their scope for regulatory and ethical oversight, and whether the risks and benefits of the research are unevenly distributed. We now finish with a few concluding remarks.

5.9   Concluding Remarks

In this chapter we have sought to examine the issues, dilemmas, and opportunities associated with opening up dialogue and debate on science, technology and innovation. We began with a short history of dialogue and debate, with a particular focus on the institutional history of the issue in the UK. We then looked in more detail at different models and motivations for institutional forms of dialogue, suggesting that while some were reasonable and authentic (honest broker and upstream models of dialogue), others were less so (issue advocate models of dialogue). We articulated what we believe to be good and bad ways of conducting dialogue and suggested criteria for classifying good practice. Finally, we examined the substantive character of public concerns, fears, and hopes, pointing to the considerable unease that many people feel with the speed, direction, and impacts of technological trajectories, not simply in terms of producing new harms but on the lifeworld as directly experienced in everyday life. We have directly addressed foundational dimensions of Responsible Innovation highlighted by Owen *et al.* in Chapter 2 – notably deliberation – (as well as dimensions of reflection and responsiveness), contributing to the substantive agenda in future programs of responsible innovation. There are four elements in such an agenda that will require further consideration.

Firstly, we need to think more about the governance of science and innovation, and to explore and clarify any role dialogue might have. Organizational pressures and traditions still tend to prevent public values from being reflected in procedures and practices of policy organizations. Public engagement activities, and large dialogue processes in particular, have had an impact. But, while some funding bodies and government departments have made some small steps and tried some experiments in "opening up" their governance processes, dialogues still tend to be seen as an add-on to established structures, rather than the start of a new sort of relationship with the public. There is, therefore, a need to move beyond thinking of public engagement in isolation, to talk about *governance in the public interest*. A report on Science, Governance, and Public Engagement (TNS-BMRB, 2011) found that many senior figures in science organizations (e.g. funding bodies and government departments) expressed a desire to reflect public interests in their governance processes better. There seems to be an appetite to do this, accompanied by uncertainty, and often cautiousness, about how. The concept and approaches of responsible innovation may be one route that organizations follow to try to incorporate a more considered version of the public good in their governance procedures.

Secondly, we need to find new ways to respond to the substantive character of public hopes and concerns: the purpose of science and technology and the underlying motivations of scientists; the trustworthiness of responsible institutions and whether they are seen to act in the public interest; the scope for inclusion and the desire for publics to feed their values into the innovation process; the speed and direction of science and whether reasonable ethical and regulatory oversight can keep up with the pace of science; whether the risks and benefits of research are unevenly distributed, and whether the culture and organization of science and innovation encourage or discourage reflection on risks, uncertainties, and ethical considerations. These collective and shared matters of concern present a material context to the governance priority articulated above.

Thirdly, we need to move beyond one-off dialogue events on particular technologies. We need an identifiable shift that goes beyond formal deliberative processes – which remain a dominant and important governance mechanism – toward a more diverse range of ways in which scientists and institutions can be exposed to public issues. These range from steps to understand and capture perspectives emerging from uninvited engagement spaces (such as the blogosphere) and various forms of conversation and knowledge exchange, through to data mining and crowdsourcing. We also need innovative ways to connect discussions on public engagement with the current and lively debate on involving users in open innovation processes (see Chapter 1) as well as broader conceptual integration with debates aimed at democratizing innovation from the bottom up. And we need to get better at collectively gathering social intelligence – in a wide range of ways – about technologies as they emerge and develop.

And fourthly, we need to test the applicability of these arguments to different contexts and political cultures. Although broadly UK-focused, we have at times situated the UK experience within a set of parallel developments, mostly in Europe. And, although our prescriptions emerge from the UK context, they nevertheless have broader purchase, speaking to more general dynamics and imaginaries of public engagement in late modern, democratic states. Nevertheless, we need to develop a more explicitly comparative analysis of the role and dynamics of public engagement across cultures and contexts, and to analyze the significance of these to emergent frameworks of responsible innovation (see also Chapter 9). We need in particular to examine the issues and dilemmas associated with opening up dialogue and debate in Global South contexts. Although not a focus of this chapter, we know from research that such contexts may have highly distinctive and divergent political cultures and contexts that offer a different set of challenges and opportunities (Macnaghten and Guivant, 2011). Opening up dialogue is never a public good in itself; its value depends on the political culture in which it is to be enacted.

References

Bodmer, W. (1985) *The Public Understanding of Science*. London: The Royal Society.

Callon, M., Lascoumes, P. and Barthe, Y. (2010) *On Acting in an Uncertain World: An Essay on Technological Democracy*. Boston, MA: MIT Press.

Carson, R. (1962) *Silent Spring*. Boston, MA: Houghton Mifflin.

Chilvers, J. (2010) *Sustainable Participation? Mapping Out and Reflecting on the Field of Public Dialogue on Science and Technology*. Summary Report. London: Sciencewise-ERC and the University of East Anglia, London.

Chilvers, J. and Macnaghten, P. (2011) *The Future of Science Governance: A Review of Public Concerns, Governance and Institutional Response*. London: Sciencewise-ERC. All the Sciencewise dialogues are at: http://www.sciencewise-erc.org.uk (accessed 1 June 2012).

Council for Science and Technology (2005) *Policy Through Dialogue: Informing Policies Based on Science and Technology*. London: Council for Science and Technology.

Doubleday, R. and Wynne, B. (2011) Despotism and democracy in the UK: experiments in reframing relations between the state, science and citizens (ed. S. Jasanoff) in *Reframing Rights: Bioconstitutionalism in the Genetic Age*. Cambridge, MA: MIT Press.

Durrant, J. (1994) Final Report, UK National Consensus Conference on Plant Biotechnology. London: Science Museum.

Van Eijndhoven, J. (1997) Technology assessment: product of process? *Technology Forecasting and Social Change*, **54**: 269–286.

van Est, R. (2011) The broad challenge of public engagement in science. *Science and Engineering Ethics*, **17**: 639–648.

See also Fiorino, D. (1989) Environmental risk and democratic process: a critical review, *Columbia Journal of Environmental Law*, **14**: 501–547.

Grove-White, R., Macnaghten, P., Mayer, S., and Wynne, B. (1997) *Uncertain World: GMOs, Food and Public Attitudes in Britain*. Lancaster: CSEC and Unilever.

HM Treasury/DTI/DfES (2004) Science and Innovation Investment Framework 2004–2014, HM Treasury, London, July 2004.

House of Lords (2000) *Science and Society – Third Report of the Science and Technology Committee*, Session 1999–2000. London: House of Lords, February 23, 2000.

Hynes P. (1989) *The Recurring Silent Spring*. New York: Pergamon Press.

Irwin, A. (2006) The politics of talk: coming to terms with the 'new' scientific governance. *Social Studies of Science*, **36**(2): 299–330.

Jones, R. (2008) When it pays to ask the public. *Nature Nanotechnology*, **3**: 578–579.

Kearnes, M., Macnaghten, P. and Wilsdon, J. (2006) Governing at the Nanoscale: People, Policies and Emerging Technologies. London: Demos, available at http://www.demos.co.uk/publications/governingatthenanoscale, (accessed 1 June 2012).

Lutts, R. (1985) Chemical fallout: Rachel Carson's silent spring, radioactive fallout and the environmental movement, *Environmental Review*, **9**: 210–225.

Macnaghten, P. and Jacobs, M. (1997) Public identification with sustainable development: investigating cultural barriers to participation, *Global Environmental Change*, **7**: 1–20.

Macnaghten, P. (2010) Researching technoscientific concerns in the making: narrative structures, public responses and emerging nanotechnologies, *Environment and Planning A*, **41**: 23–37.

Macnaghten, P. and Guivant, J. (2011) Converging citizens? Nanotechnology and the Political Imaginary of Public Engagement in Brazil and the United Kingdom, *Public Understanding of Science*, **20**: 207–220.

Macnaghten, P. and Chilvers, J. (2012) Governing risky technology, in S. Lane, F. Klauser and M. Kearnes (eds.). *Critical Risk Research: Practices, Politics and Ethics*. Oxford: Wiley-Blackwell.

Pielke, R. (2007) *The Honest Broker: Making Sense of Science in Policy and Politics*. Cambridge: Cambridge University Press.

Pielke, R. (2010) *The Climate Fix*. Basic Books: New York.

Royal Society (2004) *Nanoscience and Nanotechnologies: Opportunities and Uncertainties*. London: Royal Society.

Small Talk (2005) Small Talk – Discussing Nanotechnologies. available at http://www.smalltalk.org.uk/page1g.html (accessed 1 June 2012).

Stirling, A. (2005) Opening up or closing down? Analysis, participation and power in the social appraisal of technology, in M. Leach, I. Scoones, and B. Wynne (eds.) *Science, Citizenship and Globalisation*. London: Zed.

Stirling, A. (2007) Deliberate futures: precaution and progress in social choice of sustainable technology, *Sustainable Development*, **15** (5): 286–295.

Thorpe, C. and Gregory, J. (2010) Producing the post-Fordist public: the political economy of public engagement with science, *Science as Culture*, **19**(3): 273–301.

TNS-BMRB (2011) *Science, Governance and Public Engagement*. London: Sciencewise-ERC, available at http://www.sciencewise-erc.org.uk/cms/assets/Uploads/Project-files/Science-Governance-and-Public-Engagement-Nov11.pdf (accessed 1 June 2012).

Warner, M. (2002) Counter publics. *Public Culture*, **14**: 49–90.

Wiulsdon, J. and Willis, R. (2004). *See-through Science: Why Public Engagement Needs to Move Upstream*. London: Demos, available at http://www.demos.co.uk/publications/paddlingupstream (accessed 1 June 2012).

Wynne, B. (1995). The public understanding of science, in S., Jasanoff, G.E. Markle, J. C. Peterson (eds) *Handbook of Science and Technology Studies*. Thousand Oaks, CA: Sage Publications, pp. 380–392.

Wynne, B. (2006) Public engagement as a means of restoring public trust in science – hitting the notes, but missing the music? *Community Genetics*, **9**: 211–220.

6

"Daddy, Can I Have a Puddle Gator?": Creativity, Anticipation, and Responsible Innovation

David H. Guston
Arizona State University, USA

6.1 Introduction

Sam, not quite three and a half, was stomping through the street-side puddles of an Arizona spring. With more than 300 days of sunshine and less than eight inches of rain in the average year in his hometown of Tempe, I indulge him his splashing. In an impish mood myself, I admonished him: "Watch out for puddle gators!"

He looked up with a slightly startled face, paused to contemplate, and then replied, "Daddy, there is no such thing as puddle gators."

"Wouldn't it be cool if there were?"

"YES!" He added a boot-stomp into the puddle for emphasis.

Sam and I continued to discourse on the speculative natural history of puddle gators. We agreed that they should be vicious predators. While I envisioned them as salamanders with an attitude, about the size to clamp onto your finger if it probed too close to their hunting grounds in seasonal puddles, he saw them as microscopic – perhaps a little like the water bear he'd met through his book of poems about pond life.

I imagined the puddle gator for Sam, knowing that it would entertain him. I also imagined in the knowledge that there is a deep divide between my imagination and the actual ability of anyone – and certainly me! – to literally conceive such a wee beastie. But I have deep ambivalences about the research agenda of synthetic biology, a contemporary field of inquiry that could, eventually, make puddle gators a reality. Synthetic biology sees biology in distinctly engineering terms. Just as one might build a bridge

Responsible Innovation, First Edition. Edited by Richard Owen, John Bessant and Maggy Heintz.
© 2013 John Wiley & Sons, Ltd. Published 2013 by John Wiley & Sons, Ltd.

from information about what bridges look and perform like and from the materials at hand, synthetic biologists aspire to build organisms from information encoded in DNA sequences and the materials at hand from other organisms. Plug some salamander traits like size and coloring into the appropriate "chassis" of a cloneable amphibian, add some alligator teeth . . . and you've got a puddle gator.

Whether microscopic or macroscopic, puddle gators could merely be playthings, or they could be ecological intrusions. Creating a male *aegyptus* mosquito with terminator genes that would produce only unviable offspring could save untold thousands of lives lost to dengue fever (Specter, 2012). Designing a bacterium that efficiently turns sunlight and ambient carbon dioxide into a liquid transportation fuel could be a great boon for the environment (Waltz, 2009); at least until a wrenching transition past combustion is completed (perhaps with the assistance of organisms that – like corals – can fix carbon dioxide into materials for construction rather than combustion and thus store carbon rather than merely recycle it . . .). More fundamentally, doing stuff because it's cool – in a carefully controlled environment with plenty of contextual instruction – can help encourage creativity, human "flourishing" (Rabinow and Bennett, 2009) and a set of capacities to address such larger problems, even if the specific activity does not do so.

But a useful new organism provides fewer, if any net benefits if issues of ownership or intellectual property are not well resolved, or if we cannot have confidence in its use in the face of known risks or unanticipated consequences, for example, through such techniques as safety-by-design – in which organisms are designed like the modified *aegyptus* to die quickly outside the lab[1] – but also through sound insurance and liability policies and fair distribution of risks and benefits. And fostering curiosity should not foster hubris. Curiosity is not a reason for endangering others, or the environment. And just perhaps, we might also be better people, and a better society, if we did not haughtily imagine that we could map completely and plan immaculately the complexities of life, believing that living things existed on the planet for us to manipulate toward our own ends.

In this chapter, I want to explore what – beyond curiosity – helps constitute responsible innovation. Owen *et al.* in Chapter 2 articulate four dimensions of responsible innovation, arguing that anticipation, reflection, deliberation, and responsiveness are a set of common commitments necessary to satisfy some current definitions of the term. I focus here on anticipation, not only because it is a signature concept that the research center I direct (the Center for Nanotechnology in Society at Arizona State University) has tried to develop through its vision of "anticipatory governance" (Barben *et al.*, 2008; Guston, 2008), but more importantly because it is perhaps the most crucial and problematic dimension to deal with. This is not to say that reflection, deliberation, and responsiveness are uncontroversial. But, whereas there are relatively clear intuitions and broad literatures around reflection, deliberation, and responsiveness; there is less conceptual development around anticipation, and even poorer intuitions. Beyond a general exploration and definition of anticipation in the context of responsible innovation, this chapter also addresses two specific issues within anticipation: the politics of novelty, which helps center questions of responsible innovation not on the issue of the newness of innovation, but rather on its *purpose;* and the challenge of speculative ethics, which confronts the nature of our dispositions toward the future.

---

[1] See also Grinbaum and Groves discussion about the Golem in Chapter 7.

6.2   Understanding Anticipation

We can never know about the days to come/But we think about them anyway.

Those old enough may remember how a Carly Simon song eroticized a commercial for ketchup, but its connection to responsible innovation may be less obvious. The commercial – with its portraits of hungry eaters of French fries and hamburgers impatiently peering down the mouth of the ketchup bottle because its contents were so thick as to emerge so very slowly – emphasized anticipation's familiar connotation of *"keepin' me waitin'."* But Simon's lyrical contemplation of a future that is imminent but still uncertain, that is capacious but might not hold what she desires, has more to do with what I want to get out of "anticipation." We don't want to rush headlong into a future dominated by either pell-mell innovation posing as progress, or a mere extension of the unsustainable status quo. Yet *"I'm no prophet and I don't know nature's ways."* Our ignorance is vast, and the ability to predict is both over-reaching and overwrought. So we are left to anticipate.

Anticipation need not, however, be purely passive. Before the future manifests, we can do much more than pace the floor or stare at the ketchup. Etymologically, anticipation is unrelated to such relatively passive expectations (from *specere*, to look at, and *ex-*, thoroughly). It is similarly distant from other vulgar synonyms like prediction and foresight, which denote a temporally prior sensing and articulation of an actual future. Prudence, including the "prudent vigilance" advocated by the US Presidential Commission for the Study of Bioethical Issues (PCSBI) (2010; also Wiek *et al.*, 2012) for addressing synthetic biology, is likewise distant: it is a contraction of providential, from *pro-*, before, and *videre*, to see. Instead, anticipation is about building a capacity (which shares the root, *capere*, to take) in a way that is prior (*ante-*) in either time (e.g., antebellum) or position or order (e.g., antechamber).

An analogy for anticipation, properly conceived, is that of exercise. When you go to the gym to work out – performing your curls and your presses and your pulls – you are not doing those specific maneuvers because you believe that at some point in the future you will need to press a heavy beam off your chest in order to survive. You exercise that way because you believe you are building in your body a capacity to face any physical or emotional challenge life might throw at you. Anticipation thus admits contemporaneous activities like exercise, practice, and rehearsal, oriented in a non-predictive way toward an undefined future.

The group- or societal-level analogies are not as familiar on the face of it, but war-gaming and simulations are the kind of activities that often fit the bill. So are building prototypes (Selin and Boradkar, 2010), writing (Johnson, 2011; Billing, 2011) and reading (Miller and Bennett, 2008) science fiction, and creating scenarios and other approaches (Fisher *et al.*, 2008). These opportunities explore a variety of futures, not all of which – obviously – can come true, but in practice none of which need to. The point of anticipation through such activities is not to manufacture in the present a replica of the future to be compared for virtuosity against the one that unfolds. Rather, its point is to *explore*, navigate in, and even "live off the land" in a variety of terrains so that we may learn better how to survive in that "undiscovered country" of the future (via *Star Trek VI*, rather than *Hamlet*).

Similarly, Owen *et al.* in Chapter 2 elaborate that the dimension of anticipation is about:

> describing and analyzing plausible, intended and potentially unintended outcomes of and implications associated with research and its development, be these economic, social, environmental or otherwise. Supported by methodologies that include those of foresight, technology assessment and scenario development, these not only serve to articulate promissory narratives of expectation but to explore other pathways to other impacts, to prompt scientists and innovators to ask 'what if . . .' and 'what else might it do' . . . to surface issues and explore possible impacts and implications that may otherwise remain uncovered and little discussed.

This text highlights two issues in anticipation that I will now take up: the politics of novelty and the challenge of speculative ethics.

6.3 The Politics of Novelty

When I was an undergraduate, I got into an argument with my English professor. She corrected my usage, in red felt-tipped pen, when I modified "unique" with "nearly" or "rather," or something like that. It was either unique, she insisted, or it was not. There was no "nearly" about it. I argued that nothing was unique, at least across all dimensions, and that something was "nearly" or "rather" unique if it had more dimensions that were unlike other things and fewer that were comparable or familiar.

I lost this semantic argument with my English professor, but I want to reconstitute it here with the concept of novelty. I do not want to go as far as the author of Ecclesiastes (1 : 9) who declares that

> The thing that hath been is that which shall be; and that which hath been done is that which shall be done; and there is no new thing under the sun.

Rather, I want to argue that novelty in technological innovation *admits to politics* because different people will value differently the different aspects of a technology and thus judge its innovativeness or novelty differently. They may, perhaps with good reason, argue that it is novel in one context and not in another. In nanotechnology, for example, it is clear that many materials at the nanoscale have properties that are different from those same materials at the micro- or the macro-scale. They may have different optical properties or magnetic properties, or interact with biological materials differently. You wear gold jewelry, for example, because at the macro-level gold is largely inert. At the nano-level, however, gold is highly reactive and is often used to bind organic and inorganic nanomaterials. Indeed, many materials have been patented based on properties that emerge only at the nanoscale. Nevertheless, it is not self-evident that nanosize ought to be the major criterion for regulating materials for environmental health and safety.[2] Thus there is a politics of novelty around nanotechnology in which its advocates, for

---

[2] See Chapter 8 for further discussion on this point.

example, value its relative novelty for the purposes of intellectual property protection, but not necessarily for environmental health and safety regulation.

Similarly, many argue that synthetic biology is not much different from the genetic engineering that emerged about 40 years ago. Many view it as continuous even, with a millennia-old tradition of husbandry and agriculture (see, for example, Specter, 2009), and that the aspect of synthetic biology to be valued is the scientific precision and concision with which current efforts are aimed, compared with selective breeding, radiation-induced mutations, and other random or haphazard, craft-based approaches. Yet genetic engineering and synthetic biology also usher into the world organisms that, but for human ingenuity, not only would not exist but – like the terminator *aegyptus* mosquito – could not exist.

By calling this a politics of novelty, I mean to say that the decision about the novelty of nanotechnology, or synthetic biology, or geoengineering, can be settled by neither the nature nor essence of those technologies, nor by the definition nor reference to the concept of novelty itself, as my English teacher would settle uniqueness. Rather it needs to be settled – if indeed it can be settled – by a political process that references context and the particular aspects of the novelty at stake – its purposes. Indeed, it is the presence of this politics of novelty – alongside the great uncertainty and high stakes of "post-normal" science – that for me characterizes emerging technologies like nanotechnology, synthetic biology, and geoengineering. And it is largely for such emerging technologies that we face debates over responsible innovation (Hellstrom, 2003).

While adhering to this view, though, I do not want to gloss over two important fallacies lurking in the "long-view" argument about innovation, in which emerging technologies are considered as being largely continuous with, or incremental improvements upon, classical chemistry, husbandry and agriculture, or weather modification. Opposition to, or even calls for precaution or anticipation in the face of, new technologies – especially the generic opposition now seen among some non-governmental organizations like the ETC Group, Greenpeace, and others – is often met by accusations that these same opponents would have opposed now mature technologies that we take for granted, like automobiles or antibiotics.

To pose a choice in this way, first, presumes falsely that "to do" or "not to do" are the only relevant questions. In the absence of "not to do," it further presumes there is only one way that things can or do get done. A vast array of choices for responsible innovation and responsible governance exist between the determinist motto that "science finds, industry applies, man adapts" (courtesy of the Chicago World's Fair of 1933, celebrating "a century of progress") and the precautionary conundrum of calling a halt to research because we don't know enough to proceed. This choice also conceals in the depths of history the unexamined presumption that those earlier innovations worked out well. And indeed they often did – especially for us, the descendants of the winners. But there were losers, too. The more recent losses associated with automobiles or industrial chemistry are somewhat more apparent. Yet this was the case even for ancient innovations (for example, some anthropologists now imagine that *Homo sapiens* may have outcompeted Neanderthals in part because of the former's innovation of the selective breeding of wolves into dogs). Two ironies lurk here: that people who lionize the skills of innovators would enthusiastically embrace an argument for the irrelevance of human purpose in innovation; and that those who would otherwise abhor any perspective with the whiff of Social Darwinism would adopt one in which it was unproblematic to facilitate the extinction of a tribe, or clan, or city of competitors.

Not that it is appropriate to assign our ethical standards to our ancient ancestors. But that is precisely the point. The deep history of innovation – that we have been husbanding animals and breeding plants for thousands of years, taming fire and fashioning points, grinding and mixing minerals – is largely irrelevant to the question of the extent to which we should be engaging in genetic modification, or nanotechnology, today, or in the next 20 years. From napping flint to fracking fuel, the relevant question is not whether it has, is, or can be done. The relevant questions are *why might it be done*, and if it is to be done, how best to do it. These are anticipatory questions, and they suggest why it is crucial that our approach to innovation be forward-looking and, again as Owen argues, re-center responsibility in the discussion.

6.4   The Challenge of Speculative Ethics

Avery Brooks wanders an empty cityscape, wondering aloud, "We were promised flying cars. Where are the flying cars?" He's not playing Captain Benjamin Sisko in an episode of *Star Trek: Deep Space 9*, but rather he's starring in an IBM commercial reminding viewers that it is "a different world" because of the World Wide Web, and that millions of people are collaborating online, so we don't need flying cars. Are there limits to the forward-looking nature of anticipation and responsible innovation? Some (e.g., Nordmann, 2007) argue that we should not engage in what they pejoratively call "speculative ethics" because, since we "*can never know about the days to come*," we do not want to squander our scarce ethical resources on fantasy. Indeed, we probably shouldn't be asking what the speed limit for flying cars in a school zone should be.

The argument for responsible innovation, however, relies on some capacity to anticipate, albeit one that is different, as I argue above, from an always-illusory capacity to predict. Nevertheless, is this move to infuse the creative capacity that humans manifest through technology with the elixir of responsibility subject to the critique of speculative ethics? Before answering this, I want to revisit Ecclesiastes as Shakespeare does, in his "Sonnet 59," for a helpful perspective on creativity:

> *If there be nothing new, but that which is*
> *Hath been before, how are our brains beguiled,*
> *Which, labouring for invention, bear amiss*
> *The second burden of a former child.*

Shakespeare here takes poetic advantage of two denotations of "conceive." One is the etymologically older sense of a child's life taking hold in the womb. The second is the historically later, and thus even more metaphorical, notion of an idea taking hold in the mind. Both of these conceptions can lead to "laboring" and creation. In the example of the puddle gator, synthetic biology conceives (in the latter sense) of biology as engineering, in order to conceive (in the former sense) organisms that suit our preferences rather than evolution's meanderings. Here the metaphorical conception by synthetic biology anticipates the physiological one.

The critique of speculative ethics would have us believe that addressing the metaphorical aspects of conception should not occur until the physiological or material aspects were in some way imminent . . . or likely . . . or simply non-"speculative" – what is not completely clear. But surely we cannot be ethically suspect for conducting thought experiments about puddle gators, or contemplating the difference between a 20-year and a 30-year mortgage. And just as surely we cannot be suspect for imagining, and even devoting resources toward, some modest fantasies about the lives our children and grandchildren will lead. And just as surely we probably should be thinking not only about what we might leave when we are gone for those we know and love, but also what we leave for those we do not know, but to whom we (and our own children and grandchildren) are nevertheless bound by ties of community or culture or humanity, if not by love.

So we must be allowed to look toward the future, if not into it. Yet anticipation does not suppose that we can look into the future as an "it," as an identifiable object. It supposes that the future is an admixture of predetermined elements (path dependences, obdurate institutions, and the like) and critical uncertainties (Selin, 2008a). It does not see the future as something to be figured, made and imposed.

Accepting the critique of speculative ethics and dismissing anticipation may well lead to its own pathologies, for example, by ceding the field to those who are willing to engage in the folly of prediction. Without building a capacity to inquire in an anticipatory way – developing rigorous ideas about what constitutes anticipatory knowledge (see Nelson *et al.* 2008) – the linear extrapolators and hype-or-horror prognosticators dominate the discussion. Not engaging them may be a satisfying protest against the hubris of techno-science, but it allows them to set the terms of debate and thus, often, the research agendas to be pursued.

This ethical ostrich that hides from the future to focus on the present may well contribute to the perpetuation of present injustices. Properly conceived, anticipation is about working in the present to prepare for an uncertain future. But the current organization of what might be called 'future work' – the professions that engage in socio-technical innovation – is very exclusive. Opening up and diversifying these professions – creating what is sometimes called "well-ordered science" (Kitcher, 2003) – is a goal that can be shared by critics and advocates of speculative ethics. To engage fully in future work – and to make it more responsible – those new participants will need to be free to, and capable of constructing speculative visions that compete successfully with the visions of the current participants. They must be allowed to conceive by holding in mind, before gestating in the laboratory. "I have a dream . . . " – whether of electric sheep or something more responsive to the goals of equality and justice – anticipates "I have a patent."

The ethical ostrich also neglects the fact that whatever future may come will contain elements of arguable novelty, and elements whose imminence we may or may not have identified. Strictly allocating our ethical resources according to even an expansive understanding of imminence or likelihood not only means that we will pay too little attention to things that we have not properly identified as sufficiently concrete, but more importantly it allocates effort only to one part of the future equation, the likelihood, and not to the consequences. There are certainly future scenarios of such slim chance but profound impact – a civilization-killing asteroid impact, for example – that they are worth some allocation of ethical resources. But once we calculate both likelihood and consequence, we have doubled back into risk assessment – that dark wood from which responsible innovation and its focus on anticipation is, in part, attempting to lead us.

Finally, while I agree that our ethical resources are scarce and that current injustices demand more significant ethical attention, it is not altogether clear that we can grow our ethical resources by hoarding them for the present. Ethical resources are not, in fact, as fungible as money. What worked to some extent for bioethics, for example, cannot be transferred immediately to nano-ethics. This is not to say that every object requires its own ethics. But it is to say that our ethical assessments must be informed by empirical as well as theoretical inquiry, and only then will we be able to determine if we need to deploy new ethical resources. For example, nanotechnology and synthetic biology require a different array of ethical resources than the human genome project did, if only because the US Department of Defense is a major sponsor of nanotechnology and synthetic biology, and thus these agendas raise important questions of dual use, just war, targeted assassinations, and the like, which genomics did not raise. These issues are not, of course, novel in and of themselves, but they are relatively novel vis-à-vis the ethical, legal, and societal impacts of genomics.

6.5   Conclusion

A tale of three pens: I collected them all within a few minutes in the exhibition hall at the EuroScience Open Forum, held in Dublin in June, 2012. One is a small, blue pen – oddly retro in its device of the four different colors of ink one can click to use – bearing the name and logo of the European Commission and the words, "Responsible Research and Innovation." A second pen – embodying a mid-century futuristic esthetic of sterile white and cool blue bounded by stainless steel – advertises Intel with the words, "Sponsors of Tomorrow." A third pen – dun-colored with dark flecks, looking and feeling recycled – bears the Aarhuus Universitet name and logo, together with the branding of "eco-friendly" (with the hyphen here replaced by a leaf on the pen).

I don't want to read too deeply into cheap conference bling, and neither have I yet been able to verify the actual eco-friendliness of the Aarhuus pen, but the EC and Intel pens appear to be mere propaganda next to Aarhuus's apparent performance. We need somehow to assure that responsible innovation as a policy in government, and as a practice in the laboratory does not sink into empty exhortation or insipid sloganeering.

Part of this assurance is for those of us in future-work to use our anticipatory and reflexive capacities, for example, by developing scenarios (e.g., Selin, 2008b). Such an approach might be particularly useful to examine unintended consequences of innovations, for example, the kinds of odd ways that users might reconfigure or hack innovations. Part of the answer is also orienting innovation toward societal "grand challenges," as Von Schomberg suggests in Chapter 3, in order to emphasize the opportunities seized as well as the issues avoided. For each of these paths, however, we must appropriately expand our ability to include a broader set of actors in such future work (see Chapter 5), because our science and innovation policy institutions are not yet well-ordered enough to assume that the kinds of deliberations on which we currently rely are sufficient.

Such an expansion, of course, must include both lay citizens, and researchers and innovators. All should be encouraged to understand and experience their stake in helping render research and innovation responsible. While the former might greet such encouragement with indifference, the latter may respond with outright hostility. But in each of these stereotypical responses lies an ecological fallacy – the group is made up of individuals, and modern society is pluralist enough for almost any venture to start up – the real trick will be going public in a large enough way.

And while the urgency of today's emerging technologies has our attention, there will surely be a new set tomorrow, and the day after tomorrow. Education and training is thus a critical endeavor for responsible innovation, and not only for the current crop of future workers (see Chapter 2).

In the light of Sam's childhood love of the natural world, I often lament that "natural historian" or "natural philosopher" is not a career open to him. As in the puddle gator story, however, I also love the way he melds his imagination with the natural world as well – something that natural historians, and especially those turned into, say, field biologists are not often encouraged to do. Synthetic biologists, however, seem to partake in this melding of imagination and observation, and that is likely a career that will be open to him. So I also lament the continuing short-sightedness of an innovation system that does not emphasize responsibility.

For now, while Sam is still learning the rules of social behavior along with the names of the creatures in our yard, such fantasy is cool. Anticipation, deliberation, responsiveness, and reflexivity come later. But for the day he splices his first gene, I hope that he will have already learned that "Wouldn't it be cool if . . . ?" is not sufficient justification. What would be really cool is if he learned that from his science teacher, and his art teacher, and a whole host of others, and not just from me.

Acknowledgments

The author would like to thank Dan Sarewitz, Cynthia Selin, and the editors for their assistance. This research was funded by the US National Science Foundation under cooperative agreement #0937591. The findings and observations contained in this paper are those of the author and do not necessarily reflect the views of the National Science Foundation.

References

Barben, D. Fisher, E. Selin, C. and D.H. Guston (2008) Anticipatory governance of nanotechnology: foresight, engagement, and integration, pp. 979–1000 in (eds E. J. Hackett, O. Amsterdamska, M. E. Lynch, and J. Wajcman), *The New Handbook of Science and Technology Studies*. Cambridge: MIT Press.
Billing, R. (2011) Tales from the Future. Brussels: European Commission.
Fisher, E., C. Selin and J. Wetmore, (eds) (2008) *Yearbook of Nanotechnology in Society*. Presenting Futures, Vol. I, New York: Springer.
Guston, D. H. (2008) Innovation policy: not just a jumbo shrimp. *Nature* **454**:940–941.
Hellstrom, T. (2003) Systemic innovation and risk: technology assessment and the challenge of responsible innovation. *Technology in Society* **25**:369–84.

Johnson, B. D. (2011) *Science Fiction Prototyping: Designing the Future with Science Fiction*. San Rafael, CA: Morgan & Claypool Publishers.

Kitcher, P. (2003) *Science, Truth and Democracy*. New York: Oxford University Press.

Miller, C. A. and I. Bennett.(2008) Thinking longer term about technology: is there value in science fiction-inspired approaches to constructing future. *Science and Public Policy,* **35**(8): 597–606.

Nelson, N. Geltzer, A., and S. Hilgartner (2008) Introduction: the anticipatory state: making policy-relevant knowledge about the future. *Science and Public Policy* **35**(8):546–50.

Nordmann, A. (2007) If and then: a critique of speculative nanoEthics. *NanoEthics* **1**:31–46.

Presidential Commission for the Study of Bioethical Issues (PCSBI) (2010) New Directions: The Ethics of Synthetic Biology and Emerging Technologies, PCSBI, Washington, DC.

Rabinow, P. and G. Bennett (2009) Ethical ramifications of synthetic biology, 2009. *Systems and Synthetic Biology* **3**(1–4):99–108.

Selin, C. (2008a) Sociology of the future: tracing stories of technology and time. *Sociology Compass* **2** (60):1875–95.

Selin, C. (2008b) The Future of Medical Diagnostics. Scenario Development Workshop Report No. CNS-ASU Report #R08-0001, Center for Nanotechnology in Society, Arizona State University, Tempe, AZ.

Selin, C. and P. Boradkar.(2010) Prototyping nanotechnology: a transdisciplinary approach to responsible innovation. *Journal of Nanotechnology Education* **2**(1/2): 1–12.

Specter, M. (2009) A Life of Its Own. The New Yorker (Sep. 28), http://www.newyorker.com/reporting/2009/09/28/090928fa_fact_specter (accessed 4 September 2012).

Specter, M. (2012) The Mosquito Solution. The New Yorker (Jul. 9), p. 38.

Waltz, E. (2009) Biotech's green gold? *Nature Biotechnology* **27**:15–18.

Wiek, A., D. H. Guston, E. Frow and J. Calvert. 2012. Sustainability and anticipatory governance in synthetic biology. *International Journal of Social Ecology and Sustainable Development* **3**(2):25–38.

7

What Is "Responsible" about Responsible Innovation? Understanding the Ethical Issues

Alexei Grinbaum[1] *and Christopher Groves*[2]

[1] *CEA-Saclay/LARSIM, France*
[2] *Cardiff University, ESRC Centre for the Economic and Social Aspects of Genomics (Cesagen), UK*

7.1 Introduction

"Innovation" is the process of bringing something new into the world, through a combination of intellectual and practical ingenuity. In this chapter, we lay out a set of concepts that can help us to understand the meaning of "responsible innovation," by reflecting on the ethical significance of technological innovation.

What are the key characteristics of innovation in the contemporary world? Technological or otherwise, it typically emerges from the efforts of a community of individuals working together within a complex set of social relationships, through which financial, administrative, and other resources are secured and allocated. What innovation, whether technological or otherwise, creates is not simply a new set of techniques for doing things, but also ultimately new social practices and even institutions that transform the ways in which human beings interact with the world around them. It is, therefore, inherently a *future-creating* activity: by bringing something new into the world, it changes the world itself – perhaps incrementally, perhaps more radically. This means that, to reflect on the conceptual basis for responsible innovation, we have to acknowledge that the responsibility associated with innovation necessarily *responsibility for the future it helps to create*. Consequently, the "responsibility" in responsible innovation presents conceptual and practical difficulties that are related to the future-oriented character of innovation itself.

Responsible Innovation, First Edition. Edited by Richard Owen, John Bessant and Maggy Heintz.
© 2013 John Wiley & Sons, Ltd. Published 2013 by John Wiley & Sons, Ltd.

In this chapter, we proceed via three steps. First, we clear the ground by setting out why some of the ways in which modern societies have become used to thinking about responsibility are inadequate in relation to technological innovation. This section ends by noting that, while in one sense the nature of advanced technologies brings with it new kinds of uncertainty and moral demands, what makes us, as innovators, responsible for innovation is not in itself new, but is rather a condition of mutual vulnerability that we share because of the kind of creatures we are – animals with the capacity to manage their communal affairs through the use of reason, Aristotle's "political animals." This leads us into our second step, where we examine how the meaning of responsible innovation might be better understood by analogy with two existing, future-oriented varieties of responsibility, namely *individual parental* and *collective political* responsibility. Finally, we affirm that responsible innovation cannot simply be a matter of following a set of fixed professional rules. We go on to examine the individual and collective "virtues" necessary to exercise the quasi-parental and political forms of responsibility contained in responsible innovation, along with some of the ways in which cultural narratives can help us understand both the complexities involved in moral choice about technologies, and the limits of our capacity to take responsibility.

7.2 The Changing Meaning of Responsibility

7.2.1 From the Divine Corporation to the Sovereign Individual

On one reading, the whole intellectual and cultural history of the West represents a gradual shift away from what J. B. Schneewind (1984) calls the "divine corporation" view of the world. In this worldview, the basis of morality is a system of offices to which individuals are allotted by divine (or royal, monarchs being supposedly appointed by God) edict. Being moral and acting rightly is the same as playing one's role in this system properly. Whether what one does is right or wrong depends on how one's actions conform to immutable decrees relevant to one's position in the hierarchy: the criteria for right and wrong here are *deontological* in nature, that is, related only to a pre-existing rule (Davis, 2001). It is during this period, from Greek antiquity to scholasticism (McKeon, 1990), that we find the origins of two key elements of an understanding of responsibility: *imputability* and *accountability*.

To be responsible for a transgression is, in this tradition, to (i) be recognized as having performed a transgressive act and (ii) be required to give an account of oneself to an authority (or its representative) whose decree one has transgressed against. Responsibility therefore implies being accused of something, that is, being *held* responsible after the fact – a common-sense conception of responsibility called by the British philosopher F. H. Bradley the "vulgar" sense of the word (Bradley, 1927, pp. 1–8). This denotes the fact of authorship of an act: to hold someone responsible for having done something, it must be possible to *impute* an act to him/her after it has occurred: "she was driving when she hit him!" The legal scholar H. L. A. Hart, in his analysis of the different senses of responsibility, splits this *ex post facto* mode of responsibility into causal responsibility ("she caused the collision!"), and blame or liability – which attract punishment (Hart, 1968, Chapter 9, Part 1). But being held responsible also means someone having to *account* for what transgressions against the law are imputed to him or her. This is preserved in the etymology of the various terms that, since the fourteenth century, have emerged in Western European languages (responsibility, *responsabilité, Verantwortlichkeit*) as means of translating the Latin legal terms for accountability derived from *respondere*, "to respond," as in a court of law to one's accuser.

As we shall see, historical developments in more recent times have undermined the "divine corporation" worldview, bringing with them changes in how and why people are held accountable, by whom or what they are held accountable, and in what wrongs can legitimately be imputed to them. With these changes comes, in turn, an overall transformation in the meaning of "being responsible." Perhaps the most important element of this transformation affects what we might call the *tense* of responsibility. Under the "divine corporation" view of morality and law, responsibility tends to be a "backward-facing" condition. It exists because of what one has done, and how one's actions relate to the duties decreed by the divine "CEO" of the corporation, or his royal representative. Under a new emerging dispensation, from early modernity onward, the temporal focus of responsibility increasingly falls on a secular future (even if the ultimate significance of this future is still shaped by religious belief). Rather than duties being pre-ordained, it is up to the individual moral subject to *take* responsibility for deciding what s/he should do, and to prepare to be accountable later for the consequences. As we shall see, it is this individualist and *consequentialist* concept of forward-looking responsibility – which we accept as being of everyday as well as of legal validity – that initially appears relevant to the idea of responsible innovation. We shall also discover, however, that problems arise when we try to apply it in this context.

The "modern period" (for our purposes here, since the seventeenth century) is one characterized by emerging social complexity. Mercantile societies, as they gradually became industrialized ones, developed highly differentiated divisions of labor, in which individuals typically came to occupy several private and public roles – in direct contrast to the "offices" of the divine corporation. In his classification of varieties of responsibility, Hart describes a prospective, future-oriented meaning of the word that is relevant to such societies. *Role responsibility* is a sociological concept that implies the duties one needs to accomplish by dint of occupying a certain role in society. This is, however, not sufficient to spell out the *ethical* meaning of responsibility. One telling indication that this is so comes from Hannah Arendt's analysis of Adolf Eichmann's role as an administrator in the Nazi hierarchy, in which the gap between role responsibility and a wider responsibility to consider the moral significance of one's actions was egregiously evident (Arendt, 1963). This and other exemplary cases of the gap between one's social role and its ethical content notwithstanding, in modern societies one is often expected to judge one's own actions based on shared understandings of what the responsible "occupational" behavior appropriate to the role of doctor, mother, engineer, politician, and so on, should be (Hart, 1968, Chapter 9). One uses these ideals of responsible conduct for guidance, affirming in the process social and moral boundaries. At the same time, ideals of conduct do not tell us exactly what to do. The lack of fit between ideal and situation creates uncertainty and a need to exercise individual judgment. That role responsibility is unthinkable without some uncertainty or indeterminacy is most clearly reflected in the idea that some occupations are not just roles one *plays* but professions to which one *belongs*, and within which one is expected to exercise professional judgment,

judgment which cannot ultimately be reduced to firm rules. Role responsibility implies specific responsibilities for which one is accountable to particular social institutions, such as professional bodies and the like.

Although the meaning of responsibility in the modern period is heavily influenced by the emergence of role responsibility and the need for individual judgment that accompanies it, the indeterminacy of responsibility here ultimately goes much deeper, as the Eichmann example and others like it suggest. Increasingly, the rightness and wrongness of acts is decided according to individual or collective purposes that are subject to change, innovation, and improvisation – processes often shaped by the application of scientific knowledge. As well as being an age of proliferating roles, this is the age of Max Weber's *Zweckrationalität* and consequentialism, that is, justifying actions in terms of what they can accomplish, rather than in terms of whether or not they conform to pre-existing decrees of right and wrong. A world that can be improved, a world of technology and innovation, is essentially a world in which right and wrong *depend on outcomes*. The individuals who inhabit this world have to balance the competing demands of their roles as parents or children, workers or managers, users or developers of technology, and citizens. They are expected to engage in internal dialogue with themselves over the outcomes of the diverse activities they perform (Davis, 2001, pp. 10–11). Responsibility in this sense increasingly becomes a forward-pointing quality or virtue that one's actions can possess or lack. Insofar as it requires that moral agents anticipate the consequences of their actions, taking responsibility means to exercise foresight and to increase one's knowledge about the world and how one's actions might interact with and alter it.

The ideal consequentialist moral agent is, therefore, Jeremy Bentham's utilitarian subject, who strives to assess, with precision, the contribution each action makes to the aggregate happiness of society. Without the assurance of occupying one of the fixed "offices" (with their set duties) within the divine corporation, the individual must, as Henry S. Richardson points out (Richardson, 1999, p. 231), judge what to do solely on the basis of the social benefits an act is expected to bring about, over and above the requirements of any particular role she plays. Indeed, this ultimate criterion is meant to help decide any conflicts between the duties associated with different roles. Consequently, the individual is directly accountable to society itself, rather than to some authority outside it, whether deity or monarch.

As Richardson points out, however, this age of innovation and consequentialism is also, by its very nature, an age of surprises. With the focus on consequences, whether or not one is actually *being* responsible becomes subject to increasing uncertainty, particularly because changing situations may require a moral agent to revise or even ignore pre-existing rules and expectations.

Not only does the individual have to juggle the demands of the roles s/he inhabits, s/he also has to question the limits of these roles, and where it is appropriate to go beyond them. Moreover, when it is consequences that matter, the individual may be accountable, despite not possessing any intention to harm. It might be the case that unpredictable future events will have a retroactive impact on the way his or her conduct is judged (Grinbaum and Dupuy, 2004). This phenomenon, referred to as "moral luck" (Williams, 1981), means that the perspective of an ideal utilitarian agent is ultimately impossible to adopt, as to overcome uncertainty would require perfect foresight covering the entire span of consequences of any act. Consequently, the individual is responsible for deciding when enough foresight is enough, and when s/he must simply stop deliberating, and make up his/her mind to act. Sometimes, as in situations that are relatively routine, this is undemanding. With respect to other activities, however, the opposite is true – and technological innovation is one such.

7.2.2   Knowledge, Uncertainty, and Human Finitude

The growing reliance of societies in the modern period on the extensive use of ever more complex technologies changes the nature of uncertainty faced by the individual who takes responsibility for his/her actions. With the growing ubiquity of complex technologies and the global and intergenerational (Jonas, 1984, p. 40) reach of their effects come significant social changes that expose a tension at the heart of consequentialist approaches to responsibility – a tension between the need to *take* responsibility and the evidentiary standards by which moral agents are *held* accountable for the consequences of what they do. The future on which one has an eye when one strives to act responsibly is no longer the same kind of future as in previous historical periods, even in the early part of modernity (Adam and Groves, 2007). The future faced by humans has always been uncertain, but the quality of this uncertainty now takes on a different character.

Let us examine more closely what is involved here. As we have noted, the modern period is one in which innovation – in the broad sense of transforming the natural and social worlds for purposes which might, in fact, themselves be novel – increasingly comes to depend on scientific knowledge. Science transforms, too, how people are held responsible for the consequences of what they have done. This is clear if we consider legal evidence. Before a court, what comes to count, in general, as a true version of events is a scientifically-validated causal story. Liability in a court of law is settled with reference to scientific standards of evidence ("CCTV cameras prove that she was driving, and breathalyzer tests confirm she had twice the legal limit of alcohol in her blood"). But to be liable for one's behavior requires that one had to be aware that this sort of chain of events could have happened, and that acting in that way would have been wrong. One needs to have had the *capacity* to have foreseen the consequences of one's actions (Hart, 1968) – "she should have known that another glass of wine would put her over the limit, yet still she chose to drive." Generally, morally, and legally speaking, "capacity" here refers to a very general ability to act in accordance with moral rules, which young children and people with severe learning difficulties (for example) may not possess.

But in certain circumstances, *anyone* might be judged to be not culpable for the effects of their actions, due to their ignorance at the time of acting. Now, not being culpable due to ignorance, and not having the capacity to be morally or legally responsible are not the same. Nonetheless, there is a sense in which the nature of innovation as an activity creates ignorance in ways that *undermine* the capacity to act responsibly, as a consequentialist might understand it.

It is important to understand that this effect is not simply a matter of innovation adding new "facts" to the world, of which we just happen to be ignorant. As noted above, there is a difference between lacking "the facts" and lacking the *capacity* to understand the facts, a difference which tracks the distinction between law and morality. Being inescapably ignorant of the facts is legally significant: for example, not being in possession of the full facts regarding the potential harmful outcomes of his/her actions can, on the legal principle of reasonable foreseeability, absolve someone of liability even if s/he is found to be causally responsible for a wrong in due course (Pellizzoni, 2004). This is particularly so if ignorance about these outcomes is of a general kind, that is, no-one could have predicted the risk of causing a particular harm, given the then-current "state of the art" in a relevant body of scientific knowledge. In such circumstances, an innovator may have been a model of probity, determinedly living up to the highest demands of their occupational role and exercising due diligence and careful foresight as to potential harmful consequences. Yet because robust scientific knowledge provides the "gold standard" evidence base for due diligence, limitations on the "state of the art" also place constraints on future liability. Ignorance of "the facts," in such cases, may be *exculpatory* ignorance, in a legal sense.

Legal systems may, therefore, face significant difficulties in principle in dealing with new technologies: this is the legal face of what Ulrich Beck has called "organized irresponsibility" (Beck, 1999, p. 149). Scientific knowledge gives us an evidentiary standard suited to a consequentialist concept of responsibility. Scientific evidence is how we assess the quality of someone's foresight after the fact, and we expect people taking responsibility (particularly in certain socially-important roles) to use such evidence as the basis for exercising foresight. The problem is that science is often badly suited to understanding the consequences of the actions it enables us to perform, particularly when they introduce novel entities (like nuclear reactors, genetically-modified organisms (GMOs), and so on) to the world, because important aspects of how these function in the world may not be covered by the state of the art. By assembling data and creating explanatory hypotheses about how it works, scientific understanding tracks the world the past has made. But creative action and innovation *point forward*, opening up the world the past has created and adding new entities to it that change the way it works. The world that scientific understanding extrapolates into the future – with its gaze still directed toward yesterday – might tomorrow no longer exist. Innovation therefore creates a problem of knowledge, which has legal implications.

This problem of knowledge, which makes law lag behind the reality of innovation, also opens up a deeper and properly moral problem of capacity, which has to do with human finitude rather than scientific ignorance, though it is related to it. In societies that have become thoroughly dependent on advanced technologies, the background of human action has changed. No longer coherently imaginable as Nature, eternal, and unchanging, it has become an amalgam of natural processes and technological artifacts that intimately interact with them. In Alfred Nordmann's phrase (Nordmann, 2005), advanced technologies thus become *naturalized* technologies. The more complex our technologies become, and the more embedded in the social and natural worlds, the more like unfathomable "black boxes" they become – perhaps even to their creators. The more intimately they interact with nature – and with each other – the more "autonomy" they have in creating unpredictable effects. Being ignorant of the future impact of one's innovations may, therefore, become the norm rather than the exception. As Ian Hacking (1986) notes, new technologies may interact with other bits of the world (including other technologies) to create unpredictable negative outcomes, "interference effects." What may have been well understood in the lab or on the testbed alters the world (and is perhaps altered itself) in unforeseeable ways when released "into the wild." We have come to rely on scientific knowledge to create the innovations that help us to transform the world, but we cannot expect it to also enable us to calculate the ethically relevant consequences of using it, even though that is exactly what consequentialist morality requires of us.

As a result, the legal problem of exculpatory ignorance becomes a moral problem linked to human finitude. Humans are finite beings in several ways: because of limitations on their knowledge and of the boundedness of their lives in space and time; because of the diversity of conflicting values that guide their lives (truth, beauty, pleasure, justice, solidarity, etc.); and because the meaning of their existence is doubly *conditioned*. On the one hand, they are born into a social and natural world they have not themselves made, and on the other, whatever they create or shape by acting on the world itself becomes then an objective condition of their lives and to some degree escapes their control over it (Arendt, 1998/1958, pp. 9–10). This multifaceted sense of finitude is challenged by the promise of technological mastery that comes with scientific knowledge. The prospect of unending progress and infinite creative possibility opened up by scientific investigation creates a sense of separation from Nature that is different from the sense of being "thrown" into an already existing world, because it rests upon the promise that human beings have the power to transform this world in accordance with their desires. But the experience of living with naturalized technologies brings into the foreground again the doubly conditioned character of human life. Living with technologies offers up new forms of uncertainty and insecurity, making us *more* human (in the sense of contributing to the evolution of what Arendt calls 'the human condition') rather than superhuman.

If scientific knowledge cannot, therefore, ultimately give us the guide for action that consequentialism requires and thus overcome human finitude, then the resulting lack of moral capacity is a deficiency that is *inherent to the culture of consequentialism itself*. This is underlined by the inadequacy, in relation to innovation, of certain tools generally employed by consequentialist moral philosophers to resolve problematic situations where a good intention might produce bad outcomes (like Hacking's negative interference effects). For example, the "principle of double effect" states that an intention to create beneficial outcomes (e.g., via technological innovation) may be judged permissible, even if it may also produce bad effects so long as (i) these effects are not intended, (ii) the desired outcome does not require these bad effects to happen, and (iii) that the intended good effect should not be grossly outweighed by expected bad effects (Timmons, 2002, pp. 78–80). If technological innovation fills this bill, then we can consider ourselves to have taken a responsible choice in pursuing it. Yet we face here, once again, the problem of foresight. Given that interference effects are highly unpredictable, and may have uncertain consequences that vary enormously in seriousness, the principle of double effect, with its criterion of proportionality, is not applicable (Yara, 2011, pp. 154–155).

If the experience of naturalized technologies reveals to us the inadequacy of one concept of responsible, forward-looking action, however, it also drives home that one can still be *held* morally responsible by society for what happens, even if one is ignorant (through no fault of one's own) of the *specific* potential harms at the time of acting. Hacking points out that, even if we cannot reliably predict the consequences of new innovations, we *can* know that new technologies by their very nature tend to produce "interference effects." Further, we can expect that some unforeseen side-effects of technologies may turn out to be positive, but that many will likely be negative. Given that, in technological societies, a huge variety of complex technologies are ubiquitous, and may be strongly interdependent with natural systems, such interference effects must be expected to be relatively common, and will range from relatively innocent to extremely serious in nature. As a result, one knows one is taking what may be a serious risk, and that moral luck is, therefore, a factor in how one will be judged (Nagel, 1979). Even if such risks may, legally speaking, be legitimated by provisions such as development risk defense (Newdick, 1988; and Lee and Petts in Chapter 8), there remains a moral question here that bears on legal matters.

If we recognize that we may be held morally responsible for the results of innovation, we still need a way of thinking about how to actively *take* responsibility that escapes the problems associated with consequentialism that we have described. This is by no means easy. Given the "autonomy" of naturalized technologies, we can expect that any interference effects may be extended in space, be latent for long periods of time (perhaps even lifetimes), and may be cumulative, perhaps persistent, and possibly irreversible. The release of a technology into the world, through the journey from research, through innovation, to market, becomes itself a kind of experiment, with the world as the laboratory (Krohn and Weyer, 1994). The spatial scales at which interactions between technologies, and between technologies and nature, occur may extend to encompass the entire globe (as evidenced by the traces of persistent organic pollutants and other chemicals found in species from the Poles to the Equator). Further, the timescape (Adam, 1998) of some of these interactions – the reach of their intended and unintended effects into the future – may be extremely long, or even, in principle, unending, as in the case of genetic engineering's irreversible transformation of biological entities.

In summary, if, as we have suggested, a "modern" conceptualization of responsibility makes us into consequentialists, then we have to exercise foresight about our actions, particularly when seeking to innovate. But insofar as we rely on knowledge (and in particular science) for foresight, we appear to *lack the capacity* for foresight – because our attempts to understand the consequences of our actions are simultaneously undercut by attempts, whether by ourselves or by others, to change the world we are trying to understand. If, as Hacking suggests, we know we can "expect the unexpected," what – as consequentialist moral agents – do we do with this knowledge? Because of their potential seriousness, we are called upon to anticipate global and long-term future consequences of our actions. People and non-humans distant in time and space become our moral neighbors. But how can we act responsibly toward them if we concentrate on the consequences of our actions? If these extend beyond our foresight, then are we pushed toward paralysis (Grinbaum, 2006) rather than toward action?

7.2.3 Reciprocal and Non-Reciprocal Responsibility

One response to this consequentialist crisis is to propose that we become deontologists again and search for a set of fixed rules on which we can rely in the face of uncertainty. To do this, however, we have to find an immovable point on which to stand, one which does not refer, as consequentialists must, to some method for calculating the relative balance of the benefits and costs of an action. Perhaps we could rely on an account of a "special moral sense" that human beings possess and which guides them in the face of uncertainty, or rely on "the intuitions of the 'best people'," those (like scientists or business people) whose points of view tend to be accorded a special status and authority in modern societies? (Richardson, 1999, p. 232). Such suggestions, however, are question-begging ones in an age characterized by Weber's *Zweckrationalität*, where rationality depends on results, and any other form of justification must appear to be only an illegitimate argument from authority.

We could consider another kind of deontological ethics, however. We could look for guidance on how to *act responsibly* within the structure of our basic relationships with other humans. For example, a series of classical liberal and republican philosophers, including Locke and Rousseau (along with earlier thinkers like Hobbes), depicted our social relationship with others as being, essentially, contractual – although they did this in different ways, which philosophers classify into "contractarian" and "contractualist" positions (Darwall, 2003). The existence of society assumes an implicit and fundamental contract in which reciprocal rights are guaranteed and enforced by legal authority. Under the terms of such a contract, I demonstrate my responsibility as a citizen by ensuring I act only in ways that do not infringe other citizens' legal and moral entitlements – in the expectation that they will reciprocate by doing the same. Beneath all the role responsibilities we may have, then, we are fundamentally citizens *whose fundamental responsibility is to reciprocally respect each others' rights*.

Does this help, however, when we are thinking about humans outside our community, non-humans, and future generations of people and/or non-humans? Here, the assumption that morally-significant relationships are reciprocal ones falls down. Contractarianism, for example, represents the basis of reciprocity as mutual advantage – that, in other words, I gain from not harming you because then you will not harm me. However, people on the other side of the world who we may be able to harm via the interference effects of our technologies may well not be able to "harm us back": if there is no possibility of reciprocity, then no obligation falls upon us. Even more problems are encountered with respect to non-humans who cannot, by their nature, enter into such contracts. The problem is yet more intractable when considering future humans, who are logically unable to enter into such contracts. We do not and cannot, in principle, stand in a reciprocal relationship to the future generations of people who will inhabit the world shaped by the innovations we create. Our relationship to them is entirely non-reciprocal (Groves, 2009), as we have the power to completely change the conditions in which they will live, while they enjoy no comparable power over us.

This observation does, however, give us a chink of light, through which a better path toward understanding the "responsibility" in responsible innovation might be glimpsed. Our power over future generations – amplified by our reliance on technological innovation and the likelihood of interference effects – is what, according to the German philosopher Hans Jonas (1984), places upon those who live in technological societies a historically unprecedented responsibility for the future. Robert E. Goodin (1985, pp. 170–172) agrees, and spells out some implications of our power over future people: any responsibility we have to future people derives from their *vulnerability* to our actions, and not from a social contract. The position in which we stand vis-à-vis future people is analogous to our relationship with a dependent, such as a child or someone in desperate need. More widely, being vulnerable to others – yet not necessarily reciprocally so – may be seen as a condition which derives from human finitude (Løgstrup, 1997), and as such is hardly unprecedented in and of itself. This condition imposes upon us, as individuals apart from whatever particular social roles we may play, a basic obligation to care for others whom our actions may affect.

At first sight, this might not seem to help us much. We have reached what appears to be a troubling philosophical insight – that the power of technology potentially creates novel (and problematic) relationships between those alive now and future people. In other circumstances, relationships between present and future people might be mediated by institutions with stability designed into them – such as investment funds, state welfare services, and so on. But intergenerational relationships shaped by our reliance on technology are mediated only by "naturalized" artifacts that seem to have an uncanny life of their own, beyond our control. What can the innovator do, faced with this insight? When consequentialism is of no help, must s/he therefore stand paralyzed, facing the gap between his/her own finite capacities and the seemingly logical demand that s/he take on unlimited responsibility (European Commission, 2008), exposed to the uncertainties of moral luck and the possibility of future blame and liability? In the next section we explore a different approach to responsibility. We show how to draw from the vulnerability of future people some useful insights that help us think about the prospective responsibilities implied by responsible innovation.

7.3   Beyond the Sovereign Individual: Collective Responsibility, Desire, and Cultural Narratives

7.3.1   Passion Sits Alongside Reason

The problem of responsible innovation stems, as we have seen, from a contradiction that affects the social authority possessed by scientific knowledge. This is the contradiction between the promise of knowledge without intrinsic limits, and the limits that actually emerge when the products of this knowledge, in the form of technology, generate radical uncertainty about the future. Hence, the downfall of consequentialist ethics in addressing the actual problems of responsible innovation that we have discussed above. Human desire is yet another part of the human condition that also possesses no intrinsic limits. Unconstrained by the voice of reason, passions can reinforce themselves with unbounded strength for an indefinite period of time. They provoke emotions, whose contribution to moral judgment stands on a par with the input of a consequentialist calculation of costs and benefits associated with one's action: hence, the necessity to take them into account in addressing the problems of responsible innovation. We begin by a brief sketch of emotional attitudes that society exhibits, and suffers, with regard to technology.

The twentieth century was replete with reflections and reactions on what was perceived as the failed promises of rational science and the enlightened man. From the Holocaust and the Gulag on the social side, to Chernobyl, Fukushima, the debacle of GMOs, intrusions of privacy, and contaminated medicines (from hemophilia blood products in the 1980s to cardiac drugs in the 2010s) on the technological side, all of these catastrophic events involved unforeseen consequences of technological innovation as either leading vectors or helpful mediators of evil. The psychological and moral experiences that these events induced in human societies had a traumatic character (Frankl, 1946), in which the claims of a trusted authority were unexpectedly found to be untrustworthy – thus disrupting widely held cultural assumptions about the place of science in society as a reliable interpreter of the world (see Chapter 6, for further discussions on trust). Yet most societies still react with hope and excitement to the promise of new technologies, even as they preserve the memory of past technological catastrophes. Thus the traumatic loss of trust continues to reverberate to this day.

One of the temptations of this trauma is to see it as total and irrevocable, marking out a radical discontinuity between the present of "open-source" science and the past "ivory-tower" science, and one that – to return to epistemological issues – discloses insurmountable gaps in knowledge that mean we cannot predict what our actions will mean to future generations. The existence of this radical separation between us and them is one way of reading Hans Jonas's remark (Jonas, 1984) that we, as members of technological societies, bear a historically unprecedented responsibility to future generations. If this responsibility is genuinely unprecedented, then, to be genuinely responsible innovators, do we need to innovate in the realm of responsibility too, perhaps to the extent of entirely jettisoning the ethical traditions we have inherited? Yet such a conclusion may lead us nowhere. If we decide we need an entirely new kind of responsibility, then our decision leaves us amidst the ruins of old concepts of responsibility, carefully distilled in the course of human history, without any obvious path to take.

As an alternative, one option is to simply reverse the standards of proof, and make "being responsible" identical with "being precautionary." One could demand (to take things to an extreme) that innovators provide evidence that their innovations are safe with complete certainty, even where potential harms are scientifically recognized to be merely plausible. This is, however, insufficient for an account of moral responsibility. Although the precautionary principle is based on an acknowledgment of the pervasiveness of uncertainty, by itself it represents little more than a negative version of foresight-based consequentialism: grounding decisions on worst-case scenarios still requires that we foresee what these might be, and that we make a judgment whether the benefits of acting are "proportionately" better than the potential hazards of doing so (Dupuy, 2007; Marchant, 2003).

Without any firm guidelines on when exactly precaution must end, we are left caught between an unjustifiable policy of precaution and an unjustifiable policy of *laissez-faire*. The ever-present possibility of paralysis between these options drives home the importance of *emotional* reaction to innovation, and with it the analogy between the trauma of scientific authority and individual trauma: just as an individual trauma sufferer may retreat entirely from the world, unable to deal with its demands, societies may demand that technologies – or individual researchers – be certified as being entirely innocent, as being either free from potential hazards or being required to extend their foresight through additional research to ferret out every possibility of harm. Even more radically, voices may be raised against technological rationality as such, representing scientific knowledge as infected with a will to exploitation, and even totalitarianism. Counterposed to these demands are often found consequentialist responses from exasperated scientists: there is no innovation without risk, so if you want the benefits of new technologies, accept the risks! Such responses, however, miss the point: in technological experiences of trauma, the authority of confident pronouncements about the balance between "benefits" and "risks" is precisely what is at issue. Where the criteria provided by instrumental and consequentialist reason fail, *we are left with emotion or passion as the basis of judgment.* Consequently, we cannot expect that trying to decide how to proceed on a rule derived from decision theory, based on exploring the rationality of different ways of weighing benefits against risks, can be an adequate response, even if the decision rule we come up with is beautifully precautionary in nature. What is needed is a recognition that our situation, although technologically unprecedented in the history of humanity, *is not ethically unprecedented*, and rather than simply inventing new decision rules which individuals or organizations can apply, we need to look back and seek to learn from the moral thought of the past about styles of ethical thought which can be effectively applied to our present, "passionate" situation. As we shall see, these lessons may be more complex and demanding than simply learning a rule.

7.3.2   Non-Consequentialist Individual Responsibility

If technological societies are marked by experiences that tempt us with fantasies of radical discontinuity – that things are no longer as they were, that "we" and our contemporaries are special just because of *when* we are alive – then one suitably sceptical path forward may be to carefully explore *continuities*, rather than demanding the wholesale invention of a new morality entirely innocent of the alleged sins of scientific rationalism. Given that, as we have seen, the responsibilities of innovators derive from the vulnerability of future people to their actions, can we draw any useful analogies with other roles or forms of subjectivity whose identity revolves around handling vulnerability?

It is first of all important to note that, contrary to a commonly-held view that a victim of wrongdoing of any kind enjoys a superior moral standing over the ordinary man, being vulnerable does not equate with being right, nor being righteous. Victimhood caused by the feeling of vulnerability does not suffice on its own to determine the meaning of action, but merely serves as one of its motivations. As Robert Musil wrote, "Even a sex-murderer is, in some cranny of his soul, full of inner hurt and hidden appeals; somehow the world is wronging him like a child, and he does not have the capacity to express this in any other way than the way he has found works for him. In the criminal there is both a vulnerability and a resistance against the world, and both are present in every person who has a powerful moral destiny" (Musil, 1990/1913, p. 39). Hence the need, once the moral dimensions of vulnerability are explored, to add to our ethical thinking a different component taking us beyond a mere observation of this condition. However, we first focus on vulnerability as a factor of individual responsibility.

We mentioned previously that the relationship between present and future people was more akin to that between caregivers and dependents or children than between adult contemporaries, given that it generates non-reciprocal responsibilities. Yet this is not perfectly comparable, by any means. For example, the dependents of caregivers (and children in particular) are not "future people," but present people whose potentialities we assume are particularly sensitive and malleable, and who are vulnerable as a result. This point, however, means we can make a useful comparison between a parental duty of care and a similar duty which might be appropriate for innovators, based on an analogy between "naturalized" technologies (technologies, that is, with something like an autonomous existence of their own) and children.

We might say that parents are required to care for children in such a way as to encourage certain kinds of character traits and behaviors aligned with social norms.

Parents may be thought of as having a duty to future people (and to their children's contemporaries) not to raise offspring who ignore their responsibilities to others. Their responsibility to future people is, therefore, mediated by their responsibilities to their children, and vice versa. Further, the role of parent is without the kinds of well-defined limits we may expect to find drawn around an occupation, to which explicit role responsibilities might attach. What characterizes the role of parent is, first, caring for a child's capabilities and ensuring that they are given the opportunities to develop them, which requires a thickly detailed understanding of what makes for a valuable set of such capacities (or "good character," if you prefer). The parent is not expected to have the capacity of superior foresight regarding future consequences, which, as we have seen, is an expectation that technological societies both promote and undermine. The capacities required are other than this, belonging to the set of personal characteristics that has traditionally been called "virtues." The purpose of raising children on this pattern is to make them fit them for adulthood, for relative, then full, autonomy, and for taking responsibility on their own account.

Are innovators parents of their innovations in this sense? As they are unleashed to live a "life" of their own in a complex world, technologies can develop a certain autonomy – though one that obviously does not make them identical to human children, particularly because technological innovation carries an aura of novelty that, arguably, human procreation does not. During early elaboration stages, technologies are dependents with sensitive and malleable potentialities, in which it is hoped the ingenuity of innovators will help produce – in concert with the sleeping powers of nature that are called to life by the innovator – particular virtues. These typically include the efficient production of "right impacts"; that is beneficial, intended effects (see Chapter 3), together with the kind of stability set out in ideas of "safety by design" (Kelty, 2009), and the broader social character of a technology implied by the concept of the "social constitution of technologies" (Grove-White, Macnaghten, and Wynne, 2000). Such obvious virtues can even be formulated in the ordinary language of moral values rather than technical specifications: to rephrase the slogan promoted by one technological company, not only the innovator but technology itself must not "be evil." Those involved in research and development therefore partake, in many ways, in preparing their technological children for maturity – although we should note that if naturalized technological artifacts with the potential for unforeseeable interference effects are children, then they are certainly endowed with a special social status – not truly alive yet decidedly not simply inanimate slaves . . . They may not be capable of maturity in the sense that we take human children to be, but they cannot simply be fixed in the position of eternal childhood either – for to do so is to be unjust to their caring and responsible "parents."

We see the problems that arise from such an "infantilization" of technology in the precautionary tendencies of contemporary governance of innovation. For example, the European Code of Conduct for Responsible Nanosciences and Nanotechnologies Research contains a principle of accountability that reflects the traumatized precautionary stance we examined above: "Researchers and research organizations should remain accountable for the social, environmental, and human health impacts that their research (in nanosciences and nanotechnologies) may impose on present and future generations" (European Commission, 2008). This reference to future generations without any time limit for accountability, from the point of view of consequentialist ethics, subjects the innovator-parent to unbounded hazards of moral luck. It is notable that we do not accept such infantilization of technology in relation to many past inventions. Today, we do not hold the inventor of the locomotive, telephone, or internal combustion engine responsible for any negative impacts that these technologies have exercised on humanity since the nineteenth century. It does not occur to us to blame high costs of electricity and an ensuing increase in poverty on Edison or Faraday, or illnesses caused by inhalation of particulates on Rudolf Diesel. However, if "should remain accountable" were replaced with "care for the vulnerability of technology users" within a finite time span of individual quasi-parental responsibility, then such an excessive extension of responsibility would be altogether removed.

Let us pause at this point to review the usefulness of the analogy with parental care. It is informative to the extent that it illustrates how the future-oriented responsibilities of innovators, based on vulnerability, can be understood in terms of what mediates between present and future for caregivers and for innovators – respectively, children and technological innovations. The duty of care for the vulnerability of future people becomes concrete, as a result, in the idea of a duty to "teach" or "encode" the virtues in children or in created artifacts. But before we ask which virtues should be taught in this way, the analogy itself leads us to examine, beyond the individual dimension, the relationship between the innovator and the wider social order. To what extent does the technological innovator adopt a particular *collective, hence political*, role, in addition to the "parental" one?

7.3.3   Collective Political Responsibility

Our analogy with parental responsibilities was presented to illustrate an important continuity between responsible innovation and extant conceptions of responsibility, to avoid an excessive and paralyzing concentration on the uniqueness of technological responsibility. We now examine a further continuity: between responsible innovation and *collective, political responsibility*. This is relevant to innovation as bringing new social practices and even institutions that transform the ways in which human beings interact with their peers and the world around them.

Society often believes that the innovator creates in order to serve some identified social need. The innovator herself may indeed be motivated by the desire to mend social injustice or to do social good. In her innovation, however, she contributes to a process that often reshapes the social and natural worlds in unforeseeable ways. In this sense, innovators are (*pace* Shelley, 1970/1821) the unacknowledged legislators and co-creators of the world. They thus adopt a political responsibility as part of a particular professional group engaged in a collective endeavor.

Hannah Arendt's analysis focuses on the collective aspect of responsibility and its implications for social groups. A German Jew who fled Germany in 1933, Arendt chose to turn her experience of ethical and social trauma into something beyond a question of her own, or anyone's, individual ethics. She did not ask whether an individual is good but whether his or her conduct is good for the world s/he lives in, and she emphasized the political dimension of her thought: "In the centre of interest is the world and not the self" (Arendt, 1968, p. 151). The social structures observed by Arendt directed her attention to the notion of collective responsibility. By definition, collective responsibility occurs if the following two conditions are met: a person must be held responsible for something she has not done, and the reason for her responsibility must be her membership in a group which no voluntary act of hers can dissolve. Thus, all nuclear scientists share political responsibility for the human condition in a world full of atomic power plants and nuclear weapons, irrespective of their degree of personal involvement in the industry; or all scientists in general partake in shaping the world, whatever their individual research disciplines might be. Collective responsibility looms large, not in considerations regarding individual actions based on personal convictions about what is right, but in *political considerations of a group's conduct.* In contrast to, for example, Karl Jaspers (1947), Arendt maintains that collective responsibility is a concept quite distinct from the concept of guilt. She argues that the notion of collective guilt only serves to exculpate those individuals who are actually legally guilty of specific evils, while collective responsibility is a moral and political, but not a legal, phenomenon, and relates to collective well-being under changing technological realities. This form of responsibility arises when complex social forces become important that cannot be reduced to individual will or intent, but the responsibility for the consequences of the action of such forces is, nevertheless, attributed to individuals who compose the group: this is the case for innovation!

Collective political responsibility rests on historical continuity, flowing from the past and reaching out to embrace the future. The individual who recognizes his or her implication in collective responsibility recognizes that who s/he herself is, what s/he values and how s/he acts – in other words, his or her own identity – is inseparable from a social identity that is historical in nature, and rooted within particular institutions. Taking responsibility means assuming an account of the history of the institutions to which one belongs, and which shape who one is, as much as it means assuming responsibility for shaping the future consequences of what they do with an eye on wider well-being. Weighing the rights and wrongs of an action here goes beyond, for example, simply concentrating on the narrow technical benefits of an invention. The innovator, as bearer of a political responsibility specific to his or her social role, has to ask herself about the *wider social and political significance of what she intends to accomplish, and what her actions may accomplish despite her intentions.* Here, the limitations of traditional considerations of role responsibility are again apparent: the responsibilities one assumes when playing a role are a medium through which one enters the political sphere, and the role itself is but a gate that leads to an arena where moral judgment takes place.

On a group level, Arendt's conditions for collective responsibility fully apply to Nordmann's "naturalized technologies." The perceived autonomy of these artifacts is due to the fact that the internal functioning of complex technological devices remains opaque for the layperson. Science is perceived as a mysterious force that produces useful artifacts, that is, a kind of modern magic. However, even if we acknowledge the autonomy and ubiquity of modern technology, the layperson will distinguish it from magic or fairy tales in that s/he knows that there exist living people, namely scientists and engineers, whose participation in the inner workings of science and technology is direct: they are the initiates. Hence, their collective responsibility: as seen by society, any scientist is engaged in "secret" production of artifacts that will leave a deep mark on every man's life. No act of his or her own, even if s/he exits the institution of science completely, will return the scientist to the status of layperson, as long as his or her past scientific training and occupation remain known to the group. Particularly paradoxical cases of political responsibility arise when scientists working in a certain discipline are held responsible for what has been done in a very different domain. The intra-scientific differences that are evident to the initiates remain socially invisible, and, as a consequence, politically irrelevant.

7.3.4   The Virtues of Responsible Innovation

We have argued, so far, that responsible innovation means taking responsibility in ways that are, respectively, quasi-parental and collectively political in nature. The quasi-parental way of taking responsibility implies a limited kind of individual responsibility that focuses upon the duty of care for the malleability of technological artifacts and the vulnerability of their future users. However, being vulnerable is no guarantee that either the technological artifact or the person will act virtuously: a victim may turn into a persecutor of those who took care of him/her, given the right circumstances. If the innovator who takes care of the "virtues" of his or her creations is blamed for any unintended consequences, the reaction will primarily be internal rather than external: s/he will feel ashamed and in conflict with his or her own conscience, rather than being liable in the eyes of society and perhaps punished under the law. The latter, political form of responsibility is collective, and the "politics" to which it refers is not the usual kind. The relevant line of division within society runs, not between opposed alliances (such as those on the political left and the right) that represent contrasting interpretations of the "public good," but between technological initiates and technological laypeople, who may very well vote identically at elections, but may well not form the same opinion where the contribution of technological innovation is at stake. How these two groups can live together, and what they ought to do in order to maintain peaceful coexistence, is the central challenge posed by the innovator's specific political vocation. Its collective dimension implies that no one person, however knowledgeable about science and technology, can single-handedly answer this question. The timescale over which evolves the division line between laypeople and the initiates is larger than the scale of usual politics and its actors are diffused and impersonal: on the left (or right), naturalized technologies, on the opposite side, a world-wide constituency of their users crossing all national and natural frontiers. Decision-making in this political configuration is often implicit, and its consequences take years, if not decades, to become visible.

Among the two types of non-consequentialist responsibility we have discussed, quasi-parental responsibility in particular relies on "teaching" certain virtues. This is fundamental, as moral judgment that depends on passion as well as reason includes an emotional evaluation of the technological artifact and the innovator who created it. Preparing to assume such kinds of responsibility is typically not a part of the training received by scientists, industrial entrepreneurs, or managers of scientific institutions. The non-consequentialist character of responsible innovation we have suggested must require particular forms of education. Without wanting to map out in detail what the virtues of the innovator might be, or the educational means of creating them, we present in the closing pages of this chapter a framework for thinking about them.

7.3.5 Narratives Take over Where Cost–Benefit Analysis Fails

7.3.5.1 Desire and Motivation

A silent alchemist who once unleashed natural processes in the darkness of a laboratory has, with the centrality of innovation to globalized, technological societies, become a political individual whom we call an innovator or technological entrepreneur. The political question asked by contemporary technological societies of such individuals is: in the first place, why would innovators *wish* to make a pact with the sleeping powers of Nature? What did they *want to achieve*? Both the goal and the very *desire* to achieve it are ethically suspect and subject to scrutiny. Here, we should pause and reflect on the problem of desire as such, and more generally on the place of passion in the judgment of moral responsibility; for when human desire is implicated within any ethical framework governing one's actions, what counts is whether there are clearly demarcated limits to it, and not simply whether acting brings results which fulfill the desire. As Davies and Macnaghten (2010) note in a seemingly paradoxical finding in their study of lay perceptions of technology, "getting exactly what you want may not ultimately be good for you." What exactly does this imply for responsible innovation?

We answer this question from a philosophical and practical point of view that rests on two pillars. The first, as we have already discussed, is that by their very nature science and technology, like any creative process, exceed the limits of prudence. There is continuity between the human condition that they contribute to create and the condition, explored in literature, of a hero who confronts powerful natural forces. In his well-known poem "The Age of Anxiety," W. H. Auden contrasts the demands of pure engineering: "The prudent atom//Simply insists upon its safety now, //Security at all costs," with the forces that govern and reward desire and ambition: "Nature rewards//Perilous leaps" (Auden, 2011/1947, p. 7) Hence, if responsible innovation is something more than a rephrased safety protocol, it must inevitably address, not just reason, but also the passion which inhabits a courageous innovator preparing to make a perilous leap.

This analogy between modern innovator and literary hero might help to reveal unexpected moral difficulties to be faced by the former. Scientific discovery and its ensuing transformation into successful technology depend on multiple factors: assiduous research, for sure, but also serendipity and favorable business opportunities. We learn from literature that the latter are not morally innocent: by saying "O opportunity, thy guilt is great," Shakespeare famously made in *The Rape of Lucrece* a moral judgment so puzzling that it either calls for a mythological personification of "guilty" chance (his own solution) or, for the analytic mind, it reveals the need to open up the Shakespearean shortcut from "opportunity" to "guilt," by spelling out what elements may form this chain of logic. This is where the moral suspiciousness of desire comes into play. Under some circumstances, getting exactly what one wants may lead one to unforeseen disasters and catastrophes: "be wary of what you wish for . . . " These circumstances exist when what *may* potentially be wished for is itself boundless, like the never-ending technological progress, which can be the cause both of great expectations and of the disruption of the community (Dupuy, 2010).

This moral conundrum is not unknown in history. The notion that too much success incurs a supernatural danger, especially if one brags about it, has appeared independently in many different cultures and is deeply rooted in human nature (Dodds, 1951, p. 30).

Ancient Greek mythology, and later Greek thought, distinguish between four different kinds of circumstances: successful action may provoke jealousy of the gods (*phthonos*), it may lead to divine retribution (*nemesis*), it may cause complacency of the man who has done too well (*koros*), or it may lead to arrogance in word, deed, or thought (*hubris*). *Hubris* is condemned by the Greek society and punished by law, but reaction to the other three is more subtle. *Phthonos* and *nemesis* are dangerous and must be feared. The attitude that the Greeks have toward *koros* is rather ambivalent: the complacency assumed in this notion makes someone's life untenable, however *koros* can hardly be avoided, for it goes hand in hand with ambition, or the inability to put an end to one's desire of great achievements, called *philotimia*. In a telling example, a modern commentator connects Ulysses's hardships with his *philotimia* in a way that bears striking resemblance to the innovator and his or her limitless desire to bring new technologies to life: "[it] condemns Ulysses to a hard life, for he must constantly live up to the height of new dangers, unless the reputation of his past deeds be tarnished. Peace of mind is forbidden to him, because he depends on a reputation placed under continuous threat" (Gangloff, 2006, pp. 103–104, our translation from French). In the later centuries of Greek thought we find an explicit argument describing the moral condition of a man who has achieved great technical feats as "always on fire from fervor," his soul "consumed by a continuous suite of loves, hopes, and desires," the reason being that "the sweetness of success lures him into a painful ordeal of the worst misfortunes" (Festugière, 1954, our translation from French). Thus perfect success forbids peace of mind, and, by way of analogy between ancient and modern ethical thought, this is at the same time a part of the innovator's human condition and a moral problem of its own. The impossibility to limit one's desire endlessly amplifies ambition, and the only way to escape from this eternal fire is via balancing one's desire with humility that would help to restore one's mind to peace. How exactly this can be achieved, and whether this is at all possible, cannot be answered in full generality; what needs to be done instead is an educational effort that would teach the individual to compensate his or her own virtue of scientific ambition with virtuous lucidity, inasmuch as the moral standing of this ambition is concerned, thus contributing to an accrued sense of innovator's responsibility.

7.3.5.2   Cultural Narratives

The second pillar is the importance of *stories* for ethical thinking. Several recent publications insist on their relevance, both practically observed and theoretically motivated, for understanding public perception of new technologies (Davies and Macnaghten, 2010; Dupuy, 2010; Ferrari and Nordmann, 2010; Grinbaum, 2010). Ancient and modern narratives become part and parcel of the social reading of technology, making it impossible to tackle ethical questions that it raises without an evocation of mythological personifications of various technical feats and the ensuing moral punishment, for example, Prometheus, Daedalus, or Pandora. Thinking about moral questions with the help of stories is to virtue ethics what cost–benefit analysis is to consequentialism, and the ever more evident irrelevance of consequentialism to the present science–society situation makes it urgent to resort to other tools of dealing with the growing number of problems. We survey here two such stories that are particularly relevant for the analysis of responsibility. As with all myths or narratives, they do not contain a direct answer to the moral question that they explore. Rather, they proceed by encouraging the scientist and the innovator to reflect on the sides of moral judgment that typically are not a part of his or her rational toolkit. If consequentialism cannot but fail to predict the exact future consequences because of their high uncertainty, one can still imagine what future ethical implications might be by resorting to cultural narratives. Their interpretation may reveal a surprising degree of analogy with the scientific and technological work of modern scientists and engineers.

The first story concerns Rabbi Judah Loew of Prague, to whom a legend ascribes the creation of an artificial man called the Golem of Prague. Rabbi Loew wrote, "Everything that God created requires repair and completion" (Sherwin, 2004, p. 53). On this interpretation of a Biblical verse in *Genesis* 2 : 3, which isn't uncommon in the Jewish tradition, the world was "created to be made": God has not finished his creation and therefore human beings receive a mandate to act as "God's partners in the act of creation," by developing raw materials and unleashing the sleeping powers of Nature. Not only is innovation *per se* free of sin; it is encouraged and praised as a mandatory activity in one's fulfillment of his human potential. Like modern technology that is said to serve societal needs, in the Jewish tradition human creativity is always purposeful: Judah Loew creates the Golem of Prague, not on a whim or for pleasure, but in order to protect the city's Jewish community from the many threats they encountered in the gloomy streets of Prague in 1580. Once unleashed, the golem obeyed Judah Loew's commands and successfully protected the Prague ghetto for about 10 years. Then, according to one popular version of the story, the golem went berserk, at which point Judah Loew was summoned and told to do something to stop the golem's wrongdoing. He "unmade" the golem by a procedure that was, "technically" speaking, the reverse of the method he had used to make him.

This legend exemplifies several typical features of the many golem stories in Jewish literature that may cast new light on modern science and technology. In reflecting on such stories, we may learn more about the complexities of moral judgment. Points of comparison between the golem legends and modern techno-science include: (i) purposefulness: a golem is made on purpose by a human creator with a specific goal in mind, while modern technology is often justified before society as being created in order to serve identified social needs; (ii) reversibility: a golem can be both made and unmade through a fixed procedure, while modern technological innovation can change the world so dramatically that one can hardly envisage going back; (iii) machine-like obedience: the creator commands his creation at will and the latter obeys the former, while modern naturalized technologies gain a form of autonomy that demands they be granted a special, intermediate social and moral status; and (iv) responsibility: when the golem's actions become harmful, the community tells Judah Loew to repair the damage. Responsibility for the golem's conduct falls upon his creator rather than upon the golem himself, and this in spite of the fact that the golem behaved and looked more or less like an autonomous human being. This is strikingly similar to the quasi-parental responsibility of the innovator we have discussed earlier.

The second story concerns Mary Shelley's novel about Victor Frankenstein, which displays a different set of characteristics (Shelley, 2009/1818). Unlike Judah Loew, Frankenstein, who created a monster, cannot undo what he had done: the monster would not obey him and escapes his power altogether. The process unleashed here is irreversible, but even as it begins to produce terrible consequences (as the story develops the monster kills several people), Frankenstein keeps his moral perplexities to himself. He evidently refuses to acknowledge any political dimension of his action. His responsibility with regard to society, which happens not to be imposed on him by legal or any other external threat to his own person, proceeds exclusively from his own conscience. And although he is perturbed by the monster's actions, he does not reveal that he has created it, nor does he admit what he knows of its deeds, thus allowing one person falsely accused of murder to be executed. What places him in this position is the modern version of what Augustine of Hippo called the "lust of the eyes" (Augustine, 2000/398, Chapter 35; O'Neill, 1993, pp. 155–59), the desire for scientific truth and technical achievement above any other effect produced by the innovator's desire. The story then goes on to explore the consequences of Frankenstein's failure to admit his political responsibility. Soon the monster promises to put an end to both his and others' suffering if Frankenstein makes for him a second artificial creature to become his wife. Seduced by an easy technical solution to the problem of social evil, Frankenstein complies and begins to work on the second monster, only to realize a little later that by making this new creature he would unleash yet another irreversible process out of his control. He refuses to finish the second being and flees the country and all human company, apparently unable to cope with a moral burden.

Shelley's verdict is unequivocal: Frankenstein's creative activity was morally wrong, for it failed to stand up to the moral and political challenges it had itself generated. But why *precisely* was it wrong? Unlike Judah Loew, Victor Frankenstein created the monster without a particular societal goal – is this the source of evil? Or is it the lack of reversibility? Or the lack of control, whereby the monster's autonomy placed him altogether out of his creator's control? A small episode in the novel reveals further complexity by proposing a parabola about the source of evil in the monster, which we can interpret as a story about good and evil in modern technology (Pavlopoulos, Grinbaum, and Bontems, 2010, Chapter 5): after the monster's initial escape from Frankenstein, he finds refuge in a hovel next to a small house inhabited by a blind man and his two children. By observing the family and reading their books, the monster learns human language. Gradually he warms up to the poor family and starts secretly to help them. One day, longing for mutual kindness, he decides to come out to his hosts. First he enters into a conversation with the blind man and is received warmly by him. But when the children arrive and see the monster, they beat him and throw him into the street. At this moment the monster puts an end to his righteous conduct and turns to wrongdoing.

This episode mingles the usual theme inherited from the Golem legends (that social success and the moral status of one's novel creation depend on the purity of the creator's intentions), with the unpredictability of nonetheless morally relevant consequences, otherwise known as moral luck (see above). Shelley contends that evil influence in the monster is not necessarily due to a lack of reversibility in the original innovation, nor of course to Frankenstein's revealed evil intentions, but to the human conduct on which the monster models his own behavior. When the blind man's children beat the creature, he learns from experience and, henceforth, starts to spread evil himself. Taking this episode as a metaphor for the condition of modern technology, one might contend that the responsibility for misuse of technological innovation belongs with the society rather than the inventor; technology would not be prone to misuse *per se*, nor would such misuse be inevitable. If it occurs, then it is rooted in the environment in which technology operates rather than being encoded deterministically in the technical object. In other words, as we frequently hear today, moral judgment depends on how technical objects are used, while the existence of the object itself is neither good nor bad.

Yet Shelley gives reasons to doubt this interpretation. Whether the source of the monster's wrongdoing is in his creator or in a random chain of events that happened to the monster after his escape, Victor Frankenstein still feels an unbearable responsibility that forces him to flee and abandon both his work and his world. Hence, evil done by the monster has something to do with Frankenstein himself. When the latter halts the creation of the second being, it is not because he suddenly mistrusts the monster's promise to live peacefully in the woods with his future partner. Rather, he realizes that episodes such as the meeting between the monster and the blind man's children are inevitable because they are a consequence of his own finiteness, and of the dark side that is inherent to Frankenstein as human creator. Angelic, purely righteous beings cannot subsist, as Melville will make clear a few decades after Shelley's novel by putting to death his Billy Budd (Melville, 1924; Rey, 2011). Frankenstein knows that his political responsibility for what the monster will do to society, although not limitless, is nevertheless very real: he cannot come to terms with his conscience, affirms his own responsibility, although no legal threats are made against him, and flees society.

To some extent, the innovator today is put in all these different situations at once: on the one hand, society exerts pressure on him if his work proves harmful; on the other, by turning inwards and interrogating his or her own conscience, the innovator must make a choice between his or her ambitions and desires, and face moral judgment even if (or perhaps, especially if) they are successfully realized. Yet there is no universal answer as to how to translate the lessons of old stories into action in the present. Even as one strives to possess the requisite virtues of the responsible innovator: to bind one's desire, to check ambition by humility, and to maintain both internal interrogation and external dialogue about the meaning of one's actions, there is no guarantee that moral luck in the uncertain future will not mean that one's efforts to act responsibly will not turn out to have unintended consequences. Whatever choices are made, the final verdict on a distinction between responsible and irresponsible innovation is not in our capacity to make. No one can vouch that his action is an adequate expression of the virtues of a responsible innovator: rather, living up to the demands of responsibility is a lifelong process.

7.4 Conclusion: Responsibility and Meaning

Narratives teach continuity and comparison, and it is through developing such reflective skills about the cultural meaning of innovation that the virtue of responsibility can be developed. By tracing out, as they unfold, how the consequences of action ramify through time in unpredictable ways, narratives can also teach the limits of foresight and rational prudence. One finds such limits, too, by pursuing a purely analytic approach. Thus the downfall of consequentialist ethics exemplified by the notion of moral luck and the failure to take into account passion and desire call for alternative tools for ethical reflection, and virtue ethics supplies such instruments in the form of narratives. A refusal of virtue ethics to carry out moral judgment too hastily, before all its complexities can be fully contemplated, is a necessary ingredient of the moral education that the scientist should receive in the framework of responsible innovation.

Yet responsibility is only one of the virtues. Others, relevant to the scientific endeavor, perhaps include integrity, impartiality, honesty, lucidity, or openness. But even practicing all these virtues is no ultimate guarantee that good intentions, schooled by a sensitivity to vulnerability, shaped by quasi-parental care and tempered through responsive dialogue and political deliberation, will not produce bad effects. It is the meaning of action as a moral phenomenon that ultimately matters. As Musil reminds us, this meaning cannot be exhausted by excusability or inexcusability of occasional bad effects (Musil, 1990/1913, p. 38), for, on the one hand, political consequences of innovation for the ways in which people live in a society and its impact on the human condition will exceed the scope of any hasty judgment. On the other hand, the judgment itself involves two types of actors: the human innovator, of course, but also the naturalized technology in its capacity of semi-autonomous force that possesses the power to help shape our common destiny. As a result, as far as the innovator is concerned, the final verdict on whether he or she has acted responsibly or irresponsibly remains pending. As Paul Tillich wrote, "In the anxiety of guilt and condemnation doubt has not yet undermined the certainty of an ultimate responsibility." The occurrence of bad consequences, therefore, is not a final ethical verdict. The truly final word in moral judgment will remain with the meaning of one's action: "If, however, doubt and meaninglessness prevail, one experiences an abyss in which [...] the truth of ultimate responsibility disappears" (Tillich, 2000/1952, p. 174). The courage to deal with a complex process that creates such meaning is the best evidence for responsible innovation.

References

Adam, B. (1998) *Timescapes of Modernity: The Environment and Invisible Hazards*. London: Routledge.

Adam, B. and Groves, C. (2007) *Future Matters: Action, Knowledge, Ethics*. Leiden: Brill.

Arendt, H. (1994/1963). *Eichmann in Jerusalem: A Report on the Banality of Evil*. New York: Penguin Books.

Arendt, H. 1998/1958. *The Human Condition*. Chicago: Chicago University Press, (2nd edn).

Arendt H. (2003/1968) Collective responsibility, in: H. Arendt, *Responsibility and Judgment*, New York: Schocken Books.

Auden, W. H. (2011/1947) *The Age of Anxiety*. Princeton University Press.

Augustine (2000/398) *Confessions*, Oxford: Clarendon Press.

Beck, U. 1999. *World Risk Society*. London: Polity Press.

Bradley, F. H. 1927. *Ethical Studies*. 2nd edn. Oxford: Clarendon.

Darwall, S. L. 2003. *Contractarianism, Contractualism*. Oxford: Blackwell Science.

Davies S. R. and P. Macnaghten, 2010. Narratives of mastery and resistance: lay ethics of nanotechnology, *Nanoethics*, **4**, 141–151.

Davis, W. (2001) Introduction, in *Taking Responsibility: Comparative Perspectives*. (ed. Davis, W.) Charlottesville, VA: University Press of Virginia, pp. 1–27.

Dodds, E.R. (1951). *The Greeks and the Irrational*, University of California Press.

Dupuy, J.-P. (2007) Rational choice before the apocalypse. *Anthropoetics* **13**(3), 237–261.

Dupuy J.-P., (2010) The narratology of lay ethics, *NanoEthics*, **4**, 153–170.

European Commission (2008) Recommendation on 'A Code of Conduct for Responsible Nanosciences and Nanotechnologies Research'. C(2008) 424, Brussels.

Ferrari A. and A. Nordmann, 2010. Beyond conversation: some lessons for nanoethics, *NanoEthics*, **4**, 171–181.

Festugière, A.-J. (ed.) 1954. *Corpus Hermeticum*. Les Belles Lettres, Paris.

Frankl, V., (2006/1946) *Man's Search for Meaning*, Beacon Press.

Gangloff, A. (2006) *Dion Chrysostome et les Mythes*, Paris: Editions Jérôme Millon.

Goodin, R. E. (1985) *Protecting the Vulnerable: A Reanalysis of Our Social Responsibilities*. Chicago: University of Chicago Press.

Grinbaum, A. 2006. Cognitive barriers in the perception of nanotechnology, *Journal of Law, Medicine and Ethics*, **34**(4), 689–694.

Grinbaum A., (2010) The nanotechnological golem, *Nanoethics*, **4**, 191–198.

Grinbaum A. and J.-P. Dupuy, (2004) Living with uncertainty: toward a normative assessment of nanotechnology, *Techné*, **8**(2), 4–25.

Groves, C. (2009) Future ethics: risk, care and non-reciprocal responsibility. *Journal of Global Ethics* **5**(1), 17–31.

Grove-White, R., Macnaghten, P., and Wynne, B. (2000) Wising Up: The Public and New Technologies, IEPPP, Lancaster.

Hacking, I. (1986) Culpable ignorance of interference effects, in MacLean, D. (ed.) *Values at Risk*. Totowa, NJ: Rowman & Allanheld, pp. 136–154.

Hart, H. L. A. (1968) *Punishment and Responsibility*. Oxford: Clarendon Press.

Jaspers K. (2000/1947) *The Question of German Guilt*, Fordham University Press.

Jonas, H. (1984) *The Imperative of Responsibility: In Search of an Ethics for the Technological Age*. Chicago, London: University of Chicago Press.

Kelty, C. 2009. Beyond implications and applications: the story of 'Safety by Design'. *NanoEthics* **3**(2), 79–96.

Krohn, W. and Weyer, J. 1994. Society as a laboratory: the social risks of experimental research. *Science and Public Policy* **21**(3), 173–183.

Løgstrup, K. E. (1997) *The Ethical Demand*. Notre Dame and London: University of Notre Dame Press.

Marchant, G. E. (2003). From general policy to legal rule: aspirations and limitations of the precautionary principle. *Environmental Health Perspectives* **111**(14), 1799–1803.

McKeon, R. 1990. *Freedom and History and Other Essays*. Chicago: University of Chicago Press.

Melville, H. 1992/1924 *Billy Budd*. TOR Books.

Musil R. (1990/1913) *Precision and Soul*. The University of Chicago Press.

Nagel, T. (1979) Moral luck, in *Mortal Questions* (ed. Nagel, T.). Cambridge: Cambridge University Press, pp. 24–38.

Newdick, C. (1988) The development risk defence of the Consumer Protection Act 1987. *The Cambridge Law Journal* **47**(03), 455–476.

Nordmann, A. (2005) Noumenal technology: reflections on the incredible tininess of nano. *Techne* **8**(03), 3–23.

O'Neill, J. (1993). *Ecology, Policy and Politics*. London: Routledge.

Pavlopoulos, M., Grinbaum, A., and Bontems, V. (2010) Toolkit for Ethical Reflection and Communication on Nanoscience and Nanotechnology, CEA, Saclay, www .observatorynano.eu/project/catalogue/4ET/ (accessed 20 December 2012).

Pellizzoni, L. (2004) Responsibility and environmental governance. *Environmental Politics* **13**(3), 541–565.

Rey, O. (2011) *Le Testament de Melville: Penser le Bien et le Mal avec Billy Budd*, Gallimard.

Richardson, H. S. (1999) Institutionally divided moral responsibility. *Social Philosophy and Policy* **16**(2), 218–249.

Schneewind, J. B. (1984) The divine corporation and the history of ethics, in Rorty, R., Schneewind, J.B., and Skinner, Q., eds. *Philosophy in History: Essays on the Historiography of Philosophy*. Cambridge: Cambridge University Press, pp. 173–192.

Shelley, P. B. (1970/1821). A defence of poetry, in *Political Writings Including "A Defence of Poetry"*. (ed. R. A. Duerksen), New York, Appleton-Century-Crofts Inc.

Shelley M., 2009/1818. *Frankenstein, or the Modern Prometheus*. Oxford University Press.

Sherwin B., (2004) *Golems Among Us: How a Jewish Legend Can Help Us Navigate the Biotech Century*, Chicago: Ivan R. Dee Publisher.

Tillich P. 2000/1952. *The Courage to Be*. Yale University Press.

Timmons, M. 2002. *Moral Theory: An Introduction*. Totowa: Rowman & Littlefield Publishers.

Williams B., 1981. *Moral Luck*, Cambridge, Cambridge University Press.

Yara, T. 2011. Uncertain risks and consensus building: the HIV crisis as a case study. *Journal of Philosophy and Ethics in Health Care and Medicine* **5**, 151–167.

8

Adaptive Governance for Responsible Innovation

Robert G. Lee[1] *and Judith Petts*[2]
[1]*University of Exeter, Law School, UK*
[2]*University of Southampton, Faculty of Social and Human Sciences, UK*

8.1 Introduction

Emerging technologies (nanotechnology, genomics, genetically modified (GM) crops, synthetic biology, geoengineering, etc.) create the possibility of novel materials, new life forms, and opportunities not offered in nature; indeed sometimes deliberately intervening in the "natural." But opportunity is accompanied not only by data and model uncertainty, but often also by ambiguity, sheer ignorance, and indeterminacy (e.g., Rowe, 1994; Stirling, 2008; Wynne, 1992). These may be widely drawn, for example, in terms of what futures individuals and societies would wish for; the purposes and motivations of innovation and those who innovate; the direction of travel and future impacts of science that is still in the very early and experimental stages of discovery, and the unforeseen repurposing of technologies (so-called "dual use" technologies) that could bring beneficial as well as harmful or even dangerous outcomes. Risk may also be drawn more narrowly and immediately in terms of the potential threats to human health and the environment of technologies that come onto the market and into use.

Unfortunately, innovation does not flow through some simple linear chain with clear and definable points of potential interruption for control or even debate – from bright idea, through experimentation, demonstration, and testing, to production and assimilation into markets, use and disposal at end of life (see also Chapter 1). Rather, innovation is a complex, nonlinear and collective process enacted over varying but often very long (decadal) timescales and over multiple sectors (scientific, industrial, retail, financial, etc.).

Responsible Innovation, First Edition. Edited by Richard Owen, John Bessant and Maggy Heintz.
© 2013 John Wiley & Sons, Ltd. Published 2013 by John Wiley & Sons, Ltd.

Scale is often not just local but global (raising fundamental problems in terms of *where* innovation is governed and not just *how*). A vast range of actors (from individuals to corporates and states) are involved, each having their own objectives and interests, and who are acting in differing cultural and economic contexts which influence perceptions of what is the "responsible" thing to do and what are acceptable outcomes. As observed by Stirling (2008, p. 98) "the directions taken by technology at a variety of scales are increasingly recognized as being open to historic contingency, individual creativity, collective ingenuity, economic priorities, cultural values, institutional interests, stakeholder negotiation, and the exercise of power."

Against this background, calls for a new and, importantly, adaptive framework for the governance of innovation have been emerging. This idea of "governance" acknowledges that government is not the only important actor. Indeed, in a basic sense even command and control regulatory systems require some partnership between the regulator and the regulated (Ayres and Braithwaite, 1992). Beyond this, developing notions of "risk governance" understand that decisions about potential unknown but systemic risks have to be understood as the outcome of complex interplays between multiple actors, not least in that converging technologies are embedded in the larger contexts of societal processes (e.g., van Asselt and Renn, 2011).

Therefore, the new governance framework implies a move away from a reliance on the top-down risk-based, regulatory approach to one that attempts to set the parameters of a system within which people and institutions behave, such that innovation achieves desired outcomes (Roco, 2008; and Chapter 3). Science and innovation can be shaped in responsible ways (Guston, 2008). The new framework will be characterized by: (i) anticipation as early as possible of plausible impacts and consequences; (ii) reflection about what is being done and what different outcomes might emerge and their acceptability, and about individuals' responsibilities and accountabilities; (iii) open discussion and debate involving all those who seek to innovate as well as those who may be affected; and (iv) responsiveness and flexibility so that options are kept open and decisions and controls can be reversed or changed in the light of new knowledge, aspirations, and priorities (see Chapter 2).

A governance framework with these characteristics does not seek to discourage innovation or to impose moratoria on development. It is one that understands precaution (as in the sense of the precautionary principle (Fisher, 2002; de Sadeleer, 2010; Stirling, 2009)) not as some kind of rule upon which to base decisions, but a process to follow when regulation is especially subject to intractable uncertainty. This process recognizes that emerging technologies raise questions which are trans-scientific in nature (Weinberg, 1972). That is, they extend beyond issues of risk and risk management to fundamental questions about the direction, application, and control of innovation (e.g., RCEP, 2008).

Our task in this chapter is to introduce the components and characteristics of this governance framework. Other chapters (e.g., Chapter 5, Chapter 2, and Chapter 3) consider in more detail their operation. First, by way of context we position responsible innovation within the broader concern about the need for the opening up of traditional, expert-led risk characterization, and management approaches which underpin technology development and regulation. The chapter then focuses on the notions of responsibility and accountability and how innovation at the earliest stages of research, and by scientists themselves, can be more open and reflective. We then turn to consider the types of regulatory tools that might bring more formal accountability to the governance of innovative technologies and their products, focusing on the points within the innovation and product network at which regulatory intervention might be appropriate and effective. However, we will show that there are shortfalls in the regulatory toolkit when dealing with innovation and novelty. The consequences of these are considered. We suggest that there is a necessary dependence on soft law and co-operative approaches to embed notions of responsibility in the early stages of research and innovation. This leads us to consider the fundamental principles of an effective governance framework and to reflect on progress in, and requirements for, development of the essential tools to ensure anticipation, reflection, deliberation, and responsiveness. We use nanotechnologies as a frequent example, because compared to some technologies that are still nascent they (at least in terms of the first and second generation nanotechnologies) have gone from the lab bench to use and so it is possible to examine multiple opportunities for governance.

8.2   Risk and Adaptive Governance

Traditionally, risk management frameworks have sought to manage the impacts of technological innovation at the point at which decisions are required concerning individual technologies, when possible impacts are amenable to identification and, hence, decisions can be taken about their acceptability. At these points management depends on effective risk characterization and responses from a range of related actors. Notwithstanding the inherent limitations of understanding impacts and responses to them, the problem is that a focus on the point of risk identification may be too late. It may also be suboptimal because of the inability to capture and affect the myriad of sectoral interests and the globally dispersed points of innovation (particularly around production and use).

Thus, settling questions about the impacts of new materials and technologies consistently and in a timely fashion using risk-based regulatory frameworks is increasingly difficult. Collingridge (1980) characterized this as a technology control dilemma: not enough is known in the early stages of a technology to establish the most appropriate controls, and yet by the time problems (e.g., in terms of human and environmental health) start to emerge the technology may be too entrenched within society to be changed without major disruption. Collingridge suggests that one response to the dilemma lies in corrigibility and the development of technology by means of steps that are easily corrected if shown to be mistaken.

To take the example of nanomaterials, there are genuine health and safety concerns in relation to human exposure and a degree of acceptance of the potential for health and environmental risks emanating from free, engineered nanoscale materials. It is also possible that fixed nanoparticles might pose a threat over their lifecycle (Chaudhry *et al.*, 2005). However, the extent to which fears over safety are well-grounded is itself a matter of uncertainty, as the hypothesized risks posed by nanomaterials are far from fully investigated. This type of information asymmetry is a common reason for regulatory intervention and it has certainly prompted a number of reviews of the efficacy of present regulatory structures (Frater *et al.*, 2006; Defra, 2006; FSA, 2006; HSE, 2006; RA/REng, 2004; RCEP, 2008). In general, while existing regulatory frameworks are considered to have the potential capacity to control possible nanotechnology risks, adaptation of regulatory frameworks would be required (at both national and international scale) to achieve this. But even then regulation might only be able to deal with the physical risks that can be identified, such that the building blocks for regulation in terms of definitions, metrics, standards, and protocols can give it effect in framing criminal sanctions. Risk as yet to be identified and understood would remain a problem.

For nanotechnologies available now there are still fundamental societal, political, and economic questions around ownership, the direction of innovation and distribution of gains and losses. In relation to future nanotechnologies (often referred to as third and fourth generation technologies) fundamental ethical and political questions still need to be debated (for example, around human identity, performance, and privacy) (RCEP, 2008).

The debates around the governance of innovation fit then within a much wider context, which has gathered pace over the last three decades, concerning the assessment and management of technological risk. In a "Risk Society" (Beck, 1992) there is recognition of the dangers of uncontrolled and unregulated science and technology. But traditional risk assessment approaches, which have underpinned regulatory control, are fundamentally limited. The International Risk Governance Council (IRGC) (IRGC, 2009) through multiple case studies usefully summarizes 10 deficits in risk assessment, encompassing difficulties around the gathering and interpretation of knowledge about risks and perception of risks, combined with disputed or potentially biased or subjective knowledge, and with deficits of knowledge related to systems and their complexities. The answers delivered in risk assessment typically depend on the framing of the analysis – not just "what" informs the framing but importantly "who" (e.g., Harrimoes, 2001; Jasanoff, 1990; Stirling, 2008; Wynne, 1987).

Risk governance literature has consistently stressed the principles of communication and inclusion, integration of all relevant knowledge and experience, and repeated reflection about uncertainty, ambiguity, and complexity. The risks and benefits of new technologies have to be debated and reflected upon as they can rarely be considered in terms of "how safe is safe enough?" but rather "how much uncertainty is the collective willing to exchange for some benefit(s)?" (van Asselt and Renn, 2011).

Analytic-deliberative approaches have been presented and increasingly tested as potential means to counter failures to recognize different framings of risk (Macnaghten, 2010; Renn *et al.*, 1995; Stern and Fineberg, 1996). By emphasizing the involvement of multiple perspectives and voices (scientists, risk analysts, stakeholders, and, importantly, members of the public) at all stages of assessment, through discussion and challenge of information and views, it is argued that fairness of decision process, competency of assessment, as well as social learning can be enhanced (Renn *et al.*, 1995; Webler, *et al.*, 1995).

The testing of analytic-deliberative processes has gathered pace but has often been "downstream," for example, around the point of application of risky technologies such as the siting of a nuclear waste repository. Such real-world tests have consistently shown that well-designed deliberative processes can allow all participants (and particularly the lay public) to move quickly from little knowledge and no opinions on a risk issue to understanding the key issues of even the most complex scientific and technological developments. But what most frequently emerges are fundamental concerns and divergent views about the need for the technology in the first place, as well as questioning about why people/organizations want to develop it, what they are going to gain from it, and what other impacts it might have – that is, questions of purpose, motivation (Chapter 2 and unforeseen risks (e.g., Bhattachary *et al.*, 2010; Doubleday, 2007). In other words there is a demand for more than risk management, at a much earlier intersection with the innovation ecosystem. The argument therefore to go "upstream" in terms of deliberation and public engagement has become loud (e.g., Pidgeon and Rogers-Hayden, 2007; Stilgoe and Wilsdon, 2007 – see also Chapter 5). But certainly in the UK, governmental views of this have still often been restricted to promoting understanding and debating fears around a potentially controversial technology in advance of significant application (as has happened around the multiple public debates on GM crops) (Pidgeon *et al.*, 2005). It is still about risk regulation, rather than a more vital discussion about science, values, and what society expects from technology-based innovation (Stilgoe, 2007; and Chapters 3 and 4). So rather than just upstream engagement and downstream control (both are essential) innovation governance debates have increasingly focused on the notion of "responsible" innovation.

8.3   Responsibility and Accountability

Responsibility, etymologically derived from the word response, or to answer, implies a communicative structure. Responsible innovation seeks to achieve desirable outcomes (Chapter 3)). This is seen not as an aim in itself but rather as a contributing factor to the overall good (explored, for example, by Von Schomberg (2011) in relation to Information and Communication Technologies (ICT)). So responsible (research and) innovation implies a *dialogue* between those involved in the process of innovation and wider society "with a view to the (ethical) acceptability, sustainability and societal desirability of the innovation process and its marketable products . . ." (Von Schomberg, 2011, p. 9; Von Schomberg, this volume). This implies a mutuality of interest and a collective responsibility for scientific advance.

Such a notion of "responsibility" is widely drawn and conforms to common understandings of the term as referring to a capability of fulfilling an obligation, as well as a quality of being trustworthy or reliable (Oxford English Dictionary (OED)). Thus a researcher may be some way from envisioning the technological end use of an innovative breakthrough, but is not absolved from responsibility for reflecting on where the findings might lead, or from a degree of stewardship over the research that reflects the trust that scientists might wish society to place in them. This could be a challenging role for a researcher who prefers to perfect the science first and think about the implications later, which in turn may leave a "fundamental gap between the technologically-enhanced power of industrialized societies to create futures, and our ability as agents within these societies to take responsibility for the kinds of futures we create" (Groves, 2006). Certainly, as science has become increasingly connected with application, and most recently with many of the global or "grand" challenges (sustainable development; climate change; health; food and water security, etc.), questions of responsibility have become much harder to ignore.

Nanotechnology became a test case for a new model of responsible scientific governance. Specifically, the European Union considered that the uncertainties of nanotechnology justified some form of early governance through a "Code of Conduct for

Responsible Nanosciences and Nanotechnologies Research" (EC, 2008). However, difficulties arose when one of the key principles suggested that researchers should "remain accountable" for the social, environmental and human health impacts that their research may impose on present and future generations. The word "remain" would suggest that researchers already face some degree of accountability for the consequences of their research, but that this might also be extended in scope (to include, e.g., social consequences) and time (to include future generations). In practice, however, it is difficult to envisage quite what accountability currently faces scientific researchers, beyond those enshrined in conventions of scientific research or in contracts with funding bodies. These place demands on researchers that are in general much more narrowly and immediately drawn; for example, in terms of duties not to fabricate results or misapply funds.

The main objections voiced about the principles in the European Code related to the language of "accountability." It was thought to be an unrealistic and unfair obligation to place upon researchers and ill-suited to a spirit of open-minded and creative inquiry through research. Interestingly, the objection in certain countries, such as Germany and France, was that the term accountability was close to the juridical idea of liability, which can be defined as being charged with a legal obligation that might be enforced by private or public law. Although this might seem to be a case of the concept being lost in translation, it would be foolish to overlook this objection. In English, being accountable refers to the sense of being called to account for, or to answer for conduct or the discharge of a duty (OED). The dictionary offers the closest single word as "amenableness," and as such implies a legal connotation; one would generally speak of a person being amenable to the jurisdiction of a court.

From broad areas of responsibility we might choose to narrow in on more discrete points of accountability in order to ensure that there is some answerability for egregious, perhaps reckless or negligent, failures. But arguably the principle in the Code of Conduct was mistaken in its choice of a principle of accountability on researchers for sweeping consequences of multiple species of harm across differing timeframes. It would have been better to have adopted notions of responsibility in the sense of requiring some reflection by the researcher on unwelcome possibilities over time, and wider debate and engagement on these issues in order to engender a sense of care and responsiveness (see also Chapter 2). This does not mean that there is no room for accountability. Researchers might be called to account on certain issues (such as laboratory safety or pollution) and some of the wider duties envisaged by the Code within accountability structures, but possibly at a much later point in the chain of innovation.

The time dimension of responsibility is important – that is, are we considering responsibility after the fact or before? If concerned about regulatory concepts of liability and blame, particularly when science and innovation is so uncertain then a prospective or anticipatory view of responsibility, that is more about care and responsiveness than liability, is appropriate (Pellizzoni, 2004; and Chapters 7 and 2). Importantly, taking care has to be a collective responsibility given the understanding of innovation as involving a network of actors and actions (Chapter 1). It is as much about the process of doing science and innovation as their products. What motivates a scientist, and with what purpose they embark on particular research is as important as how they do their work (Stilgoe, 2010).

In governance terms, frameworks and appropriate tools have to be created to assist the funders of research and scientists to reflect on their aims and the possible outcomes and to do this in as open a manner as possible. Some of the UK Research Councils have been trialing a number of new mechanisms to prompt this. For example, the Engineering and Physical Sciences Research Council (EPSRC) formed a Societal Issues Panel (SIP) in 2007 to advise the Council directly. Importantly, it stressed the need for the Council to broaden funding decision processes to encompass not just oversight through traditional ethical requirements, but more fundamentally to publicly question which areas of science should be funded (i.e., seeking to understand how to spend public money in the public interest). Public engagement through deliberative processes has been one mechanism to open discussion on the purposes of science and innovation. Some large-scale engagement processes have been organized before funding programs have commenced (e.g., around nanotechnologies for health care) (Jones, 2008)) in order to help understand how the public might respond to new technologies, and whether some forms of innovation (and hence scientific funding through public bodies) might be considered unacceptable. In other cases (e.g., the synthetic biology public dialogue (Bhattachary *et al.*, 2010) initiated by the UK Biotechnology and Biological Sciences Research Council (BBSRC) and EPSRC) there was a focus on exposing funded scientists to the range of public views on an issue, not least to assist in the development of effective ongoing communication and engagement. Public engagement might be decried as merely orchestrated talk, but certainly members of the synthetic biology community have responded that it is "dialogue or bust" in terms of the development of the field (Macilwain, 2010).

Requiring applicants for funding to think through the implications of their research has been trialed through novel forms of "risk registers" to encourage researchers to think about the wider implications of their intended research at the point of application for funding (Owen and Goldberg, 2010). When research has been funded the EPSRC has also tested a "stage gate" process (drawn from strategic innovation management but with echoes of Collingridge (1980) and corrigibility). Traditionally, for example, in product development, a decision to move to the next stage of work is contingent on passing through a decision "gate," often focused on technical feasibility and market development. In the EPSRC, geoengineering research program stage-gating was used for one of the first projects looking at candidate particles for solar radiation management. The stage gate went considerably beyond the questions that would normally be asked through peer review or university ethics committees or under current regulations, by requiring dimensions of anticipation and responsiveness of the researchers to think about future potential applications of the technology and to put in place mechanisms to understand wider public and stakeholder views. This trial has encountered a number of difficulties (Macnaghten and Owen, 2011), not least because the decision criteria were not developed and applied until after the project had been funded. However, this was very much an experiment (see Chapter 2 for more details).

Whether "upstream" public engagement, or research risk registers, or stage gating – the fundamental issue is that *all parties are clear on the expectations*. Whether it is a member of the public who takes part in a dialogue process and who wants to know what difference their contribution will make, or a scientist who wants to understand the purpose of being required to think about the future application of the products of their research and to engage non-traditional stakeholders in this debate. In both instances participants will be challenged by their engagement.

Such experiments are part of a natural rhythm to responsible innovation supported by soft law processes, based on self-regulation and the assumption of responsibility, early in the innovation cycle, which might evolve into more hard law structures of accountability as the contours of the risks begin to emerge.

8.4   The Rationale for Regulation

Ordinarily, in liberal market economies, regulation is via the market, and the expression of market choice directs goods and services resulting from technological innovation to their most desired end use. Given the inherent efficiency of this market ordering, intervention to constrain it may be inappropriate, except where there is reason to believe that the market process is failing for some reason. Over time, broad reasons for intervention develop, such as external costs or other "externalities" generated by activity. This may give rise to broad regulatory objectives for protective legislation to safeguard those who otherwise bear the social costs, such as consumers, workers, the environment, and so on. It may become apparent that there are certain products, such as foodstuffs, where the costs of poorly-exercised market choice (in terms of buying unsafe food) could be particularly high. Equally there may be certain points in a product life cycle at which a product could become more dangerous (e.g., in the hands of a child or when abandoned at the end of life). In this way, regulations may be shaped according to three axes, namely product type (toys, food, pharmaceuticals, etc.), points in the product lifecycle (research and development (R&D), introduction to the market, end of life, and the like) and objective (worker or consumer safety, environmental protection, etc.).

Alongside this there are considerations of regulatory method. At one end of the spectrum, goods posing little foreseeable harm may be considered safe to circulate freely on the market, with no prior approval and with little warning or labeling as to use. At the opposite end of the scale, substances may be so hazardous that they need to be banned from sale. Between these two extremes there is a range of regulatory possibilities. These may mandate particular action with sanctions for breach (so-called "command and control" measures) or they may seek to influence conduct either through processes of providing information (such as labeling), or through providing economic incentives or disincentives (e.g., through the tax system) to alter behavior. Along this spectrum of regulatory instruments is advice, so that an objective might be pursued by the promotion of an advisory standard. This might be done where there is insufficient knowledge (toxicological, economic, epidemiological, etc.) to develop a binding standard, even though this may be thought desirable, leaving an advisory standard as the only feasible option.

This suggests that when dealing with novel applications of a technology, at least in the initial stages, it may be necessary to resort to soft law instruments. Over time, better risk characterization may allow the introduction of more precautionary stances and these can be supported by mechanisms such as labeling (Stokes, 2011). Later still, risk assessment processes may lead to the finding of possible harm and there may then be various sorts of restrictions employed to limit impact. Whether these are restrictions on sale/use or some form of licensing to engage in sale or other activity, these types of processes are likely to be in the nature of command and control. This term refers to a form of direct regulation which makes demands of those subject to it, with non-compliance leading to sanctions (Steinzor, 1998). However, although the imposition of sanctions implies a hard law structure, in practice, compliance under such systems may be accompanied by soft law approaches (Sinclair, 1997). This is because the regulator is likely to view the most severe sanctions (such as criminal penalties or revocation of a licence) as very much a weapon of last resort. In reality, the task becomes one of steering the regulated community away from such measures by a process which starts with education and persuasion.

To support this, soft law instruments such as codes of practice or guidance may be deployed, and, if successful, it may prove unnecessary to revert to the weapons in the hard law armory. So, while regulation of novel technologies and products may be able to strive for little other than a soft law approach, this is only a second best approach in the sense that experience shows that at the margins some stick might usefully be required to accompany the soft law carrot (Robalino and Lempert, 2000; Sinclair, 1997).

The shifting terrain of regulation, from soft to hard and back to soft again would suggest that the type of regulatory device to be employed is neither certain nor fixed for all time. It may adapt over time, in accordance with an appreciation of changing behaviors under conditions of regulation. Basically, regulation pursues two tasks. The first lays down broad conditions of how the market operates. The second does something quite different, by intervening in the market as a corrective to market failure. It is possible to demonstrate how both of these are present in relation to research and innovation. In advance of goods being placed on the market, in the early stages of product innovation, the market corrective process of regulation is unlikely and is difficult to devise amidst widespread contingency concerning the possible outcomes and endpoints of R&D. At this point, wider governance mechanisms, rather than hard law regulation, will be better suited to promote collective responsibility along the chain of innovation. Later, after market introduction, further product-specific regulation may be introduced in an attempt to curb or internalize social costs arising out of identifiable hazards presented by the product.

Before, (re)turning to questions of innovation governance, we explore accountability mechanisms enshrined in law at the point at which products are brought to the market.

8.5   Risk Regulation and Accountability for Product Safety

There is much risk regulation which focuses both on products and their lifecycles, as well as activities and their potential for harm. So wide-ranging is this regulation that much of it will be capable of adaptation where novel risks arise out of technological development. However, this is a process that will take time and, as indicated above, it may involve the transition from initial soft law approaches to hard law responses in due course. This may give the impression that, at the most risky point, at which novel materials, products, or applications emerge (where there is little experience of their use or behaviors) there is an almost lawless environment, or at least one in which there is little control other than some form of appeal to the good sense of the producer to operate with caution. This is not quite so, however, since it overlooks a large body of general, background law that is almost certainly applicable.

To begin with, in Europe, there are general liability regimes, to be found in measures such as the General Product Safety (GPS) Directive (European Community, 2001) or General Food Law (GFL) Regulation (178/2002/EC). The GPS regime provides that only "safe" consumer products (not including food and drink – see below) may be placed on the market. A product is safe if it presents no risks to consumers, or only the minimum risks compatible with the product's ordinary use. Note that this is a different notion of "safety" to that which is found in the Product Liability Directive considered below. Under the Directive it is permissible for EU Member States to introduce a due diligence defense and the UK has done so. As there is no limitation period in most countries for criminal offences, prosecution could theoretically be brought some years after placement on the market, where risks are slow to materialize. Because this is a Directive, it is differently transposed across the Member States of the EU (Faure, 2000), but on the face of it, and especially if no due diligence defense is invoked, the wording of the Directive is strict.

The General Food Regulation (often referred to as the General Food Law (European Community, 2002) also provides that only safe food and drink may be placed on the market. Safe food is food which is not injurious to health and is fit for human consumption. Interestingly, for these purposes, Art 14(4) expressly provides that, in assessing whether food is injurious to health, regard should be had (inter alia): "not only to the probable immediate and/or short-term and/or long-term effects of that food on the health of a person consuming it, but also on subsequent generations" and "to the probable cumulative toxic effects." Again, the UK has introduced a due diligence defense. It might also be worth mentioning in this category of general safety laws, the Environmental Liability Directive (European Community, 2004), which establishes a common framework for liability with a view to preventing and remedying damage to animals, plants, natural habitats and water resources, and other damage affecting land. Strict liability (that is, liability without the need to prove fault) attaches where such damage is the result of emissions to the environment from certain specified occupational activities, which tend to be those operating under environmental permits under EU law.

Perhaps the most important of these measures is the Product Liability Directive (European Community, 1985) which introduces strict liability for harm caused by product defects. According to Article 6 of the Directive: "A product is defective when it does not provide the safety which a person is entitled to expect, taking all circumstances into account . . . ." This is a potentially useful formulation when considering risks posed by novel materials incorporated within products, since consumer expectations of the safety of the product may have developed prior to any change in the product's composition. The notion of safety which a person "is entitled to" expect means that test is usually represented as one of legitimate (objective) rather than actual (subjective) expectation. Commentators (Miller and Goldberg, 2004) have suggested that this means that the cost and practicability of a safer design and/or risk-utility analysis may form part of the assessment. This is a matter of some controversy. By including issues such as cost, practicality, utility, and the like one runs the risk of diluting the core concept that liability should be strict. Limiting factors such as cost or practicality of precaution are used in civil law in determining breach of duty, which assigns liability for risks which could be foreseen. Owen *et al.* in Chapter 2 rehearse the reasons why this approach may be less than satisfactory in the context of technological innovation and the European strict liability regime was introduced precisely to remedy such shortfalls.

There are a variety of possible defects that one could envisage, both in manufacture and design, but this could clearly also include informational shortfalls, such as the failure to warn of potential hazards under types of use. Liability attaches to the "producer" of the product, but this also goes beyond the manufacturer to include a party importing a product into the EU. Liability is strict, so, on the face of it, even if the producer could not have foreseen or prevented harm there can be liability. However, it remains necessary to prove causation – that it was the product that caused the harm complained of; in the language of Article 4: "The injured person shall be required to prove the damage, the defect, and the causal relationship between defect and damage." This proof of causal relationship may remain a considerable challenge under conditions of uncertainty attaching to novel substances. Moreover, there are two defenses. A limitation period is introduced by Article 11 under which: "... rights conferred upon the injured person pursuant to this Directive shall be extinguished upon the expiry of a period of 10 years from the date on which the producer put into circulation the actual product which caused ... damage." Given longer tail manifestation of harm (think asbestos) attaching to certain substances, this has the potential to bar significant product liability claims. Finally, there is a state of the art defense under which a producer may avoid liability where it can be shown "that the state of scientific and technical knowledge at the time when he put the product into circulation was not such as to enable the existence of the defect to be discovered" (Article 7(e)).

Though much-criticized, this "development risks defense" represents a conscious balancing act between industry and consumer interests, and was introduced when the pharmaceuticals industry, in particular, lobbied on the theme that absolute liability would deter innovation. Moreover, in some of the European cases, the Court of Justice has tended to try to balance out liability by referring back to the recitals in the Directive. This includes recital 2 which states: "Whereas liability without fault on the part of the producer is the sole means of adequately solving the problem, peculiar to our age of increasing technicality, of a fair apportionment of the risks inherent in modern techno-logical production..." and also recital 7 which states: "Whereas a fair apportionment of risk between the injured person and the producer implies that the producer should be able to free himself from liability if he furnishes proof as to the existence of certain exonerating circumstances...." Thus, where the development risk is adopted by Member States it has clear capacity to dilute the strict liability principles of the regime in a manner to which the Court may prove sympathetic. In so doing, however, the economic rationale of the Directive is weakened, as the idea is to internalize the costs of risk into the price of the product. If this is done successfully then it would follow that, over time, safer products would gain some market price advantage, thereby providing encouragement for greater R&D – so called "technology forcing" (Stapleton, 2006).

If we assume that producers are unlikely to knowingly place a defective product on the market, then routes to liability are likely to lie in shortfalls in development. This can include inadequate research underpinning the product, perhaps because of too great a focus on product design as opposed to issues like toxicity testing and even considerations of how a product might be used. Failure to monitor accessible data on the use and behavior of products, such as available warning signs or other potential indications of risk (including accumulative or synergetic effects) can heighten the prospect of liability; so too can poor decision-making about warnings or instructions for use, or failures to take advice from regulatory agencies. In the face of these prospects of liability, it is of course open to parties in an innovation chain to construct their own processes of risk allocation. This is done through what the EU institutions generally refer to as contractual liability structures, but which in practice rests upon warranties (about issues such as quality) and indemnities in the supply chain. This allocation of risk will prompt insurance coverage. In practice, the role of insurance in this area may be to cover exercises of product recall rather than to respond to liability and will generate some private standard-setting through the use of premium weighting, based on performance monitoring, together with variable deductibles and other incentives for safe behavior.

Even without product safety and liability legislation, civil law systems may respond in the event of loss or damage caused by technologies. A duty may arise where those involved in innovation can envisage that certain acts or omissions on their part could lead to foreseeable injury to a range of parties unless care is taken. Facing such a duty, it may not be difficult to establish its breach where there is a departure from good industry practice. However, it must be borne in mind that the defendant's conduct is to be assessed according to standards applicable *at the time of any negligent action*, and not by the standards known at a later point in time when litigation ensues (Harrington, 2002). In considering whether or not the duty owed has been breached, the courts will generally take into account three issues, namely: the risk of injury; the practicability of any precautions which might have been taken; and the importance of the object to be attained in the running of the enterprise. Broadly, the greater the risk of injury, the greater the onus upon the innovator to introduce precaution, and it becomes less and less likely that any benefit said to be inherent in the innovation will override any risk of injury to the claimant (Landes and Posner, 1987).

One might conclude from this overview of the general law of product safety that there are background mechanisms of accountability from the outset of any innovative activity which might have harmful effects. However, these accountability principles are limited in civil law by notions of fault, driven largely by principles of foreseeability. Overlaid on this are stronger civil or even criminal law structures of strict liability, but these too are diluted by available defenses. Moreover, all of these formulations depend on satisfying tests of causation which might be difficult to prove, especially amidst prevailing uncertainty. Therefore, the task becomes one of revisiting more specific frameworks of regulation in order to adapt these to accommodate the risks which may attach to novelty arising out of research and innovation.

8.6   The Adaptation of Risk Regulation

In the face of rapid technological advance, regulators are likely to face considerable difficulties in fulfilling their regulatory brief, given the novelty of materials and their capacity for new applications not previously falling within the regulatory domain. Even if it is clear about the need to bring new substances within regulation, gaps in toxicological and other data may render this problematic (Lee and Jose, 2008). In such circumstances some form of self-regulation may carry great appeal as the best way to engender anticipatory and proactive management of emerging risks, and integrate areas of concern. This type of thinking lay behind rather unsuccessful voluntary reporting initiatives for nanotechnologies in the UK (Defra, 2006) and the USA (US EPA, 2009) and behind the EU's "Nanotechnology Action Plan" (European Commission, 2005) in Europe. The appeal here is to ethical behavior, transparency, and inclusiveness in the process of innovation, with the suggestion that industry might gain by integrating societal considerations into the development of technologies. At this stage, these types of appeals may be supported by soft law instruments, such as codes of practice, as happened with nanotechnology in both the UK (Insight Investment *et al.*, 2008) and Europe (EC, 2008), see above. Such soft law instruments derive much legitimacy from the processes of engagement through which they emerge, though we would argue that the *type* of deliberative processes which may lie behind the development of such soft laws is fundamental to good governance, irrespective of this legitimating function.

Eventually, better knowledge of risk, together with shared understanding of the technologies, will allow the development of hard law instruments such as regulations, where necessary. These may be new, or they are more likely to be an adaptation of existing regulation to cover new developments (see below). These hard law measures can appear strict, or even punitive (Baldwin, 2004). An example would be of regulations that allow activity only to be conducted if it is licenced; here the licence can be revoked and the business closed or criminal penalties imposed in the absence of compliance with the licence conditions. Surprisingly quickly, this type of licensing mechanism has been put into place in Europe to facilitate carbon capture and storage and one could envisage this model being used for other geoengineering activity, such as seeding plankton to draw carbon dioxide into an ocean. However, regulators rarely want, or may not be able to afford, to use the sanctions that attach to such command and control structures. In practice, while these serve to underpin the regime, the vast majority of regulatory activity lies in education, persuasion, and appeals to corporate social responsibility, supported by more soft law in the form of guidance or standards (Ayres and Braithwaite, 1992; Gunningham and Grabosky, 1998).

The time taken to move from self-regulation to incorporating novel materials or activity within existing regulation will generally depend on the knowledge base surrounding technological development. Risk assessment processes necessarily involve elements of uncertainty and indeterminacy, but it may be that a paucity of available scientific knowledge regarding the properties of novel materials or activities will limit the capacity for hazard characterization and assessment, as has been the case for nanomaterials. For example, in the absence of appropriate dose-response and exposure data to help resolve questions regarding the appropriateness of safety thresholds, it may be more appropriate to act in a precautionary manner. This will certainly be so where a credible threat has been identified, even if its scope and impact is scientifically uncertain. The existing regulatory framework has to begin a process of adaptation to allow transparent and proportionate decision-making, which may need to proceed on a case-by-case basis, and which will be subject to review as new information becomes available. This adaptation process can be considered in the light of the possible shortcomings in existing regulatory coverage. This can be done by reviewing common regulatory devices to ensure the protection of the environment and human health, which may need to be the subject of adaptation in the face of innovation (Frater *et al.*, 2006).

One common form of regulation is to set a threshold to restrict the presence of a substance in a product so that it is reduced to a volume quite clearly regarded as safe. This threshold can be set in different ways. Assuming that there is no outright ban then the substance may be limited according to its weight, percentage of the product, or concentration. For novel substances, however, there may be no such threshold, and any particular threshold may be difficult to establish and defend. In the case of nanomaterials, there may be a particular difficulty here. Existing thresholds will have been set in accordance with established safe levels for conventional (bulk) substances. The reason why nanomaterials may have been incorporated into the product may be precisely because these exhibit different properties to their conventional counterparts (RCEP, 2008). Precisely because this is the case, however, there is a danger that any regulatory thresholds will be inappropriately pitched to capture risks arising from the inclusion of nanomaterials. Indeed it may be that the conventional substance has itself never been the subject of a threshold, being regarded as entirely safe, with the need for some restriction only becoming apparent as information becomes available. There are a wide variety of consumer goods, ranging from food through cosmetics to electronics, where this approach is taken.

A similar issue arises where certain substances of concern are listed in order that they may be regulated. This approach is famously taken in European chemicals regulation under the Regulation on the Registration, Evaluation, Authorization, and Restriction of Chemicals (REACH) (Lee and Vaughan, 2010). Each separate use of a "substance of very high concern" ("SVHC") as listed in Annex XIV of REACH will be subject to authorization by the Commission. Without a time-limited authorization the substance cannot be placed on the market in the EU. A number of substances will be automatically considered as SVHCs, triggering authorization requirements, including: carcinogens, mutagens and reproductive toxins. Substances which are persistent, bio-accumulative, or toxic will be included in this category, as will substances which are very persistent or very bio-accumulative. Moreover, other substances (including novel substances) may be identified and added on a case-by-case basis. An everyday example of this listing approach is available in the area of waste management. In the EU, the List of Wastes, which replaced the "European Waste Catalogue" (EC, 2000/532/EC), provides for the classification of wastes, and signals, by the addition of an asterisk, which wastes should be considered hazardous. Like any list, the List of Wastes may need to be updated, but without such revision the particular controls on the disposal of hazardous substances may be ineffective over time. To take one example, no amendment has been made to the list to take account of the possible presence of nanomaterials in waste streams.

Because of the continual need to update schedules or lists of materials, a preferred approach, especially when allowing goods to enter the market, is to single out products which are novel for regulatory scrutiny, while allowing products equivalent to those already on the market to circulate freely. Schemes requiring that products, not seen as like or equivalent to authorized products, must be approved before being placed on the market, depend on a judgment call by the producer of such goods, who should draw the attention of the regulator to the product in order to gain regulatory approval. This ought to be done for novel materials, but if, say, nanoparticles of salt are used in foodstuffs, in order to reduce the quantity of salt used, is this then a novel food or not? The capacity of pre-market authorization processes to identify potential risks in this example depends on a determination about whether the product is treated as being *equivalent* to authorized products, such as conventional salts, already on the market. Note, that reform of the European regulation on Novel Foods (EC Regulation 258/97, 1997) stumbled, in 2011, over how to handle technological innovation in food, namely whether to ban food produced from clones and their offspring.

The UK Royal Commission on Environmental Pollution (RCEP, 2008) recommended a review of REACH, not least because the 1 tonne threshold for registration of a material is too high to capture potentially problematic effects of a very large number of nanoparticles, and stressed an incremental approach (favored by the European Commission) to consideration of regulatory control, as new evidence and understanding is collated. In this case an approach that more specifically focuses on the functionality of specific new materials (as opposed to merely a focus on the general technology that creates them) was advocated. Incremental development has to be supported by clarity about priorities – in the case of nanomaterials for testing those with functionality which suggests that they might pose the greatest risk.

Another possibility currently being explored, and in some contexts implemented, is additional product labeling. Soon, in the EU, all cosmetic products (EC Regulation No. 1223/2009 on cosmetic products, Article 19) and foodstuffs (EC Regulation No. 1169/2011 on the provision of food information to consumers, Article 18) containing engineered nanomaterial ingredients will be required to carry the label "nano" before being placed on the market. Such measures hold the attraction that they slot easily into existing EU consumer protection legislation, which has long focused on values of information disclosure and informed consumer choice. Given that manufacturers and suppliers are already subject to a host of legal provisions on the labeling of products, it makes sense to add "nano" to the regulatory repertoire without disrupting existing legislative rules and routines. As well as the familiarity of product labeling as a regulatory device, nano-labeling offers the added benefit of establishing some degree of certainty in an otherwise uncertain and complex market. Since, as explained above, the tools and techniques needed to characterize nanomaterials are lacking, or available in relation to only a limited proportion of the nanotechnology sector, in their absence legislatures are understandably reluctant to introduce more interventionist means of regulation, notwithstanding considerable pressure to ensure that the products and processes of nanotechnology are brought under control. Labeling helps to create certainty over market entry conditions and product content, even if it leaves unanswered other important questions about nanotechnology's potential social and ethical implications. Its capacity to overlay existing legislative frameworks is, however, also one of its more problematic features, because it assumes that the current use of product labels is an appropriate and effective way of mobilizing consumer and citizen interests. The extent to which labels provide consumers with genuine instruments of choice is debatable, not least because the content and use of pseudo-scientific terms like "nano" are limited. Moreover, by restricting opportunities for consumer engagement and choice to the market place, the utility of product labeling is time and space limited to the supermarket. The question is, without other meaningful processes to provide information, promote engagement, and engender open disclosure, what does the label "nano" really convey (see also Chapter 13)?

Where substances are regulated, one issue is whether they are fully regulated throughout their lifecycle. As noted earlier, the tendency to a linear view of lifecycles is limiting and partial. For example, nanomaterials may form part of the laboratory waste stream and their flushing away with waste waters will not be at the end of their life but the beginning of a new life in the aquatic environment. Any review of regulation reveals that certain points in the life cycle (such as placing a product on the market) are commonly singled out for regulatory attention at a convenient point at which controls may be instigated. This often piecemeal approach may be exacerbated by the background to regulatory intervention and the tendency to regulate in an *ad hoc* fashion following some form of crisis (Haines, 2009). This hardly provides the most considered approach to when, across the life cycle of a substance, risks might materialize. With novel materials there is at least the risk that this point in the lifecycle may be quite different to that of other types of substances falling within regulation. In one sense, this is simply a matter of risk characterization, but it is easy to overlook if we place too much faith in our capacity to adapt existing regulation to suit technological advance.

Finally, it is important to note that often what is regulated is not a product but a process. This type of regulation is commonly found in the areas of health and safety at work and in environmental protection. So, for example, environmental permitting will authorize industrial processes and activity subject to conditions, including a condition that the process employs best available techniques. Under these sorts of command and control structures, technical standards will underpin permit conditions in order to ensure environmental protection. To take an example, the Groundwater Regulations 1998 prohibit the release to the environment of List I substances and restrict the release of those substances in List II. As with the sorts of lists considered above, these need to keep abreast of the behavior of substances and should identify the unique properties and potential risks associated with the novel substances. There are exemptions under the regulations, but these are inevitably reliant on technical knowledge of the risks posed to the environment by substances either singly or acting synergistically with other substances. Protective laws concerning safety, health, and environment are often iterative in nature, in the sense that experience drawn from untoward incidents in the past can lead to safer futures. The problem with novelty is that there may be little experience to draw upon. Moreover, this experience is transformed under regulation into quite practical instruments, such as safety data sheets to assist in the workplace management of hazardous substances. Where there is the lack of sufficient information and knowledge on toxicological hazards and appropriate exposure limits it may be difficult to provide the relevant data and undertake the necessary risk assessments.

8.7   Adaptive Innovation Governance: Limits and Needs

Our discussion of governance tools within the overall innovation ecosystem suggests that there may be a continuum, from engendering responsibility through self-regulation and soft law measures to introducing more formal accountability through regulation. However, the analysis confirms that no single element is either more important or robust than any other, not only because of the uncertainty and ambiguity surrounding emerging technologies, but because the points (sectoral, spatial, temporal) for interruption and control within the system are hugely diffuse. Tools need to be *adapted and adaptive* (i.e., responsive to changing societal views and expectations about technologies). In this context we return here to summarize the underlying limits to innovation governance.

First, are issues of scale. Science and innovation have "gone global." Multi-national collaborative research is now common place (for example, as supported by the EU Framework programmes). Emerging technologies break through traditional disciplinary boundaries and inherently open up opportunities for new clusters of research. So collaborative research not only steps across multiple national funding regimes but also inherently crosses multiple international, cultural, and ethical settings in which research is conducted and regulated. Not only do different codes of practice support the research, but even opening up science to public challenge and debate will bring different degrees of support for such activities, engagement, and experience. The UK is leading European experience in this regard.

The end-products of technology development will influence the scale at which regulation can be implemented and achieved. It is the propensity of products to have global reach that poses one of the greatest regulatory difficulties (Reynolds, 2003). While we have stressed the European regulatory environment of product control, regulation is, nevertheless, strongly national in focus and sensibilities. Thus, for example, for some countries the uncertainty and ambiguity around GM technology has had a significant impact on the development of the technology, while for others the issue has been of marginal importance (e.g., UK versus USA). Mandatory common labeling could be a technical barrier to trade and the EU and US are already pursuing divergent policies in relation to consumer labeling (Carter and Gruère, 2003). An international convention (in the style of the United Nations Persistent Organic Pollutants Convention) was considered for nanomaterials by the RCEP review (2008). But the conclusion focused on the sheer complexity of achieving this and the fact that, in practice, it would be unmanageable. In the end the Commission concluded that the simple but potentially powerful tool of international open exchange of information across science, government, and industry was most appropriate. Roco (2008) reflected this in his suggestion that a multidisciplinary forum or consultative group with members from various countries is needed to assist with adaptation of existing regulation, building capacity, and designing new international agreements and partnerships.

The second limitation is the sheer speed of innovation – and the "tyranny of urgency." The RCEP (2008) concluded in relation to novel materials that regulators face a "Sisyphean task" as innovation is forcing new products onto the market at rates that are orders of magnitude faster than can be hoped to be managed with the available resources. Resultant fears of being "out of control" can prompt calls for moratoria on development, as has happened in Europe and the US (Arnall, 2003). The question is whether selective moratoria might be an appropriate precautionary measure in particular circumstances.

Science itself is moving at such a pace that developments in one country (for example, in synthetic biology in the USA) could significantly impact on science in another. The UK Research Council's concern that scientists need to be ready to engage with public questioning if scientific advancement was announced in the US was actually behind the anticipatory move to a public dialogue (discussed above).

The third limitation is around understanding how, when, and with what purpose to engage multiple stakeholders and the public. While the "deliberative turn" (Goodin and Dryzek, 2006) has now captured policy attention, certainly in the UK government narratives have too often seemed to focus on the instrumental idea of "gaining public confidence" around new technologies (e.g., HM Government, 2005) as opposed to processes of collective reflection around notions of care and responsiveness (see also Chapter 5). The problem is that public engagement when done well (i.e., when it is inclusive of all key interests, is representative of the range of possible views, is well informed, allows for challenge of stated views and evidence, and is done early enough that the outcomes can effect decisions) can be time-consuming (over weeks or months) and expensive. The skill sets required to design and run an effective dialogue process are considerable. Engagement exercises to date have nearly always been time-limited: that is, they might capture a range of views at a point in time. They have often been questioned as to how representative the views expressed are of those of the wider public: but this is to misunderstand their purpose. Importantly, inclusion and dialogue do not necessarily reduce conflict or lead to greater acceptance of a technology. Even the important attempts by the UK research councils to build engagement and deliberation into decisions about research funding require a degree of honesty about the extent to which outcomes are likely to change. And of course, publicly-funded research is just one piece in the innovation jigsaw. Key decisions and agendas are often driven elsewhere – not least in the private sector.

An alternative to one-off engagement exercises might be initiatives that contribute to the "social intelligence" function of governance. RCEP (2008) recommended this as a means of providing ongoing opportunities for public and expert reflection and debate, reflecting the view that, to make a difference, public engagement has to be more a part of day-to-day science than a one-off exercise (Stilgoe, 2007; and Chapter 5). Tools such as Real Time Technology Assessment (Guston and Sarewitz, 2002) could be one means to understand and map how knowledge, perceptions and values develop over time. They could feed into exploration by some sort of international forum that explores normative questions around the direction and control of innovation, as well as issues of risk and regulation. Importantly, however, it is the individual scientist and innovator that must be challenged on an ongoing basis as to what motivates them. The training of young scientists has a crucial role to play in engendering notions of responsibility.

8.8   Conclusion

Responsible innovation will require adaptation of traditional regulatory tools and systems. But regulatory systems can only seek to control and to conduct surveillance once risks can be adequately characterized. Given the uncertainties and indeed sheer ignorance around the characteristics (physical, function, and use) of emerging technologies this might come too late in the innovation system to limit harm, or to be capable of effective implementation once a technology has become embedded in everyday use. Emerging technologies challenge societal priorities for the future. Yet processes of governance allow little opportunity for reflection on the purposes and motivations of science and innovation in this respect. Furthermore, the global context in which new technologies emerge across multiple and diffuse sectors and groups, with varying priorities, aspirations, and ethical views, severely challenges governance. This is why it is important to set out principles to underpin governance frameworks which can adapt to new knowledge and can seek to develop social intelligence around the direction and control of innovation. These principles must include anticipation of the future, reflection on R&D purpose and objectives, ensuring inclusion of stakeholders, users, and wider publics in the debate, and adjusting the direction of innovation in response (see Chapter 2). The innovation governance framework will be reliant in its early stages on notions of responsibility enshrined in various forms of soft law instruments. We may be heavily dependent on these, pending eventual capacity for the adaptation of more formal regulatory structures. Such processes are reliant on an opening up of innovation to societal debate as a pre-requisite for the good governance of adaptive innovation.

References

Arnall, H.W. (2003) Future Technologies, Today's Choices. Nanotechnology. Artificial Intelligence and Robotics. A Technical, Political and Institutional Map of Emerging Technologies, Greenpeace Environmental Trust, London.

Ayres, I. and Braithwaite, J. (1992) *Responsive Regulation*, Oxford University Press, Oxford.

Baldwin, R. (2004) The new punitive regulation. *The Modern Law Review*, **67**, 351–383.

Beck, U. (1992) *Risk Society: Towards a New Modernity*, Theory, Culture and Society Series, Vol. **17**, Sage Publications, London.

Bhattachary, D., Pascall Calitz, J, and Hunter, A. (2010) Synthetic Biology Dialogue, TNS-BMRB, UK, http://www.bbsrc.ac.uk/web/FILES/Reviews/1006-synthetic-biology-dialogue.pdf (accessed 19 December 2012).

Carter, C.A. and Gruère, G.P. (2003) International approaches to the labelling of genetically modified foods. *Choices*, **18**(2), 1–4.

Collingridge, D. (1980) *The Social Control of Technology*, Open University Press, Milton Keynes.

Chaudhry, Q., Thomas, M., Boxall, A., Aitken, R.J., Hull, M. (2005) The Manufacture and Use of Nanomaterials in the UK. DEFRA Report CB01070, London.

Defra (Department for Environment, Food and Rural Affairs) (2006) A Scoping Study to Identify Gaps in Environmental Regulation for the Products and Applications of Nanotechnologies, Defra, London.

Doubleday, R. (2007) Risk, public engagement and reflexivity: alternative framings of the public dimensions of nanotechnology *Health Risk and Society*, **9**(2), 211–227.

European Commission (2005) Nanosciences and Nanotechnologies: An Action Plan for Europe 2005–2009 (Brussels: COM(2005) 243 final)

European Commission (2008) Commission Recommendation of 07/02/2008 on a Code of Conduct for Responsible Nanosciences and Nanotechnologies Research (2008) 424 Final.

European Commission (2009) Regulation No. 1223/2009 on Cosmetic Products.

European Commission (2011) Regulation No. 1169/2011 on the provision of Food Information to Consumers.

European Community (1997) Regulation (EC) No 258/97 of the European Parliament and of the Council of 27 January 1997 Concerning Novel Foods and Novel Food Ingredients.

European Community (2001) General Product Safety (GPS) Directive (2001/95/EC).

European Community (2002) General Food Law, Regulation (178/2002/EC).

European Community (2004) Directive 2004/35/EC of the European Parliament and of the Council of 21 April 2004 on Environmental Liability With Regard to the Prevention and Remedying of Environmental Damage.

Faure, M. (2000) Product liability and product safety in Europe: harmonization or differentiation? *Kyklos*, **53**(4), 467–508.

Fisher, E. (2002) Precaution, precaution everywhere: developing a 'common understanding' of the precautionary principle in the European community. *Maastricht Journal of European and Comparative Law*, **9**, 7–28.

FSA (Food Standards Agency) (2008) A Review of Potential Implications of Nanotechnologies for Regulations and Risk Assessment in Relation to Food, FSA, London. Note that although the Report has a 2008 publication date, a draft version was presented to the FSA Board and available in 2006.

Frater L., Stokes, E. Lee, R.*et al.*, (2006) An Overview of the Framework of Current Regulation Affecting the Development and Marketing of Nanomaterials – A Report for the DTI, OSI, London.

Goodin, R. and Dryzek, J. (2006) Deliberative impacts: the macro-political uptake of mini-publics. *Politics and Society,* **34**(2), 219–243.

Groves, C. (2006) Technological futures and non-reciprocal responsibility. *The International Journal of the Humanities,* **4**(2), 57–61.

Gunningham, N. and Grabosky, P. (1998) *Smart Regulation: Designing Environmental Policy*, Oxford University Press, Oxford.

Guston, D.H. (2008) Innovation policy: not just a jumbo shrimp. *Nature,* **545**, 940–941.

Guston, D.H. and Sarewitz, D. (2002) Real-time technology assessment. *Technology in Society,* **24**, 93–109.

Haines, F. (2009) Regulatory failures and regulatory solutions: a characteristic analysis of the aftermath of disaster. *Law & Social Inquiry,* **34**(1), 31–60.

Harrimoes, P. (ed.) (2001) Late Lessons from Early Warnings: The Precautionary Principle, 1896–2000. Environmental Issue Report 22, European Environment Agency, Brussels.

Harrington, J. (2002) Red in tooth and claw: the idea of progress in medicine and the common law. *Social and Legal Studies,* **11**, 211–232.

HM Government (2005) Response to the Royal Society and Royal Academy of Engineering Report: 'Nanoscience and Nanotechnologies: Opportunities and Uncertainties', Department of Trade and Industry, London.

HSE (Health and Safety Executive) (2006) Review of the Adequacy of Current Regulatory Regimes to Secure Effective Regulation of Nanoparticles Created by Nanotechnology, HSE, London.

Insight Investment *et al.* (2008) Information on the Responsible Nano Code Initiative (Responsible NanoCode), http://www.nanoandme.org/downloads/The%20Responsible %20Nano%20Code.pdf (accessed 20 December 2012).

IRGC (International Risk Governance Council) (2009) Risk Governance Deficits: An Analysis and Illustration of the Most Common Deficits in Risk Governance, IRGC, Geneva.

Jasanoff, S. (1990) *The Fifth Branch: Science Advisers as Policy Makers*, Harvard University Press., Cambridge.

Jones, R. (2008) When it pays to ask the public. *Nature Nanotechnology,* **3**, 578–579.

Landes, W.M. and Posner, R.A. (1987) *The Economic Structure of Tort Law*, Harvard University Press, Cambridge, MA.

Lee, R. and Jose, P.D. (2008) Self-interest, self-restraint and corporate responsibility for nanotechnologies: emerging dilemmas for modern managers. *Technology Analysis and Strategic Management,* **20**(1), 113–125.

Lee, R. and Vaughan, S. (2010) Reaching down: nanomaterials and chemical safety in the European Union. *Law Innovation and Technology,* **2**(2), 193–217.

Macilwain, C. (2010) Without effective public engagement there will be no synthetic biology in Europe. *Nature,* **465**, 867.

Macnaghten, P. (2010) Researching technoscientific concerns in the making: narrative structures, public responses and emerging nanotechnologies. *Environment and Planning A,* **41**, 23–27.

Macnaghten, P.M. and Owen, R. (2011) Good governance for geoengineering. *Nature,* **479**, 293.

Miller, C.J. and Goldberg, R.S. (2004) *Product Liability*, Oxford University Press, Oxford.

Owen, R. and Goldberg, N. (2010) Responsible innovation: a pilot study with the U.K. engineering and physical sciences research council. *Risk Analysis,* **30**, 1699–1707.

Pellizzoni, L. (2004) Responsibility and environmental governance. *Environmental Politics,* **13**(3), 541–565.

Pidgeon, N.F., Poortinga, W., Rowe, G. *et al.* (2005) Using surveys in public participation processes for risk decision-making: the case of the 2003 British GM Nation public debate. *Risk Analysis,* **25**(2), 467–480.

Pidgeon, N.F. and Rogers-Hayden, T. (2007) Opening up nanotechnology dialogue with the publics: risk communication or 'upstream engagement? *Health, Risk and Society,* **9**, 191–210.

RA/REng (Royal Society and Royal Academy of Engineering) (2004) *Nanoscience and Nanotechnologies: Opportunities and Uncertainties*, Royal Society, London.

RCEP (Royal Commission on Environmental Protection) (2008) Novel Materials in the Environment: The Case of Nanotechnology. 27th Report, The Stationery Office, London, www.official-documents.gov.uk/document/cm74/7468/7468.pdf (accessed 26 July 2012).

Renn, O., Webler, T., and Wiedemann, P. (eds) (1995) *Fairness and Competence in Citizen Participation: Evaluating Models for Environmental Discourse*, Kluwer Academic Press, Boston, MA.

Reynolds, G.H. (2003) Nanotechnology and regulatory policy: three futures. *Harvard Journal of Law and Technology,* **17**(1), 180–210.

Robalino, D. and Lempert, R. (2000) Carrots and sticks for new technology: Abating greenhouse gas emissions in a heterogeneous and uncertain world. *Integrated Assessment,* **1**(1), 1–19.

Roco, M.C. (2008) Possibilities for global governance of converging technologies. *Journal of Nanoparticle Research,* **10**, 11–29.

Rowe, W.D. (1994) Understanding uncertainty. *Risk Analysis,* **14**(5), 743–750.

de Sadeleer, N. (2010) The precautionary principle in EU law. *Aansprakelijkheid, Verzekering & Schade,* 173–184.

Sinclair, D. (1997) Self-regulation versus command and control? Beyond false dichotomies. *Law and Policy,* **19**(4), 529–559.

Stapleton, J. (2006) Evaluating goldberg and Zipursky's civil recourse theory. *Fordham Law Review,* **75**(3), 1529.

Steinzor, R.I. (1998) Reinventing environmental regulation: the dangerous journey from command to self-control. *Harvard Environmental Law Review,* **22**, 103.

Stern, P.C. and Fineberg, H. (eds) (1996) *Understanding Risk: Informing Decisions in a Democratic Society*, National Academy Press, Washington, DC.

Stilgoe, J. (2007) *Nanodialogues: Experiments in Public Engagement with Science*, Demos, London.

Stilgoe, J. (2010) A question of intent. *Nature Climate Change,* **1**(7), 11.

Stilgoe, J. and Wilsdon, J. (2007) *The Nanodialogues: Four Experiments in Public Engagement in All Talk? Nanotechnologies and Public Engagement*, Institute of Physics, London.

Stirling, A. (2008) Science, precaution and the politics of technological risk: converging implications in evolutionary and social science perspectives. *Annals of the New York Academy of Sciences,* **1128**, 95–110.

Stirling, A. (2009) The precautionary principle, in *Blackwell Companion to the Philosophy of Technology* (eds J.-K. Olsen, S.A. Pedersoen, and V.F. Hendricks), Blackwell, Oxford.

Stokes, E. (2011) You are what you eat: market citizens and the right to know about nano foods. *Journal of Human Rights and the Environment,* **2**(2), 178–200.

US Environment Protection Agency (2009) Nanoscale Materials Stewardship Program: Interim Report, EPA, Washington DC.

Van Asselt, M.B.A. and Renn, O. (2011) Risk governance. *Journal of Risk Research,* **1**(4), 431–449.

Von Schomberg, R. (ed.) (2011) Towards Responsible Research and Innovation in the Information and Communication Technologies and Security Technologies Fields. European Commission, Brussels.

Webler, T., Kastenholz, H., and Renn, O. (1995) Public participation in impact assessment: a social learning perspective. *Environmental Impact Assessment Review.,* **15**(5), 443–464.

Weinberg, A.M. (1972) Science and trans-science. *Minerva,* **10**, 209–22.

Wynne, B. (1987) *Risk management and Hazardous Waste: Implementation and the Dialectics of Credibility*, Springer, Berlin.

Wynne, B. (1992) Uncertainty and environmental learning: reconceiving science and policy in the preventive paradigm. *Global Environmental Change,* **2**(2), 111–127.

9

Responsible Innovation: Multi-Level Dynamics and Soft Intervention Practices

Erik Fisher[1] *and Arie Rip*[2]

[1]*Arizona State University, Consortium for Science, Policy and Outcomes, USA*
[2]*University of Twente, The Netherlands*

9.1 Introduction

While issues of scientific responsibility and the social control of technology have been raised and addressed throughout the post-WWII science-policy era, there is now a surge of interest in "Responsible Innovation" (RI) and its cognate expressions, "Responsible Development" and "Responsible Research and Innovation" (RRI). This seeks to extend scientific responsibility so as to include future societal impacts of technological development, and is particularly visible for emerging high technosciences like nanotechnology. While early forms of technology assessment (TA) sought to balance the positive and negative effects of introducing new technology, the balancing act was seen more as the responsibility of political processes than of scientific ones. By contrast, RI/RRI distribute this responsibility *throughout* the innovation enterprise, locating it even at the level of scientific research practices. Although this interest started out at the level of policy discourse, the fact that it was articulated there at all, and has subsequently been taken up more widely, marks it as an expression of broader concerns, which we suggest are related to ambivalences distinctive of late modernity. The promise of progress through biotechnology and now nanotechnology is accompanied by concerns about their eventual impact and attempts at governance. RI/RRI is emerging as a way to address these concerns and attempts at governance, without losing faith in the promise of progress.

Responsible Innovation, First Edition. Edited by Richard Owen, John Bessant and Maggy Heintz.
© 2013 John Wiley & Sons, Ltd. Published 2013 by John Wiley & Sons, Ltd.

The ambivalence that relates to addressing promises as well as concerns is visible in the definition of responsible development of nanotechnology given in the 2006 National Nanotechnology Initiative (NNI) (Reprinted from [National Research Council. 2006] Copyright (2006) The National Academies Press).

> Responsible development of nanotechnology can be characterized as the balancing of efforts to maximize the technology's positive contributions and minimize its negative consequences. (...) It implies a commitment to develop and use technology to help meet the most pressing human and societal needs, while making every reasonable effort to anticipate and mitigate adverse implications or unintended consequences.

This optimistic definition recognizes that unintended negative consequences are perhaps unavoidable, but without considering why. It then affirms the possibility of mitigation, and of balancing "efforts" to maximize benefits and minimize costs. No reference is made to the challenges of resolving conflicts between diverse interests that will inevitably come into play in such cases, or to processes of contestation and their (partial) resolution. The continuing debates and regulatory impasses over genetically modified organisms (GMOs) show the difficulties associated with RI/RRI in practice. Of course, it is precisely struggles such as these that proponents of RI/RRI are seeking to avoid, as is evident in declarations of intentions to "get nanotech right" (Krupp and Holliday, 2005).

It is exactly because of widespread ambivalences in modern societies, such as those between technologically optimistic and pessimistic attitudes, that RI/RRI has not only become a key term in policy discourse, particularly in Europe, but is also being taken up by institutions such as research funding agencies and research consortia, and even at the "lab-scale" – as is evident in attempts for change within university and industrial research practices. This situation gives rise to multi-level dynamics – for example, funding agencies may refer to policy discourse about RI/RRI in setting soft requirements for research proposals which may, over time, in turn lead to changes in research practices. In this chapter we will discuss initiatives at different levels and some of their dynamics. We then focus on two types of intervention-oriented activities that concretely support and stimulate aspirations for RI/RRI: socio-technical integration research (STIR) and constructive technology assessment (CTA). In conclusion, we return to tensions in the concept and practices of RI/RRI, particularly in the light of its prospects for effectiveness and institutionalization.

9.2   Discourse and Activities at Different Levels of Governance

The policy discourse of RI has a symbolic function, displaying a willingness to "do better" in handling new science and technology in society, but it also has practical implications. This is particularly visible for nanotechnology, with the implementation of the US twenty-first Century Nanotechnology Research and Development Act (NRDA) of 2003 (US Congress, 2003), and the uptake of the 2008 EU Code of Conduct for Responsible Nanoscience and Nanotechnologies Research by European Member States (European Commission, 2008).[1] But funding agencies, research consortia and even industrial branch

---

[1] Roco *et al.* (2011) evaluate what has been done, mainly in the USA.

organizations also feel the need to address RI/RRI, and see opportunities to show that they are pro-active. Once the notion is visible, further actors start to refer to it, thus reinforcing its rhetorical strength.[2] Meanwhile, science organizations and firms feel credibility pressures, and respond to them, defensively or pro-actively. It is this multi-level constellation of declarations and activities that carries the move in the direction of RI/RRI, more so than any particular type of initiative, which may seem considerably less effective by itself.

In policy documents, RI/RRI signifies a broad, if fairly vague, aspiration for socially acceptable (and perhaps in some cases, socially accountable) forms of emerging technologies. There is now also more specific articulation on how to address this general challenge, including the proposition of novel governance mechanisms. Von Schomberg (2012), for example, articulates a values-based framework, derived from European Union treaties and other foundational documents; Macnaghten and Owen (2011) introduce a stage-gate process for UK research council projects; and Guston (2006, 2007) emphasizes centers for RI that act as boundary organizations.

9.2.1 International and Bi-Lateral Meetings

The discourse of RI/RRI is not limited to policy documents. There have been a variety of meetings, some taking up the topic because it is fashionable, others being part of a larger effort to "do something" about RI/RRI, and yet others linked to policy discussions. An early and somewhat sustained effort was the International Dialogue on Responsible Development of Nanoscience and Nanotechnology, starting in 2004 but eventually running out of steam.[3] Recently, at least five international workshops that included an explicit focus on RI were held in an 18-month period.[4] These have involved a range of public policy officials, advisors, experts, including (in some cases) both social and natural scientists and (occasionally) private and civil society sector participants. Workshops were held in The Hague (2010), the Woodrow Wilson Center (2011),[5] the European Commission (2011),[6] the French Embassy in the UK (2011),[7] and ASU's Washington, D.C. Center (2012). Several of these had public outreach components, for

---

[2] For example, the Glasgow-based Institute of Nanotechnology, which ran the Observatory Nano Project, has shifted to promote the project in terms of RI/RRI. In the announcement of its fourth and final report on Regulation and Standards for Nanotechnologies (Observatory Nano, 2012), the Institute says: "*The key lesson from the report [is]: Promoting responsible Research and Innovation (RRI), using multistakeholder approaches and addressing EHS [environment, health & safety], ELSA [ethical, legal & societal aspect] and regulatory issues throughout the entire lifecycle of products.*"

[3] The International Dialogue on Responsible Development of Nanoscience and Nanotechnology was set in motion by Mike Roco (US National Nanotechnology Initiative) and Renzo Tomellini (European Commission's Nanotechnology Program) in 2004. The idea was, and still is, to have informal interactions between government officials and other actors in the nano-world, with reference to responsible development as one reason why coordination is important. After the first meeting in Alexandria, Virginia, there was a delay because of political difficulties, but then meetings were held in Tokyo (2006) and Brussels (2008), with the next meeting planned in Russia (although it has not yet materialized). Such meetings offer reporting on developments, including ELSA and experiences with public dialogues, but are also space for interaction. Their advantage is that they can be inclusive: there is no official mandate or link to an authority, so there are no actual or symbolic barriers to participation. (This brief description is based on (unpublished) interviews and participant observation by Arie Rip; see also Roco *et al.* (2011) for a similar evaluation.)

[4] More recently, the Danish EU Presidency organized a conference on Science in Dialogue, towards a European model for responsible research and innovation, Odense 23–25 April 2012.

[5] The STIR project's fourth international workshop (http://cns.asu.edu/stir/workshops.php?ws=4).

[6] See Sutcliffe (2011)

[7] http://www.ambafrance-uk.org/Franco-British-workshop-on.

instance, the Wilson Center and French Embassy workshops had live or video webcasts; and all included the participation of policy officers.

Several of these meetings sought to enable or stimulate new developments, in addition to taking stock of existing work and attempting to define and specify what the topic means. Most notably, the EC workshop actually developed an articulated vision of RRI that has contributed to concrete strategy. Similarly, the Wilson Center workshop included discussion of a proposed definition for RI, which has since been refined and utilized in policy documents (e.g., Von Schomberg, 2011 on ICT). It was also explicitly aimed at creating a diverse and international network for "socio-technical integration," including on the agenda roughly equal numbers of social scientists, natural scientists and engineers, and policy officers from nearly a dozen nations, as well as being attended by members of a charitable foundation. The ASU workshop included representatives from the UK as well as two-dozen US federal agencies, and led to a follow-up presentation on RI to the US National Science Foundation's Engineering Directorate.

9.2.2   Legislative Initiatives

While RRI is now also used in reference to synthetic biology, converging technologies and geoengineering, for nanotechnology in particular there is legislation in the US, and there have also been requests to Member States of the European Union to implement a Code of Conduct for nanotechnology research.

In the US, the Twenty-first Century NRDA of 2003 (NRDA, US Congress, 2003) established the legal foundations for the US NNI, which was created in 2000 (Fisher, 2009). Notably, the NRDA designated the National Research Council (NRC) *"to assess the need for standards, guidelines or strategies for ensuring the responsible development of nanotechnology"* (US Congress, 2003). Additionally, it authorized the creation of a societal research center meant to, among other things, *"identify anticipated issues related to the responsible research, development, and application of nanotechnology"* (*ibid.*). These provisions, along with the law's "integration mandate" (Fisher, 2005: p. 326), helped establish the umbrella term of "responsible development" that has served as the basis for follow-on activities in the US.[8] Follow-on activities led to the establishment of the Center for Nanotechnology in Society (which we discuss below) as well as several reports by the NRC, including the 2006 report we have quoted above. They also include the 2004, 2007, and 2011 NNI strategic plans, which all list four goals, the fourth being to "Support the responsible development of nanotechnology" (e.g., NSTC, 2011). The NRDA provisions cited here represent only a part of the larger legislative text and the broader social and political context to which it responds. The legal language taken as a whole reflects competing narratives about the promise and peril of nanotechnology that appeared in US popular and policy discourses prior to the law's enactment (Fisher and Mahajan, 2006a). The narratives show up in the legislation in the form of an unresolved tension *"between the two perceived policy alternatives of rapid versus responsible nanotechnology development"* (Fisher and Mahajan, 2006a: p. 13). This tension is echoed in the efforts of funding agencies, which we will come to shortly.

In the European Union, the 2008 proposal for a Code of Conduct for Responsible Nanoscience and Nanotechnologies Research (EC, 2008) was preceded by a consultation,

---

[8] The integration mandate requires "integrating research on societal, ethical, and environmental concerns with nanotechnology research and development" (US Congress, 2003: Sec 2 (b)).

but it had an earlier history, starting with the 2004 International Dialogue meeting (see note 3) where Roco and Tomellini pushed for a Code of Conduct. Tomellini maintained the effort, and was able, after wide consultations, to have a Code of Conduct (text plus guidelines) formulated. The restriction of the code to "research" was necessary because, at the time, the remit of the European Commission was limited to research. But the code is broader, and refers also to public understanding and the importance of precaution. There are explicit links to governance: the guidelines *"are meant to give guidance on how to achieve good governance"* as the Commission further specifies:

> Good governance of N&N (nanosciences and nanotechnologies) research should take into account the need and desire of all stakeholders to be aware of the specific challenges and opportunities raised by N&N. A general culture of responsibility should be created in view of challenges and opportunities that may be raised in the future and that we cannot at present foresee (Reprinted from European Commissions Code of Conduct for Responsible Nanotechnologies Research. Available at: http://ec.europa.eu/research/science-society/index.cfm?fuseaction=public.topic&id=1303 Last accessed 15/11/12 Copyright (2008) European Commission).

A "general culture of responsibility" cannot of course be created by the European Commission, but they clearly see themselves as contributing to such *de facto* governance.

The Code of Conduct has been discussed by the Member States, and they have to report on its uptake. An evaluation is foreseen for 2013. In the meantime, the thrust is maintained through dedicated meetings and publications, as well as presentations by EU DG Research and Innovation staff at conferences and workshops. Thus, the overall notion of RRI is alive and well in Brussels, some pushing it actively, others going along somewhat grudgingly. While the EU Science in Society Program will be disbanded, the new R&D Framework Program Horizon 2020 will integrate RRI in all programs.[9]

The Framework Programs are R&D funding programs, but in their goals and in the instruments that are devised they are much closer to policy than those of national-level research funding agencies. The sponsoring of research also occurs through private, charitable foundations, sometimes with large budgets and dedicated portfolios, like the Wellcome Foundation in the UK, and the Bill and Melinda Gates Foundation located in the US. Such private foundations have more freedom to set requirements on proposals than national-level funding agencies. Their portfolio of projects often has a strong societal orientation and can be set up with interaction involving stakeholders – thus operationalizing the notion of responsible research.

9.2.3 Research Funding Agencies

National-level research funding organizations are involved in three ways. First, they can adapt their procedures and requirements. Important RI/RRI precedents occurred when merit review was introduced at the National Science Foundation, and when the UK Research Councils required a dissemination paragraph in research proposals submitted

---

[9] As EU Commissioner for Research, Innovation, and Science, Máire Geoghegan-Quinn phrased it in her opening speech for the EU Presidency Conference on Science in Dialogue, towards a European model for responsible research and innovation, Odense, 23 April 2012: *"Horizon 2020 will support the six keys to responsible research and innovation … and will highlight responsible research and societal engagement throughout the programme"* (quoted from the official text handed out at the conference) (Geoghegan-Quinn, 2012).

to them. Recently, the National Science Board proposed to correlate more closely with one another the two separate NSF merit review criteria during the peer review process. The two criteria, "intellectual merit" and "broader impact," which are associated with scientific quality and societal relevance, respectively, have had a delicate relationship with one another (Holbrook, 2005). Broader impact has been associated with numerous societal issues, ranging from ethics, TA, public outreach, minority representation in science and (building on the 1980s US focus on "technology transfer") with dissemination (Roberts, 2009).

More recently, "valorization" of research has become a fashionable term in Europe, for Ministries of Science and national funding agencies. Taking a broader view of valorization, so as to include embedding in society, activities that go with RRI are becoming more important, and have to be included in research proposals. An example is the requirement to have extended impact statements in some of the programs of the EU Seventh Framework Program. How to do this is still experimental, but it is judged and given equal weight as the traditional judgment dimensions (scientific quality of the proposal; management quality of the project). Learning will occur, including some operationalization of RRI. As is evident in both the US and EU cases, the ambivalence conveyed by the markedly different ways used to evaluate R&D – with promotion of quality science and control of undesirable social impacts marking two extremes – are becoming institutionalized in multi-level attempts to integrate previously separate goals (at the legislative level) and mechanisms (at the agency level).

Second, research funding organizations can develop special programs of research around RRI. One example is the Dutch program Maatschappelijk Verantwoord Innoveren (MVI), which translates as "Societally Responsible Innovating," while the official English title of the Program is Responsible Innovation, (see www.nwo.nl/mvi). This started in 2009, after a long and difficult period of preparations, but is now reasonably successful. The Norway Research Council's Ethical, Legal and Societal Aspect (ELSA) program was to some extent modeled on the Dutch MVI program, but with a smaller budget, and a simpler structure. Other Norwegian Research Council's programs, especially those concerning functional genomics (FUGE) and nanotechnology (NanoMat), which had ELSA components and were in collaboration with the ELSA Program, strongly resonate with the US "integration mandate" (Fisher, 2011). This could be the beginning of a broader approach to funding R&D for the Research Council. A first sign is that the new funding programs Nanomat2021 and Biotech2021 require ELSA components to be integrated in all proposals.[10] Yet another example is to be found in Genome Canada's interest in funding collaborative projects that integrate social and natural scientific research in a functional manner. These "integrated projects" can produce social scientific findings, for instance derived from the documenting of stakeholder values, that feed back and redirect the natural science research design. This intention was elaborated in a white paper entitled "Pathways to Integration" (Genome British Columbia, 2011).

Third, research funding organizations can play a role in implementing government policies on RI/RRI. For example, in the US, the National Science Foundation responded to NRDA in 2005 by issuing a call for proposals to establish a Center for Nanotechnology in Society. During the course of the competition, the NSF decided to split the award funds

---

[10] Nanomat2021 adds: "if relevant." The NRDA contains a similar caveat (see Fisher and Mahajan, 2006a).

in order to allow it to establish multiple Centers for Nanotechnology in Society – one at Arizona State University (CNS-ASU) and the other at the Centers for Nanotechnology in Society-University of California at Santa Barbara (CNS-UCSB).

Research Councils UK, in 2007/2008, identified "Nanoscience from Engineering through Application" as one of their "Grand Challenges," and phrased it as an attempt to compete internationally by exploiting technoscientific opportunities, and conveying the sense of urgency that goes with it. Subsequently, there were consultations with stakeholders about specific challenges (in health care (Jones, 2008), and in carbon capture) before the actual funding of proposals, and the research call on nanotechnology for carbon capture had an explicit requirement for RI/RRI (Owen and Goldberg, 2010). This is in contrast with their earlier funding of Genetics and Society Research Centres. This RI/RRI approach has been extended to recent UK research council-funded geoengineering projects, one of which required a RI/RRI stage-gate process, in which public engagement plays a role (cf. Macnaghten and Owen, 2011; Parkill and Pidgeon, 2011).

9.2.4 Intermediary Organizations and Consortia

There are additional relevant organizations at the meso-level. These can be branch organizations (and in nanotechnology, they often try to push their members to pay more attention to possible risks and the need to engage with stakeholders and publics). There are regional clusters, and, in the world of science, research consortia and forums for strategy articulation and anticipatory coordination: the American National Science and Technology Council (NSTC) subcommittees and European Technology Platforms (ETPs) being examples. The NSTC, for instance, requested the NSF to hold a workshop on the societal implications of nanoscience and nanotechnology in 2000 (Roco and Bainbridge, 2001). ETP Nanomedicine had paragraphs on ethics in its original strategy document, and there are interesting references to RI/RRI, reflecting a particular perspective on RI/RRI as helping to making innovation more credible.[11]

The CNS-ASU has become a hub for a wide array of research and engagement activities, both nationally and internationally. Under the rubric of real-time technology assessment (RTTA) (Guston and Sarewitz, 2002), these activities range from research and innovation system analysis and public opinion polling to collaborations with scientists and engineers and large-scale public engagement forums. RTTA activities are conceptualized in terms of anticipatory governance (Barben *et al.*, 2008), which includes an ensemble of "foresight" (Selin, 2011), "engagement" (Cobb, 2011), and "integration" (Fisher, 2007) activities. The CNS-ASU has also become a destination for numerous international scholars, students, and practitioners from more than 20 countries, and has played a role in a number of national and international efforts and collaborations to develop concepts and practices for RI. It also develops educational and research tools

---

[11] The Report of the Round Table exercise, A Report on the Nanomedicine Environment: NanoMed Round Table Extended Report (NanoMed 2010) discussed Patient Needs, Ethical and Social Aspects, Economic Impact, Regulation, Communication, and said (in the report of the working group on regulation, at p. 29), under the heading *"Establishing mechanisms of credibility for responsible innovation"*: *"Given the hype about new technologies, and both the anxieties and over-expectations that the general public may have as a result, there is a need for society to establish and promote mechanisms that offer credibility and authority. This supports and encourages responsible practice in the development of innovative products. Institutional mechanisms that facilitate a common perspective with regard to clarity, objectivity, and common practice for credibility and authority will help to guide and facilitate responsible innovation."*

that have been taken up in universities, nanoscale science and engineering centers, and policy forums.

In the Netherlands, the national R&D consortium NanoNed (2005–2010), funded through a special funding program for knowledge infrastructure, included a TA subprogram.[12] Its successor, NanoNextNL, which was funded by the same knowledge infrastructure program and started research in 2011, again had a TA subprogram, and now also a risk analysis subprogram. The research portfolio of NanoNextNL has a stronger orientation toward domains of application. It was decided to accept the European Code of Conduct for Responsible Nanoscience and Nanotechnology Research as a guideline. A further way in which RI/RRI is operationalized is through the requirement that all PhD students funded through NanoNextNL should also do a TA nanotechnology project, and perhaps include it as a chapter in their eventual PhD thesis.[13]

A recent development is the establishment of centers for the study of RI, such as the Exeter Business School Chair in RI held by Richard Owen, the Oslo Research Group on RI, led by Ellen-Marie Forsberg (see www.hioa.no) and the Observatory of RI at the Ecole des Mines de Paris (www.debatinginnovation.org; and Chapter 10) with an initial focus on RI in the financial sector.[14]

9.2.5   Concrete Activities

Concrete RI/RRI activities can take different forms. They can consist of laboratories altering their practices in any number of ways, whether by adopting new training materials, for instance as a result of interacting with the CNS-ASU, or when laboratory directors invite others into their labs in order to build a greater awareness of social and ethical contexts. This latter phenomenon began occurring in the early nano years, with mixed results,[15] and has become more and more widely practiced (as in the STIR program, discussed below). Actions that seek to protect the lab from "outsiders," on the other hand, may seem to work against RI/RRI aspirations. These can be construed as attempts to define RI/RRI on scientists' own terms. For instance, the National Nanotechnology Infrastructure Network has produced a series of posters that labs in their network can obtain and hang on their walls. One in particular is rather striking: a scientist looks up from her microscope and reassuringly tells the viewer, "*I consider every aspect of my research, including what happens with it outside of the lab,*" while a field of wheat placidly waves behind her. One take-home message is that controversies like

---

[12] The total budget of the consortium was €240 million, half of which was funded through the knowledge infrastructure funding program, the other half contributed by participants. See www.nanoned.nl. The inclusion of a TA component was part of the visionary leadership of David Reinhoudt (University of Twente), who had seen the emerging discussion about nanotechnology and society in the US, and wanted to be pro-active. Arie Rip was invited to set up and lead the TA program, which had a strong focus on constructive TA.

[13] For the portfolio of research themes, see www.nanonextnl.nl. The implementation of the requirement for PhD students may turn out to be difficult because of the reluctance of their supervisors (and perhaps of the students as well) to create space to allow the making of a serious effort.

[14] The Observatoire awarded the 2012 Dufrénoy Prize for RI on June 18, 2012 for remarkable initiatives in the field of RI in the financial services industry. The award goes to the Reserve Bank of India for its precautionary approach to the regulation of derivative markets, to EGAMO for the development of cooperative democratic principles in asset management and to MyHemera for its potential for a transparent assessment of complex financial products.

[15] Erik Fisher was invited in 2003 by Roop Mahajan to join his nanoscale engineering lab. The two went on to document the practical results of their collaborations (Fisher and Mahajan, 2006b) and later the conditions under which their collaborations were both enabled and constrained (Fisher and Mahajan, 2010). Robert Doubleday was invited at roughly the same time by Marc Welland, but was expected to play more of a pedagogical rather than a collaborative role (Doubleday, 2007).

that associated with GMOs can be placated by more socially responsive science and engineering. Whether the poster will facilitate such responsiveness is another question.[16] The important point is that what counts as "good laboratory practices" can be extended to include broader considerations. The chemical companies formulating codes of conduct for nanotechnology have included health and safety considerations for lab and production workers. Wider impacts of their nanotechnology-enabled products would then be the responsibility of their strategy and communication departments.

Concrete activities can also take the form of attempts to broaden ongoing innovation trajectories, or to create frameworks to guide such activities. An early example of the latter is the "Nano Risk Framework" developed by the chemical company DuPont in partnership with the NGO Environmental Defense. The framework was created in order to "get nanotech right" (Krupp and Holliday, 2005) and for the purpose of "ensuring the responsible development of nanoscale materials" (DuPont and Environmental Defense, 2007). Laurent (2011), after discussing how a French company producing nanotubes tried to integrate risk aspects, describes in detail how a key actor in the nanotubes project initiated an attempt by the French Ministry of Health to create a nano-responsible standard in the context of the *Comité Européen de Normalization*, to be taken up in the work of the International Standardization Organization (ISO) (TC 229), and mobilizing industry, as well as civil society organizations. The project started in 2009, had its internal tensions (between industry and NGOs) and tried to articulate a French position in international forums, transcending the dichotomy between the precautionary "no nano inside" and the promissory "exploiting the promise of nano." There was no clear outcome, but the project left its traces in France and in the international standardization discussions.

9.3   Two Cases of "Soft" Intervention

In the overall multi-level picture that we have sketched so far, the activities of different actors (with their own positions and perspectives) combine to work toward RI/RRI. There are also attempts to intervene based on a diagnosis of what is happening and how this can be modulated. Such "soft" interventions are conceptualized and tried out in practice by Science and Technology Studies (STS) scholars, as well as actors interested in governance of, and governance frameworks for, nanotechnology. A number of such projects have been funded in Europe and America (Bird and Fisher, 2011; Von Schomberg and Davies, 2010). By way of example, we will zoom in on two "soft" interventions in which we have been involved ourselves. The first, STIR, has produced concrete changes at the micro-level, taking meso-level developments and macro-level discourses into account in order to build multi-level capacities for anticipatory and reflexive governance. The second, CTA, plays out on the meso-level, and refers to actor's strategies as well as macro-level trends toward more reflexive co-evolution of science, technology, and society.

9.3.1   STIRing the Capacities of Science and Innovation Practitioners

STIR is a form of collaborative inquiry between natural scientists and engineers on the one hand, and social scientists and humanities scholars on the other, that has been

---

[16] The poster series is entitled "Responsible Research in Action." See http://www.sei.nnin.org/.

shown to broaden and enhance R&D decision-making processes.[17] An "embedded" social science and/or humanities scholar conducts a "laboratory engagement study," which feeds back social scientific observations into the field of study over a 12 week period (Fisher, 2007). The embedded scholar engages her hosts in what can turn out to be "high impact" critical reflection as an ongoing part of their normal routines and activities. The collaborative interactions are mediated by a semi-structured decision protocol (Fisher, 2007), which serves as a stable boundary object and basis of dialogue for the participants.

The results of the interactions are then assessed in terms of a framework of "midstream modulation" (Fisher *et al.*, 2006), which charts sequential modes of reflexivity and action. "Midstream" refers to research and innovation decisions that implement, or enact, strategic visions and objectives. Midstream modulation plays out in three iterative phases:

- *De facto* **modulation** involves a suite of interacting social and ethical contexts that affect decisions, even those made during routine scientific and engineering activities. Expert and specialist practitioners, whether conducting a laboratory experiment or designing a regulatory policy, seldom reflect in a systematic way on these contexts – for better or for worse.
- *Reflexive* **modulation** involves recognizing and systematically reflecting upon these social and ethical contexts of decision-making, while otherwise carrying out normal routines and practices. Nothing changes except for increased awareness of the broader context within which an individual or an organization is acting.
- *Deliberate* **modulation** involves putting the increased *reflexive awareness* generated in the previous step to work during research or strategic decision-making. This may be done to improve either the products or the processes of decisions. It typically results from the practitioner perceiving a broader variety of either decision alternatives or decision values to be at play in her actions.

The engagement studies map out the social and institutional contexts of the lab, including formal and informal policies, sponsors, and other actors and discourses.[18] Embedded scholars typically start off in a single laboratory but can then circulate to additional sites, including other laboratories, clinics, regulatory agencies, and legal venues (e.g., Conley, in review). Recently, several groups of researchers have made plans for STIR "rotations," in which sequential 12-week studies are conducted across multiple university, private-sector, government, and civil society sites within a larger network or sociotechnical system.

The laboratory engagement approach is intended to integrate critical, social scientific observation, inquiry, and analysis directly into the practice of scientific research and innovation activities in real-time. The social scientific feedback generated by STIR activities can productively disrupt expert practitioner routines (Wynne, 2011), serving to

---

[17] STIR has been taken up in over 30 public and private laboratories in a dozen nations across North America, Europe and East Asia. An initial project in 2009 was funded at just over US $1 Million, with half coming from the National Science Foundation and the rest from a dozen or so collaborators. The NSF award helped support research and training activities, including workshops in the US, Europe and Asia for an international network of science and innovation scholars based in a dozen nations. It also established STIR as an associated project of the CNS-ASU.

[18] As stated in the NSF project proposal, STIR studies investigate *"what counts as responsible innovation at the macro-level of public policy, the micro-level of laboratory research, and the meso-level of institutional structures and practices that connect them."*

problematize laboratory practices, research administration and evaluation, and strategic decisions, which in turn leads to concrete changes in material practices, research directions, and strategic decision-making (e.g., Schuurbiers, 2011). These changes in practice have been observed at the individual and collective level. STIR interventions can not only lead to action, they can build capacities to enable longer-term and more broadbased modulations.

For instance, Fisher's pilot study documented alterations in the experimental design, set-up, and materials used to synthesize carbon nanotubes in a university mechanical engineering laboratory (Fisher and Mahajan, 2006b). He also documented changes in the disposal methods and research conduct practices of the laboratory. Each of these instances was correlated with the engagements between Fisher (as an "embedded humanist") and the other members of the laboratory whose decision processes were modulated. Revisiting the laboratory 18 months later, Fisher learned of additional and lasting effects that the researchers stated had continued to take place as a result of the earlier STIR engagements. Similar changes in research practice, organizational culture, and public outreach have been documented in other STIR studies (e.g., Conley, 2011; Domareski, 2011; Flipse *et al.*, 2012; Schuurbiers, 2011).

Such changes in practice are consonant with both scientific and societal values, suggesting that common ground between historically divergent values can be cultivated even on the laboratory floor. This is significant given that pressures of RI have been observed, in other contexts, to emphasize divergence between the "health" of science and that of society (McCarthy and Kelty, 2010). STIR studies have documented changes in practice in settings as diverse as university bench science, research administration, and strategic communication within corporations (e.g., Fisher *et al.*, 2010; Flipse, 2012). STIR findings have, in turn, helped shape research policy and program solicitation at the national level in Europe and North America, and the program has been referred to as an example of RI activities formally included under the NNI's fourth goal of "responsible development" (NSTC FY, 2011).[19]

While changes in material and strategic practices can inspire confidence, their significance extends beyond the instrumental. Collaborative inquiry in the STIR program raises deeper questions. While STIR makes no pretense of "representing" any particular group or special interest, it is animated by a commitment to the common interest, and to probing the cultural and institutional conditions that both enable and constrain its pursuit (Lasswell, 1970). If STIR has succeeded in working intimately with the science and innovation enterprise, in doing so it has sought to newly confront the enduring modern theme of segregation between technical and humanistic approaches.[20]

9.3.2 Constructive Technology Assessment (CTA) of Newly Emerging Science and Technology

Issues now labeled as RI/RRI have been identified before, notably in the mid- to late 1980s in the Netherlands, in the government's Policy Memorandum on Integration of

---

[19] Thus, not without irony, what began as an exploration of the possibility and utility of socio-technical integration as a means for RI (Fisher and Mahajan, 2010) has, in producing positive examples, now officially become part of the very enterprise it set out to investigate.

[20] Poets and public intellectuals from Wordsworth to C.P. Snow have lamented this segregation, which has become a distinct focus of genomics and nanotechnology policy (Fisher, 2005).

Science and Technology in Society (Ministerie van Onderwijs en Wetenschappen, 1984). On the basis of the Policy Memorandum, a Netherlands Organization for TA (now Rathenau Institute) was established in 1986. One of its projects was to develop the approach of CTA (Daey Ouwens *et al.*, 1987), with two key elements: to broaden technology development by including more aspects and involving more actors, and to do so on the basis of an understanding of the dynamics of technology development and its embedding in society. Development of CTA methodologies occurred in STS studies, linked to evolutionary economics of technological change (cf. Rip *et al.*, 1995; Schot and Rip, 1997), and it was positioned as part of an overall move toward more reflexive co-evolution of science, technology, and society (Rip, 2002).

Further development of CTA methodology and practice for emerging technologies, such as nanotechnology, was made possible in the 2000s through dedicated funding from the consortium NanoNed (cf. above). As Rip and Te Kulve (2008) show, a CTA activity consists of (i) the building of sociotechnical scenarios of possible technological developments and the vicissitudes of their embedding in society (based on extensive document study and field work) and (ii) the organizing and orchestration of workshops with a broad variety of stakeholders. The scenarios help to structure the discussion in the workshops (Robinson, 2010) and stimulate learning about possible strategies (Parandian, 2012). Therefore, it is important to have scenarios of high quality and relevance, which can be seen as legitimate by workshop participants.[21]

CTA activities take into account what happens on a variety of "work floors": research laboratories, conferences, workshops, agenda setting and planning meetings, roadmapping events, and public debates anticipating issues related to technology developments. A corollary is that the CTA actor has to move about, observe and actively circulate in locations where actors are shaping the emerging paths of technology and how it will become embedded in society.

For the workshop interactions it is important to have "enactors" of technology developments as well as "comparative selectors" (from potential users to regulators and NGOs), with their differences in perspective, as participants.[22] The workshops then function as bridging events, where participants can (in Garud and Ahlstrom (1997)'s felicitous phrase) *"probe each other's realities."* There will also be a future orientation, because the positions and interactions, as visible in the scenarios, will come alive because their protagonists are present. With the right mix of participants, what happens will reflect ongoing dynamics in the wider world, so the workshop will be like a micro-cosmos. The workshop is also a protected space, where participants have the opportunity to consider alternatives and the possibility of modifying their strategies and eventual interactions in the real world without there being immediate repercussions. Still, the wider world has its own dynamics, and these are important for eventual uptake and effect of the CTA exercise.[23]

---

[21] Quite some effort has to be put into the creation of robust socio-technical scenarios (Robinson, 2009). Thus, they become a product in their own right, which can be put to further use, also by participants. Scenarios add substance to the interactions in a workshop, which make them different from participatory exercises with the goal of including more actors and thus democratizing technological development (a goal that is occasionally projected on CTA, e.g., by Genus (2006).

[22] This terminology, and the diagnosis of a structural difference in perspectives, was introduced by Rip (2006), drawing on the work of Garud and Ahlstrom (1997) who used the somewhat unfortunate terminology of "insiders" and "outsiders."

[23] Marris *et al.* (2008) have shown this for an interactive TA exercise about field tests of genetically modified vines in France. Their point is reinforced by what happened subsequently: productive co-construction of the design of the field tests between local stakeholders and researchers ensued, but five years later (August 2010), the test fields were destroyed by critics of GMO. (The story is told in LMC (2010), from the perspective of the actors involved in the co-construction.)

While this methodology has been successfully applied in the nano-world, some reflection is in order. First, the scenarios speak to an enactor perspective in their projection of further development of a new technology. But CTA actors introduce twists, showing unexpected (for enactors) shifts and repercussions. And the workshops allow other actors, with other perspectives, to speak and be heard.

Second, emerging technologies, like nanotechnology, live on promises, so choices have to be made about which topics and developments to focus on. Which expectations should be taken into account as more realistic and/or more important? What is seen as important also depends, of course, on the position from which such expectations are voiced, for example, by an enactor or by a comparative selector. The CTA analyst has a responsibility here, and must build on her knowledge of the domain and its dynamics.[24]

Third, for emerging technologies the goal of CTA is to broaden design and development as this occurs at an early stage. Thus, it has an upstream bias: better outcomes result from doing better at an earlier stage.[25] It is a bias, because it is the overall co-production process that leads to eventual outcomes: there is no determinism. But the bias cannot be avoided if one wants to do better in handling new technology in society. The implication is that CTA activities, say of nanotechnology, should not be one-off exercises. There must be further activities that modulate the co-production process.

9.4 Concluding Observations on Governance

STIR and CTA are not themselves RI/RRI; rather, they probe, support, and stimulate the ability of actors to take up RI/RRI by offering concrete ways of productively broadening their activities. Of course, this depends on the extent to which the (temporary) soft intervention is taken up as a part of research and innovation activity – and to the extent that it represents a new way of "doing" science and innovation that accords with a broader array of values and concerns. Still, one can contrast this with the route governments often take: government agencies and policy makers do not themselves perform RI/RRI, they incentivize it by creating requirements (such as the integration of ethical, legal, and societal implications (ELSI)/ELSA, or following a code of conduct, etc.), or providing for social scientific research and engagement activities (as in the US Centers for Nanotechnology in Society). They prescribe (softly), while STIR and CTA problematize and invite. In both cases, there may be willingness with the research and innovation actors to "do" RI/RRI, as well as reluctant uptake because of credibility pressures on science and technology. These pressures take a distinctive form in late modernity, which is characterized by self-referential processes, such as policies that reflexively take their anticipated effects into account. All this is becoming part of the governance of new science and technology in contemporary society, and institutionalization may occur in terms of organizational arrangements and changed practices. As we discuss below, the new governance element is that research and innovation actors are *now held co-responsible for taking societal*

---

[24] The challenge of choosing which future developments to discuss is a generic one. Nordmann and Rip (2009) have considered ethical assessment of nanotechnology in this light (and criticized the way ethicists tend to address the challenge).

[25] Upstream public engagement (in the UK and elsewhere) has the same bias, but in contrast with CTA it focuses on actors with little or no agency. Upstream public engagement may well remain an empty exercise. Even if there is pressure for the views and discussions reported to be taken up by policy makers (when they see fit), this can remain limited to only shifting the locus of the upstream bias.

embedding and potential impacts into account. What social and institutional forms that will take is still an open question. RI/RRI is a pluralistic phenomenon, whose meaning is far from fixed or stable. This makes it easy to refer to in policy discourses, as an umbrella term. It also makes it easy for actors to neglect it. It is striking how RI/RRI is being taken up by intermediary organizations (including funding agencies) and consortia. Whatever their reasons, they are becoming important nodes in the multi-level dynamics of RI/RRI.

In order for RI/RRI to mean something, research and innovation actors will need to change their practices – which are embedded within particular contexts and against a larger backdrop of institutions and norms that structure behavior. Insofar as aspirations go beyond incremental amelioration (or mere relabeling and impression management), however, such changes will lead to tensions with these established, contextual elements. For instance, responsibilities, whether they are new, existing or modified, invoke the notion of socially-sanctioned roles, such as established divisions of moral labor. Divisions of moral labor are evident in the culturally-accepted responsibility of scientists to work for progress by conducting good basic research, while others (regulators, citizens, professional ethicists, etc.) are responsible for controlling the societal impacts of the application of this science. Thus, for scientists to take responsibility for considering broader social aspects of science will necessitate confronting and renegotiating such divisions of moral labor.

For the challenge of RI/RRI, the key division of moral labor is the functional separation between on the one hand promotion and on the other control of research, technology, and innovation. The separation of promotion and control in modern societies is heir to the industrial revolution of the eighteenth and nineteenth centuries, where technology development became a separate activity, carried out by engineers and located in firms and public or semi-public research institutes. Culturally, a mandate allowing new technologies to be developed as such emerged and, since the engineers were successfully positioned as contributing to social progress, the mandate, therefore, had to be accepted, almost by definition. Institutionally, an indicator of the separation between promotion and control is the division of labor between government ministries, some promoting the development of new technologies and innovation, while other ministries have to consider impacts and regulation (Rip *et al.*, 1995).[26]

The phrase "responsible innovation" attempts to transcend this existing division of moral labor. As we have shown, there are policies and activities attempting to bridge the separation of technology development and attempts at control because of projected societal impact. The existing division of moral labor is still strong, as can be seen in how "RI/RRI" is interpreted differently on the two sides of the fence. Some government agencies and civil society organizations emphasize "responsible," arguing that this can sometimes lead to the curbing of innovation. Technology developers, on the other hand, put "innovation" upfront, seeing "responsible" as modulation of innovation which maintains their "licence to operate." Still, there is an opening in the sense that anticipation of societal impacts is now seen as being also a responsibility of technology developers (McCarthy and Kelty, 2010).

While the dichotomies, tensions, and ambivalences (innovation vs. responsible, developers vs. users, promotion vs. control) remain visible, interactions and mixed approaches

---

[26] TA emerged within this regime of handling technology in society, and was institutionalized at the control side of the division of labor – to the point of being qualified, by technology promoters, as "technology harassment."

intended to resolve or "balance" them are cropping up. Meanwhile, the interactions may have the effect of heightening the tensions, or at least making them more visible. The heightened tension could cause the situation to collapse, to reaffirm the existing divisions, or, as seems to be the case, to evolve further. The domain of nanoscience and nanotechnologies, for example, is evolving to be a site for experimentation and learning – including controversy. One can see various actors exploring (even if reluctantly) possibilities (Rip and Shelley-Egan, 2010). This is leading to modifications of the division of moral labor, albeit incrementally.[27] When some stabilization occurs, there will be *de facto* governance of nanotechnology, that is, steering and shaping of action that has some legitimacy, even if there is no formal authoritative basis, as in law and regulation (Rip, 2010). The experimentation and mutual learning that occur in and around nanotechnology are now being taken up for other emerging and converging technologies, such as synthetic biology, neurotechnology, and so on, and ambitious technological ventures such as geoengineering.

Thus, what started out as policy discourse may lead to arrangements and behaviors that endure, their actual forms shaped and reinforced by the multi-level dynamics, rather than through policy specification and its implementation as such. The process can be seen as what political scientists have called "cumulative incrementalism" (Hill, 1997). Depending on how the tensions and divisions of moral labor play out, however, RI/RRI could take several different forms. In the US, the outcome may issue in arrangements that are partially stabilized through collaborative assurance (Guston, 2000), while tensions, and occasional antagonistic interactions, remain a source of periodic renegotiation and renewal. In Europe, the situation could develop into neo-corporatism, in which distinct social sectors – such as industrial actors, professional science associations, government actors, and various civil society organizations – act as somewhat coherent interest groups that work toward a common goal (such as that represented by a code of conduct). New science and technology create indeterminate situations where different and contrasting futures are considered. If approaches like STIR and CTA become an integral part of the governance of newly emerging science and technology, the governance features will have reflexive elements.[28] Maybe that is the best we can hope for.

References

Barben, D., E. Fisher, C. Selin, and D. H. Guston. 2008. Anticipatory governance of nanotechnology: foresight, engagement, and integration, pp. 979–1000 (eds E. J. Hackett, O. Amsterdamska, M. E. Lynch, and J. Wajcman), *The New Handbook of Science and Technology Studies*. Cambridge: MIT Press.

Cobb, M. 2011. Creating informed public opinion: citizen deliberation about nanotechnologies for human enhancements. *Journal of Nanoparticle Research,* **13**(4): 1533–1548.

Conley, S.N. (in review) Activating Transformative Capacities: Socio-Technical Integration in Canadian and British Genetics Laboratories (in review).

---

[27] For new technologies, the point has been made that technology development is distributed, so that responsibilities must be distributed as well (Von Schomberg, 2007).

[28] As one of us (AR) has argued, this would be reflexive neo-corporatism, see Randles *et al.*, 2012.

Conley, S.N. 2011. Engagement agents in the making: on the front lines of socio-technical integration. commentary on: "constructing productive engagement: pre-engagement tools for emerging technologies" *Science and Engineering Ethics* **17**(4):715–721.

Daey Ouwens C, Hoogstraten, P. van Jelsma, J., Prakke, F. and Rip, A. *Constructief Technologisch Aspectenonderzoek. Een Verkenning*, Den Haag: Staatsuitgeverij (1987) (NOTA Voorstudie 4).

Domareski, J. 2011. Responsible innovation network. *Genomics and Society: Social Science and Humanities Research in Genomics,* (4), Spring,13 .

Doubleday, R. 2007 The Laboratory Revisited. *NanoEthics* **1**(2), 167–176.

DuPont and Environmental Defense (2007) Nano Risk Framework, http://apps.edf.org /documents/6496_nano%20risk%20framework.pdf accessed 23 December 2012.

European Commission (2008) European Commissions Code of Conduct for Responsible Nanotechnologies Research, http://.ec.europa.eu/nanotechnology/pdf/nanocode -rec pe0894c-en.pdf , accessed 24 December 2012.

Fisher, E. (2005) Lessons learned from the ethical, legal and social implications program (ELSI): planning a societal implications research program for the national nanotechnology program. *Technology in Society* **27**: 321–328.

Fisher, E. (2007) Ethnographic invention: probing the capacity of laboratory decisions. *Nanoethics* **1**(2):155–165.

Fisher, E. (2009) Legislative and Regulatory Framework. Nanotechnology and FDA-Regulated Products: The Essential Guide, Food and Drug Law Library, Washington, DC.

Fisher, E. 2011. Editorial overview: public science and technology scholars: engaging whom? *Science and Engineering Ethics* **17**(4):607–620.

Fisher, E., S. Biggs, S., Lindsay, and J. Zhao. 2010. Research thrives on integration of natural and social sciences. Correspondence. *Nature* **463** 1018.

Fisher, E., R.L. Mahajan, and C. Mitcham (2006a) Midstream modulation of technology: governance from within. *Bulletin of Science, Technology and Society* **26** (6):485–496.

Fisher, E. and R.L. Mahajan, 2006b. Contradictory intent? US federal legislation on integrating societal concerns into nanotechnology research and development. *Science and Public Policy* **33**(1):5–16.

Fisher, E. and Mahajan, R.L. (2006c) Midstream modulation in an academic research laboratory. Proceedings of the American Society for Mechanical Engineers International Mechanical Engineering Congress and Exposition, Chicago, Illinois, November 5–10.

Fisher, E. and R.L. Mahajan (2010). Embedding the humanities in engineering: Art, dialogue, and a laboratory. in Gorman, M.E. (Ed.), *Trading Zones and Interactional Expertise: Creating New Kinds of Collaboration*. ed. M.E. Gorman,MIT Press, Cambridge, MA and London, England, pp. 209–230.

Flipse, S.M., van der Sanden, M.C.A., and Osseweijer, P. (2012) Midstream modulation in biotechnology industry – redefining what is 'part of the job' of researchers in industry. *Science and Engineering Ethics* doi: 10.1007/s11948-012-9411-6.

Garud R. and Ahlstrom D. (1997) Technology assessment: a socio-cognitive perspective, *Journal of Engineering and Technology Management*. **14** 25–48.

Genome British Columbia (2011) Pathways to integration. GSEAC Subcommittee on Pathways to Integration, March 23.

Genus, A. (2006), Rethinking constructive technology assessment as democratic, reflective, discourse. *Technology Forecasting and Social Change* **73**, 13–26.

Geoghegan-Quinn, M. (2012) http://ec.europa.eu/commission_2010-2014/geoghegan-quinn/headlines/speeches/2012/documents/20120423-dialogue-conference-speech_en.pdf.

Guston, D.H. (2000) Retiring the social contract for science. Issues in *Science and Technology* (summer) available: http://www.issues.org/16.4/p_guston.htm, accessed 24 December 2012.

Guston, D.H. 2006. Responsible knowledge-based innovation. *Society* **43**(4): 19–21.

Guston, D.H. 2007. Toward centres for responsible innovation in the commercialized university. *Public Science in Liberal Democracy: The Challenge to Science and Democracy*, (eds. P.W.B. Phillips and J. Porter) 295–312. Toronto, Canada: University of Toronto Press.

Guston, D. H. and D. Sarewitz. (2002) Real-time technology assessment. *Technology in Society* **24**:93–109.

Hill, M. (1997) *The Policy Process in the Modern State*. Prentice Hall: London.

Holbrook, J. B. 2005. Assessing the science–society relation: the case of the US National Science Foundation's second merit review criterion. *Technology in Society* **27**: 437–451.

Jones R. (2008) When it pays to ask the public. *Nature Nanotechnology* **3**, 578–579.

Karen, P. and Pidgeon, N. (2011) Public Engagement on Geoengineering Research: Preliminary Report on the SPICE Deliberative Workshops. Understanding Risk Working Paper 11–01, June 2011.

Krupp, F. and Holliday, C. 2005. Let's get nanotech right. *Wall Street Journal* Management Supplement, B2.

Lasswell, H.D. (1970) Must science serve political power? *American Psychologist* **25**:2, 117–123.

Laurent, B. (2011) Democracies on trial. Assembling nanotechnology and its problems. Thèse de Doctorat, Ecole des Mines de Paris.

LMC (Local Monitoring Committee) (O. Lemaire, A. Moneyron, J. E. Masson), (2010) "Interactive technology assessment" and beyond: the field trial of genetically modified grapevines at INRA-Colmar, *PLoS Biology* **8**(11), (1–7) (Separately Paginated).

Macnaghten, P., and O. Richard (2011) Good governance for geoengineering. *Nature* **479**: 293.

Marris, C. Rip, A. and Joly, P.-B. Interactive technology assessment in the real World: dual dynamics in an iTA exercise on genetically modified vines. *Science, Technology & Human Values* **33**(1) (2008) 77–100.

McCarthy, E. and C. Kelty. 2010. Nanotechnology and responsibility. *Social Studies of Science* **40**(3) 405–432.

Ministerie van Onderwijs en Wetenschappen (1983–1984) Integratie van Wetenschap en Technologie in de Samenleving. Beleidsnota (Policy Memorandum: Integration of Science and Technology in Society),'s-Gravenhage:Tweede Kamer, 18 421, nrs. 1-2.

NanoMed (2010) The Report of the Round Table Exercise, A Report on the Nanomedicine Environment. NanoMed Round Table Extended Report, http://www.philosophie.tu-darmstadt.de/media/institut_fuer_philosophie/diesunddas/nordmann/nanomed.pdf accessed 24 December 2012.

National Research Council (2006) A Matter of Size: Triennial Review of the National Nanotechnology Initiative.

National Science and Technology Council Committee on Technology, and Subcommittee on Nanoscale Science, Engineering, and Technology (2011) *National Nanotechnology Initiative Strategic Plan*, Washington, DC, Government Printing Office, February 2011.

Nordmann, A., and Rip, A. (2009) Mind the gap revisited. *Nature Nanotechnology* **4** 273–274

Observatory Nano (2012) Final Observatory NANO 2012 Report. Press Release, March 2012, http://www.innovationsgesellschaft.ch/en/index.php?section=news&cmd =details&newsid=621 accessed 24 December 2012.

Owen, R. and Goldberg, N. (2010) Responsible Innovation: A Pilot Study with the U.K.

Parandian, A. (2012) Constructive TA of newly emerging technologies. stimulating learning by anticipation through bridging events. PhD thesis, Technical University Delft, defended March 12, 2012.

Randles, S., J. Youtie, D. Guston, B. Harthtorn, C. Newfield, P., Shapira, F., Wickson, A., Rip, R., Von Schomberg, N. Pidgeon 2012 A trans-Atlantic conversation on responsible innovation and responsible governance. (eds.H. van Lente, C. Coenen, T. Fleischer *et al.*), *Proceedings of the third S.NET Conference in Tempe, Arizona, November 2011*, Heidelberg: Akademische Verlaggesellschaft AKA/IOS Press, pp. 169–179.

Rip, A. (2002) *Co-Evolution of Science, Technology and Society*. Expert Review for the Bundesministerium Bildung and Forschung's Förderinitiative 'Politik, Wissenschaft und Gesellschaft' (Science Policy Studies), Managed by the Berlin-Brandenburgische Akademie der Wissenschaften. Enschede: University of Twente.

Rip, A. (2006) Folk theories of nanotechnologists *Science as Culture* **15**: 349–365.

Rip, A. (2010): De facto governance of nanotechnologies. (eds Goodwin, M.; Koops, B.-J.; Leenes, R) *Dimensions of Technology Regulation*. Nijmegen, pp. 285–308.

Rip, A. and te Kulve, H. (2008) Constructive technology assessment and sociotechnical scenarios. (eds E. Fisher, C. Selin, M.W., Jameson) *The Yearbook of Nanotechnology in Society Volume I: Presenting Futures*, Berlin: Springer, pp. 49–70.

Rip, A., Misa, T. J. and Schot, J. (eds.), (1995) Managing technology in society. *The Approach of Constructive Technology Assessment*, London and New York: Pinter Publishers.

Rip, A. and Shelley-Egan, C. 2010. Positions and responsibilities in the 'real' world of nanotechnology. (eds Von Schomberg R., Davies S.) *Understanding Public Debate on Nanotechnologies: Options for Framing Public Policies: A Working Document by the Services of the European Commission*. European Commission, Brussels, pp. 31–38.

Roberts, M. R. (2009). Realizing societal benefit from Academic Research: analysis of the National Science foundation's broader impacts criterion. *Social Epistemology* **23** (3–4): 199–219.

Robinson, D.K.R. (2009), Co-evolutionary scenarios: an application to prospecting futures of the responsible development of nanotechnology. *Technological Forecasting and Social Change* **76**, 1222–1239

Robinson, D.K.R. (2010) Constructive technology assessment of emerging nanotechnologies. Experiments in interactions. PhD thesis, defended November 25, 2010.

Roco, M. and Bainbridge, W. S., (eds.) 2001: *Societal Implications of Nanoscience and Nanotechnology*. Boston, MA: Kluwer Academic Publishers, http://www.wtec.org /loyolainanolNSET.Societal.Implications/nanosi.pdf (accessed 3 December 2008).

Roco, M.C., B. Harthorn, D. Guston, P. Shapira (2011), Innovative and responsible governance of nanotechnology for societal development. *Journal of Nanoparticle Research,* **13**(9), 3557–3590.

Schot, J. and Rip, A. (1997) The past and future of constructive technology assessment, *Technological Forecasting and Social Change,* **54** 251–268.

Schuurbiers, D. 2011. What happens in the lab: applying mid-stream modulation to enhance critical reflection in the laboratory. *Science and Engineering Ethics* **17**(4):769–88.

Selin, C. 2011 Negotiating Plausibility: Intervening in the Future of Nanotechnology. *Science and Engineering Ethics* **17**(4): 723–737.

Stephanie, B. and E. Fisher. 2011. Science and technology policy in the making: observation and engagement. Special issue of *Science and Engineering Ethics*. **17**(4): 607–849.

Sutcliffe, H. (2011) A Report on Responsible Research and Innovation for the European Commission, Matter, http://ec.europa.eu/research/sciencesociety/document_library/pdf _06/rri-report-hilary-sutcliffe_en.pdf accessed 24 December 2012.

US Congress (2003) 21st Century Nanotechnology Research and Development Act of 2003, Public Law No. 108–153.

Von Schomberg, R. (2007) From the Ethics of Technology Towards and Ethics of Knowledge Policy. Working Document of the Service of the European Commission, http://ec.europa.eu/research/science-society/pdf/ethicsofknowledgepolicy_en.pdf accessed 24 December 2012.

Von Schomberg, R.(2011). *Towards Responsible Research and Innovation in the Information and Communication Technologies and Security Technologies Fields*. European Commission, Brussels.

Von Schomberg, R. (2012) Prospects for technology assessment in a framework of responsible research and innovation in a M. Dusseldorp and R. Beecroft (eds), *Technikfolgen Abschätzen Lehren. Bildungspotenziale Transdisziplinärer Methoden*, Springer Vs Verlaf für Sozialwissenschaften, Wiesbaden, pp. 39–61.

Von Schomberg, R. and S. Davies (eds.), Understanding public debate on nanotechnologies. *Options for Framing Public Policy, Brussels*: Commission of the European Communities, (2010).

Wynne, B. (2011) Lab work goes social, and vice versa: strategising public engagement processes. *Science and Engineering Ethics* **17**(4): 791–800.

10

Responsible Innovation in Finance: Directions and Implications

Fabian Muniesa[1] and Marc Lenglet[2]
[1]*Centre de Sociologie de l'Innovation, Mines ParisTech, France*
[2]*European Business School, France*

10.1 Introduction

Debates on responsibility and irresponsibility in the financial services industry have recently become prominent due to the part played by financial innovation in the global financial crisis of the late 2000s, which has been repeatedly emphasized by practitioners, commentators, and researchers alike. From the rapid development of applied mathematics and financial engineering from the 1970s onwards, to the more recent construction and diffusion of sophisticated financial instruments, such as credit derivatives or the development of algorithmic trading, "innovation" in the financial services industry (examples of which are given in Box 10.1) is both understood as a field of intense creativity (and technical imagination) in the development of financial solutions and opportunities, and as a particularly telling illustration of unintended consequences, negative externalities, feedback loops, technological dangers, and regulatory failures (Bookstaber, 2007; Engelen *et al.*, 2011; Lépinay, 2011; MacKenzie, 2006, 2011; Millo and MacKenzie, 2009; Taleb, 2007; Tett, 2009). And, yet, probably due to the unprecedented pace of innovation in that sector, the financial services industry does not seem to have developed a culture of public assessment and technical precaution comparable to that of other sectors, such as biomedicine, biotechnology, nanotechnology, energy engineering, or telecommunications (Callon and Lacoste, 2011). It is striking, for example, that, despite the spread of metaphors of "toxicity" in accounts of financial products involved in the subprime crisis of the late 2000s (practitioners and commentators alike talk about "toxic assets" or "toxic products"), principles of testing and vigilance, such as the ones put forward in the pharmaceutical industry, are still marginal in the financial sector.

Responsible Innovation, First Edition. Edited by Richard Owen, John Bessant and Maggy Heintz.
© 2013 John Wiley & Sons, Ltd. Published 2013 by John Wiley & Sons, Ltd.

Box 10.1 Some examples of financial innovations

Financial innovations are manifold and take different forms. They can either populate our everyday lives (like the credit card or the ATM) or, on the contrary, can apparently remain outside our surroundings. Since the beginning of the financial crisis of the late 2000s, financial innovations that have been criticized for their huge impact on the well-being of societies include, notably:

Credit Default Swaps (CDS): the purpose of these contracts is to gain protection from a potential default by the underlying issuer, who can be a private actor like a company or a public actor like a State in the case of Sovereign CDS. Should such a default occur, the seller of the CDS commits to the reimbursement of the buyer, which in turn would have made a series of payments (usually referred to as the CDS "spread").

Collateralized Debt Obligations (CDOs): these are a type of asset-backed securities (ABS) issued by "special purpose entities" (SPEs, sometimes called "special purpose vehicles" or SPVs), which are legal entities created with a view to fulfilling a very specific and temporary task. CDOs are constituted by different tranches issued by the SPE and collateralized by obligations (bonds for instance). Each tranche has a different risk profile, serves different return rates and can be sold to different investors.

Mortgage-Backed Securities (MBS): these are another kind of ABS, created through a technique known as "securitization" and involving the transformation by a SPE of pools of assets (made up of mortgages in this case, having been purchased from lenders such as banks) into tradable securities. MBS can be made of residential mortgages (thereby contributing to a RMBS) or commercial mortgages (thereby contributing to a CMBS), resulting in a different structuring of the instrument.

Among the major downsides generated by such innovations was the fact that these developed historically as a way to circumvent the Basel Accords through the transfer of risks from banks (structuring and selling those securities) to third-parties (buyers of tranches of those securities), while at the same time contributing to the fragmentation of information and the dissemination of risks that were thereby made very difficult to trace back and were most probably unidentifiable. For a historical account of the development of CDOs, see Tett (2009); for an anthropological account of collateral practices, see Riles (2011).

It is also interesting to note that the notion of responsible innovation, which has been subject to extensive discussion in the field of technology assessment and in science and technology policy (see other chapters in this volume), is rarely present in finance – the notion of responsibility being mostly referred to two recurrent forms: on the one hand, "socially responsible investment" (investment vehicles promoting environmental sustainability and social fairness, for example) and on the other hand "corporate social responsibility" (business self-regulation encouraging compliance with regulations and ethical standards). Being too often restricted to these two expressions, "responsibility" in the financial sphere does not provide any place for the sound questioning or the concern of externalities at the core of financial innovation proper: the perimeters of responsible innovation in finance are yet to be explored.

In the present chapter, we draw from a recent policy-oriented investigation that seeks to ground measures for the advancement of responsible innovation in finance within an account of several dimensions of responsibility in that area (Armstrong *et al.*, 2012). The purpose of the chapter is to clarify the several meanings that responsible or irresponsible innovation can have in finance, and to illustrate them with some examples. The first section presents these several meanings and the second section comments briefly on how these meanings may be considered in the organizational spaces in which complex financial innovation is handled at a design stage, inside investment banks.

10.2   Perspectives on Responsible Innovation in Finance

How can we map the various meanings of responsibility and irresponsibility in financial innovation? The layout proposed in this section is the outcome of both a literature review and discussions with practitioners and researchers from a variety of backgrounds.[1] For each broad meaning of what "responsible innovation" could mean in finance, we identify a general philosophical intuition, which we then refer to in terms of practical interpretations.

10.2.1   Perspective on Function

When can a particular financial innovation be said to be "responsible" and what exactly makes it responsible? One initial way of considering an answer to such a question would be to consider the "function" of financial innovation, as put forward by mainstream economists. Within this line of thought, a responsible innovation in finance is one that fulfills the functions of finance in the economy (this is synonymous with considerations of purpose discussed in Chapters 2 and 3). Silber (1983) and Merton (1995) are crucial references within this functionalist view of financial innovation, which is considered to be justified when and if it serves the economic functions of finance. Those functions are, following Merton (1995): the provision of a medium for exchange, the funding of economic enterprise, the transfer of resources, the management of risk, the coordination of distributed decisions, and the resolution of problems of asymmetric information. This of course refers to functions that are considered as being positive by the economic theorist: in this case Robert C. Merton, the reputable North-American economist, Nobel laureate in economics, and recognized contributor to the development of options pricing, portfolio selection, and valuation methods for complex derivative securities (see also Merton and Bodie, 2005). This particular view presupposes that the functional and ethical debate has already been settled. For example, the idea that making money with money or increasing personal wealth could be considered a legitimate function of financial innovation. All in

---

[1] These discussions took place in 2011, as part of the activities of the "Working Group on Responsible Innovation in Finance," a standing working group of the Observatory for Responsible Innovation, a think tank established at Mines ParisTech (the Ecole des Mines de Paris) in France. For more details on this initiative, see Armstrong *et al.* (2012) and Callon and Lacoste (2011).

all, this focus requires the presence of a moral (in this case also scientific) authority that defines what the correct and acceptable functions of financial innovation are.

Within the financial services industry, this functionalist perspective usually translates into the emphasis on a supervisory view. A regulator, considered as an external, disinterested observer, scrutinizes financial reality in terms of previously defined general functions, and provides an assessment that may subsequently be taken into account in measures of sanction or reward. This view is implicitly present in the narratives of financial regulation (e.g., Gray and Hamilton, 2006; Spencer, 2000). The involvement of academic economists in policy proposals can allow for a variety of perspectives, inspired by the economic assessment of the function and functioning of financial regulation and the translation of this assessment into regulatory recommendations (e.g., French *et al.*, 2010).

10.2.2   Perspective on Moral Rules

An analogous but slightly different perspective would put the emphasis on moral rules. The point here relies on the balance between financial innovation on the one hand, and transcendent moral principles, with an explicit reference to Kantian metaphysics (Longuenesse, 2005; Uniacke, 2005) on the other. Such a philosophical position toward responsible innovation requires a shared understanding of moral considerations and, therefore, social apparatuses that foster the compliance of individual behaviors, together with the deployment of coercive actions and mechanisms of exclusion in order to remove faulty agents from regular collective life. Although techniques of government may also evolve toward the subjective acceptance of discipline and control (Foucault, 2007), emphasis is put on authority. But authority is legitimate because it guarantees the respect of moral principles – which implies, in part, a strong presence of religious narratives.

Such a perspective finds its financial expression through the deployment and reinforcement of regulatory authorities, with particular attention toward sound principles of action and the promotion of environmental, societal, and ethical sensitivity (Blommenstein, 2006; Boatright, 2007, 2010; McHugh, 2006). The case of Islamic finance is of particular relevance here, as a possible illustration of the interpenetration of moral doctrine in financial innovation, with the creation of Shari'a-compliant financial products allowing the reconciliation of theological imperatives on the one hand and economic development on the other (Maurer, 2005, 2006).

10.2.3   Perspective on Internalized Values

Another understanding of responsible innovation in finance shifts focus toward internalized values. Here, the innovation would come as a result of moral agents: that is, agents for whom morality would come as a naturally embedded form of action. The "legislator," being reintegrated within the very act of decision-making, shares of course a portion of the Kantian view, but emphasis is definitely put on the subjective, and the ability of actors to reflexively perceive and question their ways of engaging in the financial arena. Values sit at the core of such a perspective and lead us to the rereading of the sociological tradition, from Weber to Parsons (e.g., Parsons and Shils, 1951), with the idea that human action depends on internalized moral hierarchies, which in turn reflect social orders (see Bourdieu, 1977).

In practical terms, this means that directions for conduct work well when they are internalized in the form of personal values. This sort of perspective leads quite naturally to stress the importance of education and learning institutions, as vectors of socialization taking into account the very act of transmitting values. Financial elites can be made privy to such questions during their curricula, where the acquisition of technical financial knowledge would be paralleled with critical approaches and discussions toward ethical outcomes. The MBA Oath at the Harvard Business School, an initiative intended to make future MBA graduates commit to responsible values, such as integrity, accountability, and sustainability, can serve as an example of this type of struggle to make future financiers more responsible (Anderson and Escher, 2010; see also Khurana, 2007; Starkey and Tiratsoo, 2007). In general, debates on responsibilities in financial debacles leading to a reconsideration of business schools as vehicles for the transmission of values strongly partake in this perspective on responsible innovation as a matter of socialization.

10.2.4 Perspective on Aggregate Consequences

But responsibility can be thought of from a different perspective, focusing on unintended and negative outcomes relating to the considered innovation. With this perspective in mind, a responsible innovation would take into account, at the very early stages of its development, its negative potentialities and effects (see Chapter 6). The inscription of innovation in such a frame of thought would amount to replacing the classical synchronic dimension of innovation by a diachronic approach (Jonas, 1984). Indeed, responsibility implies the considering of forthcoming consequences related to the deployment of current action. Being in a position to influence a forthcoming world implies the ability to think about the successful dissemination of the contemplated innovation: the focus is then put on accountability, with an emphasis on negative externalities and references to the "risk society" (Arnoldi, 2009; Beck, 1992; Giddens, 1990; Luhmann, 1993).

Looking into financial innovation from this vantage point, these ideas translate into calls for the enhancing of modeling capacities, with a view to mitigating forthcoming dangers under unintended or even unforeseeable, cascading situations (Hutter and Power, 2005; Power, 2007). Internal critique of financial innovation pointing to the use and effect of flawed models, deficient probabilistic thinking, and insufficient reflexivity as the main forms of irresponsibility does side with this perspective to a large extent (Ayache, 2010; Mandelbrot and Hudson, 2004; Taleb, 2007). Responsibility in financial innovation means better scientifically-grounded innovation, more skillful and intelligent innovators and more refined forecasting and risk assessment methodologies. But it also means taking into account the effects of escalation in intelligent innovation and the development of unintended systemic consequences, feedback loops and collective accidents.

10.2.5 Perspective on Accountability

A fifth possible understanding of responsibility refers to the authorship of action rather than to the principles that may guide it. Here, being responsible amounts to accepting the potential liabilities related to the innovative product or practice, with the idea that these can be traced. In this view, the pivotal point rests on the idea that somebody may be in a position to stand and respond to forthcoming questioning, once identified. The innovator is responsible for her creation and the creation's consequences, as pointed out in the case of Mary Shelley's Frankenstein (see Chapter 7) insofar as she remains present and accountable, especially in the cases in which the innovation turns out to be problematic. Not only does this mean that the respondent acknowledges the necessity of an answer for something and toward someone (Hache and Latour, 2010; Levinas, 1969, 2003), but it also entails the ability to sign (that is, leave a trace) as the author (Agamben, 2009).

In the financial services industry, such a definition of responsibility amounts to the deployment of auditing devices, together with disclosure mechanisms for the attribution of liabilities. The Sarbanes–Oxley Act of 2002, for instance, was enacted after a series of accounting scandals, which prompted the development of organizational practices such as the individual signature of documents accounting for decision-making, as an attempt at tracing responsibility down to the individual's level (Coates, 2007; Fairfax, 2002). More generally, practices of verification that have come to characterize what researchers in accounting studies have called "the audit society" exemplify this idea of responsibility as accountability (Power, 1997).

10.2.6   Perspective on Precaution

Responsibility can also be made sense of in terms of precaution and vigilance, both developed through safety protocols to be followed by the participants in the innovation. What is at stake here is the ability to follow an escape route, should the innovation prove dangerous and toxic; hence its resonance with the so-called "precautionary principle" (Dratwa, 2002). Philosophically speaking, it resonates with the avoidance of excesses and a specific attention or "care" toward the innovative action, paying attention to proportionate levels of engagement and being aware that experiments sometimes result in failures. With this perspective, we are not far from Spinozist views on ethics (Deleuze, 1988) or the considerations on pathology later suggested by Canguilhem (1989). Another comparison could be drawn from pharmacovigilance practices, involving careful representations of what the market is and how it is in fact used as a genuine and fragile testing device, where drug recall is part of its structure (Daemmerich, 2004).

Such an approach is sometimes used in the financial services industry, for instance when it comes to the definition of capital buffers with a view to mitigating "systemic risk" ("minimum capital requirements" in Basel Accords parlance; see Drumond, 2009 and also Izquierdo, 2001). A better dissemination of this perspective within the financial sphere would entail the organization of arenas for the discussion of innovation, together with the characterization of risk pockets and the institution of recalling protocols. A recent example can serve to further illustrate this view: contrary to those countries where they developed in an unregulated space, over-the-counter derivative markets (that is, markets for a certain class of financial instruments traded directly between two parties, with no necessity to have the transaction made on an exchange or through a third-party intermediary) were developed in a regulated space in India. This space notably involved product specifications, the qualification of market participants, the deployment of effective reporting systems, together with a series of acknowledged responsibilities for those market participants willing to trade such products (Epstein and Crotty, 2009; Gopinath, 2010).

10.2.7 Perspective on Democracy

Responsibility can also be understood as a way to foster debates between empowered stakeholders: a responsible innovation would be made discussable by all concerned parties, so that potential or forthcoming controversies can be collectively addressed by concerned actors. Indeed, innovation can often be the subject of antagonistic visions, materializing different interests and positions at stake: democratic devices allowing for deliberative approaches to emerge are used in fields such as nanotechnology, nuclear policy, medicine, and biotechnology (Callon *et al.*, 2009; Jasanoff, 2005; Latour, 2004; Rip *et al.*, 1995), see Chapter 5 for further discussion.

How does this perspective translate in the area of financial innovation? Beyond classical (though recent) approaches toward corporate social responsibility (Basu and Palazzo, 2008; Freeman, 1994), some initiatives relating to the financing of large industrial projects (activities sometimes referred to as "project finance") usually include public participation in decision-making processes (Wright and Rwabizambuga, 2006). A financial world that would fully comply with this viewpoint would, for instance, be one in which a "hybrid forum" is constituted for every important act of innovation. Although ideas of public scrutiny and democratic participation are discussed in the domain of corporate social responsibility or socially responsible investment, these seem to be missing in the area of financial innovation proper (with regards to the development of complex financial instruments or sophisticated trading technologies for instance) in the global financial world of the early 2010s.

10.3 Some Directions for Further Reflection

We have listed seven possible perspectives on responsible innovation, with indications of possible implications in the area of finance. Our focus is not on ordinary financial practices of accounting and investment, but on what practitioners, commentators, and researchers call financial innovation, that is, the development of new financial products and financial technologies. The key, pressing issues concerning financial innovation in the wake of the financial crisis of the late 2000s are threats to stability within the financial services industry, undesirable chain reactions, disruptions in the financing of economic activities, exacerbation of social asymmetries and social unrest, with political consequences. In the early 2010s, controversy has been sparked regarding the benefits and dangers of novel financial instruments such as ETFs (exchange-traded funds), hybrid complex MTNs (medium-term notes), sovereign CDS (credit default swaps on sovereign debt) and liquidity swaps, and on new trading practices such as HFT (high-frequency trading) – Box 10.2. In our view, the call for responsibility in these issues is a call that navigates in all the perspectives that we have highlighted.

Box 10.2 Some definitions

ETF: is a financial instrument combining the nature of an investment fund, while being traded like securities, such as equities, on a stock exchange. ETF can be used to track an index (e.g., the Dow Jones) or may be constructed to represent a sector (e.g., the healthcare industry), a country or a definite class of assets (e.g., commodities).

MTN: is a debt security allowing a company to obtain a flow of cash tailored according to its financing needs. MTNs are usually paid back after 5–10 years; the volume of MTN issuance has recently witnessed a very important growth, both in the EU and the US.

HFT: refers to a form of trading involving the use of quantitative models and computerized algorithms to implement trading strategies with a very short time horizon. Positions relating to HFT can be held for less than minutes, and involve numerous transactions performed within milliseconds (sometimes even microseconds) with machines inputting, modifying, and deleting orders within the same time frame. HFT is usually deployed by proprietary firms (hedge funds) or proprietary desks (within investment banks) and requires advanced technical knowledge and important technological capacities. Its defendants contend that HFT contributes to liquidity formation and price-discovery mechanisms in markets, while its opponents underline the lack of meaning resulting from such transactions, as compared to the classical features of a financial market (that is, financing the "real" economy).

But *where* are these products and services developed? An empirical look at the ordinary, actual practice of financial innovation is of use in developing directions for further reflection in this regard. Professionals of financial innovation working inside investment banks and credit institutions follow internal organizational processes. In the financial services industry, the notion of New Product Committee or New Product Approval refers to the organizational structures and group meetings in which the development and launch of a new product or a new service are discussed inside the investment bank, risks and opportunities are assessed, decisions are validated, and tasks and responsibilities are attributed (Armstrong *et al.*, 2012). Product approval processes have been in use for quite a long time, for instance taking the form of project development groups. But the institutionalization of New Product Committees or New Product Approval as such is a quite recent phenomenon. Traces of their emergence may be found in the framework of the Basel II Accords (BCBS, 2006, p. 267). Regulators have since been introducing the idea of a mandatory approval for new products (AMF, 2006; BCBS, 2008, 2011; CCLRF, 2005, art. 11–1; FSA, 2011, p. 16; JFSA, 2007, p. 9; SIFMA, 2011).

New Product Committees in the financial services industry are generally open to a multiplicity of concerned parties, but these are limited to the internal perimeter of the credit institution or the investment firm. Participants are members of the teams in charge of financial engineering and trading, risk analysis, legal compliance, accounting, and clearing and settlement. There is no widely shared practice of widening the perimeter of New Product Committees and introducing participants external to the firm. There are no industry-wide guidelines for the governance of New Product Committees, which is defined internally. Worries and concerns can generally be expressed by relevant departments within these spaces, although sometimes a marked sense of hierarchy, an over-emphasis on competition, or a harsh climate of professional progress may lead to situations in which some actors refrain from expressing concerns or are simply not heard. In principle, New Product Committees can also assess and evaluate the evolution and effects of a service or product once it has been released into the market, therefore opening a cyclic revision process and preventive steps that can be implemented before the innovation is too widely disseminated, and hence difficult to restrain. New Product Committees are also instruments for the traceability of decisions and responsibilities. Decisions result in the production of documents signed by involved parties, which therefore certify that signatory parties are made accountable. But New Product Committees are sometimes also seen as an administrative burden, impairing the unleashing of financial imagination (traders and financial engineers generally hold this view), and these organizational measures are not always popular among bank employees. The fact that New Product Committees somehow produce legitimacy and allow new products to join the chain of existing products may not be sufficient to make them an attractive feature. Compliance officers and other actors in charge of regulatory verification inside the financial firm play an important role in New Product Committees: yet they are often caught between contradictory commitments (toward the firm on the one hand and toward the regulator on the other).

Armstrong *et al.* (2012) indicate how, once conveniently retooled, New Product Committees could turn into appropriate organizational instruments for the development of responsible innovation in finance when considered from the various angles indicated above. The New Product Committee is an environment in which the purpose or function of the financial innovation can be articulated and justified (more or less) publicly. The role of the compliance officer could be strengthened and improved, so that it would not remain limited to warranting regulatory verification, but rather be more oriented toward raising issues and formulating objections, in order to transform the New Product Committee into a robust relay with regulators. As part of the organizational culture of the investment bank, New Product Committees can also strengthen the penetration of responsibility into professional habits through, for example, the conditioning of career development by participation in them. The New Product Committee is also the place in which the limitations of financial modeling can be acknowledged, and thus compensated by discussion on qualitative considerations, and also by commitment to revision and reassessment of the innovation and its behavior once introduced on the market. Membership of New Product Committees is already a form of personal accountability and this can be improved with a long-term commitment of participants, including the recalibration of their economic incentives. The New Product Committee can be a place where issues of calibration and dissemination are systematically raised, following a clinical perspective and in connection with an industry-wide initiative for setting indicative precautionary thresholds for the size and scope of an innovation. Finally, New Product Committees allow a deliberative process, in which the voicing of concerns could be improved with procedures and codes of conduct that foster an equal distribution of voice among participants, and perhaps with the invitation of external observers. With these remarks, which should not be read as a way to trivialize the difficulties pertaining to the crafting of responsible innovations in finance, we intend to contribute to a reopening of a debate on these issues, and foster a renewed perspective on the governance of innovation inside investment banks.

10.4 Conclusion

Responsible innovation in finance is today more a challenge than a structured field. The global financial crisis of the late 2000s has exacerbated the public debate on responsibility and irresponsibility in the financial services industry. In particular, it has put forward two crucial topics that are characteristic of responsible innovation at large. The first is the problem of unanticipated risks of innovation and the second is the problem of the involvement of potentially affected actors in the innovation process (Callon and Lacoste, 2011). Lessons from industrial and scientific domains in which the discussion on responsible innovation is characterized to some extent by a more advanced level of maturity (such as in biomedicine, biotechnology, nanotechnology, energy engineering, or telecommunications) are today increasingly inspiring policy discussions and professional ventures. Science and technology studies as a field of study have been at the forefront of the development of the topic of responsible innovation in this regard, and have a significant contribution to make to the theory and practice of financial innovation that goes above and beyond mainstream economics. Indeed, understanding such perspectives might help us better understand the embedded nature of innovation, its cultural and material determinants, its tacit assumptions, and the views and concerns of often silent participants and stakeholders. This might provide us with sounder representations of what is at stake with financial innovations (see, for example, MacKenzie, 2006, 2011). We conject (and hope) that this approach will prove relevant in the development of policy initiatives for the development of responsible innovation in finance. At the same time, as this chapter shows, we think that disciplinary openness is necessary, and that the notion of responsibility in financial innovation needs to be tackled from all possible angles, including the philosophical one.

Acknowledgments

The work on which this chapter draws has been supported by the Observatory for Responsible Innovation, Mines ParisTech, France. We thank Diane-Laure Arjaliès, Margaret Armstrong, Daniel Beunza, Michel Callon, Guillaume Cornut, Stéphane Delacôte, Nadège Jassaud, Bruce Kogut, Annalivia Lacoste, Michèle Leclerc-Olive, Yuval Millo, Jean-Claude Monod, Alexandre Pointier, Michael Power, Valérie Rabault, Yamina Tadjeddine, and Christian Walter for their comments on earlier versions.

References

Agamben, G. (2009), *The Signature of All Things: On Method*, Zone Books, Brooklyn, NY.

AMF (Autorité des Marchés Financiers) (2006), La Commercialisation Des Services d'Investissement Et Des Produits Financiers: Analyse Des Rapports Adressés à l'AMF en 2004, Autorité des Marchés Financiers, Paris.

Anderson, M. and P. Escher (2010), *The MBA Oath: Setting a Higher Standard for Business Leaders*, Portfolio, New York.

Armstrong, M., G. Cornut, S. Delacôte, M. Lenglet, Y. Millo, F. Muniesa, A. Pointier and Y. Tadjeddine (2012), Towards a practical approach to responsible innovation in finance: New Product Committees revisited, *Journal of Financial Regulation and Compliance,* **20**(2), 147–168.

Arnoldi, J. (2009), *Risk: An Introduction*, Polity Press, London.

Ayache, E. (2010), *The Blank Swan: The End of Probability*, John Wiley & Sons, Ltd, Chichester.

Basu, K. and G. Palazzo (2008), Corporate social responsibility: a process model of sensemaking, *Academy of Management Review,* **33**(1), 122–136.

BCBS (Basel Committee on Banking Supervision) (2006) International Convergence of Capital Measurement and Capital Standards, Basel Committee on Banking Supervision, Basel.

BCBS (2008) Principles for Sound Liquidity Risk Management and Supervision, Basel Committee on Banking Supervision, Basel.

BCBS (2011) Basel III: A Global Regulatory Framework for More Resilient Banks and Banking Systems, Basel Committee on Banking Supervision, Basel.

Beck, U. (1992), *Risk Society: Towards a New Modernity*, Sage Publications, London.

Blommenstein, H.J. (2006), Why is ethics not part of modern economics and finance? A historical perspective, *Finance and the Common Good,* **24**(1), 54–64.

Boatright, J.R. (2007), *Ethics in Finance*, John Wiley & Sons, Ltd, Hoboken, NJ.

Boatright, J.R. (ed) (2010), *Finance Ethics: Critical Issues in Theory and Practice*, John Wiley & Sons, Ltd, Hoboken, NJ.

Bookstaber, R. (2007), *A Demon of Our Own Design: Markets, Hedge Funds, and the Perils of Financial Innovation*, John Wiley & Sons, Ltd, Hoboken, NJ.

Bourdieu, P. (1977), *Outline of a Theory of Practice*, Cambridge University Press, Cambridge.

Callon, M. and A. Lacoste (2011), Defending responsible innovation, *Debating Innovation,* **1**(1), 19–27.

Callon, M., P. Lascoumes and Y. Barthe (2009), *Acting in an Uncertain World: An Essay on Technical Democracy*, The MIT Press, Cambridge, MA.

Canguilhem, G. (1989), *The Normal and the Pathological*, Zone Books, Brooklyn, NY.

CCLRF (Comité Consultatif de la Législation et de la Réglementation Financières) (2005), Regulation 97–02 of 21 February 1997, Relating to Internal Control in

Credit Institutions and Investment Firms, Comité Consultatif de la Législation et de la Réglementation Financières, Paris.

Coates, J.C. (2007), The goals and promise of the Sarbanes–Oxley Act, *Journal of Economic Perspectives,* **21**(1), 91–116.

Daemmerich, A. (2004), *Pharmacopolitics: Drug Regulation in the United States and Germany*, The University of North Carolina Press, Chapel Hill, NC.

Deleuze, G. (1988), *Spinoza: Practical Philosophy*, City Lights Publishers, San Francisco, CA.

Dratwa, J. (2002), Taking risks with the precautionary principle: food (and the environment) for thought at the European Commission, *Journal of Environmental Policy and Planning,* **4**(3), 197–213.

Drumond, I. (2009), Bank capital requirements, business cycle fluctuations and the Basel Accords: a synthesis, *Journal of Economic Surveys,* **23**(5), 798–830.

Engelen, E., I. Ertürk, J. Froud, S. Johal, A. Leaver, M. Moran, A. Nilsson and K. Williams (2011), *After the Great Complacence: Financial Crisis and the Politics of Reform*, Oxford University Press, Oxford.

Epstein, G. and J. Crotty (2009), Controlling dangerous financial products through a financial pre-cautionary principle, *Ekonomiaz,* **72**, 270–291.

Fairfax, L.M. (2002), Form over substance: officer certification and the promise of enhanced personal accountability under the Sarbanes-Oxley Act, *Rutgers Law Review,* **55**(1), 1–64.

Foucault, M. (2007), *Security, Territory, Population: Lectures at the Collège de France, 1977–1978*, Palgrave Macmillan, New York.

Freeman, R.E. (1994), The politics of stakeholder theory: some future directions, *Business Ethics Quarterly,* **4**(4), 409–421.

French, K.R., M.N. Baily, J.Y. Campbell, J.H. Cochrane, D.W. Diamond, D. Duffie, A.K. Kashyap, F.S. Mishkin, R.G. Rajan, D.S. Scharfstein, R.J. Shiller, H.S. Shin, M.J. Slaughter, J.C. Stein and R.M. Stulz (2010), *The Squam Lake Report: Fixing the Financial System*, Princeton University Press, Princeton, NJ.

FSA (Financial Services Authority) (2011) Product Intervention, Discussion Paper DP11/1, Financial Services Authority, London.

Giddens, A. (1990), *The Consequences of Modernity*, Polity Press, Cambridge.

Gopinath, S. (2010), Over-the-counter derivative markets in India: issues and perspectives, *Financial Stability Review,* **14**, 61–69.

Gray, J. and J. Hamilton (2006), *Implementing Financial Regulation: Theory and Practice*, John Wiley & Sons, Ltd, Hoboken, NJ.

Hache, E. and B. Latour (2010), Morality or moralism? An exercise in sensitization, *Common Knowledge,* **16**(2), 311–330.

Hutter, B. and M. Power (eds) (2005) *Organizational Encounters With Risk*, Cambridge University Press, Cambridge.

Izquierdo, A.J. (2001), Reliability at risk: the supervision of financial models as a case study for reflexive economic sociology, *European Societies,* **3**(1), 69–90.

Jasanoff, S. (2005), *Designs on Nature: Science and Democracy in Europe and the United States*, Princeton University Press, Princeton, NJ.

JFSA (Financial Services Agency, Japan) (2007) Inspection Manual for Deposit-Taking Institutions, Financial Services Agency, Tokyo.

Jonas, H. (1984), *The Imperative of Responsibility: In Search of an Ethics for the Technological Age*, The University of Chicago Press, Chicago, IL.

Khurana, R. (2007), *From Higher Aims to Hired Hands: The Social Transformation of American Business Schools and the Unfulfilled Promise of Management as a Profession*, Princeton University Press, Princeton, NJ.

Latour, B. (2004), *Politics of Nature: How to Bring the Sciences into Democracy*, Harvard University Press, Cambridge, MA.

Lépinay, V.A. (2011), *Codes of Finance: Engineering Derivatives in a Global Bank*, Princeton University Press, Princeton, NJ.

Levinas, E. (1969), *Totality and Infinity: An Essay on Exteriority*, Duquesne University Press, Pittsburgh, PA.

Levinas, E. (2003), *Humanism of the Other*, University of Illinois Press, Urbana, IL.

Longuenesse, B. (2005), *Kant on the Human Standpoint*, Cambridge University Press, Cambridge.

Luhmann, N. (1993), *Risk: A Sociological Theory*, Walter de Gruyter, Berlin.

MacKenzie, D. (2006), *An Engine, Not a Camera: How Financial Models Shape Markets*, The MIT Press, Cambridge, MA.

MacKenzie, D. (2011) The credit crisis as a problem in the sociology of knowledge, *American Journal of Sociology,* **116**(6), 1778–1841.

Mandelbrot, B. and R.L. Hudson (2004), *The (Mis)Behavior of Markets: A Fractal View of Risk, Ruin and Reward*, Basic Books, New York.

Maurer, B. (2005), *Mutual Life, Limited: Islamic Banking, Alternative Currencies, Lateral Reason*, Princeton University Press, Princeton, NJ.

Maurer, B. (2006), *Pious Property: Islamic Mortgages in the United States*, Russell Sage, New York.

McHugh, F. (2006), Thinking ethics while learning finance, *Finance and the Common Good,* **24**(1), 38–46.

Merton, R.C. (1995), Financial innovation and the management and regulation of financial institutions, *Journal of Banking and Finance,* **19**(3–4), 461–481.

Merton, R.C. and Z. Bodie (2005), The design of financial systems: towards a synthesis of function and structure, *Journal of Investment Management,* **3**(1), 1–23.

Millo, Y. and D. MacKenzie (2009), The usefulness of inaccurate models: towards an understanding of the emergence of financial risk management, *Accounting, Organizations and Society,* **34**(5), 638–653.

Parsons, T. and E.A. Shils (1951), Values, motives, and systems of action, in *Toward a General Theory of Action: Theoretical Foundations for the Social Sciences*, (eds T. Parsons and E.A. Shils), Harper & Row, New York, NY, 45–275.

Power, M. (1997), *The Audit Society: Rituals of Verification*, Oxford University Press, Oxford.

Power, M. (2007), *Organized Uncertainty: Designing a World of Risk Management*, Oxford University Press, Oxford.

Riles, A. (2011), *Collateral Knowledge: Legal Reasoning in the Global Financial Markets*, The University of Chicago Press, Chicago, IL.

Rip, A., T.J. Misa and J. Schot (eds) (1995), *Managing Technology in Society: The Approach of Constructive Technology Assessment*, Pinter, London.

SIFMA (Securities Industry and Financial Markets Association) (2011) The Current Economic Environment and its Impact on Retail Investors, Securities, Industry and Financial Markets Association, New York.

Silber, W.L. (1983), The process of financial innovation, *American Economic Review,* **73**(2), 89–95.

Spencer, P. (2000), *The Structure and Regulation of Financial Markets*, Oxford University Press, Oxford.

Starkey, K. and Tiratsoo, N. (2007), *The Business School and the Bottom Line*, Cambridge University Press, Cambridge.

Taleb, N.N. (2007), *The Black Swan: The Impact of the Highly Improbable*, Random House, New York.

Tett, G. (2009), *Fool's Gold: How Unrestrained Greed Corrupted a Dream, Shattered Global Markets and Unleashed a Catastrophe*, Free Press, London.

Uniacke, S. (2005), Responsibility and obligation: some kantian directions, *International Journal of Philosophical Studies,* **13**(4), 461–475.

Wright, C. and A. Rwabizambuga (2006), Institutional pressures, corporate reputation, and voluntary codes of conduct: an examination of the Equator Principles, *Business and Society Review,* **111**(1), 89–117.

11

Responsible Research and Innovation in Information and Communication Technology: Identifying and Engaging with the Ethical Implications of ICTs

Bernd, Carsten Stahl,[1] Grace Eden,[2] and Marina Jirotka[2]
[1]Centre for Computing and Social Responsibility, De Montfort University, UK
[2]Oxford e-Research Centre, Oxford University, UK

11.1 Introduction

The concept of "responsible (research and) innovation" (RRI) can refer to a number of separate but interlinked questions: who is responsible? what are they responsible for? why are they responsible? or what are the consequences of these responsibilities? are just some of the more obvious ones. This chapter will discuss some of the most pertinent of these questions with reference to information and communication technologies (ICT). It will do this by describing the context, background and findings of the European research project "Ethical Issues of Emerging ICT Applications" (ETICA) as well as the currently on-going UK research project on a "Framework for Responsible Research and Innovation in Information and Communication technology" (FRRIICT).

The chapter will start with a brief discussion of concepts of responsibility and responsible innovation that will allow the identification of important aspects that a responsible approach to ICT will require. It will then build a FRRIICT by discussing two different approaches to RRI, as represented by the two projects. This will lead to a

Responsible Innovation, First Edition. Edited by Richard Owen, John Bessant and Maggy Heintz.
© 2013 John Wiley & Sons, Ltd. Published 2013 by John Wiley & Sons, Ltd.

discussion of further research, as well as policy requirements that need to be addressed in order for research and development in ICT to live up to the expectations of responsibility.

11.2   Conceptualizing Responsibility and Responsible Research and Innovation in ICT

One of the first definitions of RRI is offered by Von Schomberg in Chapter 3 and Von Schomberg (2011, p. 9) who suggests that it can be understood as *"a transparent, inter-active process by which societal actors and innovators become mutually responsive to each other with a view on the (ethical) acceptability, sustainability and societal desir-ability of the innovation process and its marketable products (in order to allow a proper embedding of scientific and technological advances in our society)."* For the purposes of this chapter it is worthwhile briefly to unpack the ideas behind RRI in order to better understand how these ideas are related to ICT.

11.2.1   Responsibility as a Social Ascription

Such a conceptual unpacking requires a brief look at the concept of responsibility (see also Chapter 7). The etymological roots of the term come from responding or answering (Lewis, 1972), which is reflected in the French *responsabilité* (Etchegoyen, 1993), as well as in the German *Verantwortung* (Bayertz, 1995). This is a first important indication of the relational nature of the term. Responsibility can be understood as a social construct that establishes relationships between a set of different entities. Primary among them are the subject and the object. The subject is the entity that is held responsible. The object is that which the subject is responsible for. This relationship between a subject and an object is the core of the vast majority, if not all, responsibility ascriptions. Examples of this core responsibility relationship can be the responsibility of parents for their children, of politicians for their policies, of a criminal for her crime, or the responsibility of the storm for the damage it caused. This core relationship needs to be supplemented with other aspects for a responsibility ascription to be workable. Further ingredients are the norms according to which the subject is responsible for the object as well as the mechanism by which this relationship is established. Both norms and mechanisms differ for different types of responsibility, such as moral, legal or role responsibilities. In the case of legal responsibility the law is likely to provide the norm and a court, judge, or jury may attribute it. Professional responsibility requires professional rules and professional bodies to implement these. Depending on the type, there are different types of purpose of responsibility ascriptions. Responsibility can aim at retribution or revenge. For the purposes of this chapter on RRI in ICT we hold that responsibility is a prospective exercise (Chapter 7) that aims to achieve some desirable social state. Retrospective responsibility ascriptions (such as holding a copyright infringer legally responsible for a past infringement and sentencing them to a pay a fine) can also be understood to serve a forward-looking goal, such as re-socializing them into society or ensuring future compliance with copyright legislation.

Responsibility ascriptions are normally meant to have practical consequences. This requires consideration of the conditions for successful ascriptions. These conditions can refer to any of the individual components of an ascription (e.g., subject, object, norms), or to the mechanism of defining and enforcing consequences or sanctions arising from a responsibility ascription. There is much literature on some of these conditions. A key topic, for example, is the question of who, or what, can count as the subject of responsibility. The traditional response, both in law and in ethics, has been that it should be the individual human being. Conditions that such individual human responsibility subjects are normally assumed to meet include a certain level of knowledge of the situation, freedom to act and influence outcomes, power to affect the object, and a set of personal characteristics such as rationality, intentionality, reason, or self-control. It is immediately obvious that many of these touch on significant philosophical problems, such as freedom of will or freedom of action. In addition, however, there has been significant debate about whether other entities can be considered responsibility subjects. Possible candidates are groups of individuals (French, 1992), corporations (Werhane, 1985), and also technical artifacts (Allen, Smit, and Wallach, 2005; Floridi and Sanders, 2004). Depending on who or what is considered a legitimate subject of responsibility ascription, the other components will vary.

It is easy to find examples of responsibility relationships that relate to ICTs. There are several big issues that are widely discussed and have led to significant regulation and legislation. The two primary examples here are privacy/data protection and intellectual property. The responsibilities of different actors in this area (for example, the responsibility of social network sites such as Facebook to safeguard users' privacy, or the ownership of biometric data by governments or companies) are highly contested. Other examples of responsibility in ICT refer to the role of software developers in assuring quality and functionality, the responsibility of companies for usability, or the responsibility of regulators for appropriate use of data.

These are currently contested issues in existing technologies, which can be exacerbated with regards to novel technologies that are currently being researched and developed. Looking at von Schomberg's earlier definition, one can now see that he touches on some aspects, such as possible subjects (innovators and societal actors), some of the aims to be achieved (sustainability, acceptability, desirability of products), but leaves others open (exact nature of the object, conditions, mechanisms of ascription). This is not surprising, partly because responsibility ascriptions are always an evolving network where novel circumstances require redefinitions and adjustments. The present chapter contributes to the process of such redefinitions.

11.2.2 Responsible Research and Innovation as Meta-Responsibility

As the previous section has shown, responsibility relationships that touch on ICT as subject, object, or in some other form are nothing new. There are already large amounts of definitions of responsibility in the area (Stahl, 2004). These may be collective, individual, professional, role, moral, legal, and other responsibilities. Many of these responsibilities are interlinked and mutually constitutive. A software engineer, for example, may have a professional responsibility to develop a system for a customer on time and to a specified quality. She will have legal responsibility to comply with existing regulation, for example, data protection or copyright law. She may feel a moral responsibility to ensure that users are treated fairly in the system and a responsibility toward her peer software engineers to ensure transparency of her code. She can have a role responsibility as team leader to ensure responsible behavior by her team members, which may put upon her a responsibility to define responsibilities of others to meet shared goals. It may, therefore, be better to speak of a web of inextricably interlinking responsibilities.

Understanding this web of responsibilities is not trivial, as many of these responsibilities will take different forms and will have different degrees of visibility and external validity. The different responsibilities may be mutually supportive, but they may also be contradictory. For example, our software engineer has been asked to code a piece of software that may infringe a user's privacy. There is a dilemma here in terms of what her responsibility may be to bring this issue into discussion. What if senior-level managers are aware of the breach? The conflict occurs when someone needs to be held accountable for acting upon the implementation of such code. The negotiation and arbitration between the different types of responsibilities may be explicit, but they may also be tacit and implicit.

RRI as a relatively novel concept has to incorporate the fact that it enters a well-established playing field. Responsibility in research and innovation is nothing new and, as outlined above using the example of ICT, is already expressed in a web of responsibilities. It is unlikely that RRI will make a difference and affect science and technology research and innovation in a sustainable way if it is turned into one more responsibility ascription or relationship in an already well-populated field. Instead, we suggest, RRI should be conceptualized as a higher level responsibility or a meta-responsibility. This meta-responsibility is *a responsibility for responsibilities*. RRI can aim to align responsibilities, to ensure they move in a particular way. RRI can define socially desirable consequences that existing responsibilities can work toward and develop responsibility relationships that ensure that the achievement of such desired aims is possible.

In this chapter we explore this idea of RRI as a meta-responsibility in the field of ICT. Before going into detail it is helpful to have a brief look at the current state of discussion of RRI more broadly. This will allow clarification of which areas are in need of further understanding and thus which contributions to knowledge are required. On this basis we explore two pieces of research on RRI in ICT, which allow us to return to the content of RRI in ICT and beyond.

11.2.3   Responsible Research and Innovation: the Four "P"s

The reason why RRI has recently gained currency is due, to a large extent, to the real, or potential impact that a number of technical innovations can have, or are perceived to have on our lives. In the area of ICT this can, for example, relate to the ability to communicate in novel ways, for example, through social media, or the potential of large scale ubiquitous monitoring or surveillance through automatic sensor systems. Innovation can be understood as the process of making some type of potential phenomena useful for human lives through "creation of better or more effective products, processes, services, technologies, or ideas that are readily available to markets, governments, and society."[1] This raises the question of when such an innovation can be considered responsible. A look at current work on RRI in other fields shows that it is a concept that is meant to mediate the consequences of technical and other innovations on our individual and social lives. While innovation is associated with social benefit and economic growth, understanding its implications now takes on a new sense of urgency because technical and scientific

---

[1] See Wikipedia, available http://en.wikipedia.org/wiki/Innovation (accessed 10 July 2012).

innovations are happening on a global scale and at increasing speed. At the same time the social authorities who regulate innovation work or its evaluation are no longer clear (see Chapter 8 for further discussion). In a globalized world it is not obvious what is perceived to be good or on what grounds such normative evaluations can be made. This adds to the complexities of developing approaches to incorporating RRI concepts into current governance frameworks.

In this context of the globalization of research and the fragmentation of research governance, the questions loom large regarding what is considered to be desirable, desirable to whom, for what purposes, and how can we use technology to achieve it. Since we have no agreed substantive view of what is good, right, and desirable, RRI can be understood as an attempt to give a procedural answer to the question of how to deal with the uncertainties around innovation. One way of characterizing these processes is to use an alliteration that allows us to keep track of some of the core features of RRI in ICT, namely the four "p"s, which are: product, process, purpose and people. The purpose of using the four "p"s is to draw attention to the fact that, in addition to the widely recognized importance of both product and process of technical development, the purpose of the development needs to be considered and people involved in the innovation need to be incorporated in RRI (see Chapter 2 for further discussion of products and purposes and the importance of inclusive deliberation). In this chapter we will not be able to discuss all of these comprehensively, but will give an account of some of them in some more depth, in so far as they are relevant to ICT.

In the light of this complexity of responsibilities, their interlinking aspects and dimensions, the current chapter will draw a picture of RRI in ICT. Returning to the four "p"s, we start with a look at aspects of the product.

11.3   Building a Framework for RRI in ICT

Having briefly outlined some of the conceptual foundations of RRI (e.g., the concepts of responsibility in relation to ICT innovation, the idea of RRI as meta-responsibility and the four "p"s), we now provide an outline of two research projects which aim to explore the specifics of RRI in ICT. The first, the EU project ETICA explores ethical issues of emerging ICTs, whereas the second, the UK Engineering and Physical Sciences Research Council (EPSRC) project on a Framework for Responsible Research and Innovation looks at the current landscape of RRI within the UK ICT research community.

11.3.1   Product: ICTs and Their Ethical Implications

One way of approaching the question of RRI in ICT is to explore the ethical issues that future and emerging ICTs are likely to raise. This is what the ETICA project set out to do. It was funded under the European Union's Seventh Framework Programme and ran from April 2009 to May 2011. The idea of ETICA was to explore the ethics of emerging ICTs by following these four main aims:

1. Identify emerging ICTs.
2. Identify ethical issues likely to be raised by those ICTs.
3. Evaluate and rank these issues.
4. Provide recommendations on appropriate governance structures to address these.

This section will briefly highlight the main findings of each of the first three steps and will then turn to the question of governance below.[2]

11.3.1.1   Identification of Emerging ICTs

The ETICA project was predicated on the idea that, in order to facilitate a proactive approach to the ethics of novel ICTs, policy makers, researchers, research institutions, funders, and other actors in innovation processes need to gain a sound understanding of which technologies are likely to be relevant, and what their capabilities and constraints will be. While an exact knowledge of the future is elusive, as predictions cannot be certain, one can study current work in research and development to gain a sound understanding of emerging technologies. This follows the principles of technology foresight research, which aims to explore possible futures in order to allow the making of decisions that are likely to promote desirable states (Cuhls, 2003).

The methodology employed to identify emerging ICTs during the ETICA project was a structured discourse analysis of documents containing visions of future technologies. Two types of documents were analyzed: (i) high-level governmental and international policy and funding documents, and (ii) documents published by research institutions.

During data analysis more than 100 technologies, 70 application examples and 40 artifacts were identified. These were synthesized into the following list of emerging ICTs. Note that the term "emerging ICT" is used for any high-level socio-technical system that has the potential to significantly affect the way humans interact with the world. A good example of such as system would be "ambient intelligence" which can be understood as a vision of a generalized, embedded and ubiquitous technology deployment in the human environment to further a broad range of human purposes (Sadri, 2011). Such systems are deemed to be emerging if they are likely to be socially and economically relevant in the coming 10–15 years. The ETICA project highlights the following 11 ICTs.

- Affective Computing
  (use of computing to measure or express human emotions)
- Ambient Intelligence
  (ubiquitous and pervasive computing environment)
- Artificial Intelligence
  (representation of intelligence through artifacts)
- Bioelectronics
  (combination of biological materials or principles with electronics)
- Cloud Computing
  (remote shared computing services)
- Future Internet
  (novel technical infrastructure for networked services)
- Human-machine Symbiosis
  (direct combination of humans and artifacts)

---

[2] This chapter does not provide the space to discuss any of the issues discussed here in depth. However, all project deliverables and findings are available in full from the project web site (www.etica-project.eu). A more detailed account of the overall project can be found in Stahl (2011a).

- Neuroelectronics
  (link between computing and neurosciences)
- Quantum Computing
  (utilization of quantum effects for computing purposes)
- Robotics
  (embodied artificial agents, typically somewhat autonomous)
- Virtual/Augmented Reality
  (representation of reality through technical means).

For each of these technologies a detailed description was developed that indicated their definition, history, likely uses and constraints. For the purposes of this chapter it will be sufficient to give a brief overview of some of the shared features these technologies are expected to display. These include:

- Natural interaction
  (use of ICTs becomes similar to interaction with humans)
- Invisibility
  (as a result of miniaturization or embedding of artifacts)
- Direct link
  (either physical implant, direct contact (e.g., wearable ICT) or through sensors)
- Detailed understanding of the user
  (emerging ICTs will require a highly detailed model of the user to fulfill their tasks)
- Pervasiveness
  (ubiquitous embedding of ICTs in the human and natural environment)
- Autonomy
  (ability of ICT to act without direct user input)
- Power over the user
  (ability to structure the space of action of the user)
- Market driven
  (allocation decisions are reached through commercial exchange mechanisms).

For the purposes of the ETICA project, as well as this chapter, it is not crucial to know whether all of these aspects will materialize. Instead, the interesting question is whether these predicted futures allow us to come to a better understanding of what could be done now in order to make sure that the ethical and social consequences of the technologies are beneficial. Or, to put it differently, the question is whether we find ways of dealing responsibly with the technologies and their expected consequences.

11.3.1.2   Ethics of Emerging ICTs

The above list of shared features of the technologies gives an indication of possible ethical issues. During the ETICA project the consortium analyzed each of the technologies and explored the literature to see which ethical issues were predicted to be raised by them. Again, all this chapter can do here is to give a high-level overview of the approach and of those ethical consequences of the emerging technologies that were found in the literature.

In order to identify likely ethical issues of emerging ICTs, a literature analysis of the ICT ethics literature from 2003 onwards was undertaken. This started out with a novel bibliometric approach that mapped the proximity of different concepts in the ICT ethics literature.[3] Using this bibliometric analysis as a starting point, a comprehensive analysis of the ICT ethics literature was undertaken for each technology.

The ethical analysis showed that there are numerous ethical issues that are discussed with regard to the technologies. The number and detail of these ethical issues varies greatly. This variation is caused by the differing levels of detail and length of time of discussion of the technologies. Ethical issues shared by several of the emerging ICTs can roughly be divided into issues that are already being researched and regulated, and those issues that are currently less tangible and further removed from current debates. The widely discussed ethical issues of emerging ICTs include *privacy, security, trust, liabilities, and digital divides.* Some of these were represented on the bibliometric map, others were not visible because this particular representation of the bibliometric data did not display them. Being widely discussed does not imply that they will remain unchanged. In fact, many of these issues will take new forms. Privacy, for example, is a well discussed issue that has led to a wealth of literature, and is even recognized as a human right (Humphreys, 2011). There are numerous cases in which technical systems and their affordances have created novel types of privacy issues. In the UK, for example, one could observe the government's attempt to collect genetic data in a national DNA database or to create a national ID system, both of which were met with strong opposition. Similar cases from the private sector have been discussed in depth, for example, with regards to Google's right to collect data for the Streetview application, the appropriateness of contextual advertisement, and many more. In the light of current technical developments, privacy is likely to become even more prominent due to new quantities of data, new ways of linking it, and maybe even new types of data (e.g., emotion-related data) which may raise qualitatively new issues. What these issues have in common, however, is that they are currently on the social and political agenda and are recognized as important and in need of further attention.

Less predictable ethical issues arising from the emerging ICTs tend to be centered on difficult conceptual issues, such as human identity, the relationship between humans and technologies, and relationships among individuals or groups. Individual identities may change due to the way we interact with technology. What we perceive to be normal may partly be a function of the affordances (Gibson, 1977; Norman, 1999) that technologies offer us and, therefore, is potentially subject to change. A good example of this is the difficult distinction between therapy and human enhancement (Bostrom and Sandberg, 2009; Coeckelbergh, 2011). Technical interventions that can be used to treat diseases can, in many cases, be used to improve human performance. Drugs that were developed to stop memory loss, for example, may help healthy university students improve their exam performance. Related issues can arise due to the way in which new technologies can change power relationships and traditional balances between individuals and groups, and this is the very area where prediction of future uses and likely outcomes may be impossible. Such changes can affect not only local cultures and collective self-views, but the ways in which societies might be organized. This does not have to be morally problematic, but it may well be in some respects. The scale of the change means that potential ethical issues need to be monitored closely.

---

[3] A detailed account of the methodology used in the ethical analysis can be found in Heersmink *et al.* (2011).

11.3.1.3   Evaluation of Emerging ICTs

The evaluation of emerging ICTs and their ethical issues was undertaken from four different perspectives:[4]

- **Law**:
  The analysis was based on the principles of human dignity, equality, and the rule of law. A review of 182 EU legal documents revealed that the legal implications of emerging technologies were not adequately reflected, that is, did not relate to the specific issues the technologies raise.
- **(Institutional) ethics**:
  The earlier ethical analysis was complemented by looking at opinions and publications of European and national ethics panels or review bodies, such as the European Group on Ethics in Science and New Technologies, the Nuffield Council on Bioethics, the German Ethics Council, to name but a few. Furthermore, the review covered the implied normative basis of technology ethics in the EU.
- **Gender**:
  A review of the gender and technology literature showed that, in the case of five technologies, such gender implications had already been raised in the literature. However, for the majority of the technologies no research on their gender implications had been undertaken.
- **Technology assessment**:
  This analysis asked how far ICTs are developed and what are their prospects of realization. The expected benefits and possible side effects were discussed, as well as the likelihood of controversy arising from the different technologies. The technology assessment perspective included the other assessments and aimed to provide a general insight into the consequences of the technologies.

The evaluation found that several of the technologies are so closely related that they should be treated in conjunction. Building on the criteria of the likelihood of coming into existence and raising ethical debate, the following ranking was suggested:

1. Ambient Intelligence
2. Augmented and Virtual Reality
3. Future Internet
4. Robotics, Artificial Intelligence and Affective Computing
5. Neuroelectronics, Bioelectronics, and Human-Machine Symbiosis
6. Cloud Computing
7. Quantum Computing.

This ranking allows the prioritization of activities and policies. Overall, the ETICA project addressed the product dimension of RRI in ICT by identifying those technologies which are likely to require being dealt with responsibly, and which possible ethical and social consequences they may have that need to be taken into account. While such an ethically sensitive foresight analysis is important to feed into the process of RRI, it

---

[4] A full discussion of these steps of evaluation, the methodologies used and the findings can be found in deliverable D3.2 "Evaluation Report" which is available from the deliverables section of the ETICA project web site at www.etica-project.eu.

is by no means enough to lead to better technologies or consequences. One further central aspect that needs to be understood is how those individuals who actually create the technologies – the engineers, researchers, and developers – see the technologies, their consequences and the responsibilities that they or others have in ensuring that the technologies are socially beneficial. In order to assess this question in more depth, the chapter now discusses the fundamental ideas and preliminary results of another project, which will highlight the aspect of people in RRI in ICT.

11.3.2   People: Landscape of ICT Ethics

In the UK, the Framework for Responsible Research and Innovation (FRRIICT) project began in September 2011 and is conducting the first comprehensive investigation of ICT researchers' notions of Responsible Research and Innovation and the role this might play in the next decade of ICT research. Responsible research invites researchers, policy makers, and funders to reconsider the influences of near and long-term research strategy on the shaping of funding priorities, taking into account the potential consequences to social, environmental, health, and behavioral well-being. The RRI initiative creates an opportunity for reflection, where decisions about research goals are made not exclusively on the grounds of their technical or scientific attributes; so that, in addition to addressing technical grand challenges, RRI asks all stakeholders to consider the potential impacts, risks, and uncertainties of research outputs to wider society.

As part of the FRRIICT project, a landscape study is being conducted to understand current perceptions and attitudes toward RRI, using semi-structured interviews with researchers – those who seek funding – and with portfolio managers – those who manage funding calls, within the EPSRC ICT portfolio. The goal of the interviews is twofold; in the case of researchers we are interested in how professional responsibility is conceptualized within specialist domains, and how ethical issues might be identified, discussed, and resolved as research projects unfold. In the case of the portfolio managers we are interested in the processes and procedures that motivate the identification and direction of long-term funding strategy (e.g., horizon scanning and researcher-led workshops) which, in turn, influence the development of themed funding calls. In addition to these two groups, we are including other stakeholders, such as industry, professional organizations and charities, in our discussions around the potential future societal consequences of ICT research and how RRI may be embedded into current processes.

With a focus on what is commonly referred to as *upstream activities* (Fisher, Mahajan, and Mitcham, 2006), encapsulated in research policy and strategic direction, and *midstream activities* (where bench work and R&D activities take place: see Chapter 9), we can begin to create a picture of the current ICT research and innovation cycle with an aim of providing a set of recommendations and good practice that could be adopted by the EPSRC and the ICT research community. This may provide an opportunity for reshaping research policy and funding governance to include a new conception of responsibility that extends beyond conventional, although important, notions associated with ensuring "experimental reproducibility" when working in the laboratory and with following research process guidelines (such as gaining "informed consent" when involving human participants, or sufficiently protecting data). We present brief preliminary findings below and discuss foreseeable challenges to implementing RRI in actual practice, as well as the potential for RRI to be implemented as a resource for creativity rather than a constraint for innovation, as underlined by Von Schomberg in Chapter 3.

As part of our preliminary research interviews were undertaken with 16 ICT researchers, ranging from professorial to post-doctoral positions, and across domains from cybersecurity, artificial intelligence, robotics, eHealth, natural language processing to human–computer interaction. Additionally, seven EPSRC portfolio managers who facilitate research funding in these and other areas, as diverse as theoretical computer science, visualization, and photonics, were interviewed in early 2012. In the interviews we aimed to find out how both funders and researchers frame the relationship between scientific research, professional responsibility and the ways in which research outputs might impact society.

A noteworthy distinction has consistently appeared across both funder and researcher interviews that may underpin general perceptions of professional and social responsibility. For many researchers there is a correlation between the location of their research (within the spectrum of "fundamental" to "applied" (cf. Calvert, 2006)) and how, or even *if* they should be concerned with the potential societal consequences of their research outputs. The proximity of research outputs to uptake and use by potential user communities may be considered as a commonsense understanding of the ways in which research may have a direct influence on society; the closer it is to being taken up by, or embedded in society, the greater the societal impact is likely to be. However, it can be argued that even blue skies research has societal consequences, even though these may materialize in the longer-term. The EPSRC funds at a Technology Readiness Level (TRL) of between 1 and 3, which is defined as the lowest level of "technology readiness." This is where basic principles are identified, technological concepts formulated, and experimental research conducted to validate those principles and concepts. At TRL 1–3, fundamental scientific research is conducted. However, many projects within the ICT portfolio fall within a "gray area" somewhere between fundamental and applied research. Most researchers we interviewed described their projects as a mix of fundamental and applied. The distinction has been articulated as that between the *prototype*, a working system that could, quite soon, be iterated into a fully-developed product, and the *demonstrator*, whose purpose is to show the utility of the science, with its potential commercialization many years into the future. In both cases fundamental research, which may focus on algorithm and infrastructure design, is conducted alongside software engineering and human interface development. The potential for research outputs having either long or short-term utilization leads to a series of often tacit presumptions for many of our interviewees about their professional responsibility, social obligations, and whether or not they should consider how their research outputs may lead to either positive or negative consequences within wider civil society.

Within the spectrum of fundamental to applied, we find a further distinction is made by researchers, many of whom identify their own work as being either "generic" or "application-oriented." Both types of research address highly technical, scientific challenges through experimental design and intensive laboratory work. However, those who frame their work as generic, on the whole, conduct their research at arms-length to any potential user community; whilst those who describe their research as application-oriented work in close partnership with some designated user community for the duration of a research project. In this way, the potential *context of use* of research outputs is drawn upon as a justification allowing researchers to distance themselves from any kind of professional responsibility related to societal consequences, risks, and uncertainties.[5]

> The research that we do doesn't inherently tell you how to use this research. So, we built a robot that can throw balls 6 meters compared to 1 meter from previous versions. So, there is no kind of moral value associated with that, it's more of a performance. We're focused on the performance. How you use that performance is not our part I think (R-05).

The view that fundamental research is somehow independent to the concerns of contemporary society is found mostly when research outputs contribute to the development of "enabling technologies," which can be described as technologies that could be adopted across a wide variety of domains (e.g., healthcare, military, industrial or domestic settings) and for any number of uses. In contrast, for those who conduct application-oriented research, the potential social consequences of their outputs might be more obvious to them.

> You have this machine in your house 24/7 then it will potentially collect a lot of data about you. Video data, audio data it tracks what you are doing and it monitors what you are doing. It tracks and monitors whose coming into the house, the phone calls you make and potentially other data. So the question is; how do people perceive that? Is that a problem? If yes, in what way? And how can we design systems to address these issues and to give people the feeling that you take them seriously (R-03).

Even though researchers differentiated between these two orientations (generic and application-oriented), they nevertheless stated that in all cases potential negative consequences, risks, and uncertainties should be obvious and unmistakable before any decisions are made to change the direction of an ongoing research path or to halt it completely. For many, the most obvious issues center around personal data; its security, confidentiality, and personal privacy. Outside of the realm of personal data protection and human subject consent many researchers and funders struggle to identify potential negative consequences of ICT research. In research areas where devices are manufactured, only minimal concern has been expressed in relation to environmental factors. One researcher suggested that because they are not *directly* involved in the manufacturing process, those issues are of no concern to their research.

> I don't specify how things get made. I specify what I want on the chip and then the manufacturers are responsible for putting it there by whatever means they use (R-10).

On the whole, ICT researchers take a very strong stance that there should be no oversight of research strategy unless there is an obvious social consequence to projected outcomes. They also tend to share a suspicion of activities aimed at projecting likely outcomes of research and a resistance to the introduction of foresight methodologies for the purposes of predicting possible future consequences, risks, and uncertainties. This is an interesting response, as research funding is prioritized at present through foresight and horizon scanning techniques. However, this resistance could be attributed to researchers being

---

[5] The displayed text indicates quotes transcribed from participant interviews.

unfamiliar with RRI concepts, as the current focus of such exercises remains largely on the potential positive, transformative effects of technology.

To summarize, in fundamental research, societal consequences are framed as being identifiable only within their *contexts of use*, and in application-oriented research the possibilities of industry and user adaptation may change the *trajectory of a technology* in unforeseen ways.

> Any research can always have negative consequences. We take a lot of precautions in what we are doing but you can never fully predict whether there might be negative consequences or not. It would be completely unrealistic and dishonest if I said; 'oh, there will never be any negative consequences of my research'. You can't say that. Who knows how someone else might use our research. You can never predict (R-03).

Some of the researchers we interviewed have suggested that rather than asking the ICT research community to predict in advance the potential outcomes of their research they could be asked instead to "respond to changes consequentially" as they arise (see Chapter 2 for further discussion of iteration and responsiveness). Others have suggested allowing "sufficient discussion" around the possible positive and negative consequences of research within institutions and amongst colleagues so that academic stakeholders "felt there'd been a broad airing and discussion around what the challenges might be." These types of activities could be developed further within emerging RRI frameworks and may be seen as a "responsive" tailoring of RRI by the ICT researchers them-selves, rather than the imposition of a top-down "governance" model. When considering researchers' responses that consequences, risks, and uncertainties need to be obvious, their general distrust of the use of foresight methodologies, and their cautious sugges-tions for improvements to current processes, we can conclude that there will be many challenges to implementing RRI in actual practice. A more approachable and accept-able RRI framework could facilitate discussion amongst the researchers themselves in the initial phases of research, in an informal and non-binding manner where Chatham House Rule[6] applies, ensuring free and open discussion. RRI also aims to facilitate a step forward "from public engagement to public dialogue" where researchers facilitate workshops and engage the public directly in order to understand their concerns and to iteratively provide feedback on research strategies. These two activities (ICT community reflection amongst colleagues, and engagement with the public in a dialogue about the societal consequences of research outputs) appear, at the moment, to be difficult chal-lenges to address with regard to researchers current commitments to the scientific and technical challenges of their domains. We need to take researchers' concerns seriously if RRI is to be embedded into the research process.

We suggest that there are many challenges to developing policy and regulation in an arena where attempting to predict the potential uses of ICT research outputs is a tenuous one, and where there may *not* be obvious risks or harms, as in other areas of research such as geoengineering or nanotechnology. Indeed, there may be significant differ-ences between ascertaining risks and uncertainties in computer science, and those in the physical and life sciences (e.g., nanotechnology, geoengineering and synthetic biology).

---

[6] When a meeting, or part thereof, is held under the Chatham House Rule, participants are free to use the information received, but neither the identity nor the affiliation of the speaker(s), nor that of any other participant, may be revealed.

For instance, software and hardware may be released without adherence to health, safety, and other risk assessment procedures, excluding data protection and informed consent discussed previously. In contrast the potential consequences to society might be more obvious in the physical and life sciences because researchers conduct experiments with materials or manipulate the properties of matter, whether they are biological, botanical, or synthetic.

Even so, the ICT research community should begin to consider ways in which reflective governance mechanisms and public consultations can extend greater influence upon the direction of long-term funding strategy, such that decisions about research goals are inclusive of the concerns of wider society and take into account their influences on society, environment, health, and behavior. Policy in this area will also need to be harmonized with research strategy on a global level, if this is feasible, perhaps through the newly formed Global Research Council (GRC),[7] in order to mitigate any risks to competitive advantage as a contributor to and stakeholder of worldwide scientific outcomes. This could provide an opportunity for GRC member states to remain ahead of the technology innovation curve and act as shapers and facilitators of innovation rather than run the risk of RRI being considered a constrainer of research. While it is open to debate whether such a global strategy would be feasible, it is easy to see that it would be desirable with respect to setting minimum standards and spreading costs equally.

11.3.3   Process: Governance of RRI in ICT

Having now discussed both the ETICA and FRRIICT projects, which address different but complementary aspects, one can ask what steps are necessary in order to ensure that new ICTs are being built responsibly. We discuss this question by first going through the recommendations that arose from the ETICA project, and then looking at further research that is required in order to ensure such an RRI approach to ICT.

Current ways of dealing with the ethics of technology, whether they are embedded in European research funding (e.g., FP7) procedures such as the ethics review, or whether they are used outside of European funding, tend to be based on biomedical ethics. Biomedical ethics developed from the Nuremberg trials as a reaction to the Nazi's and others' atrocities committed in the name of scientific research. Formulated in the Declaration of Helsinki (World Medical Association, 2008), these principles continue to be developed. They have proven to be successful in many respects and they can guide action with regard to established ethical issues and legal requirements. However, the applicability of bio-medical ethics to ICT research can be questioned. It is not *a priori* clear that the aim of the technical development is justified. Bio-medical ethics is based on informed consent to research processes and tends to neglect the research product. Particularly within the EU Framework Programme, this approach has led to a tick-box attitude that sees ethics as a legal compliance issue, divorced from application context and broader societal discourses. This position contravenes much ethical thinking and ethical traditions. RRI will need to move beyond this status quo. The ETICA recommendations on governance and approaches therefore include recommendations to policy makers

---

[7] www.globalresearchcouncil.org, www.nsf.gov/news/news_videos.jsp?cntn_id=124178&media_id=72475&org=NSF.

to provide a political framework conducive to a proactive engagement with ethics and to ICT researchers, organizations, and the civil society concerned with the question of how to affect social reality.

11.3.3.1   Recommendations for Policy Makers

Policy makers have an important role in creating the regulatory framework and the infrastructure to allow ethics to be considered in ICT. If emerging ICTs are to be developed in a responsible manner that allows the identifying and addressing of the social and ethical problems outlined above, then a framework and infrastructure for the development of responsibility needs to be provided. Such a framework should cover at least the following three main areas of policy activity:

- ***Provide a regulatory framework which will support Ethical Impact Assessment for ICTs:*** This recommendation addresses the institutional framework that will be required to recognize responsibilities, and develop mechanisms for discharging them. The idea of an "Ethical Impact Assessment for ICTs" was chosen because it can draw on precedent from areas of the environment, privacy, or equality. Researchers are often familiar at least with some types of prospective assessment, such as risk assessment, and may be willing to engage with ethics on this level. This may explain why one attempt to implement RRI relied on principles of risk management (Owen and Goldberg, 2010). A framework for ethical impact assessment in ICT could provide incentives to engage with relevant issues. It could, thereby, encourage discourses that may lead to the development of specific responsibilities.
- ***Establish an ICT Ethics Observatory:*** While the first set of recommendations aimed at providing a procedural framework for identifying and addressing ethical issues in ICT, this set of recommendations aims to provide the content required for an Ethical Impact Assessment. The work undertaken by the ETICA project, for example, provides important pointers toward possible ethical issues to be considered. Individuals involved in technical development are often not experts in these matters. A shared repository of ethics-related theories, practices, methodologies, and so on is a necessary condition of the development of widely shared good practice. One of the tasks of the FRRIICT project will be to develop a first prototype of such an observatory.
- ***Establish a forum for stakeholder involvement:*** This final recommendation for policy makers points to the necessity of institutionalizing important discourses that allow civil society and other stakeholders to engage on a content level with the policy – as well as technical – community. Such a forum is required to ensure that responsible innovation covers not only specific technical interests and perspectives but is allowed to reflect broader societal concerns.

11.3.3.2   Recommendations for Industry, Researchers, and Civil Society Organizations

Industry, researchers, and other individuals or organizations should adhere to the following recommendations in order to be proactive and allow innovation to be socially responsible. If the institutional framework, background, repository, and societal discourses are present, then the conditions will be favorable for the incorporation of ethics and reflexivity into technical work and application usage.

- *Incorporate ethics into ICT research and development:* This recommendation aims to ensure that ethical reflexivity is realized within technical work. Furthermore, it aims to sensitize stakeholders to the difficulties of discharging their responsibilities.
- *Facilitate ethical reflexivity in ICT projects and practice:* This set of suggestions aims to ensure that the different stakeholders realize that ethics is not a predetermined and fixed structure. Ethical issues are context-dependent and need to be interpreted in the particular situation. Interpretive flexibility (Doherty, Coombs, and Loan-Clarke, 2006) of technology renders it desirable not only for the participants in a technology development project to engage collectively in the initial definition of ethical issues that are to be considered, but also to review this initial definition continuously and engage with stakeholders involved in other stages of the technology development process.

11.4   Critical Reflections

The policy recommendations arising from the ETICA project as outlined above arose from a specific and technology-centered perspective, and will need to be interpreted in the light of the findings of the FRRIICT project. A core question is that of the reflective governance mechanisms in which RRI for ICT will develop. ETICA recommended a regulatory framework to promote an ethical impact assessment. This was motivated by the need to develop some kind of incentive for ICT researchers and practitioners to engage with responsibility issues. The concept of impact assessment was chosen because researchers tend to be familiar with other types of impact assessments, such as environment, risk, or equality impact assessments. Such impact assessments are usually compulsory but may take different forms. The idea was that by requiring such an ethical impact assessment, ICT researchers would need to engage with the issues but would not be forced to do so in a particular way.

While this idea is, in principle, still valid, it raises questions. Owen and Goldberg (2010) used mechanisms of risk assessment to encourage researchers to engage with RRI with mixed success (see Chapter 2 for a critique). Furthermore, the findings of the FRRIICT landscape study suggest that researchers may not react positively to what they perceive as external pressure to deal with ethics and responsibility. In addition, there is a danger that a compulsory ethical impact assessment may turn into a further box-ticking exercise. An initial attempt to formulate the principles of such an assessment (Wright, 2011) suggests that this might indeed be the way it could be perceived.

11.4.1   The Meta-Responsibilities of RRI

This brings us back to the earlier suggestion that RRI could be viewed as a meta-responsibility, as a responsibility for the definition and realization of responsibilities. Having explored the ethical issues of emerging ICTs, as well as the perception of stakeholders in the UK ICT field, we can now offer a more precise definition and content of RRI in ICT.

RRI is a social construct or ascription that defines entities and relationships between them in such a way that the outcomes of research and innovation processes lead to socially desirable consequences. Of course, socially desirable consequences may be very different for different stakeholders and so the diversity of viewpoints needs to be taken into account and negotiation made possible in whatever framework we suggest. RRI contributes to existing vibrant networks of existing responsibility relationships and ensures that these become compatible and synergetic. The activities of RRI will encompass the following aspects:

- Description of subjects of responsibility in ICT (e.g., researchers, professional bodies, funders, policy makers)
- Attribution of objects to subjects (e.g., sustainability, usability, privacy, transparency)
- Facilitation of discourses on norms, values, and ethical foundations
- Design of sanction and incentive structures
- Reflection on preconditions for successful responsibility relationships.

All of these points are already incorporated in existing responsibility ascription. The meta-aspect of RRI is that they are usually done on a local or *ad hoc* level and are often in conflict, or even contradictory. RRI will require a higher level discussion of what diverse groups within different societies want to achieve through their technologies, and then consider how to identify and negotiate those aims and how they might be achieved.

The last point – the reflection on the preconditions for successful responsibility relationships – may be the most difficult one. The question of when responsibility may have desired effects is surrounded by conceptual and empirical uncertainties. It is rather safe to say, however, that one of these conditions will be to ensure that researchers, developers, and practitioners in ICT understand the problems surrounding ethics and responsibility and accept that it is in their interest, not only as ICT professionals, but also as citizens, to engage with these questions. This leads to a clear need to embed such questions into ICT education from primary to tertiary levels (Stahl, 2011b). An understanding of ethics and responsibility is a necessary (albeit not sufficient) condition for researchers to take such issues seriously (see Chapter 2 for further discussion on education, training, and capacity). Such an understanding can lead to an intrinsic motivation to deal with the ethics of ICT. This intrinsic motivation will likely have to be combined with an extrinsic motivation, as represented by a reflective governance framework. The relationship between these two drivers for engaging with RRI will be subject to empirical review and policy discussion.

11.4.2   Further Research

This chapter has shown that work on RRI in ICT is still in its infancy. Despite a long tradition of exploring ethical issues of ICT going back to the very beginnings of the technology (Wiener, 1954), and despite a rich field of research in computer and information ethics (Floridi, 2010; Himma and Tavani, 2008; van den Hoven and Weckert, 2008), we are far from having generally acceptable and accepted ways of dealing with these issues. This prior work can sensitize researchers, practitioners, and policy makers, but it gives little guidance on how to *practically* deal with issues when they arise.

RRI as a meta-responsibility does not have to dwell on the details of individual responsibility relationships (e.g., what is the responsibility of the software engineer), but it will need to develop a framework that will allow the definition of individual responsibilities and the relationship between different instances of responsibility.

The ICT Ethics Observatory recommended by the ETICA project, which is now being developed as a prototype in the FRRIICT project under the title of Observatory for RRI in ICT, can be understood as a mechanism of facilitating coherent and consistent responsibilities across the ICT field. This means that it will need to reflect the conceptual uncertainties and the contested nature of many ethical issues. At the same time it will have to provide substantive and procedural guidance to the different stakeholder groups. In addition, its success will depend on the willingness of the ICT community to make use of it and contribute to it.

There are additional considerations of preconditions for RRI in ICT that need to be taken into consideration. One important aspect of this is the socio-economic environment in which ICTs are developed and used. The majority of ICT research expenditure (and therefore its subsequent outcomes) is spent in private companies. These are normally driven by a profit motive and will disregard RRI if it appears to contravene this profit interest. There is thus a question about the relationship of RRI and profits that needs to be explored and that points toward an incorporation of ideas of business ethics into RRI. And one should admit that there is at least the potential for a conflict of interest. But RRI does not have to oppose profits and one can make a strong and evidence-supported argument that early attention to ethical and social aspects is in the interest of companies. However, one should also be honest enough that RRI may oppose some activities or products that companies would find beneficial.

Another aspect of RRI in ICT that the FRRIICT project has started to touch upon, but that will need closer attention, is the role that policy makers, and in particular research funders play as responsibility subjects in their own right. Much of the attention of the ETICA and FRRIICT project was focused on the technologies and the researchers who develop them. It should be clear, however, that in many cases the ethical issues of a technology are largely shaped by funding calls and funding decisions. Research funders may sometimes be in a better position to understand and evaluate the social impact of a technology than individual researchers or research groups. Funders not only provide the resources but often shape specific calls and have an overview of related research, which can allow them to develop a more detailed understanding of the social context of the research and its possible consequences. This raises the question of how the responsibilities of funders can be expressed and how they might be related to other responsibilities, a key question for the meta-responsibility of RRI.

A final point worth mentioning is the overall democratic legitimation of publicly funded research, and the role that civil society can and should play in RRI for ICT. Von Schomberg's opening definition of RRI prominently underlined the role of societal actors, but leaves open who these actors are and how they can be incorporated into ICT research. This is reflected by the ETICA recommendation to establish a forum for stakeholder involvement. While this idea of societal feedback is probably plausible for publicly funded research in democratic societies, it is by no means clear how it could be implemented. It is even less clear how it could be evaluated (Rowe and Frewer, 2000). And finally, there will be costs associated with it which would need to be justified by empirically confirmed benefits of such engagement.

All of this shows that much work is to be done in order to develop a practical and beneficial overall FRRIICT. Such a framework will need to draw upon the manifold activities in other areas of research and innovation. The present chapter has provided an insight into some current activities and demonstrated that RRI is best conceptualized as a meta-level activity that influences existing and novel responsibility relationships. We believe that this understanding of RRI can help further the goal of achieving desirable and desired results within ICT, as well as in other fields and disciplines.

Acknowledgments

The research leading to these results has received funding from the European Community's Seventh Framework Programme (FP7/2007–2013) under grant agreement no 230318. The authors acknowledge the contribution of the consortium members to the research which was summarized in parts of this chapter.

This research benefited from the activities undertaken in the project "Framework for Responsible Research and Innovation in ICT," EPSRC reference EP/J000019/1.

References

Allen, C., Smit, I., and Wallach, W. (2005). Artificial morality: top-down, bottom-up, and hybrid approaches. *Ethics and Information Technology,* **7**(3), 149–155. doi: 10.1007/s10676-006-0004-4

Bayertz, K. (ed.) (1995). *Verantwortung: Prinzip oder Problem?* Wissenschaftliche Buchgesellschaft.

Bostrom, N., and Sandberg, A. (2009). Cognitive enhancement: methods, ethics, regulatory challenges. *Science and Engineering Ethics,* **15**(3), 311–341.

Calvert, J. (2006). What's special about basic research? *Science, Technology & Human Values,* **31**(2), 199–220.

Coeckelbergh, M. (2011). Human development or human enhancement? A methodological reflection on capabilities and the evaluation of information technologies. *Ethics and Information Technology,* **13**(2), 81–92. doi: 10.1007/s10676-010-9231-9

Cuhls, K. (2003). From forecasting to foresight processes – new participative foresight activities in Germany. *Journal of Forecasting,* **22**(2–3), 93–111. doi: 10.1002/for.848

Doherty, N. F., Coombs, C. R., and Loan-Clarke, J. (2006). A re-conceptualization of the interpretive flexibility of information technologies: redressing the balance between the social and the technical. *European Journal of Information Systems,* **15**(6), 569–582.

Etchegoyen, A. (1993). *Le Temps des Responsables.* Julliard.

European Commission (2011) Work Programme 2012, Capacities, Part 5, Science in Society, Brussels, http://ec.europa.eu/research/participants/portal/page/capacities ?callIdentifier=FP7-SCIENCE-IN-SOCIETY-2012-1(accessed 12 October 2012).

Fisher, E., Mahajan, R. L., and Mitcham, C. (2006). Midstream modulation of technology: governance from within. *Bulletin of Science, Technology and Society,* **26**(6), 485–496. doi: 10.1177/0270467606295402

Floridi, L. (ed.) (2010). *The Cambridge Handbook of Information and Computer Ethics.* Cambridge University Press.

Floridi, L., and Sanders, J. W. (2004). On the morality of artificial agents. *Minds and Machines,* **14**(3), 349–379. doi: 10.1023/B:MIND.0000035461.63578.9d

French, P. A. (1992). *Responsibility Matters.* University Press of Kansas.

Gibson, J. J. (1977). The theory of affordances. In R. E. Shaw and J. D. Bransford (eds.), *Perceiving, Acting and Knowing* pp. 67–82. Hillsdale: Lawrence Erlbaum Associates.

Heersmink, R., van den Hoven, J., van Eck, N., and van den Berg, J. (2011). Bibliometric mapping of computer and information ethics. *Ethics and Information Technology,* 13(3), 241–249.

Himma, K. E., and Tavani, H. T. (2008). *The Handbook of Information and Computer Ethics*. Hoboken, NJ: John Wiley & Sons, Ltd.

van den Hoven, J. and Weckert, J. (eds.) (2008) *Information Technology and Moral Philosophy* (1st edn). Cambridge University Press.

Humphreys, S. (2011) Navigating the Dataverse: Privacy, Technology, Human Rights: Discussion Paper, International Council on Human Rights Policy, Geneva, Switzerland, www.ichrp.org/en/zoom-in/new_report_dataverse_privacy (accessed 07 July 2011).

Lewis, H. D. (1972). The non-moral notion of collective responsibility. In P. A. French (ed.), *Individual and Collective Responsibility: Massacre at My Lai*. pp. 116–144. Cambridge, MA: Schenkman Publishing Co.

Norman, D. A. (1999). Affordance, conventions, and design. *Interactions,* 6(3), 38–43. doi: 10.1145/301153.301168

Owen, R., and Goldberg, N. (2010). Responsible innovation: a pilot study with the U.K. engineering and physical sciences research council. *Risk Analysis: An International Journal,* 30(11), 1699–1707. doi: 10.1111/j.1539-6924.2010.01517.x

Rowe, G., and Frewer, L. J. (2000). Public participation methods: a framework for evaluation. *Science, Technology & Human Values,* 25(1), 3–29. doi: 10.1177 /016224390002500101

Sadri, F. (2011). Ambient intelligence: a survey. *ACM Computing Surveys,* 43(4), 36.1–36.66. doi: 10.1145/1978802.1978815

Stahl, B. C. (2004) *Responsible Management of Information Systems*. Hershey, PA: IGI Publishing.

Stahl, B. C. (2011a). IT for a better future: how to integrate ethics, politics and innovation. *Journal of Information, Communication and Ethics in Society,* 9(3), 140–156. doi: 10.1108/14779961111167630

Stahl, B. C. (2011b). Teaching ethical reflexivity in information systems: how to equip students to deal with moral and ethical issues of emerging information and communication technologies. *Journal of Information Systems Education,* 22(3), 253–260.

Von Schomberg, R. (ed.) (2011). *Towards Responsible Research and Innovation in the Information and Communication Technologies and Security Technologies Fields*. Publication Office of the European Union, Luxembourg, http://ec.europa.eu/research /science-society/document_library/pdf_06/mep-rapport-2011_en.pdf (accessed 01 November 2011).

Werhane, P. H. (1985). *Persons, Rights, and Corporations*. Prentice Hall.

Wiener, N. (1954). *The Human Use of Human Beings*. New York: Doubleday.

World Medical Association (2008) Declaration of Helsinki – Ethical Principles for Medical Research Involving Human Subjects. http://www.wma.net/en/30publications /10policies/b3/17c.pdf (accessed 23 August 2012).

Wright, D. (2011). A framework for the ethical impact assessment of information technology. *Ethics and Information Technology,* 13(3), 199–226. doi: 10.1007/s10676-010-9242-6

12

Deliberation and Responsible Innovation: a Geoengineering Case Study

Karen Parkhill,[1] *Nick Pidgeon,*[1] *Adam Corner,*[1] *and Naomi Vaughan*[2]
[1]*Cardiff University, School of Psychology, UK*
[2]*University of East Anglia, School of Environmental Sciences,*
Norwich Research Park, UK

12.1 Introduction

Geoengineering has been defined as the *"deliberate large-scale manipulation of the planetary environment to counteract anthropogenic climate change"* (Royal Society, 2009, p. 1). The diverse range of putative technologies that have been proposed for manipulating the climate in response to anthropogenic activity are currently subject to a great deal of scientific uncertainty, with the risks and benefits poorly understood. But beyond the considerable scientific uncertainties around geoengineering technologies, the very concept of intentionally manipulating the Earth's climate system raises a range of social and ethical issues that include acceptability, informed consent, and governance (Corner and Pidgeon, 2010). Indeed the UK's Royal Society states that any geoengineering research that may impact on the environment, or any moves toward deployment of geoengineering measures should not proceed without dialogue between, for example, policy-makers, scientists, and publics (Royal Society, 2009). While scientists may be able to outline the range of options for geoengineering, it is ultimately society which must judge their acceptability (Royal Society, 2009; Corner and Pidgeon, 2010). This in turn raises questions over how we can best meaningfully engage with such diverse actors, and how such engagement can contribute to the responsible innovation of these potentially world-changing technologies.

Responsible Innovation, First Edition. Edited by Richard Owen, John Bessant and Maggy Heintz.
© 2013 John Wiley & Sons, Ltd. Published 2013 by John Wiley & Sons, Ltd.

Many emergent technologies are accepted into society with little fanfare, yet due to the *"spectres of public resistance against technoscience (e.g., agricultural biotechnology)... lurking in the discursive background"* (Felt and Fochler, 2010, p. 221; see also Grove-White, Macnaghten, and Wynne, 2000), those involved in the introduction and governance of technologies which are believed to have the potential to "mobilize populations" (Poumadère, Bertoldo, and Samadi, 2011), have been especially cautious about how their induction into the public sphere occurs (Pidgeon *et al.*, 2012). Past modes of engagement with publics can be characterized as Decide, Educate, Announce, and Defend (DEAD) – (see Hartz-Karp, 2007), with a view to persuading publics, by tackling the now highly criticized "knowledge deficit model," to support new policies or technological developments.

Participatory processes have been developed in response to numerous criticisms of previous forms of engagement, not least the desire to move away from *"the well-entrenched linear model of science communication and its embedded values"* (Felt and Fochler, 2010, p. 220). As Chapter 5 by Sykes and Macnaghten has depicted, there are numerous reasons – normative, instrumental and substantive – underpinning the development of participatory processes (see also Fiorino, 1990). In addition to the logics for participatory processes set out by Sykes and Macnaghten we feel it is important to briefly explore why substantive reasons have emerged as such an important rationale for engagement. Indeed, for us, substantive reasons are why we are particularly passionate about the inclusion of publics in engagement processes.

Substantive reasons have emerged out of discussions concerning the expansion of sources of legitimate knowledge, in particular recognizing the value and importance of lay knowledge and social intelligence (Wynne, 1992, 1993: also see Fiorino, 1990). For Wynne (1991, p. 114), public understanding of science is not about experts or scientists educating publics, instead it *"represents an iterative process between lay people and technical experts rather than a narrowly didactic or one-way transmission of information packages"* (see also Petts, 2008). Additionally, for some, participatory processes are representative of a citizen's right to be involved in decision-making about science and technology, and it is such involvement, which – in part – affords them their citizenship (Fiorino, 1990; Irwin, 1995, 2001). Jasanoff (2003, p. 243) suggests that what is needed is a move away from "technologies of hubris," where science is the authority on mapping out future impacts and development trajectories, to including "technologies of humility," which *"would engage the human subject as an active, imaginative agent, as well as a source of knowledge, insight, and memory."* Such a shift would allow "plural viewpoints and collective learning" (Jasanoff, 2003, p. 240) – "co-intelligence" (Hartz-Karp, 2007, p. 2).

A number of key criticisms have been levied against participatory processes (see Chapter 5). First, questions have been raised over *which* publics are invited to take part. Petts (2008, p. 826) notes that *"[m]any formal engagement processes... tend to privilege the middle-class and the educated."* A more subtle reflection on this point is offered by Wynne (2007, p. 107), who points out that in the enthusiasm for promoting such approaches, in Europe in particular, a gradual co-option of publics has taken place by policy and science institutions – such that participation with "invited" publics often inadvertently forces (science-led) framings onto proceedings. He contrasts this situation with the more creative possibilities offered by "uninvited" public participation, in particular for challenging ordinarily unacknowledged normativities.

A second key criticism of participatory processes is that they may occur too late, when positions are entrenched or "*after a controversial social or ethical question has arisen in relation to a new technology*" (Rogers-Hayden and Pidgeon, 2007, p. 345). In some circumstances, engagement processes have been accused of simply attempting to mitigate such controversy – ironically often leading to its exacerbation (Jasanoff, 2003; Rogers-Hayden and Pidgeon, 2007). Tokenism is also an accusation when "*engagement comes too late to influence significant decisions or applications that are locked in by commercial or other constraints*" (Rogers-Hayden and Pidgeon, 2007, p. 345).

To avoid tokenism, "upstream engagement" has been advocated by a number of researchers (Grove-White *et al.*, 1997; Grove-White, Macnaghten, and Wynne, 2000; Royal Society, 2004; Wilsdon and Willis, 2004). It involves "*[d]ialogue and deliberation amongst affected parties about a potentially controversial technological issue at an early stage of the research and development process and in advance of significant applications or social controversy*" (Rogers-Hayden and Pidgeon, 2007, p. 346; also see Grove-White, Macnaghten, and Wynne, 2000), and is increasingly being presented as a means to more fully embrace normative and substantive reasons for participation (Chapter 5). A specific challenge of upstream engagement is that the technologies under discussion often only exist "*in terms of future-oriented promise rather than as material reality*" (Macnaghten, 2010, p. 24). As such, there is a possibility that discussions become too focused on normative assessments of technology and science. Stirling (2007) argues that upstream engagement should not be pursued as a means for "legitimising technological choices," nor should it be a method for "closing down" public contestation. Instead, he suggests that "*the truly innovative potential for 'upstream engagement' lies in 'opening up' broader attention to the full range of potentially viable choices*" (Stirling, 2007, p. 293). Through careful, critical reflection both on the aims of engagement and on ways to promote "meaningful interaction" with interested parties (Jasanoff, 2003, p. 238) – whereby publics feel enabled to take part in such discussions – innovative upstream public engagement processes are able to access publics as socio-techno-scientific citizens (Macnaghten, 2010). By this we mean varied publics are able to "*offer opinions, discuss the issues, and reflect on future politics and their contingencies*" across technical *and* socio-cultural dimensions (Macnaghten, 2010, p. 24).

Although raising significant challenges, including the unfamiliarity and ethereal status of many such technologies, evidence from sociological approaches to public engagement with upstream technologies (e.g., Pidgeon and Rogers-Hayden, 2007; Barben *et al.*, 2008), has concluded that people *are* often perfectly able to reason about and debate such risk and technology issues. While people will typically come with very limited technical knowledge of the topic, many will engage enthusiastically with the subject by drawing upon a range of shared cultural narratives and resources regarding the ways science is located in (and shapes) society, and about both the promise and perils of scientific "progress." Examples here include shared discourses about the morality of interfering with "natural" systems (Bloomfield and Vurdubakis, 1995; Macnaghten, 2010) or the trustworthiness and perceived interests of social institutions promoting and regulating scientific developments (Bickerstaff, Simmons, and Pidgeon, 2008; Pidgeon *et al.*, 2009).

Although a full discussion of both the extensive strengths and weaknesses of participatory processes in all of their forms, as well as this growing and important set of literature, is beyond the scope of this chapter, we hope the value of upstream engagement has been made clear. It should be noted that we see upstream engagement as one aspect of responsible innovation, contributing to the characterization and integration "of broader social concerns in a proactive manner" into research programs and the development of technologies as early as possible (Macnaghten, 2010, p. 23). In particular, we propose that the substantive reasons underpinning participatory processes and the benefits of upstream engagement mean it is well placed to contribute significantly to responsible innovation.

What constitutes responsible innovation has already been discussed extensively in earlier chapters of this volume (see, for example, Chapters 2 and 3). The aim of this chapter is to discuss responsible innovation in relation to geoengineering as a practical example, through the examination of empirical work derived from an upstream engagement exercise on the topic of geoengineering with members of the public. In the following sections we detail what geoengineering is, very briefly, what public attitude and engagement work has already taken place, how our analysis – building upon the framework proposed by Owen *et al.* in Chapter 2 – differs from this existing work, and the method and methodology underpinning the empirical work on which this chapter is based.

12.2   Public Perceptions of Geoengineering

In essence geoengineering (also known as climate engineering) aims to reduce the average global temperature by using either solar radiation management (SRM) techniques to reduce incoming sunlight (i.e., increasing the Earth's albedo), or carbon dioxide removal (CDR) techniques to remove carbon dioxide from the atmosphere and redress the imbalance of carbon dioxide causing accelerated climate change (Royal Society, 2009; Buck, 2012). Some suggest that geoengineering could be used to ameliorate specific climate change impacts, for example, lower temperatures regionally or alter ocean chemistry at a localized scale (MacCracken, 2009), however, this is not the focus of present research given implementation feasibility constraints. Over the last several decades geoengineering has moved from the fringes of science and science fiction, and is gaining traction with a small but growing number of scientists within mainstream science (Poumadère, Bertoldo, and Samadi, 2011; Pidgeon *et al.*, 2012).

There exists a wide variety of proposed techniques under each of the broad headings of SRM and CDR. Such techniques range from the relatively benign, for example, painting buildings white under SRM, and afforestation for CDR,[1] to what could be described as more intrusive, for example, stratospheric particle injection under SRM, and ambient air capture and storage of carbon dioxide for CDR (for an overview of many of the techniques see Vaughan and Lenton, 2011; Royal Society, 2009). It is important to note that even the "benign" forms of geoengineering, for example, biochar, would need to be operationalized at a hitherto unseen scale to have a significant impact (Jamieson, 1996).

A second key point is that many of the techniques of geoengineering currently do not exist – they are in some respects potential "future-oriented promise[s]" (Macnaghten, 2010, p. 24). We use the word "potential" as currently most of the ideas are being discussed

---

[1] Of course what constitutes "benign" is open to interpretation and highly dependent on context and social assumptions. For example, re-and-afforestation on the surface seems benign, but if there are competing land-use issues, this could potentially become a highly politicized and sensitive social and environmental justice issue. There are also numerous potential physical environment impacts of re-and-afforestation at a large scale that may not be considered "benign," for example, fertilizer run-off, albedo impacts at high latitudes, hydrological cycle interactions, and so on.

and reviewed not just based on their technical feasibility, but increasingly on moral and ethical dimensions (Corner and Pidgeon, 2010; Gardiner, 2011), and issues around responsible governance (Royal Society, 2009; Rayner *et al.*, 2010; Asilomar Scientific Organizing Committee, 2010; Poumadère, Bertoldo, and Samadi, 2011; Macnaghten and Owen, 2011). Those involved in such discussions (including publics and governments) may deem geoengineering an unacceptable development strategy. Given the importance of the social and ethical dimensions of geoengineering, together with the move toward upstream engagement processes with publics (and its accompanying benefits), commentators have called for research which explores public (un)acceptability of geoengineering in principle, and particular techniques of geoengineering specifically.

To date, relatively little public perceptions work on geoengineering has been completed (for a review of existing work see Corner *et al.*, 2012). Of that which has been undertaken, much has focused on using quantitative survey techniques to gauge public knowledge of geoengineering – confirming it is low (e.g., Leiserowitz *et al.*, 2010; Spence *et al.*, 2010; Poumadère, Bertoldo, and Samadi, 2011; Pidgeon *et al.*, 2012) or that the term "geoengineering" is ambiguous (e.g., Mercer, Keith, and Sharp, 2011) – and that there is a generic preference for CDR techniques over SRM (e.g., Spence *et al.*, 2010). Pidgeon *et al.* (2012; see also Mercer, Keith, and Sharp, 2011) in a preliminary analysis of interview data found that the term geoengineering is unfamiliar to interviewees, who often confuse it with "geothermal" techniques for producing energy. Once interviewers briefly explained what geoengineering is, initial reactions of interviewees included excitement, fear, anger, and disbelief.

A small number of qualitative studies, employing deliberative upstream engagement processes have taken place over the past two to three years, beginning with the Royal Society (2009), followed by Experiment Earth? ("EE" – carried out by Ipsos-MORI (2010) but funded by the Natural Environmental Research Council (NERC, UK), and lastly the set of workshops on which the empirical evidence of this chapter is based (more detail about this is given in Section 12.3). Such work has found that participants had serious concerns over safety, wished for geoengineering activities to be linked with mitigation activities, were more likely to support techniques which were deemed more "natural," and were worried about the reversibility of certain geoengineering techniques (ibid.; also see Corner, Parkhill, and Pidgeon, 2011, for a fuller examination of EE). It is beyond the scope of this chapter to give a "state of the art" review of all geoengineering public perceptions work and beyond (see Corner, Parkhill, and Pidgeon, 2012). In the following section we will give details of the empirical study on which this chapter is based, including how we have analyzed the data, and how this analysis has been informed by thinking through responsible innovation.

12.3 Exploring Public Perceptions of Geoengineering: an Empirical Study

12.3.1 Context

In 2010 the Engineering and Physical Sciences Research Council (EPSRC), the NERC and the Science and Technologies Facilities Council (STFC) – all UK-based funding bodies – released a funding call with the aim *"to fund research which will allow informed and intelligent assessments about the development of geoengineering technologies"* (EPSRC/NERC, 2010). As a result of a review process, two projects were awarded funding: (i) Integrated Assessment of Geoengineering Proposals (IAGP – of which the authors of this chapter are formally a part) and (ii) Stratospheric Aerosols for Particle Injection (SPICE). The aim of IAGP is to develop a mechanism by which existing, proposed, and as yet un-imagined geoengineering proposals could be assessed against criteria ranging from the technical to socio-cultural. As such, computer modeling (climatic and engineering) and, stakeholder and public engagement activities form the work of IAGP. Whereas IAGP does not focus on any particular geoengineering technique, SPICE, by way of contrast, seeks to investigate the potential means, efficacy, impacts, and modes of delivery of a particular form of SRM – stratospheric particles. One basic hypothesis that SPICE researchers wish to test is that stratospheric particles can be injected via a 20 km pipe held up by a large balloon. As with IAGP most of the intended work will involve laboratory-based and computer modeling. However, there is one work package where the researchers wished to scale-down the 20 km pipe and balloon to a 1 km test-bed, with the aim of exploring the engineering challenges of using this mechanism, and the accuracy/efficacy of using computer models to predict the pipe and balloon movement. The SPICE proposal did not involve any real world testing of the cooling properties of stratospheric particles, and would only consist of pumping fresh water.

Due to a stated commitment to responsible innovation, and on the recommendation of a review board, the Research Councils implemented a stage-gate process where they withheld the funding for the test-bed work package until the lead investigator of SPICE was able to collate evidence, which could then be reviewed by an expert panel who would make a recommendation to the Research Councils on whether or not to release the funds (see Macnaghten and Owen, 2011; and Chapter 2, for an overview of the state-gate process). As part of the evidence needed, EPSRC requested that IAGP researchers with expertise in public deliberative engagement work complete an "extra" work package on geoengineering, culminating with a specific focus on the SPICE project. Accordingly, a research team led by Prof. Nick Pidgeon and Dr Karen Parkhill set about designing, collecting, and analyzing data to assist the stage-gate evidence gathering.

12.3.2   Method: Deliberating SPICE

After extensive piloting, three deliberative workshops were completed in three cities (Cardiff, Norwich, and Nottingham) within the UK. Each workshop had between 8 and 12 participants ($n = 32$) sampled theoretically along demographic criteria (e.g., gender, age, educational qualifications, socio-economic groupings) to attempt to ensure we captured a diverse spread of opinion and life circumstances.

The workshops were completed over 1.5 days with a homework task given to participants overnight. Importantly the SPICE project was not discussed until day 2. During day 1 participants were guided through a set of activities, with the focus funneled down from climate change as a general topic to specific geoengineering approaches. Geoengineering was situated as one of three possible societal responses to climate change, with conventional mitigation and adaptation comprising the other two. Framings of "naturalness," "climate emergency," "CDR dealing with the causes of climate change" were explored fully as and when they emerged as discourses from participants, but were not introduced by the research team (see Corner, Parkhill, and Pidgeon, 2011, for more detailed discussion of different framings in upstream engagement on geoengineering).

The analysis on which this chapter is based stems from the materials collected on day 1, that is, *before* the SPICE project was discussed. In the first instance, this included small group discussions on initial reactions to geoengineering, only after broad definitions of geoengineering, SRM and CDR were given. Small group discussions also occurred after an expert gave an overview of some of the proposed techniques (CDR – biochar and ambient air capture; SRM – stratospheric aerosols and cloud brightening). It was emphasized that these were just some of the many ideas for geoengineering being thought about by scientists. All of the workshops were facilitated by the IAGP Cardiff University team. Also in attendance was an expert on climate science and geoengineering. All group discussions were audio- and video-recorded to aid transcription. All transcripts were carefully reviewed to ensure participants' quotes were accurately transcribed. After transcription all transcripts were anonymized. For more detailed information see Parkhill and Pidgeon (2011).

12.3.3 Analysis

The analysis completed for the stage-gate (Parkhill and Pidgeon, 2011) carefully inter-rogated the data exploring public perceptions of, in particular, the proposed SPICE 1 km test-bed, and thus focused on the discussions on day 2. However, to be able to contex-tualize the findings, we also briefly analyzed data from day 1 which could illuminate perceptions of SRM and CDR more broadly. In summary, and for reasons of brevity, that analysis found that CDR techniques are considered more favorably than SRM, with stratospheric aerosols of particular concern. The basis for this concern was that these techniques might distract from mitigation and were too far-fetched, with the addi-tional difficulty of predicting long-term impacts and governance issues (e.g., difficulty of garnering international agreement, issues of territoriality, and how to regulate misuse). With regards to the SPICE test-bed, we concluded that participants had significant con-cerns regarding the deployment of geoengineering techniques, in particular stratospheric aerosols, but were willing to entertain small-scale research if governance and regula-tory structures were already in place or being developed, and if research findings were shared freely.

The present analysis has applied a different analytic lens to some of the data presented in Parkhill and Pidgeon (2011), and other data from the same workshops excluded from that first analysis. In particular we have – in part – developed our analytic lens from Chapter 2 by Owen *et al.* For a reminder of the four dimensions see Box 12.1 below.

Box 12.1 Four Dimensions of Responsible Innovation (Chapter 2)

1. *Anticipatory* – describing and analyzing those intended and potentially unintended impacts that might arise, be these economic, social, environmental or otherwise. Supported by methodologies that include those of foresight, technology assess-ment, horizon scanning, and scenario development, these not only serve to artic-ulate promissory narratives of expectation but to explore other pathways to other impacts, to prompt scientists and innovators to ask "what if . . . ?" questions.

2. *Reflective* – ethically reflecting on such narratives of expectation and the social transformations these might bring, the underlying purposes and motivations and their potential impacts; what we know and do not know, the associated uncertainties, areas of ignorance, assumptions, questions, and dilemmas.

3. *Deliberative* – *opening up* such visions, impacts, and questioning to broad, collective deliberation through processes of dialogue, engagement, and debate, *inviting* and *listening* to wider perspectives from publics and diverse stakeholders.

4. *Responsive* – using this collective process of reflexivity to *influence the direction and pace* of the innovation process itself through effective mechanisms of governance. This should be an *iterative, inclusive, open,* and *adaptive learning approach* with dynamic capability.

These dimensions, together with a focus on the concept of "social intelligence" (Wynne, 1992, 1993) – that is, exploring data where publics engaged in critical reflection on science and knowledge – led us to ask the following questions during the analysis:

- What do varied publics believe are the intentions and motivations (of scientists, governments, and so forth) behind the development of geoengineering techniques?
- What do publics believe are the desired outcomes of geoengineering techniques?
- Do publics believe there are wider products/impacts of geoengineering? What of scientific (un)certainties?
- Who do publics feel is responsible for responding to climate change and investigating geoengineering? What role, if any, do publics feel they have in the responsible innovation of geoengineering?

12.4   Public Perceptions of Geoengineering through the Lens of Responsible Innovation

12.4.1   Intentions

Our participants largely regarded scientists, engineers, and designers as innovators working for the common good. It was often assumed that scientists were acting with altruism, attempting to brainstorm different ways of responding to climate change and that geoengineering was one example of this. To such participants, innovators are *"the smart kids on the block working on these things"* (William, Norwich). Additionally, even if participants did not necessarily support geoengineering, they could see value in the underlying intention of trying to do good:

> I guess the more ideas that come through the scientists and engineers are going to come up with, it's going to generate more ways of doing it.
>
> (Barbara, Norwich)

Such discourses marry with previous research that shows there is an element of idealism around the general notion of science:

Science is an icon of modern society... "science" (in general) enjoys high public esteem and interest in surveys yet suffers apathy and worse in many specific encounters (Wynne, 1991, p. 112 – emphasis in original; also see Chapter 5).

Whilst the idealization surrounding science was a dominant discourse, science as something objective was not. Some participants suggested that the results of science are open to interpretation:

> Well, computer modelling I think they could probably make it work to their favour, whatever happens.

> (Iowerth, Cardiff)

However, as stated, most participants felt confident that the intentions of scientists and innovators are good, yet this did not transform into blind faith. Participants were fully willing and able to interrogate whether or not the intention of doing good, of responding to climate change, was justification for pursuing geoengineering.

When it came to the specificities of how geoengineering may materialize and be mobilized, whether or not the innovators had good intentions became less important than the *motivations of those who might fund and subsequently deploy such innovations*. This occurred at a number of scales. First, participants would shrewdly question the motivations of (industrial) sectors:

> Some of them may make money out of it anyway depending on where the [Carbon Dioxide] stores are and where the process is going to be because that's job and things and buying things and you have to make something to do that bit of processing and stuff like that.

> (Fiona, Norwich)

Of course Fiona's excerpt is not just about how new industries may be generated, it also, in some ways, speaks to the important issue of employment – a significant concern for many under present economic conditions. Some participants were more vocal in their belief that financial motivations would cause the segueing of original intentions into business opportunity – altruism to profiteering (see Buck, 2012, for a full discussion of this issue):

> Motive. Why people do it? Why are people doing it? It's not going to be cost free when you first start doing this. You can see an altruistic motive there, but people will do these things if there is a financial incentive, if there is a reason for doing it, if governments pay them to do it, if they can get a spin off from it... then people are starting to mess with our lives for their financial benefit.

> (Bert, Nottingham)

The second and most prevalent scale at which participants questioned the intentions of pursuing geoengineering was through an examination of the possible motivations in different global regions. As a starting point, participants were quick to recognize the importance of geo-politics and that there could be heterogeneous intentions on the part of different nations for pursuing geoengineering. In such circumstances, participants questioned if responding to climate change would remain the motivating factor, or if others, for example, weather modification, could possibly become the priority.

Important in such accounts is not only that our participants could envision weather modification and enhancement usurping climate change framings, but also that such possibilities would potentially be pursued despite the materialization of negative effects on other territories. Whilst potential negative effects of geoengineering were a continual source of concern, that negative impacts may be the result of weather enhancement rather than a side-effect of responding to climate change seemed particularly unpalatable to participants. Perhaps this resided in the presumed vindictiveness of a country putting their own needs above the wellbeing of others.

It was not just nation's motivations that were interrogated. Although EE? found little evidence that geoengineering would undermine participants' support for mitigation and adaptation (Ipsos-MORI, 2010), our participants felt that this would be a particular danger. To these participants, geoengineering techniques (and intervening with large engineering technologies) were seen as being easier and quicker to implement than to generate significant uptake of lifestyle change:

> People are resistant to change and someone could come up with a nice magic way of making it that we can carry on the way we are that would be the easy option.

> (Bert, Nottingham)

In such circumstances, as Bert suggests, the intention to respond to climate change morphs into finding ways that facilitate current lifestyle trajectories. Bert later reveals how he could envision geoengineering not just leading to the continuation of business as usual, but instead to an exacerbation of activities leading to worsening environmental and social injustices:

> I'm cynical about carbon capture, because it's just another way that the power station can burn coal. Because at the moment they're limited as to what coal they can burn. But if they suddenly find they can burn anything they can pull out the ground, you're going to find a mine in your back garden before very long. Because resources that were not economically viable at one time, suddenly will become, and you thought you got a nice garden but then there's an open cast mine there.

> (Bert, Nottingham)

Indeed other participants, despite preferring SRM techniques the least, were able to imagine how Western territories may pursue them in inequitable ways, perhaps through manipulating more impoverished, less powerful countries:

> I mean if you were asking to put it up somewhere where they're incredibly poor and someone at the top is corrupt, they're going to say, 'Yes, thank you very much, we'll take your money, you can put it up here' cause they're not going to have too many concerns about the people living there. If you're talking about doing it in the UK, then everybody and their auntie want ten pennies of their input put in.

> (Barbara, Norwich)

Clearly, our participants posited that there are a range of intentions and motivations that may impact on how geoengineering is pursued. The clearest message from participants, which will be explored in *Theme 3: Impacts*, is that whatever the possible good intentions (of scientists, innovators, governments, industry and so forth), *these do not necessarily ensure good or positive outcomes*. First, however, we wish to explore how our participants navigated the complexities of responsibility.

12.4.2 Responsibility

Discourses of responsibility covered a broad number of interlinked topic areas. To begin with participants were clear that everyone has a responsibility to try to respond to climate change. For some there was a greater responsibility for developed nations, due to legacy emissions and perceived wealth. For others current higher emitters were depicted as needing to take greater responsibility. It was recognized that different responses were needed, dependent on circumstances. Some participants intimated that a social contract needs to be formed between publics and innovators, whereby publics take responsibility for implementing lifestyle change to help mitigate climate change, whilst innovators lead on developing possible technical solutions including, but not limited to, geoengineering.

Whilst there was tremendous uncertainty over developing geoengineering, some participants felt it was important that innovation should not be stifled. Indeed, some suggested that it was the responsibility of others to allow innovators the freedom to develop ideas. In part, despite the unknowns and potential impacts, participants felt the consequences of doing nothing could potentially be greater than pursuing such development.

However, many participants were also concerned that geoengineering may distract from mitigation. In a modified moral hazard argument, this was less about whether or not people would be motivated to undertake mitigation given a so-called "technical fix" had been developed, but more about whether innovators would be encouraged to concentrate on mitigation given the "tempting option" of geoengineering. The basis of this concern was that our publics envisioned there to be a limited skills base available and thus innovators would have to choose which to pursue: mitigation or geoengineering.

Participants felt it was the responsibility of innovators to ensure that their ideas are safe and safely developed. This meant thinking through exhaustively the impacts geoengineering might have, including the improbable. For many this meant incremental development stages, freely sharing knowledge (including successes and failures), and not allowing hubris to emerge. For the latter, previous science controversies acted as a precautionary heuristic:

> ... it's scientists' ability to satisfy and negate the risk before going that far. I'm struggling to think of an analogy. Thalidomide. Everybody was reassured that Thalidomide was going to be a safe drug and we're still living with the consequences ... And for an experiment of that nature, stratospheric aerosols, God forbid you had a catas[trophy] – but there was something that had not been considered.

> (Riley, Norwich)

Concerning decisions over whether or not to pursue the development and eventual deployment of various forms of geoengineering, participants felt that it was the role of innovators to provide rigorous evidence as it became available. As such, participants implied that geoengineering techniques should be subject to continual regulatory and scientific governance processes – constantly interrogated through scientific rigor. Ultimately though, many participants felt it was the role of politicians to decide if geoengineering should be pursued. For some participants, this politicization of science could lead to procrastination, missed opportunities and unnecessary delay:

> Like Owein said, you know with the air capture, that's the only thing that's actually proven to definitely work, all these are still ... well, these two [cloud brightening and stratospheric aerosols] mostly are still unknown and now so they've got this [ambient air capture] taking a long period of time, well if it's known to be working why don't they just set it up somewhere and so what if it takes 30 years ....

> (Morgan, Cardiff)

It was also apparent that new governance structures need to be developed and that ultimately responsibility should not necessarily rest with individual nations. This was particularly the case with SRM techniques. Yet participants also felt it important that individual nations should be able to pursue their own geoengineering development paths and not be dictated to by the "intergovernmental geoengineering committee": it should act more as an overseer, helping to co-ordinate and regulate action.

Participants were concerned that governance structures be rigorous enough to prevent manipulation, with individual wealthy nations taking control by merit of their financial position:

> Will the rich and powerful countries get to decide? Cost must come into it somewhere because some of these developing countries, there's no way they're going to be able to afford some of these whizzy ideas.

> (Beven, Cardiff)

Indeed, participants suggested it was the responsibility of richer nations to facilitate developing countries' involvement, and that, even before deployment, as many nations as possible be involved in decision-making. It is interesting that so much emphasis was placed on the role of governments (national and international). Participants would nearly always default to this scale in discussions of the governance of geoengineering. Whilst participants accepted that some geoengineering activities could be led by industries and commercial entities, it was assumed that even these activities would be monitored and regulated by the wider governance structures already discussed.

Discussions of responsibility inevitably also included thinking through accountability and the inherent potential difficulties of attributing this, especially in the event that something went badly wrong. SRM techniques were seen as particularly problematic given the complex nature of interactions that may occur with this type of intervention. Participants envisioned territorial disputes arising from negative effects, which may be associated by the "victim" country with those deploying SRM:

> How do you prove that that [SRM] was why it happened? So we'd say well we didn't do it, it was gonna happen anyway.

> (Orville, Norwich)

It was not necessarily the case that those deploying geoengineering would deliberately attempt to avoid taking responsibility (although this was certainly seen as a possibility) for negative impacts, but that participants were sympathetic to problems of tracking causality.

Of significant concern to most participants was the notion that we may be burdening futures through the development of geoengineering, refusing to "assume responsibility" for excess carbon dioxide (Adam and Groves, 2007). Such thoughts coalesced around both the long-term commitment necessary if SRM geoengineering was pursued (i.e., the need to continue the intervention whilst excess carbon dioxide is present, or face a more dramatic rise in temperature than even current trends of global warming), and the legacy of CDR producing vast "waste" stores:

> As we are trying to save the planet are we leaving the problem for someone else to deal with it?
>
> (Frank, Norwich)

> All of those things they have, even the air capture, where you're going to store it. All of these things seem, well they're artificial aren't they, they're artificially trying to make it better but the problem, if we don't change the way we are, it's still going to be there.
>
> (Marge, Nottingham)

In this sense, our participants recognize how "future-transforming processes" cause "future making" to slide into "future taking" (Adam and Groves, 2007, p. 79). As also by discussed Adam and Groves (2007), some of our participants questioned whether we would be able to develop institutions capable of adapting and extending into the future, particularly as the burden of excess carbon dioxide is likely to keep increasing:

> Fiona   How long can they control it for if we're gonna keep moving in the same fashion because –
>
> Frank   Yeah and what are the implications of it?
>
> Fiona   will the controls be able to manage in another 100 or 200 years time? (Norwich)

12.4.3 Impacts

In the main, as has been noted before, the "wider products" (Chapter 2), of geoengineering most focused on by participants were the unintentional, unknowable amorphous "side effects" (Ipsos-Mori, 2010; Parkhill and Pidgeon, 2011). In this sense, whilst innovators were expected to have thought through how geoengineering interventions interact with complex interlinked systems, there was also the full expectation that, due to limits of what is knowable, some potential impacts may be "overlooked." Even with careful, iterative, rigorous development and governance, participants questioned how prepared we would be after such testing:

> . . . it's all still only on trial isn't it? And research, we don't really know what would happen on such a big scale, they might have done little bits on dropping water droplets rather than having a boat shooting up water . . . But when they start doing it [cloud brightening] with these boats . . . and throwing up all that, you never know what might happen.
>
> (Iowerth, Cardiff)

CDR and SRM were both believed to have potential impacts, however, the potential scale of impact for SRM was seen as much larger. Similar to Genetically Modified Organisms (GMOs) (Grove-White *et al.*, 1997; Marris, 2001), the complexity of the systems involved meant participants felt attributes of control were highly unlikely:

> You attempted to cure one problem and actually create another problem by changing the weather patterns elsewhere in the world. I can't believe that it would be local.
>
> (Henry, Norwich)

Negative impacts were not the only potential wider products. Participants also felt that developing geoengineering could lead to other forms of innovation:

> Well the pro is that people are actually thinking about it and looking for ways to mitigate the problems that we've got ... And I guess the more ideas that come through the scientists and engineers are going to come up, it's going to generate more ways of doing it ... Until you throw the idea in it doesn't generate other ideas and once you do then people – it's a stepping stone to something else ....
>
> (Barbara, Norwich)

Whilst SRM was predominantly the focus for thoughts concerning wider, large-scale impacts of geoengineering, as we have stated previously (Parkhill and Pidgeon, 2011), participants were keen that all forms of geoengineering should be subject to careful regulation. Participants recognized that both SRM (due to both intended and potential unintended impacts) and CDR (due to the core aims of manipulating the carbon cycle) would have global implications.

The focus on side-effects and other forms of innovation as the wider products of geoengineering is, however, a rather narrow categorization. In reality, wider products are not just the technical, material manifestations of geoengineering or their potential effects: also included are socio-cultural (e.g., potential environmental and social injustices) and political (e.g., new governance structures).

12.4.4   The Role of the Public

Deliberative engagement as part of a democratic process assumes that publics should (and wish to) be involved in decisions over whether or not to pursue geoengineering. In addition, Section 12.1 made clear that there is value in engaging with publics to include varied viewpoints and ensure co-intelligence is created (Wynne, 1991, 1992, 1993; Hartz-Karp, 2007). However, we found that it took a great deal of effort to persuade our participants that, despite their apparent lack of technical expertise in science, engineering or governance, they had valuable input that they could offer. Often it was implied that they could not contribute to decision-making through the use of "they", "them", and "others" rather than "we" and "us." Sometimes participants would be explicit in stating that due to the complexity and scale of interventions being discussed under geoengineering, they could only have a limited input:

William   No we need to do this [investigate geoengineering] but the answers I think are a bit – well they're beyond me anyway.

Frank   Yeah, I don't think the answers can be done by a layman. That's gonna take someone more intelligent than me to sort it out. (Norwich)

Sentiments such as those expressed by William and Frank were particularly pointed when discussing what were deemed as more "tech heavy" and "extraordinary" approaches to geoengineering (e.g., ambient air capture and stratospheric aerosols). For such approaches some participants felt it was much more important to have "experts" input and that ultimately politicians should decide on whether or not they are pursued. In part this seems to be based on whether or not they could envision the techniques as part of either their or wider societies present and future material reality. By way of contrast, techniques such as biochar were associated with "ordinariness" (Parkhill *et al.*, 2010) by drawing upon their current material experience (Butler, Parkhill, and Pidgeon, 2011) of familiar mundane tasks, such as gardening, and with participants much more comfortable with suggesting how they might manifest. For example, they speculated that drier countries may be more inclined to use biochar as they perceived it may help such countries keep moisture in the soils and thus help their crops.

Participants also questioned if, given the emergent stage that most geoengineering techniques are at, it was even worthwhile for them to take part in deliberations. They struggled with understanding what help their ruminations could be when the techniques are likely to radically change throughout the development process. Such struggles were indicative that, at times, participants would get "lost" in the details of a technique. Once brought back to broader dimensions (such as intentionality, responsibility, governance, impacts, ethics, and so forth), most participants seemed comparatively more comfortable deliberating. Of course what this also underscores is the importance that deliberation and engagement are "*[s]ustained interactions between decision-makers, experts, and citizens, starting at the upstream end of research and development*" (Jasanoff, 2003, p. 242 – emphasis added).

Regardless of whether or not they felt comfortable and able to be engaged on such issues, some participants felt they have a limited ability to influence development trajectories or governance decisions, which is analogous to findings related to public engagement in GMOs (Grove-White, Macnaghten, and Wynne, 2000):

I just don't think my opinions would matter and things are going to happen whether I dislike it or not.

(Ruby, Nottingham)

Cynicism and disenfranchisement regarding current deliberations seemed to be derived from their experiences of past formal consultations, where they felt their concerns were usurped by the agendas of what they perceived as being more powerful actors (e.g., governments, experts, and stakeholders). Although these were qualitatively different types of engagement exercises, these past experiences meant our participants were wary and cautious of all forms of engagement exercises – including ours. However, we should also point out that most participants, despite the difficulties, did feel that publics should be engaged on a continual basis (Parkhill and Pidgeon, 2011).

12.5   Conclusion: Geoengineering – Responsible Innovation?

Public engagement has a critical role to play in the responsible innovation of geoengineering. Indeed, Owen *et al.* in Chapter 2 state the aim of their third dimension of responsible innovation (*"Deliberative"*) is to open up dialogue, relating to imaginaries and visions of social transformation that a new technology may cause, including with publics. Whilst literatures associated with public engagement processes depict core constructs of engagement (e.g., transparency, democratic decision-making, co-intelligence, and so forth) as advantageous or desirable, a commitment to responsible innovation would seem to suggest that processes of public engagement are essential and foster "technologies of humility" (Jasanoff, 2003).

On careful analysis, it is clear that our participants have incidentally engaged with the dimensions of responsible innovation that Owen *et al.* set out in Chapter 3. Most crucially, intentionality – reflecting on and probing the intentions of scientists and other stakeholders involved in the development of geoengineering – has revealed some interesting nuances to the already existing public perceptions work. Our participants did not want to stifle innovation since many of them saw it as a valued part of contemporary development. They were, however, deeply concerned that commercial interests might override the good intentions of scientists. As such they questioned the "sociology of promises or expectations" (see Chapter 13); that is, the claims put forward with regards to what geoengineering would prove able to do for society (Kearns *et al.*, 2006, p. 293). Indeed, it would be fair to comment that, whilst most of our participants were happy to discuss the perceived benefits of geoengineering, this was juxtaposed with a desire to have frank and meaningful discussions over the difficulties, challenges and uncertainties, including the perspective of innovators.

In terms of responsibility and impacts, our participants were on the whole appreciative of the role of scientists and others involved in the development of geoengineering technologies, whilst simultaneously implying that stakeholders must critically reflect on the "technoscientific imaginaries" (i.e., the future worlds which are being imagined and possibly brought into being through the development of certain technoscientific practices) and which scientists and innovators are complicit in championing (Kearns *et al.*, 2006, p. 293). This included the desire to inject a healthy dose of humility, so that innovators recognize the potential "*asymmetry between what is intended and what is merely brought about*" (Jamieson, 1996).

Concerns over the role of commercial entities in the development and future deployment of geoengineering echo an emerging concern of David Keith – a geoengineering researcher – who has recently argued against the privatization of, in particular, solar radiation technologies and has called for patents on such technologies to be banned

(Scientific American, 2012). Indeed, at the time of writing this chapter, the SPICE team researchers have also opted to cancel the 1 km test-bed, in part as it has emerged that two of the team are involved in an existing patent for the balloon technology (Nature News, 2012). As such the SPICE researchers appear to have been reflecting a growing awareness of the sensitivities surrounding SRM techniques.

Some of the concerns raised in this chapter, for example, those over commercialization and uncertainty of impacts, are reminiscent of similar discourses expressed during the GMOs controversies. Indeed, it is perhaps, in part, the earlier public concerns expressed over the role of GMO companies like Monsanto (a key commercial entity in the development and commercialization of this technology) that provide the context for our participants' sensitivities to concerns over the privatization of geoengineering. Monsanto were criticized in the 1990s and early 2000s for their domination of GMO developments and their restrictive practices of not allowing farmers to keep unused seeds for use in the following year's crop. Distrust of commercial entities in the development of GMOs is attributed as a key reason for the public contestation in Europe over their introduction (Dickson, 2000). It is not unreasonable to propose a connection between such instances and geoengineering, given that we know risk perceptions are "*sensitive to the history of controversy surrounding the issue or associated with technologies deemed similar as a context to people's attempts at making sense of an emergent technology*" (Pidgeon *et al.*, 2012, p. 4180). Geoengineering techniques share with GMOs many of the underlying issues, for example, uncertainties over impacts, potential for the paradox of control (see Chapter 2), difficulties of transboundary impacts and the fact that there are a plurality of approaches rather than a single technological pathway or discipline (Pidgeon *et al.*, 2012; also see Corner, Parkhill, and Pidgeon, 2012).

Given the discussion so far, what do our data say regarding the ways in which a process of responsible innovation may operate in a real world example? Whilst many of our participants were genuinely surprised and pleased to be engaged with, some were unsure how their participation would be utilized (the dimension of responsiveness discussed by Owen *et al.* in Chapter 2). As such it might be beneficial if the dimensions of responsible innovation were overtly discussed with publics to help them and those involved in future public engagement exercises to better situate their roles and responsibilities in the context of (geoengineering) governance. We would also suggest that those involved in developing geoengineering (and other emergent technologies) need to be visibly responsive to the dimensions of responsible innovation, particularly in the context of our discussions, listening to and reflecting on public engagement through the publishing of publically available outputs. Yet, at the same time, we would also suggest that the responsible innovation framework itself could benefit from more tangible engagement with various publics – invited and uninvited, developed and developing nations.

We do not make such a suggestion lightly – we are fully aware of the difficulties of public engagement. Yet we feel it important to underline the significant roles our publics were able to take on during their discussions. Our participants became socio-technical "scientific citizens" (Irwin, 1995; Macnaghten, 2010), philosophers, moralizers, governors, regulators, ethicists, and much more. They questioned the role of scientists, innovators, politicians, businesses and other publics. They made and challenged assumptions. They were cynical, sceptical, enthusiastic, and thoughtful, in the same breath as provocative. More often than not, they were humble. Although, as we stated earlier, public engagement processes – particularly those upstream – pose significant challenges, it is these qualities and "foibles", which make publics particularly well placed to help ensure we are at least committed to try innovating responsibly.

Acknowledgments

The authors would like to thank the UK Engineering and Physical Sciences Research Council and Natural Environment Research Council through the Integrated Assessment of Geoengineering Proposals Project (EP/I014721/1) for their support. Additional support was provided by the US National Science Foundation through Cardiff's membership of the Center for Nanotechnology in Society at the University of California at Santa Barbara (cooperative Agreement SES 0938099). We would also like to thank the IAGP advisory panel (see www.iagp.ac.uk), Merryn Thomas, Dr Joel Burton, the SPICE team and particularly Dr Kirsty Kuo for attending all of the workshops, and all of our wonderful public participants.

References

Adam, B. and Groves, C., *Future Matters: Action, Knowledge, Ethics*, Brill, Boston, MA (2007).

Asilomar Scientific Organizing Committee, The Asilomar Conference Recommendations on Principles for Research into Climate Engineering Techniques, Climate Institute, Washington, DC (2010).

D. Barben, E. Fisher, C. Selin *et al.*, Anticipatory governance of nanotechnology: foresight, engagement and integration, in *The Handbook of Science and Technology Studies* 3rd edn (eds E.J. Hackett, O. Amsterdamska, M. Lynch and J Wajcman), MIT Press, Cambridge, MA, 979–1000 (2008).

K. Bickerstaff, P. Simmons and N. Pidgeon, Constructing responsibility for risk(s): negotiating citizen-state relationships, *Environment and Planning A*, **40**, 1312–1330 (2008).

B. P. Bloomfield and T. Vurdubakis, Disrupted boundaries: new reproductive technologies and the language of anxiety and expectation, *Social Studies of Science*, **25**(3), 533–551 (1995).

H. J. Buck, Geoengineering: re-making climate for profit or humanitarian intervention? *Development and Change*, **43**(1), 253–270 (2012).

C. Butler, K. Parkhill and N. Pidgeon, From the material to the imagined: public engagement with low carbon technologies in a nuclear community, in *Renewable Energy and the Public: From NIMBY to Participation* (ed. P. Devine-Wright), Earthscan, London, (2011).

Corner, A., Parkhill, K., and Pidgeon, N., Experiment Earth? Reflections on a Public Dialogue on Geoengineering, Understanding Risk Working Paper 11-02, School of Psychology, Cardiff (2011).

A. Corner, K. A. Parkhill and N. Pidgeon, Public perceptions of geoengineering: emerging perspectives and the challenge of upstream public engagement, *WiREs Climate Change*, **3**(5), 451–466 (2012).

A. Corner and N. F. Pidgeon, Geoengineering the climate – the social and ethical implications, *Environment: Science and Policy for Sustainable Development,* **52**(1), 24–37 (2010).

D. Dickson, Science and its public: the need for a third way, *Social Studies of Science,* **30**(6), 917–923 (2000).

EPSRC/NERC, Climate Geoengineering Sandpit, http://www.epsrc.ac.uk/funding/calls /2010/Pages/climategeoengsandpit.aspx (accessed 15 August 2012) (2010).

U. Felt and M. Fochler, Machineries for making publics: inscribing and de-scribing publics in the public engagement, *Minerva,* **48**, 219–238 (2010).

D. J. Fiorino, Citizen participation and environmental risk: a survey of institutional mechanisms, *Science, Technology, & Human Values,* **15**(2), 226–243 (1990).

S. M. Gardiner, Some early ethics of geoengineering the climate: a commentary on the values of the royal society report, *Environmental Values,* **20**, 163–188 (2011).

Grove-White, R., Macnaghten, P., Mayer, S., *et al.,* Uncertain World: Genetically Modified Organisms, Food and Public Attitudes in Britain, Centre for the Study of Environmental Change, Lancaster University (1997).

Grove-White, R., Macnaghten, P., and Wynne, B., Wising up: The Public and New Technologies, Centre for the Study of Environmental Change, Lancaster University (2000).

J. Hartz-Karp, How and why deliberative democracy enables co-intelligence and brings wisdom to governance, *Journal of Public Deliberation,* **3**(1), 1–9 (2007).

Ipsos-MORI Experiment Earth: Report on a Public Dialogue on Geoengineering, Natural Environment Research Council, Swindon, www.nerc.ac.uk/about/consult /geoengineering-dialogue-final-report.pdf (accessed 15 August 2012) (2010).

A. J. Irwin, *Citizen Science,* Routledge, London, (1995).

A. Irwin, *Sociology and the Environment,* Polity Press, Cambridge, (2001).

D. Jamieson, Ethics and intentional climate change, *Climate Change,* **33**, 323–336 (1996).

S. Jasanoff, Technologies of humility: citizen participation in governing science, *Minerva,* **41**, 223–244 (2003).

M. Kearns, R. Grove-White, P. Macnaghten, *et al.,* From bio to nano: learning lessons from the UK agricultural biotechnology controversy, *Science as Culture,* **15**(4), 291–307 (2006).

A. Leiserowitz, E. Maibach, C. Roser-Renouf, *et al.,* Climate Change in the American Mind: Americans Global Warming Beliefs and Attitudes in June 2010, Yale University and George Mason University, Yale Project on Climate Change Communication, New Haven, CT (2010).

M. C. MacCracken, On the possible use of geoengineering to moderate specific climate change impacts, *Environmental research Letters,* **4**, 045107 (2009).

P. Macnaghten, Researching technoscientific concerns in the making: narrative structures, public responses, and emerging nanotechnologies, *Environment and Planning A,* **42**, 23–37 (2010).

P. Macnaghten and R. Owen, Environmental science: good governance for geoengineering, *Nature,* **479**, 293 (2011).

C. Marris, Public views on GMOs: deconstructing the myths, *EMBO Reports,* **21**(7), 545–548 (2001).

A. Mercer, D. Keith and J. Sharp, Public understanding of solar radiation management, *Environmental Research Letters*, **6**(4), 1–9 (2011).

Nature News Cancelled Project Spurs Debate Over Geoengineering Patents. Nature, http://www.nature.com/news/cancelled-project-spurs-debate-over-geoengineering -patents-1.10690 (accessed 15 August 2012) (2012).

K. Parkhill and N. Pidgeon Public Engagement on Geoengineering Research: Preliminary Report on the SPICE Deliberative Workshops. Understanding Risk Working Paper 11-01, School of Psychology, Cardiff (2011).

K. A. Parkhill, N. Pidgeon, K. Henwood, *et al*. From the familiar to the extraordinary: local residents' perceptions of risk when living with a nuclear power in the UK, *Transactions of the Institute of British Geographers,* **35**(1), 39–58 (2010).

J. Petts, Public engagement to build trust: false hopes? *Journal of Risk Research,* **11**(6), 821–835 (2008).

N.F. Pidgeon and T. Rogers-Hayden, Opening up nanotechnology dialogue with the publics: risk communication or upstream engagement? *Health, Risk & Society,* **9**(2), 191–210 (2007).

N. F. Pidgeon, B. Harthorn, K. Bryant, *et al*. Deliberating the risks of nanotechnology for energy and health applications in the US and UK, *Nature Nanotechnology,* **4**, 95–98 (2009).

N. F. Pidgeon, A. Corner, K.A. Parkhill, *et al*. Exploring early public responses to geoengineering, *Philosophical Transactions of the Royal Society (A),* **370**(1974), 4176–4196 (2012).

M. Poumadère, R. Bertoldo and J. Samadi, Public perceptions and governance of controversial technologies to tackle climate change: nuclear power, carbon capture and storage, wind, and geoengineering, *WiREs Climate Change,* **2**, 712–727 (2011).

Rayner S., Redgwell, S., Sauvulescu, C., *et al*. Draft principles for the conduct of geo-engineering research, (the Oxford Principles). Reproduced in House of Commons Science and Technology Committee, The Regulation of Geoengineering, Fifth Report of the Session 2009-2010, HC221, 18th March (2010).

T. Rogers-Hayden and N. Pidgeon, Moving engagement upstream? Nanotechnologies and the Royal Society and Royal Academy of Engineering's inquiry, *Public Understanding of Science,* **16**, 345–364 (2007).

Royal Society *Nanoscience and Nanotechnologies: Opportunities and Uncertainties*, Royal Society and Royal Academy of Engineering, London (2004).

Royal Society *Geoengineering the Climate: Science, Governance and Uncertainty*, Royal Society, London (2009).

Scientific American Researcher: Ban patent on Geoengineering Technology. Scientific American, http://www.scientificamerican.com/article.cfm?id = researcher-ban-patents -on-geoengineering-technology (accessed 15 August 2012) (2012).

Spence A., Venables, D., Pidgeon, N. *et al*. Public Perceptions of Climate Change and Energy Futures in Britain: Summary Findings of a Survey Conducted in January-March 2010. Technical Report (Understanding Risk Working Paper 10-01), School of Psychology, Cardiff (2010).

A. Stirling, Deliberate futures: precaution and progress in social choice of sustainable technology, *Sustainable Development,* **15**, 286–295 (2007).

N. E. Vaughan and T. M. Lenton, A review of climate geoengineering proposals, *Climate Change,* **109**, 745–790 (2011).

J. Wilsdon and R. Willis, *See Through Science: Why Public Engagement Needs to Move Upstream*, Demos, (2004).

B. Wynne, Knowledges in context, *Science, Technology & Human Values,* **15**(1), 111–121 (1991).

B. Wynne, Public understanding of science research: new horizons or hall of mirrors? *Public Understanding of Science,* **1**(1), 37–43 (1992).

B. Wynne, Public uptake of science: a case for institutional reflexivity, *Public Understanding of Science,* **4**(2), 321–337 (1993).

B. Wynne, Public participation in science and technology: performing and obscuring a political-conceptual category mistake, *EAST Asian Science, Technology and Society: An International Journal,* **1**, 99–110 (2007).

13

Visions, Hype, and Expectations: a Place for Responsibility

Elena Simakova[1] *and Christopher Coenen*[2]
[1]*University of Exeter Business School, UK*
[2]*Karlsruhe Institute of Technology (KIT), Germany*

13.1 Introduction

This chapter offers an analysis of responsibility with regard to emerging fields of science and technology, characterized by far reaching visions and expectations of their revolutionary potential, which can border on hype. It will consider nanotechnologies as a particular example, questioning the idea of these sciences and technologies being "fields" of focused scientific inquiry and technological development. Coming from the traditions of science and technology studies (STS[1]) and technology assessment (TA[2]),

---

[1] STS is a social science multidiscipline drawing on methodologies coming mainly from history, sociology, or anthropology to produce studies of science and technology, as well as of broadly knowledge and expertise, from constructivist perspectives. STS can also be read as science, technology, and society, particularly emphasizing research examining the roles of science and technology in society.

[2] According to Grunwald (2011), TA (i) constitutes an interdisciplinary research field aimed at, generally speaking, providing knowledge for better-informed and well-reflected decisions concerning new and emerging developments in science and technology, (ii) its initial and still valid motivation is to provide answers to the emergence of unintended and often undesirable side effects of science and technology, and (iii) it shall add reflexivity to technology governance by integrating any available knowledge on possible side-effects at an early stage in decision-making processes, by supporting the evaluation of technologies and their impact according to societal values and ethical principles, by elaborating strategies to deal with the uncertainties that inevitably arise, and by contributing to constructive solutions of societal conflicts. Grunwald identifies four partially overlapping branches of TA: TA as policy advice, TA as a medium of participation, TA for shaping technology directly, and TA in innovation processes. TA is institutionalized as a set of research policy and research bodies that are often engaged in policy advice for parliaments and other political institutions. While TA originated from the US, it is now most firmly established in Western and Central Europe.

Responsible Innovation, First Edition. Edited by Richard Owen, John Bessant and Maggy Heintz.
© 2013 John Wiley & Sons, Ltd. Published 2013 by John Wiley & Sons, Ltd.

we will develop an approach that contributes to discourse concerning the sociology of expectations, vision assessment, socio-technical imaginaries and cognate approaches (Borup *et al.*, 2006; Brown and Michael, 2003; Boenink, Swierstra, and Stemerding, 2010; Coenen, 2010a; Grunwald, 2010; Kearnes and MacNaghten, 2006; Nordmann, 2007; Nordmann and Rip, 2009; Jasanoff and Kim, 2009). This area of academic research deals precisely with a critical appraisal of emerging technologies especially associated with revolutionary claims. Examples are information technologies, nanotechnologies, biotechnologies, genomics, neurotechnologies, and so on. Social scientists and humanities scholars look at how organizations and individuals produce and interpret statements of expectation about technologies. This may occur, for example, in science and technology policy exercises accomplished for governments' demands, or individual and organizational decisions and choices with regard to emerging technologies. The field of research includes analysis of promises, imaginaries, visions, and visionaries who often present themselves as prophets; forward-looking statements contributing to the making of futures through the production of scenarios, predictions, and anticipations, as well as assessment of technological capabilities. Such processes can be highly controversial under situations of uncertainty, which entail the need to pay analytic attention to the construction of *credibility* for competing claims. We consider the place of responsibility within these visions and expectations, and by the "prophets" who make them.

Both of us, to various degrees, have been involved in TA projects, empirical research on nanotechnologies and converging technologies, as well as public engagement exercises and ELSA[3] activities. This chapter then is in part drawn from our own experiences. Being situated at the intersection of STS and TA, we developed particular insights into and sensibilities toward the role of visionary discourses in the production of technosciences. We will consider visions, hype, and expectations as constructs emerging in particular socio-historical contexts. Such an approach, however, entails certain challenges for responsible (research and) innovation (RRI) agendas.[4] It takes the discussion out of the safe waters of the objectivist understanding of sciences and technologies, and their societal implications. Instead, it stresses the uncertainties (and ignorance[5]) in evaluating promises, benefits, and risks of science and technology arising from the controversial distinctions between truth and fiction, objective and subjective, substance and description. It also throws into question the boundary between communities of assessors and assessed, which is not always clear cut. Questions of legitimacy (Grunwald, 2009), participation, and the politics of expertise (Webster, 2007a,b; Nowotny, 2007; Wynne, 2007) come forcefully to the fore. For example, the recent debate on the relevance of approaches in TA (e.g., what

---

[3] Ethical, legal, and societal aspects (of science and technology), in the US known as ELSI (ethical, legal, and societal implications).

[4] According to Grunwald (2011), new concepts of responsible innovation complement or even replace the "shaping of technology" with "the shaping of innovation" and radicalize "post-normal science" by bringing research even closer to social practice, by focusing on interventions into the social world, and on the responsibility aspects of such interventions. Such approaches also further extend the scope of consideration given to ethical issues, in particular issues of responsibility.

[5] A cognate sociological approach to ignorance is explored in a special issue "Strategic unknowns: toward a sociology of ignorance" (McGoey, 2012) of the journal *Economy and Society*, which looks at the cultivation of strategic unknowns as a resource for power relations in modern liberal societies.

is known as "vision assessment"; see, e.g., Grunwald 2009, 2010) emphasizes the importance of drawing attention to how claims about and on behalf of science and technology are produced and interpreted.[6] These approaches demand a radical re-examination of the roles of constituencies in the construction of claims for responsibility in the discourses of emerging technosciences.

In brief, this chapter first analyses a series of five historic episodes that illustrate evolving repertoires of nanofutures, and introduces notions of nano as a *flexible label*. Secondly, it discusses preliminary lessons for RRI derived from understanding nano as narratives, visions, and conflicts. Two empirical narratives are offered discussing how the notion of responsibility has been applied in conjunction with nano: first, as part of a process of "defuturization" of nano in Germany, mainly as part of TA activities and second, in university–industry relations around knowledge and technology transfer in the United States. We will conclude with a summary of our approach and some implications for RRI.

13.2   The Repertoires of Nano Futures

Nanotechnologies serve as a key focus for this chapter, to illustrate how large-scale technoscientific initiatives can be approached from a perspective which is interested in the role of expectations, scenarios, and visions of the future. In the debate on technological futures worldwide, *players* in the emerging field engage in deliberations on the attribution of responsibility for technological development. Those can be questions about whether such developments need to be *market* or *state led* (Appelbaum and Parker, 2008) and what pertinent regulatory measures need to look like. It can also be about choices and decisions concerning funding priorities. In this chapter, we will draw attention to nanotechnologies from a perspective emphasizing the *interpretive flexibility* (Pinch and Bijker, 1987) of technologies, drawing on *constructivist* approaches developed in STS. Such a stance adopts the idea that *technological properties, or promises, are not given and fixed, but are actively negotiated and subject to reinterpretation*. We will discuss how the RRI debate could be informed less by assumptions about the content of nano research (cf. also Selin, 2007) and more by understanding first how some of the players involved in this contested space (policy makers, scientists, and social scientists in our case) interact and make sense of nano. The chapter cannot and does not aim to offer an extensive global overview of activities around nano. Rather, when examining approaches to RRI, we believe that it is particularly important to develop sensibilities toward certain features of nano discourse that pose challenges for governance and consequently for RRI. Considering the scope of promises, as well as resources, attached to nano, what kind of lessons for RRI can be derived from analysis of discourses and practices around nanotechnologies? We will begin answering the question by looking closely at a series of five key, historically-successive, episodes in nano discourse, in order to try and discern patterns in the evolution of nano as an acceptable and widely adopted, technoscientific initiative.

---

[6] Such an approach can be recognized under the labels of *interpretivism, post-positivism,* or *post-essentialism.*

Episode 1 The birth of a vision

The first episode is set at the beginning of the 1980s, when, with forerunners in the 1970s, Eric Drexler and his collaborators popularized their views of nanotechnology, in particular in highly technophile circles, such as enthusiasts of space colonization. Drexler's techno-visionary book *Engines of Creation* was published in 1986. Subsequently, Drexlerian nanofuturism dominated the public image of nanotechnology in the media and in academia. In 1987, half a year before Drexler founded his non-profit Foresight Institute in Palo Alto, in the heart of the Silicon Valley in the US, he organized a Nanotechnology Symposium *Exploring Nanotechnology* at the Massachusetts Institute of Technology (MIT). He was supported by his mentor Marvin Minsky, a pioneer of artificial intelligence and a techno-visionary himself. Societal and political aspects of the emerging technology played an important role at this conference, including the potential for nano to overcome mass production; how policy makers can adapt to nano; and what kind of legislation, if any, should be enacted to control its development. On the other hand, discussions within the nanofuturist circles often continued to revolve around far-off future prospects of humanity in the universe and science-fictional notions of society.

This episode draws attention to a particular role of "enactors" (Rip, 2006) in the creation of new fields with revolutionary technological promise. Enactors are leading figures who participate in developing "*repertoires* of promises and other expectations, and strategies of how to position the future of nanotechnology and their own role in it" (Rip, 2006, p.361). It has been shown (Shapin, 2008) that contemporary promissory domains of science often depend on leading figures who act as legitimate spokespeople on behalf of these domains, or even personify them. Some scientific entrepreneurs become figures of public attention and are skilled in self-presentation. In this case promises were introduced to a particular enthusiastic community based on prominent achievements in science, combined with strong technofuturist visions.

Episode 2 Nano as an increasingly popular label

The second episode takes place at the end of the 1980s and the beginning of the 1990s. Material science research intensified. In the early 1990s, the first major scientific conferences on nanotechnology were organized. Technology assessment institutions became interested in nanotechnology at this point. Drexler and some of his collaborators increased their efforts to furnish nano as an emerging technology field and to downplay its techno-futurist origins. In 1992, Al Gore, then still an opposition leader who had just returned from the climate summit in Rio de Janeiro, organized a parliamentary hearing "*New Technologies for a Sustainable World*" in the US Congress. Drexler was one of the few experts invited to present their views. On the other hand, more and more scientists and science journalists expressed their concerns regarding Drexlerian nano visions.

This episode is illustrative of instances when "nano" began to be used as a *label* by a number of US research and development agencies, in particular in military research. As a prominent example of attempts to construct promissory fields of science and technology, nanotechnology[7] has been used as an "umbrella term" (Rip and Voß, 2009) to hold together various actors, infrastructures, and agencies. Because of the observed multiplicity of disciplines and applications that have "nano" as a prefix, it is important to understand the functioning of the shorthand "nano" in these discourses of science and technology. The prefix "nano" has been applied to both science ("nanoscience/s") and technology ("nanotechnology", "nanotechnologies") to indicate research, fabrication, and use of compounds on the so-called nanoscale.[8] In practice, there is no general consensus about the range of "nanoscale" and disputes are held about what counts as nano (research, particles, methods, theory, etc.) and are settled in each particular case.

Labeling is equally part of writing research proposals and designing descriptions of consumer goods. Being aware of labeling as part of RRI agendas is crucial for certification, safety testing, and TA. The central implications of labeling, as well as categorizations and standards (Bowker and Leigh Star, 1999), are that labels invoke assumptions about what can and what cannot be included in the unit of assessment. It is also about drawing contours around relevant institutions, groups, individuals, and practices involved in deliberations on responsibility, for example, for achieving safety of particular substances or relevance of research fields.

Episode 3   The competing repertoires of nano

The third episode is about the development of nanotechnology's public image, starting in the mid-1990s: one article in *Nature* and another one in the popular journal *Scientific American* (Stix 1996; Jones 1995) attacked Drexlerian nanofuturism for being science fiction, which should be banned from the emerging acceptable mainstream nano discourse. Subsequently, these years were marked by a growing distance between nanofuturist activism and the political or academic discourse on nanotechnology. However, a peaceful co-existence still prevailed. As late as 1998, Mihail Roco held a conference at the US National Science Foundation (NSF) on nanotechnology in connection with the annual conference of Drexler's Foresight Institute. Drexler's institute was generally perceived as a well-respected forum for the emerging nano discourse. Among speakers at the Foresight Institute were the Nobel Prize winner Steve Chu, now Secretary of Energy in the Obama administration, and Richard Smalley, another Nobelist, who subsequently turned into the most vociferous critic of Drexler (Smalley 2001; 2003a; 2003b).

The third episode helps us to begin to understand nano in terms of *competing visions*, implying both earlier, far-reaching "visionary" scenarios advocated by Drexler, and "scientistic" claims advanced by the NSF. Nano is an example of co-existing *rationalities* in public discourse – economic, social, scientific, and legal – variously enacted in different

---

[7] While the term appears to have been first used by a Japanese academic in the 1970s (Taniguchi, 1974), its early rise to some popularity took place in some parts of the US in the 1980s due to nanofuturist discourse shaped by K. Eric Drexler and others.

[8] The National Science Foundation's National Nanotechnology Initiative (USA) informs the readers that the properties of matter undergo significant changes if explored on the nanoscale, where "particles are created with dimensions of about 1–100 nm." It is claimed that such particles can be "seen" only with powerful specialized microscopes. http://www.nano.gov/nanotech -101/special (accessed 6 March 2012).

national contexts. Such various ways of portraying nano can be described in terms of *repertoires* (Te Kulve, 2006), or *narratives* (Bennett and Sarewitz, 2006), which co-exist in media and public debates on nanotechnologies. Nano also begins to connote sets of material devices and practices rendered essential for self-representation of some scientific communities, such as the probe microscopes (Mody, 2004), and dedicated laboratory spaces such as "clean rooms".

Episode 4   The emergence of large-scale technoscientific initiatives and involvement of social sciences

In the fourth period, nanotechnology is politically established. Remarkably quickly, the field became a key area of global technoscience, accumulating considerable funding. Following the publication of Bill Joy's controversial, anti-nanofuturist and anti-transhumanist essay in *Wired* in 2000 (Joy, 2000), the official, political, and academic nano discourses exorcised Drexlerian nanofuturism. While some of his visionary ideas continued to flourish in the mainstream discourse, Drexler became a *persona non grata* in policy talk, due to a remarkable effort in boundary work.[9] The dynamics of maintaining and blurring boundaries between nanotechnology repertoires thus involved decisions on whether various renditions of nano were deemed acceptable or not. For instance, the NSF in the US interpreted molecular nanotechnology as science fiction and excluded it from its funding lists (Barben *et al.*, 2008). It also authorized funding for the two Centers for Nanotechnologies in Society (CNS-ASU and CNS-UCSB).[10] The frameworks for real-time technology assessment (RTTA) were introduced as a location for anticipatory governance and the wider dimensions of nano (Guston and Sarewitz 2002; Fisher and Rip, 2012; and Chapter 9).

Nano was introduced into the policy discourse and public deliberations under different guises. The metaphor of the Internet carrying the cachet of (fast) progress and technological advantage was used in the inaugural speech for nanotechnology in the US by President Clinton (2000). The Internet as a metaphorical construct itself had a metaphorical predecessor – the information superhighway – embodying the North American values of progress, mobility, and speed (Wyatt, 2004).

The National Nanotechnology Initiative (NNI) was established in the US and endorsed in this influential public address by President Clinton's Address to Caltech on Science and Technology (2000). It became a resourceful movement with a $500 M budget in 2001, increasing in the following years. The NNI came about through substantial preparatory work in the 1990s, including the assembling of statements of support from government, academia, and industry. The ELSI/SEI program within the NNI was authorized through the twenty-first century Nanotechnology Research and Development Act. It echoed the ELSI program of the Human Genome Project, as well as Human Dimensions of Climate Change of the US Global Change Research Program and the 1999 recommendations of the President's Information Technology Advisory Committee (co-chaired by Bill Joy) (Bennett and Sarewitz, 2006, p. 316).

This episode shows the importance of *metaphors* and *analogies* in the construction of scientific fields and economies, observed earlier by researchers in STS (Hilgartner, 2007;

---

[9] Boundary-work (Gieryn, 1998) is an important concept in science and technology studies characterizing the work going into the shaping of fields of technoscience as well as how boundaries are drawn between science and non-science (e.g., pseudoscience in this case).

[10] The CNS are based at the Arizona State University (ASU) and the University of California at Santa Barbara (UCSB) and have been active since 2005 and renewed for the next five years in 2010. See Section 13.3.2 for more discussion in relation to RRI.

Simakova, 2011; Wyatt, 2004). Globally, the nano discourse displayed reliance on visual metaphors. For example, the famous IBM logo, presented by scientists (Eigler and Schweizer, 1990) as a composition of individual atoms, became an iconic represen-tation of nano through its reproduction in prominent publications, signaling the powerful industrial promise of the field. Given the "invisibility" of the nanoscale and the (strategic) presentation of research activities as "basic research" that is translatable into societally-relevant technological products, it does not come as a surprise that in numerous mass media articles "nanoguitars", "nanocars", or nanoportrayals of celebrities were used to communicate the unfamiliar topic to non-specialized publics ("the general public"). Moreover, de Ridder-Vignone and Lynch's (2012) inquiry into visualization of what is known as quantum mechanics effects[11] shows an uneasy correspondence between visionary constructs (metaphors) and "reality" on the smaller scale. They discuss the importance of artistic conventions and image galleries, which exhibit the reliance on familiar macroscale images to "make the strange familiar" to the publics.

The metaphorical constructs featured in attempts at establishing public accountability of scientific and technological developments (namely in the discourses of market-led logics[12] of commercialization and of societally-relevant outcomes of emerging techno-sciences, whereby consumers are presented as the ultimate beneficiaries of nano research), as well as of "upstream" public engagement. Publics are called upon[13] to voice their views on the societal adoption of such technoscientific developments, stimulated by and as part of the increasing reliance of policy language on the ideas of public deliberations (Irwin, 2006).

The widespread ELSA/ELSI activities involved a considerable number of social sci-entists, philosophers, and humanists engaged in various forms of interaction with scien-tists and policy makers. This included educational programs in ethics, ELSA projects, observation in scientific labs and the creation of dedicated think tanks and public engagement exercises (e.g., Nanologue; Nano Dialogue; ObservatoryNANO, Deepen-ing Ethical Engagement and Participation in Emerging Nanotechnologies (DEEPEN), NanoBio-RAISE[14], and so on, in Europe; SEI,[15] Social and Economic Issues in Nano (SEIN) in the US); a series of global and international dialogues around nanotechnol-ogy also developed (see Fisher and Rip, 2012; and Chapter 9). In these initiatives, which combined participants from sciences, social sciences, humanities, policy, and citizens, the place for responsibility was an issue at stake and was open for deliber-ation. It was not only the responsibility of individual scientists and social scientists that was a matter of discussion, often calling for self-reflection. The role of visions of nanofutures themselves began to be questioned, along with the status of social science research (Macnaghten *et al.*, 2005). The responsibilities of social science (and STS in particular) researchers in regard to representations of and interventions in nano were

---

[11] Quantum effects are only one of the ways properties of matter on the nanoscale are defined. The theoretical frameworks for nano are disputed (at least) between physical, chemical, biological, and material sciences, as well as mechanical engineering.

[12] Various evaluations and predictions of the market size and potential for nanotechnologies have been routinely made by various players. Most notable of these is one made by Lux Research, describing itself as an independent research and advisory firm providing strategic advice and ongoing intelligence on emerging technologies (http://www.luxresearchinc.com/).

[13] In the UK, one prominent call for upstream public engagement (Wilsdon and Willis, 2004) emerged after the publication of the Royal Society/Royal Academy of Engineering (2004) report.

[14] Nanobiotechnology: Responsible action on issues in society and ethics.

[15] Social and ethical issues.

assessed against previous involvements in, for example, the Human Genome Project in the US.

This variety of initiatives around nano stemmed from a lack of agreement on the roles of relevant constituencies and the focus of attention of those social scientists involved. For example, SEI stressed social and ethical *implications* of nanotechnology, assuming that citizens would wait and see/deliberate upon the adoption of new technologies, with such implications being deferred to the future (Hanson, 2011). By contrast, SEIN emphasized social and economic *issues* in nano and directed the inquiry into the nanotechnology initiatives themselves. Attempts were made to draw upon historic lessons for sources of scepticism in public acceptance of the "nanohyperbole" (Toumey, 2004). However, concerns were raised about whether nanotechnology needed to become a special case for analyses, interventions, and governance. The dangers of analogous thinking in policy further entangling nano into the dominant narratives of risk and regulation (Williams, 2006; Winner, 2003) were articulated. Critics drew attention to a heavy reliance of "ELSI-fication" of nano in metaphors and analogies, as in the comparative move from genetically modified organisms (GMOs) to nano,[16] whereby social science is understood as a set of "tools" that "reproduce an 'essentialist' understanding of the technology–society relationship – suggesting a simple relationship between the values of artifacts developed and the social outcomes when they are used" (Williams, 2006, p. 328; see also Hanson, 2011).

Remarkably, nanotechnology became accepted and propagated rather smoothly as a politically and academically established field, continuing to be the focus of wide-ranging techno-futurist visions. Such visions were promoted also with regard to so-called "converging technologies." The NBIC (understood as "convergence" of nano, bio, info, and cogno) initiative was a research and technology policy initiative introduced by Mihail Roco and William Sims Bainbridge of the NSF in 2001 (Roco and Bainbridge, 2002) and which continued until the mid-2000s. The highly visionary NBIC initiative emphasized the "human enhancement" aspect by means of the NBIC fields (Coenen, 2010a) and soon sparked controversies concerning, for example, its transhumanist underpinnings due to Bainbridge's prominent involvement with the transhumanist movement. Far from realizing its goal to become a major official research and technology policy activity, it triggered other, less technofuturist, conceptualizations of converging technologies (for example, at an EU level). The initiative also contributed to establishing far-reaching visions of "human enhancement" in the evolving discourses of nanosciences and nanotechnologies and "new and emerging science and technology" (NEST). This particular visionary "charging" of nanotechnology and the NBIC fueled debates on new forms of enhancement. Subsequently, the interest of the "human enhancement" visionaries shifted from nanotechnology to other fields, such as neuroscience and neurotechnologies.

At an EU level, it is remarkable how closely early EU activities (around the year 2000) were interconnected with US activities (for an example which focused on applications and social aspects, see Roco and Tomellini, 2002). In Germany, nano had already been established as a topic for research policy in the 1990s, but public communication on it and funding activities under the label only started forcefully at the end of the decade and

---

[16] The Canadian case of ELSI-fication of major science programs including nano (Lopez and Lunau, 2012) also demonstrates that the legal reasoning showed a strong adherence to analogies and precedents.

were then rapidly expanded against the background of US and other activities. Public and policy discourse on nano was stimulated, amongst other things, by a technology assessment study conducted in the years 2001–2003 on behalf of the German national parliament (Paschen *et al.*, 2004) and by government activities. References to public concerns regarding GMOs were frequent, as was boundary work vis-à-vis Drexlerian nanofuturism. Nano was seen as a quick successor of GMO in the public and policy discourse, emphasizing risks associated with "revolutionary" developments in science and technology. The comparison was pivotal in discussions that nano should not repeat the same mistakes, and that responsible development should be emphasized.

In the UK, nano also became the focus of public debate through references to biotechnology and associated fears of GMOs (cf. Kearnes *et al.*, 2008). A pivotal document for policy and public discourse was the (2004) Royal Society/Royal Academy of Engineering (RS/RAE) study *Nanoscience and nanotechnologies: opportunities and uncertainties*, which introduced nano with caution, defining its potential relevance and outcomes. The report also performed boundary work, exorcising any Drexlerian visions of "grey goo"[17] (Annex D, p. 109). This was achieved by presenting the vision as part of media coverage of nanotechnologies devoid of scientific foundations, and with reference to the Drexler/Smalley debate. Before that, the narrative of "grey goo" was important in the UK as part of media discourse of "self-replicating" autonomous entities going uncontrolled in society. Such rendition of nano played to heuristics regarding GM and unnatural "messing around" with nature that might cause cross-contamination and other undesirable consequences.

The nano discourse in its later stages also featured prominent industrial involvement – an important element of the rhetoric of societal relevance of emerging fields of science and technology in the United States. Rhetorically, societal relevance can be understood as one of the "patterns of moral argumentation" in the discourses of emerging technologies (Swierstra and Rip, 2007). The NNI sustained claims to novelty and societal impact of nano through the intertwinement of discourses of scientific and economic rationality, as well as technofuturist visions. Some prominent claims, for example, advanced the economic potential of nano based on the idea of miniaturization, as in President Clinton's address to the nation in 2000: "Just imagine, materials with 10 times the strength of steel and only a fraction of the weight; shrinking all the information at the Library of Congress into a device the size of a sugar cube; detecting cancerous tumors that are only a few cells in size" (President Clinton's Address to Caltech on Science and Technology, 2000).

In that period, the societal role of nano as a compelling (Nordmann and Schwarz, 2010) source of benefits to society was established. In the foundational U.S. documents (e.g., Roco and Bainbridge, 2001), making nano ultimately accountable to society is rendered equivalent to engaging multiple agencies who could take nano innovation out from universities and make it work for the public good: "Participation of multiple agencies is necessary because of the large spectrum of relevance of nanotechnology to society" (Roco, 2007a). The founders of the nano initiative explicitly acknowledged the work of amassing agencies (industries, governmental offices and research labs) – whose interest statements may match the promise of nano – as a strategy for developing the nano initiatives in a consolidated way. In preparing to present to Congress, a group of

---

[17] A doomsday scenario introduced by Drexler (1987).

founders of the nano initiative initiated extensive interactions with academe, industry and governments to develop long term visions; more than 150 experts participated in discussions (Roco, 2007a; Siegel, 1998).

The policy discourse portrayed industry as the vehicle for promoting nano innovations via tripartite collaboration with academe and government. Scenarios of nano in economic development depicted a high degree of integration of nanotechnology research with government and industry, contributing to economic well-being (Canton, 2001). Acknowledging the importance of Congressional support for the NNI, Mihail Roco admitted in an interview: "It's a personal satisfaction to envision the immense impact that nanotechnology will have in the economy and society. Because of its far reaching implications, I see this legislation as having high societal return on public investment" (Roco, 2007b). Indeed, the language of responsible innovation and its cognates began to take off along with large-scale national nanotechnology R&D programs at this time (see Fisher and Rip, 2012; and Chapter 9). The US NNI adopted a strategic goal of "responsible development", and, as noted above, funded the two Centers for Nanotechnologies in Society in line with the twenty-first century Nanotechnology Research and Development Act. The Act was signed into law in 2003, and mandated "integrating research on societal, ethical and environmental concerns with nanotechnology research and development" to ensure that nanoscale science and engineering advances "bring about improvements in quality of life for all Americans."[18] Journals and conferences started to use the label in their titles, and later a set of dedicated academic journals were established, in some of which both natural and social scientists publish (e.g., *Nanoethics; Nature Nanotechnology; Nanotechnology Law and Business*).

Episode 5 Nano futures and the governance turn

The development of nanotechnology's public image since the early 2000s has been marked by further political and academic establishment of the field, accompanied by the rise of TA, public dialogue and ELSA activities. Drexlerian and other techno-futurist visions have not been completely marginalized, but techno-futurism is mostly the preserve of visionaries' propositions which tend to focus on other fields of research and development, such as neurotechnologies or human enhancement. Civil society organizations such as the ETC Group[19] have entered the discourse, with significant impact on the mass media portrayals of nano and converging technologies.

The fifth, ongoing, episode involves a number of initiatives to gain a better understanding of the sense in which the collision of repertoires, or visions, has implications for the construction of notions of accountable, or governable, science. RRI is one of these initiatives. The ongoing conversations are about creating and understanding responses to visions, expectations, and agendas put forward by various players. The importance of such a focus is due to the competing influences of certain visions on the directions sociotechnical change would take. Visions appealing to scientific and economic rationalities

---

[18] From CNS-ASU homepage http://cns.asu.edu/. Last visited 22 July 2012.

[19] Action group on erosion, technology and concentration. See: http://www.etcgroup.org. For their influence on discourses of nanotechnology, see, for example, Coenen (2010b).

inform more recent policy documents co-authored by Mihail Roco, Roco *et al.* (2011). Societal relevance and the commercialization potential of nano (Thurs, 2007a,b) are commonly introduced through the discourses of economic rationality, which in turn differ in terms of what kind of version of "nano" they draw upon.[20] However, these visions co-exist and are in conflict with powerful visionary discourses supported by other players, as in the case of "green" nanotechnology doomsday and ecological scenarios that are seen as being mutually incompatible. They put contrasting emphasis on the benefits (e.g., the use of nanotechnologies for alternative energy production, increasing efficiency of nanomanufacturing, or for reducing pollution) and asserted or alleged dangers of nano (Schwarz, 2008). As in Shew's (2008) analysis, the "nanotech schism" between the nano mainstream and Drexlerian nanofuturism makes it problematic to create a "simple, linear story of nanotechnology" that could form a basis for ongoing deliberations. In her view, this history was "a constructed story to urge a certain vision for the field and its future" urging us to "allow the history, at least at this very early point, to admit the messiness" (Shew, 2008, p. 397).

In the domain of sciences, nano is currently characterized by claims to multi- and inter-disciplinarity. Defined in a pivotal document on responsible governance of nano (Roco *et al.*, 2011, p. 441) in terms of it being a "multidisciplinary field", nano is used as a sign of membership in particular communities, especially where claims for novelty and cutting edge science are involved: for example, scientific projects from various domains funded under the "nano" category[21]; a range of products that adopted nano as part of their label; regulatory attempts to specifically address issues around nano and establish new approaches for "education, innovation, learning, and government" (Roco *et al.*, 2011). Areas such as synthetic biology and human enhancement technologies, IT, along with others, can be presented as being variously intertwined with nano, in particular when the metaphor of convergence is applied (Roco, 2009). Such flexibility also implies opportunities for strategic uses of the nano prefix (Simakova, 2012). However, some scientists would not subscribe to the nano initiatives and would not aim to obtain funding under the nano label.[22] It has also been observed that scientists may downplay the importance of visionary statements in their everyday talk, while strategically and selectively, employing nano in presentation of their research. The "cultural response" in science to policy measures and calls for ethical assessments of scientific work is often underpinned by perception of policy being informed by inadequate expectations (e.g., fears) of nano having little to do with "normal" science (Simakova, 2012).

As part of a "governance turn" in the previous and current decades, heralding the grand narratives of democracy and responsibility of nanoscience, various assessments

---

[20] Conferences like the annual meetings of the Society for the Studies of Nanoscience and Emerging Technologies (S.NET), first held in 2009, promote an understanding of nano as a flexible label, and the need for understanding the emergence of nano-related initiatives better.

[21] Various derivatives from nano have emerged, for example, NanoTechnoScience (Nordmann, 2004, p. 52); also nanobiomedicine, nanomedicine, neuroscientific nanotechnology, nanoconvergence (as analyzed in Schummer, 2010). The distinctions between "nanotechnology" singular and "nanotechnologies" plural are liberally made in science, policy, and public discourse, and sometimes used interchangeably.

[22] Critique of nano as a "pseudoscientific" pursuit could be heard and dealt with by the proponents, for example, in the US as part of an empirical study concerning the societal relevance of nano (Simakova, 2012). In TA practice, research analysts involved in everyday exchange with scientists observe, and have to deal with, renditions of nano as a label, or even an easy way, to get funding for almost any kind of research.

of governance schemes emphasizing the societal context of technological developments have been undertaken (Kurath, 2009; Kaiser *et al.*, 2010). Similarly, when considering responsibility, institutional and policy programs supporting emerging technoscientific initiatives cannot be seen as existing independently from the assessment by and of others. Assessments are also important parts of accounting for such programs. For example (as in Roco, 2009), the NNI has been evaluated by a number of other agencies and institutes of policy advisors in the US, including the President's Council of Advisors on Science and Technology (PCAST), National Academy of Sciences, United States National Research Council, Office of Science and Technology Policy, Office of Management and Budget at the White House, Congress representatives, U.S. Government Accountability Office, as well as through NSF site visits to the scientific labs and research centers funded under the program. However, a conundrum exists for regulators and researchers alike, in that nano functions as a seemingly rich and all-embracing, but also "empty" signifier (Wullweber, 2008). Nano is seemingly capable of accommodating a variety of meanings bearing on its proliferation into public, academic, and policy discourses and practices. Even a quick overview yields a number of focal aspects of responsible innovation imported into the nano talk: environmental safety, intellectual property (IP) rights, legislation, standards, export controls, chemical and biological weapons controls, medical applications (nanoassemblers as pathogens), food labeling, health concerns (nanoparticles as asbestos), and criminal responsibility (mental states induced through advances in neuroscience).

While looking for a place for responsibility for RRI in the web of accountabilities,[23] we need to *find ways to get to grip with the roles of metaphorical constructs and vision politics*. This also demands taking into account the shifting nature of boundaries between various repertoires and communities in research policy and the boundary-work involved. Such understanding can be based on attention to how the flexible nano label functions and the politics and distribution of accountability within the scientific enterprise itself, as part of a social contract of science. For instance, if the idea is to develop a code of responsible conduct for nanosciences and nanotechnologies,[24] agreement or disagreement on whether particular areas of research (e.g., medicine) should be defined as a category under the nano label (nanomedicine) will influence which organizations, groups, and individuals will be nominated as relevant "nanoobjects", research, stakeholders, and civil society organizations.[25] Accordingly, sets of expectations, for example, in terms of patients' safety and a pool of curable diseases by means of developing medical applications will be defined.

Doubleday (2007), discussing laboratory-based collaboration between social science and nanoscience, usefully suggests, drawing on Jasanoff (2005), that "public

---

[23] Woolgar and Coopmans (2006) talk about "interlocking" accountabilities scientists are immersed in, which makes the effects (development and uptake) of technologies uncertain.

[24] For example, the European Commission's effort to design a code of conduct for responsible nanosciences and nanotechnologies research http://www.nanocode.eu/.

[25] By way of example, in a multidisciplinary research nanotoxicology workshop discussing industrial potential and benefits of nanoparticles, deliberations might occur over the category of nanoparticle itself: their sizes acceptable for the workshop disciplinary composition; their anthropogenic or natural provenance; the meaning of the boundary itself; appropriate research methods; specificity of such research in terms of "nano" toxicology rather than tackling more general problems in toxicology.

controversies and shifting government policies for science can be understood as part of a widespread renegotiation of the 'social contract'[26] between science, the state, the economy and citizens" (p.168). Contributing to the constitution and tensions between Mode 1 and Mode 2 science[27] (Gibbons *et al.*, 1994), impact agendas, and the emerging discourse of RRI (Von Schomberg, 2012; and Chapter 3), such deliberations will have implications for the assignment of individual and collective responsibility in socio-material configurations of modern technoscience. Such an approach allows room for understanding RRI in terms of *responsiveness* (Owen *et al.*, Chapter 2), and in particular responses produced to particular claims and visions concerning emerging sciences and technologies, as in the following sections.

13.3   Narratives of Responsibility

We are interested in offering for discussion particular cases where the indeterminacy and flexibility of nano is resolved for particular purposes at hand. Such resolutions bear on how responsibility is made "do-able" (McCarthy and Kelty, 2010). Our goal is to demonstrate how *making sense of nano itself is part of doing responsible innovation.*[28] In order to assess the potential for practical intervention in creating spaces for responsibility, two narratives below zoom into two particular episodes: first, processes of "futurization" and subsequent "defuturization" of nanotechnology in Germany and in the US, as analyzed and enacted in technology assessment activities and second, practices of knowledge and technology transfer between university and industry in the US.

13.3.1   Narrative 1: Nanofutures, Boundary Work and Technology Assessment Activities in the US and Germany

As shown above, discourses of nanotechnology have been permeated with societal and governance issues, and far-reaching visions of the future from very early on. These visions portrayed nanotechnology as revolutionary and potentially disruptive, demanding responsible and wise governance. Both futurist enactors, including Drexler, and policy actors made recommendations concerning the governance of nanotechnology, emphasizing its relevance for core societal issues such as sustainability. During the second half of the 1990s, and before the intensive boundary work that can be understood as "purification" (or separation of plausible scientific claims from what could be deemed quasi-utopian speculation), quasi-utopian Drexlerian visions tied to societal issues were firmly embedded in policy discourse on nanotechnology. The boundary work in policy in the 2000s marginalized nanofuturism as opposed to mainstream discourse

---

[26] As in Guston and Keniston (1994), negotiations around a social contract of science may involve "the possibility of conflict – or at least disparity of interest" (p. 5) as well as inquiries into what becomes identified, and accepted, and disputed as scientific misconduct, for example, fraud or patenting behavior.

[27] Mode 1 science is defined by separation from its social context; Mode 2, as that in which the boundaries between science, society, and industry blur.

[28] This echoes the General Principles of the European Commission Recommendation of 07/02/2008 on a code of conduct for responsible nanosciences and nanotechnologies (N&N) research "N&N research activities should be comprehensible to the public" (European Commission, 2009).

on nanotechnology,[29] but residues of quasi-utopianism in regulation policy documents remained. This led to a configuration of notions of responsibility and to the formation of discourses of a regime of technoscience under uncertainty.

13.3.1.1   How Were References to Societal Relevance and Responsibility Used for the Political Instrumentalization and "Taming" of Nanofuturism, in Particular Within Technology Assessment?

TA activities on nanofutures in the United States appear to have started with a public–private research project which ran in 1988 and 1989. It was mainly conducted by graduate students who reviewed literature, interviewed experts, and also analyzed the uses of the notion of nanotechnology. The final project report included a discussion of societal and ethical issues. The research group was heavily influenced by Drexler's visions, mentioning, for example, indefinite extension of human life as one likely impact of nanotechnology. Another likely impact that was mentioned – also as an ethical issue – was nano-based development of mood-altering drugs. When it comes to computers and material science, the authors referred to less extreme visions, however, and they also discussed public acceptance and risk perception, and gave policy recommendations. The report (Hadden, 1989) is in some aspects quite similar to the far more sober TA reports that followed in the 1990s and after 2000. In the report, however, the relationship between technology and society was inverted: it was argued that it would not be possible to regulate the manifold impacts of nanotechnology on society. Instead, it is societal changes that should be anticipated to plan for their advent. The authors recommended the creation of a new kind of advisory committee, whose role would be overseeing scientific and technological developments, publicizing them, and identifying possible problems.

The private–public project yielded many conclusions practicable for TA, but these still relied on visionary propositions. In the early 1990s, with more and more policy actors and scientists using the term nanotechnology, Drexler prioritized near-term technical options. A study on miniaturization was conducted by the Congressional Office of Technology Assessment (OTA) in 1991 in which Drexler and at least one of his followers acted as external experts. The study concluded that nanotechnology was still irrelevant from a policy perspective, and Drexler's visions were regarded as widely despised among scientists. Interviewed by Ed Regis later in the 1990s, Drexler said that he then pleaded with everyone in the nanofuturist community to "please keep the level of cultishness and bullshit down, and even to be rather restrained in talking about wild consequences which are in fact true and technically defensible – because they don't sound that way" (Regis, 1995: 210). Drexler also believed that the study above "gave a misleading, excessively futuristic cast of his overall theory" (Regis, 1995: 208).

Drexler argued similarly when invited by Al Gore to the parliamentary hearing on sustainable technologies in 1992 (U.S. Congress, Senate, 1993). He started his presentation (quite immodestly) with the remark that nanotechnology was a topic that he believed

---

[29] To give but one example: in a brief history of the rise of nano(bio)technology (Kulkarni 2007), Drexler is only mentioned once, in a passage which characterizes some nano visions in the 2000s as being "reminiscent of initial talk about nanotechnology (especially from Eric Drexler)." In this mainstream view, "talk" about nano is juxtaposed with real, material progress in nanoscience and nanotechnologies and highly visionary discourse thereby appears to be a phenomenon marginal to the rise of the field.

would one day become a dominant concern in Congress. Afterwards, however, he linked nanotechnology to the goals and trends that had been discussed in other presentations on decarbonization, dematerialization, and the development of environmentally critical technology. Mentioning his latest academic credentials in the United States and in Japan, he argued that "molecule-by-molecule control" can become the basis of manufacturing technology that is cleaner and more efficient than anything we knew at that moment. The list of nanotechnology future applications he chose was exactly tailored to the purpose of the hearing, including new molecular instruments for science and medicine, extremely compact and energy-efficient computers, materials for lighter, stronger, more efficient vehicles and manufacturing of inexpensive solar cells that are mechanically tough enough to be used as roofing and paving materials. He emphasized international competition and proposed an OTA study exclusively on nanotechnology. In conclusion, Drexler acknowledged controversies about his ideas, but expressed his belief "that molecular nanotechnology can become a basis for sustainable development, raising the material standard of living worldwide, while decreasing resource consumption and environmental impact" (page 22). His written testimony emphasized that nanotechnology would raise numerous policy issues, but years of consideration would be necessary before policies can be formulated. He only mentioned arms control as one issue that would surely arise from progress in nanotechnology. All "wilder" visions are not mentioned in this text. It ends with a warning: "Economic competitiveness and the health of the global environment may depend on timely action" (page 27).

TA activities in other countries included similar efforts to the boundary work seen in the United States since the second half of the 1990s. In Germany, for example, strategic activities within the German Ministry of Research and Education in the 1990s already had some kind of a TA component. TA institutions first started to discuss nanotechnology in the second half of the 1990s when the exorcism of Drexler and the expulsion of his ideas from mainstream discourse on nanotechnology had just started.

The situation changed when the Office of Technology Assessment at the German Parliament (TAB) began a comprehensive project on nanotechnology in the year 2001. The NNI was established in the United States, and discussions about nanotechnology and Drexlerian nanofuturism started in influential German print media. In the TAB project on behalf of the parliament, the researchers thus had to find a way of dealing with the Drexlerian visions, in the midst of frantic boundary work within the nano research and nano policy communities. At the same time the TAB researchers and other academics in Germany took notice of the new concept of "converging technologies" (in the NBIC fields; see above). While claiming a nearly all-encompassing character for converging technologies and their ethical and societal implications, the US enactors of converging technologies emphasized the "human enhancement" aspect by means of biotechnology (for example, genetic engineering), information and communication technology (including visions of "strong" artificial intelligence), and neurotechnology (for example, new brain/computer interfaces). Nanotechnology was seen by the key proponents in the debate as a fundamental enabler for most of these fields of science and technology. The TAB decided that the report for the parliament would include a chapter dedicated to the Drexlerian and other far-reaching nano visions, in addition to a chapter on ethical and societal issues, which to some extent also took into account the future implications of these visions. It was also decided that in all the other chapters, which dealt with the scientific and technological state of the art or with major potential applications areas, Drexlerian visions should play no role at all.[30]

By "isolating" nanofuturism in a separate chapter, TAB performed boundary work in the design of the report, but also gave plenty of room to the far-reaching visions. It became obvious that the content of the visions, and the ways they were used by various players in the governance of nanotechnology deserved further analysis which would have to include social science, economic, policy, philosophical, various humanist, and other expertise. In other words, the rise of nanotechnology signaled broader changes in the regime of technoscience, or even the emergence of a "new regime" as it has been called in the second half of the 2000s (Kaiser *et al.*, 2010). The TAB researchers not only argued that the hype around nanotechnology could be detrimental to the field's further development, but also criticized the hype as being "irrational" and "unworthy" of science, and as irresponsible with regard to public discourse on nano. Staying sceptical toward imminent revolutionary breakthroughs implied being sensitive to incidents of mere re-labeling of existing fields of research and development. The report argued that the enthusiasm which optimistic visions can evoke was deliberately used in the US as a means of promoting technology development, but that such a strategy of "hope and hype" is always precarious. First, there is the danger that expectations will be set too high, making disappointment of "believers" inevitable. Second, it may popularize the reverse of the optimistic futurism – a pessimistic futurism involving apocalyptic fears and visions of horror.

All German political parties in parliament highly appreciated the TAB report and subsequently used the study extensively in parliamentary initiatives and other political activities. As regards rhetoric of future prospects, all parties tended to be more enthusiastic about nano than the TAB study was, but they – as well as other political institutions – often also warned against nanofuturism in the same vein as TAB had done.

Although nanofuturism, as well as closely related futuristic sets of ideas, remains relevant to a certain extent – in particular in public communication activities – there has clearly taken place a defuturization of nano in Germany, which accompanied its political stabilization in the 2000s (Lösch, 2010; Grunwald, 2012). It appears that far-reaching visions of the future were mainly useful to draw attention to the field in a time when it represented little more than a vague umbrella term waiting to be filled with meanings. Nano was first used to restructure funding policies and existing research, and, in the course of this, a complex interplay of various efforts in boundary work led to a process in which most of these visions were excluded again from "nano", often in the name of a responsible development of nano and a responsible way of publicly communicating the emerging field.

13.3.2 Narrative 2: Responsibility as Knowledge and Technology Transfer in the United States

This narrative will look at the interpretations of technological promise of nano as achieved through industrial innovation, exploring how expectations of nano that rely on the discourse of economic rationality can be confronted with descriptions of everyday university life. As we highlighted above, this kind of expectation was pronounced strongly in the foundational statements about nano. Earlier attempts to create responsible

---

[30] See Episode 4 for a reference to the UK RS/RAE 2004 report that performed similar boundary work.

innovation centers pursued the translation of science to economic and social impact as the key responsibility of institutions of science and innovation (Guston, 2007). However, empirical studies of knowledge and technology transfer highlight the need to reconsider assumptions informing current policy expectations about how nano could yield industrially- and societally-relevant applications.

Such studies pose further questions concerning the construction of places for responsibility:

13.3.2.1   In What Sense Do University–Industry Relations, Such As Licencing, and Knowledge and Technology Transfer Hinge on Analogies?

To what extent is it possible to achieve a picture of distribution of responsibilities for knowledge and technology transfer around nano?

The NNI documents largely portray collaboration between university and industry in terms of the *linear model of innovation*: nano is presented as rapidly developing, commercializable research. University–industry collaborations are often spoken about as a key means to take promising research through "the valley of death" toward creation of technological products. It is said, for example, that by 2020 nanostructures of an increased complexity would find their way into the industrial prototyping and nanotechnology commercialization (Roco, 2009). A normative push to promote multi-stakeholder activities around nano encourages the obtaining of funding from federal and state mechanisms for collaborative research. Industrial projects are also a topic of interest and practical engagement for participants in universities attending panel discussions: in nano grantee meetings, industrial engagement forums, and scientific events. Collaborations are also an element of concern in university settings, addressed through university policies and technology transfer mechanisms. Collaborations feature in organizational reporting as, for example, mentions in web sites and annual reports, being also a focus of attention for social scientists trying to capture practices of industrial collaborations.

While policy expectations of industrial collaborations may be high, industrial collaborations, in practice, involve deliberations not only about the technical content of research projects, but also about values of collaboration (Simakova, 2011). Nano collaborations are spoken about differently in different situations and in ways that are recognized as appropriate or inappropriate. Not every piece of industrial funding is judged as acceptable, as universities assess prospects for intellectual property rights. Values of collaboration are articulated for certain audiences: some scientists would not put collaborative work on their CVs as it might be seen as compromising their reputation as academic researchers. For example, stating the negative value of collaboration is recognized as not being an acceptable social behavior. Reporting about collaborative work can be considered a mere formality that needs to strike a balance with assessors of such reports in the funding bodies.

Recent research (Simakova, 2011; 2012) shows that the use of analogies and attempts to achieve specificity of nano is part and parcel of these practices and resolutions of governance disputes in universities. *What counts as nano?* is a practical question in the everyday practices of scientists and university administration, which is often transformed into the question *who is in nano?* The practices of knowledge and technology transfer between universities and industries embody situations when the potential of nano is made sense of as part of governance processes. Formation of new research centers involves categorization of parts of university research under the nano rubric; nano rubrics are introduced in public patent databases to attract companies for licensing; positions for social science researchers looking at the social, legal, ethical, or economic issues are organized around nano.

In universities, comparative appeals to such areas as bio, material science, or engineering, are a part of defining or framing, nano. Such appeals entail deliberations about governance mechanisms pertaining to these areas as being appropriate and acceptable in conjunction with the category of nano. For example, comparing nano with bio in technology transfer would mean a possibility of drawing on a previously designed series of agreements and bureaucratic procedures around the transfer of pharmaceutical substances to and from the university campus. Drawing analogy with material sciences on a university campus known for its excellence in this discipline would portray nano as having a solid research predecessor. A reference to high-temperature superconductivity would, on the contrary, indicate a negative scenario, whereby research activities would be perceived as not delivering their promise and funding would be cut. Equally, avoiding nano as a label for particular scientific projects or technological outcomes of such projects can be part of the strategy to attract industrial sponsors deterred by the nano label due to its negative association with the safety concerns.

Many universities employ special divisions – offices of sponsored research (OSR) and technology transfer offices (TTO) – which deal with research contracts and intellectual property rights. In the university–industry interactions nano becomes accommodated into the existing governance mechanisms. In spite of the declared revolutionary potential of nano, research projects having "nano" in their titles would not necessarily receive priority treatment in terms of negotiating terms with industrial collaborators. Scientists and technology transfer officers act the web of organizational rituals and routines entailing a distribution of responsibility. The responsibility of an officer of technology transfer to achieve a workable agreement with a corporate sponsor may be curtailed by a decision not to disclose the background IP[31] of a particular collaborator. Postdocs might not sign a non-disclosure agreement (NDA) individually, but would be admitted to a collaborative research project under the auspices of a collective agreement signed by a Principal Investigator (PI). Individual scientists might be excluded from discussion of licensing terms of a particular research project. The organizational knowledge is distributed between different departments beyond TTO and OSR, and at times involves invocation of senior authority to resolve controversial situations, especially those where the public image of universities as non-profit organizations may be affected. Dealing with TTOs and OSRs may also be problematic for individual scientists. While policy often adheres to the so-called "organic" collaboration talk that promotes seamless connection between university and industry, the individual accounts often convey stories of struggle to obtain industrial funding and IPR mediated by university offices.

A significant feature of university–industry interactions that bears on the distribution of responsibility for achieving industrial collaborations is *non-disclosure*. Such secretive framings of research practice also pose questions concerning construction of knowledge about collaborative engagements for governance purposes, and equally for social science research. This practice, dictated mainly by corporate competitiveness and individual

---

[31] Intellectual property (including patents and invention disclosures).

researchers' privacy needs, seems in direct conflict with conceptualizations of responsible innovation in this volume as one that opens up, reflects, deliberates, and responds (Chapter 2). The non-disclosure arrangements intentionally keep intellectual property as "private – do not enter" until the point that patenting occurs. TTOs and SROs routinely sign NDAs with staff and faculty. The content of some scientific research projects would not be disclosed for research purposes unless it is considered a success. In fear of competition in fast moving fields, such as the semiconductor industry (another shorthand associated with nano), some industrial sponsors insist on signing NDAs *about* existing NDAs so as to conceal the interactive occasion when an initial agreement was signed to initiate a discussion.

In conclusion, this narrative has shown that nano is neither a uniform, nor homogeneous category when it comes down to everyday details of knowledge and technology transfer. The section also briefly introduces a complex and contestable web of responsibilities and accountabilities in which the amenability of the new entity (nano) to university governance mechanisms (licensing; tech transfer; industrial and government relations) is deliberated upon. Contrary to the linear model of innovation it can be argued that industrial applications of university research is a distributed process involving non-disclosure. Also, it would be naive to believe that it could be straightforwardly captured. The practices of accounting for and counting industrial collaborations are highly political, whereby such issues as funding, individual faculty privacy, as well as university public image are at stake. Identifying sites where responsibility is negotiated and attributed, as well as intervention strategies, would entail an immense reconfiguration of existing arrangements that are ingrained in the condition of non-disclosure. This would also entail rethinking assumptions, such as seamless connections in university–industry interactions, informing policy agendas and deliberations.

13.4 Narratives, Visions and Conflicts: Lessons for RRI?

In this chapter we have explored an approach to the analysis of responsibility, drawing on a perspective which is interested in expectations, scenarios, and visions concerning the future. Namely, we have shown that *what is often presented as the responsible construction of technological futures depends on competing visionary discourses and attempts to confront those.* We have also discussed two cases illustrating what we can call an "empirical response" to the grand visions of the nano initiatives. We have highlighted three key motives informing our analysis:

First, we considered nano as a label, and introduced the notions of repertoires. It follows that a focus on "nanotechnology" governance and regulation assuming that nano is a single, and straightforwardly definable, object of regulation is misleading: it ignores the abundance of metaphors, comparisons, and analogies that figure in attempts to appropriate nano into existing regulatory mechanisms as well as in the design of funding strategies. We need to stay alert to the *flexible ways in which categories and labels are applied* to configure scientific fields, policy assumptions and mobilization of governance and public engagement mechanisms. If we understand the "social contract" of science as an ongoing achievement, notions of responsible innovation require reflexive examination of assumptions and expectations attached to emerging technoscientific initiatives, including the repercussions of "visionary" communication on the perception of science and technology in certain publics.[32]

Second, we drew attention to politics *within the scientific enterprise that bear on the distribution of responsibilities* and that are often obscured by the understandings of innovation as a linear process. Knowledge and technology transfer is yet another example where ignorance is part of knowledge production (McGoey, 2012) and is cultivated as an institutional arrangement creating protected conversational spaces. *Doing responsibility in such settings is a distributed process involving politics of expertise as well as corporate secrecy.* It then turns out that when considering the responsibility of individual scientists, the everyday socio-material arrangements and accountabilities in which individual researchers operate, such as in the practices of knowledge and technology transfer, need to be taken into account and better understood in collaboration with scientists themselves.

Third, we put emphasis on the *role of "enactors"*, or key figures and organizations leading major technoscientific initiatives, in creating and offering for interpretation discourses that set certain expectations of these initiatives. Importantly, the "science for society" dimension of RRI (Owen, Macnaghten, and Stilgoe, 2012), appeals to societal relevance of new initiatives as a central strategy. Historically, be it through economic rationality, or technofuturism in search of followers, discourses have ignored the variety of players involved in the production of societal outcomes and the relations between players. Apparently, such impoverished visions of technological change, as opposed to evidence from empirical research on science and policy in practice, have been an incredibly instrumental approach in enacting and gaining support for large-scale technoscientific initiatives. In this "model", responsibility seems to be framed as paving the way for innovation into society, minimizing harm and maximizing benefit, with no opportunity for reflection or deliberation on the purposes or motivations of the science and innovation itself (see Chapter 2 for further discussion).

This is a significant issue that other chapters in this book discuss and attempt to resolve. We are conscious that drawing parallels (if not analogies) between the ways technoscientific initiatives emerge entails *responsibility for offering alternatives*, which we see as the primary task for RRI. If responsibility is seen as a process of responsiveness (e.g., to societal deliberation), (Chapter 2) it is in danger of being constantly pushed back by an instrumental model of linear science policy, which in turn is largely informed by a neoliberal model of modern Western society. Equally, if the linear model proves conducive for visions and hype, has it got limited place for RRI as we are coming to define it? Does this mean that the RRI needs to fundamentally reconfigure this model? In the US, UK, and EU the purpose of ELSI programs around nano has often been to allow nano innovation to thrive and be acceptable, with no deliberation on whether it is *desirable*, that is, the motivations and purposes (Mali *et al.*, 2012). This also bears on the

---

[32] The interplay of expectations and the entanglement of enactors' and commentators' roles in media reporting, selectively drawing on certain repertoires of nano, obviously has consequences for the distribution and interpretations of fear and hope. In recent publications in *Nature* covering the nanotechnology-lab bombings in Mexico (Philips, 2012; Corral, 2011) civil society criticism of such groups as ETC Group appears to be unfairly linked to eco-primitivist terrorism. Mexican researchers are, for example, quoted to have criticized ETC Group for using a Drexlerian doomsday scenario in public communication on nano, a communication which might create irrational fears. It is not mentioned, however, that ETC Group referred to this scenario only rarely, and mainly in the first half of the 2000s (a period of time when it still featured quite prominently also in many other, and even in official publications on nano). The *Nature* reporting also does not take into account the role of nano and NBIC enthusiasts in popularizing highly speculative visions of the future, which clearly had a potential to create strong concerns in parts of the public (as could already be seen in the debate on the above-mentioned essay by Bill Joy).

constitution of roles of social scientists and humanists that can become instrumentalized for such purposes. In turn, the impact agendas also become dependent on the winning instrumentalist versions and expectations, rarely if ever permitting the co-production of responses as a possible part of impact. One central aspect of the chapter was to question the role of leading figures in the production of credible, or publicly acceptable, renditions of technoscientific initiatives featuring responsibility and societal relevance, as well as responses to such renditions. Our emphasis on leading figures is not to aggrandize the role of visionaries and power relations that visions enact, but precisely to give examples of how responses to such visions have been produced as a way to explore alternative assumptions for governance. Our encounters with various instances and episodes where renditions of nano became contested have led us to conclude that if "responsible visions", or visions responsibly produced, are to be created and implemented in future, this is best done as part of the continuing, deliberative negotiation of the "social contract" of science.

Acknowledgments

We would like to thank Robert Doubleday and Richard Owen for their contribution to the shaping of the earlier drafts of the chapter. The chapter also benefited from the authors' earlier research and conference participation that was partly supported by the Center for Nanoscale Systems in Information Technologies, Cornell University, a NanoScience and Engineering Center of the National Science Foundation under Award # EEC-0117770, 0646547, jointly with the Department of Science & Technology Studies (S&TS) also at Cornell; Center for Nanotechnology in Society at the University of California at Santa Barbara (CNS-UCSB); the European Science Foundation; University of Exeter Business School seedcorn grant. The work on the article was supported by the European Commission FP7 Science in Society funded project EPOCH (Ethics in Public Policy Making: The Case of Human Enhancement; 2010–2012), grant number SIS-CT-2010-266660 (http://epochproject.com), and it profited from research conducted by both of us within the framework of the FP6 project CONTECS (Converging Technologies and their Impact on the Social Sciences and Humanities (http://www.contecs.fraunhofer.de/)) in the years 2006–2008.

References

Appelbaum, R. and Parker, R. (2008) China's bid to become a global nanotech leader: advancing nanotechnology through state-led programs and international collaborations, *Science and Public Policy*, **35** (5): 319-334 .

Barben, D., Fisher, E., Selin. C., and Guston, D. (2008) Anticipatory governance in nanotechnology, (eds. Hackett, E., Amsterdamska, O., Lynch, M.E., et al.). in *The Handbook of Science and Technology Studies*, 3rd edn Cambridge, MA, London: The MIT Press. 979–1000.

Bennett, I. and Sarewitz, D. (2006) Too little, too late? Research policies on the societal implications of nanotechnology in the United States, *Science as Culture*, **15**(4): 309–325.

Boenink M, Swierstra T, and Stemerding D (2010) Anticipating the interaction between technology and morality: a scenario study of experimenting with humans in bionanotechnology. *Studies Ethics Law and Technology* **4**(2), doi: 10.2202/1941-6008.1098.

Borup, M., Brown, N., Konrad, K. and Van Lente, H. (2006) The sociology of expectations in science and technology, *Technology Analysis and Strategic Management*, **18**, 3/4, 285–298.

Bowker, G. and, Leigh Star, S. (1999) *Sorting Things Out: Classification and Its Consequences*, MIT Press.

Brown, N. and Michael, M. (2003) A sociology of expectations: retrospecting prospects and prospecting retrospects, *Technology Analysis and Strategic Management*, **15**: 3–18.

Canton, J. (2001) The strategic impact of nanotechnology on the future of business and economics. Societal Implications of Nanoscience and Nanotechnology: Final Report from the Workshop held at the National Science Foundation, September 28–29, 2000, pp. 91–97.

Coenen, C. (2010a) Deliberating visions: the case of human enhancement in the discourse on nanotechnology and convergence. (eds. Kaiser, M.; Kurath, M.; Maasen, S.; Rehmann-Sutter, C.), in *Governing Future Technologies. Nanotechnology and the Rise of an Assessment Regime*, Sociology of the Sciences Yearbook 27, Dordrecht, Heidelberg, London, New York: Springer, pp. 73–87.

Coenen, C. (2010b) ETC group, (ed. Guston, D.) in *Encyclopedia of Nanoscience and Society*, Sage Publications, p. 218.

Corral, G.H. (2011) Stand up against the anti-technology terrorists, **476**, 373. doi: 10.1038/476373a

Doubleday, R. (2007) The laboratory revisited: academic science and the responsible governance of nanotechnology, *NanoEthics*, **1**(2): 167–176.

de Ridder-Vignone, K.D. and Lynch, M. (2012) "Images and Imaginations: An Exploration of Nanotechnology Image Galleries." *Leonardo* **45**(5): 447–454. http://muse.jhu.edu/ (accessed January 17, 2013).

Drexler, K.E. (1987) *Engines of Creation*. Doubleday.

Eigler, D.M. and Schweizer E.K. (1990) Positioning single atoms with a scanning tunnelling microscope, *Nature* **344**, 524–526.

European Commission, Recommendation on a Code of Conduct for Responsible Nanosciences and Nanotechnologies Research and Council Conclusions on Responsible Nanosciences and Nanotechnologies Research (2009) http://ec.europa.eu/research/science-society/document_library/pdf_06/nanocode-apr09_en.pdf (accessed 30 August 2012).

Gibbons, M., Nowotny, H., Limoges, C., Schwartzman, S., Scott, P., Trow, M. (1994) *The New Production of Knowledge. The Dynamics of Science and Research in Contemporary Society*, London: Sage Publications.

Gieryn, Th. (1998) *Social Boundaries of Science*, The University of Chicago Press.

Grunwald, A. 2005. Nanotechnology: a new field of ethical inquiry? *Science and Engineering Ethics* **11** (2): 187–201.

Grunwald, A. (2009) Technology assessment – concepts and methods (ed. A., Meijers): *Philosophy of Technology and Engineering Sciences* in Handbook of the Philosophy of Science, Vol. **9**. Amsterdam, Boston, MA, Heidelberg, London, New York, Elsevier, 1103–1146.

Grunwald A. (2010): From speculative nanoethics to explorative philosophy of nanotechnology, *NanoEthics* **4**:91–101.

Grunwald, A. (2011) Responsible innovation: bringing together technology assessment, applied ethics, and STS research, *Enterprise and Work Innovation Studies* **7**: 9–31.

Grunwald, A. (2012) Responsible nanobiotechnology: philosophy and ethics. Singapur: Pan Stanford Publ.

Guston, D. (2007) Toward centres for responsible innovation in the commercialized university. *Public Science in Liberal Democracy: The Challenge to Science and Democracy*, (eds. P.W.B. Phillips and J. Porter), 295–312. Toronto: University of Toronto Press.

Guston, D. and Keniston, K. (eds.) (1994) *The Fragile Contract: University Science and the Federal Government*, MIT Press.

Guston, D. and Sarewitz, D. (2002) Real-time technology assessment, *Technology in Society* **24** (2002) 93–109.

Hadden, S. (ed.) (1989) Assessing Molecular and Aqtomic Scale Technologies (MAST) (Special project report), Lyndon B. Johnson School of Public Affairs, the University of Texas at Austin, in association with Futuretrends.

Hanson, V. (2011) Envisioning ethical nanotechnology: the rhetorical role of visions in postponing societal and ethical implications Research, *Science as Culture*, **20**(1): 1–36.

Hilgartner, S. (2007) Making the bioeconomy measurable: politics of an emerging anticipatory machinery, *BioSocieties* **2** (3): 382–386.

Irwin, A. (2006) The politics of talk: coming to terms with the 'new' scientific governance, *Social Studies of Science*; **36**; 299–320.

Jasanoff, S. (2005) *Designs on Nature: Science and Democracy in Europe and the United States*. Princeton University Press, Princeton, NJ.

Jasanoff S., and Kim S.-H. (2009) Containing the atom: sociotechnical imaginaries and nuclear power in the United States and South Korea, *Minerva* **47**: 119–146.

Jones, D (1995) Technical boundless optimism, *Nature*, **374**, 6525, 835–837.

Joy, B. (2000) Why the Future Doesn't Need Us. Wired (Apr. 2000) http://www.wired.com/wired/archive/8.04/joy_pr.html (accessed 30 August 2012).

Kaiser, M., Kurath, M., Maasen, S., Rehmann-Sutter, Chr. Hrsg. (2010) *Governing Future Technologies. Nanotechnology and the Rise of an Assessment Regime*, Sociology of the Sciences Yearbook 27, Dordrecht, Heidelberg, London, New York: Springer.

Kearnes, M. and Macnaghten, P. (2006) Introduction: (Re) imagining nanotechnology, *Science as Culture*, **15**(4), 279 – 290.

Kearnes, M., Grove-White, R., Macnaghten, P., Wilsdon, J., and Brian Wynne (2008) From bio to nano: learning lessons from the UK agricultural biotechnology controversy, *Science as Culture* **15**(4): 291–307.

Kulkarni, RP (2007), Case study: Nano-Bio-Genesis: tracing the rise of nanotechnology and nanobiotechnology as 'big science', *Journal of Biomedical Discovery and Collaboration* 2:3. doi: 10.1186/1747-5333-2-3

Kurath, M. (2009) Nanotechnology governance: accountability and democracy in new modes of regulation and deliberation, *Science, Technology and Innovation Studies*, **5** (2), 87–110.

Lopez, J. J. and Lunau, J. (2012) ELSIfication in Canada: legal modes of reasoning, *Science as Culture*, **21**(1), 77–99.

Lösch, A. (2010) Visual Dynamics: The Defuturization of the Popular 'Nano-Discourse' as an Effect of Increasing Economization (eds. Kaiser, M.; Kurath, M.; Maasen, S.; Rehmann-Sutter, C.), Governing Future Technologies: Nanotechnology and the Rise of an Assessment Regime, Sociology of the Sciences Yearbook 27. Dordrecht, Heidelberg, London, New York, Springer: 89–108.

Macnaghten, P., Kearnes, M. B. and Wynne, B. (2005) Nanotechnology, governance, and public deliberation: what role for the social sciences? *Science Communication*, **27**: 268–91.

Mali, F., Pustovrh, T., Groboljsek, B. and Coenen, C. (2012) National ethics advisory bodies in the emerging landscape of responsible research and innovation, *Nanoethics*, **6, 3**: 167–184.

McCarthy, E. and Kelty, C. (2010) Responsibility and nanotechnology, *Social Studies of Science*, **40**: 405–432.

McGoey, L. (2012) Strategic unknowns: towards a sociology of ignorance, *Economy and Society*, **41**(1): 1–16.

Mody, C. (2004) How probe microscopists became nanotechnologists, in D. Baird, A. Nordmann and J. Schummer (eds.), *Discovering the Nanoscale*, Amsterdam: IOS Press: 119–133.

Nordmann, A. (2004) Molecular disjunctions: staking claims at the nanoscale, (eds Baird, D., Nordmann, A. and Schummer, J.) in *Discovering the Nanoscale*, IOS Press, Amsterdam: 51–62.

Nordmann, A. (2007) If and then: a critique of speculative nanoethics, *NanoEthics* 1:31–46.

Nordmann, A., and Rip, A. (2009) Mind the gap revisited. *Nature Nanotechnology* 4:273–274.

Nordmann A, and Schwarz A (2010) Lure of the 'Yes': the seductive power of technoscience. (eds Kaiser M, Kurath M, Maasen S, Rehmann-Sutter C) in *Governing Future Technologies: Nanotechnology and the Rise of an Assessment Regime*. Springer, Dordrecht, pp 255–277.

Nowotny, H. (2007) How many policy rooms are there?: Evidence-based and other kinds of science policies. *Science Technology Human Values*, **32**, 479–490.

Owen R., Macnaghten P., Stilgoe J. (2012) Responsible research and innovation: from science in society to science for society, with society. *Science and Public Policy*, **39**(6), 751–760, doi: 10.1093/scipol/scs093).

Paschen, H., Coenen, C., Fleischer, T., Grünwald, R., Oertel, D. and Revermann, C. (2004), *Nanotechnologie: Forschung und Anwendungen*, Berlin: Springer.

Philips, L. (2012) Nanotechnology: armed resistance, *Nature* **576** (488): 30.

Pinch, T. and Bijker, W. (1987) The social construction of facts and artifacts: or how the sociology of science and the sociology of technology might benefit each other, (eds Bijker, W., Hughes, T. and Pinch, T.): in *The Social Construction of Technological Systems: New Directions in the Sociology and History of Technology*: 17–50, MIT Press.

President Clinton's Address to Caltech on Science and Technology (2000) The White House Office of the Press Secretary, Los Angeles, California for Immediate Release January 21, 2000.

Regis, E. (1995) *Nano: The Emerging Science of Nanotechnology: Remaking the World Molecule by Molecule*. New York: Little, Brown and Company.

Rip, A. (2006) Folk theories of nanotechnologists, *Science as Culture*, **15**(4): 349–365.

Rip, A. and Voß, J.-P. (2009) Umbrella terms in the governance of emerging science and technology. Presented at the Spring Session 2009 'The Governance of Future Technologies' of the Working Group 'Politics, Science and Technology'.

Roco, M. (2007a) National nanotechnology initiative – past, present, future, in *Handbook on Nanoscience, Engineering and Technology*, 2nd edn, Taylor & Francis: 3.1-3.26.

Roco, M. (2007b) A One-to-One with Mike Roco. Courtesy: The National Nanotechnology Initiative, Purdue University, http://www.purdue.edu/discoverypark/dls/NNI /Mihailroco.html (accessed 1 September 2012).

Roco, M. (2009) Nanotechnology at NSF, presentation at the 2009 NSF Nanoscale Science and Engineering Grantees Conference, December 7–9, 2009, http://www .nseresearch.org/2009/presentations/Day1_Roco.pdf (accessed 21 July 2012).

Roco, M. and Bainbridge W.S. (eds.) (2001) Societal Implications of Nanoscience and Nanotechnology, National Science Foundation, Available online http://www.wtec.org /loyola/nano/NSET.Societal.Implications/nanosi.pdf (accessed 21 July 2012).

Roco, M. C., Bainbridge, W. S. (eds.) (2002) Converging Technologies for Improving Human Performance, National Science Foundation, Arlington, VA, http://www.wtec .org/ConvergingTechnologies/Report/NBIC_report.pdf (accessed 21 August 2012).

Roco, M. C., Tomellini, R. (eds.) (2002): *Nanotechnology – Revolutionary Opportunities and Social Implications. 3rd Joint EC-NSF Workshop on Nanotechnology*, Office for Official Publications of the European Communities, Luxembourg, http://ftp.cordis .europa.eu/pub/nanotechnology/docs/nano_lecce_proceedings_05062002.pdf (accessed September 3 2012).

Roco, M.C., Harthorn, B., Guston, D., and Shapira, P. (2011) Innovative and responsible governance of nanotechnology for societal development, (eds Roco, M.C., Mirkin, C.A., Hersam, M.C.) *Nanotechnology Research Directions for Social Needs in 2020*. 1st edn. Springer. pp. 561–617.

Royal Society/Royal Academy of Engineering (2004) Nanoscience and nanotechnologies: opportunities and uncertainties.

Schummer, J. (2010) From nano-convergence to NBIC-convergence: 'The best way to predict the future is to create it'. (eds. Kaiser, M., Kurath, M., Maasen, S., and Rehmann-Sutter, C.) in *Governing Future Technologies: Nanotechnology and the Rise of an Assessment Regime*, Sociology of the Sciences Yearbook 27, Dordrecht, Heidelberg, London, New York: Springer pp. 57–71.

Schwarz, A. (2008) Green nanotechnology – new challenge or business as usual? Paper presented at Conference NanoECO, Centro Stefano Franscini, Monte Verità.

Selin, C. (2007) Expectations and the emergence of nanotechnology, *Science, Technology and Human Values* **32** (2): 196–220.

Shapin, S. (2008) *The Scientific Life: A Moral History of a Late Modern Vocation*, Chicago: University of Chicago Press.

Shew, A. (2008), Nanotech's history: an interesting, interdisciplinary, ideological split, *Bulletin of Science Technology Society*; **28**; 390–399.

Siegel, R.W. (1998) Chapter 1: Introduction and overview, in (eds Siegel, R.W., E. Hu, and M.C. Roco) Nanostructure Science and Technology: A Worldwide Study. WTEC

Panel Report on Nanostructure Science and Technology: R&D Status and Trends in Nanoparticles, Nanostructured Materials, and Nanodevices. Prepared under the guidance of the IWGN, NSTC, WTEC, Loyola College in Maryland, http://clinton4.nara .gov/WH/EOP/OSTP/NSTC/html/iwgn/IWGN.Research.Directions/toc.html (accessed 13 November 2011).

Simakova, E. (2011) Collaboration talk: the folk theories of nano research, *Science as Culture*, **21** (2): 177–203.

Simakova, E. (2012), Making nano matter: an inquiry into the discourses of governable science, *Science, Technology and Human Values*, **37**(6): 604–626.

Smalley, R. (2001) Of chemistry, love and nanobots, *Scientific American*, **285**, 76–77.

Smalley, R. (2003a) Smalley responds. *Chemical and Engineering News*, **81**, 39–40.

Smalley, R. (2003b) Smalley concludes. *Chemical and Engineering News*, **81**, 41–42.

Stix, G. (1996): Trends in nanotechnology: waiting for breakthroughs. *Scientific American* **270**: 94–99.

Swierstra, T. and A. Rip. 2007. Nano-ethics as NEST-ethics: patterns of moral argumentation about new and emerging science and technology, *NanoEthics* 1:3–20.

Taniguchi, N. (1974) On the basic concept of Nano-technology. Proceedings of the International Conference on Production Engineering. Tokyo, Part II, Japan Society of Precision Engineering.

Te Kulve, H. (2006) Evolving repertoires: Nanotechnology in daily newspapers in the Netherlands. *Science as Culture*, **15**(4), 367–382.

Thurs, D. (2007a) No longer academic: models of commercialization and the construction of a nanotech industry, *Science as Culture*, **16**:2, 169–186.

Thurs, D. (2007b) Tiny tech, transcendent tech: nanotechnology, science fiction, and the limits of modern science talk, *Science Communication* **29**: 65–95.

Toumey, C. (2004) Nano hyperbole and lessons from earlier technologies, *Nanotechnology Law and Society*, **1**(4).

U.S. Congress, Senate (1993) *New Technologies for a Sustainable World: Hearing before the Subcommittee on Science, Technology, and Space of the Committee on Commerce, Science, and Transportation, United States Senate, One Hundred Second Congress, Second Session, June 26, 1992*. Washington, DC: U.S. Government Printing Office.

Von Schomberg, R. (2012) Prospects for technology assessment in a framework of responsible research and innovation, (eds Dusseldorp, M. and Beecroft, R.) *Technikfolgen abschätzen lehren: Bildungspotenziale transdisziplinärer Methoden*, Springer VS.

Webster, A. (2007a) Crossing boundaries: Social science in the policy room. *Science, Technology and Human Values*, **32**, 458–478.

Webster, A. (2007b) Reflections on reflexive engagement: Response to Nowotny and Wynne. *Science, Technology and Human Values*, **32**, 608–615.

Williams, R. (2006) Compressed foresight and narrative bias: Pitfalls in assessing high technology futures. *Science as Culture*, **15**, 327–348.

Wilsdon J. and Willis, R. (2004) See-through Science. Why Public Engagement Needs to Move Upstream, DEMOS,.

Winner, L. (2003) Testimony to the Committee on Science of the U.S. House of Representatives on the Societal Implications of Nanotechnology House Committee on Science Hearings, Wednesday, 9 April 2003.

Woolgar, S. and Coopmans, C. (2006) Virtual witnessing in a virtual age: a prospectus for social studies of E-science in *New Infrastructures for Knowledge Production: Understanding E-Science*, Chapter 1 (ed. C. Hine, 1–25. Hershey: Idea Group Inc.

Wullweber, J. (2008) Nanotechnology – an empty signifier à venir? A delineation of a techno-socio-economical innovation strategy, *Science Technology and Innovation Studies* **4** (1), 27–45.

Wyatt, S. (2004) Danger! Metaphors at work in economics, geophysiology and the internet, *Science, Technology and Human Values* **29**(2), 242–261.

Wynne, B. (2007) Dazzled by the mirage of influence?: STS-SSK in multivalent registers of relevance. *Science Technology Human Values*, **32**, 491–503.

Endnotes

Building Capacity for Responsible Innovation

Jonny Hankins
The Bassetti Foundation, via Michele Batozzi, 4, 20122 Milan, Italy

Sometimes when people ask me about my job I tell them that I am a professional blogger. This often draws a response of shock (in certain circles), and is immediately followed by the question "Oh, what do you blog about?"

"I blog about responsibility in innovation" I reply, "with a particular interest in politics, because after all to innovate is a political act."

When I talk about politics I do not necessarily mean democracy and representation, I am referring more to a notion of power, or more precisely the power to decide and implement a course of action. Innovation is political, not only in that it requires decision, a plan of action, and the means to implement and market it, but also because, to a greater or lesser extent, it has the power to change people's lives. Innovation makes and writes history. As Piero Bassetti argues: "if you want to control history you must control innovation. Innovation is politics,"[1] in the sense that while innovation is not exclusively a determiner of the future, prior access to decisions about innovation gives an advantage to the political actor. If we accept the above we would hope for a responsible use of such a powerful tool, but the question arises of how to ascribe and promote responsible behavior, and who we might expect to implement responsible thinking.

Innovation is a multi-player process and a collective endeavor, and we could blandly say that all of the players must take responsibility for their own actions, but this is a superficial statement. Does the technician who adds the water during the initial stages of research hold the same responsibility as the businessperson who invests millions in marketing a new product? Is the geologist who discovers gas in shale liable for criticism in the same way as the multinational companies practicing fracking techniques, and possibly polluting water supplies in Louisiana? I suggest not.

---

[1] Piero Bassetti is Chairman of the Bassetti Foundation for Responsible Innovation, Milan, Italy.

Responsible Innovation, First Edition. Edited by Richard Owen, John Bessant and Maggy Heintz.
© 2013 John Wiley & Sons, Ltd. Published 2013 by John Wiley & Sons, Ltd.

Hans Jonas (1984) argued that ethics is responsibility-taking for future consequences of present actions. In his opinion, modern technology influences future conditions in ways that are difficult to predict, therefore purely technological-instrumental rationality is potentially destructive. He introduced a "principle" of responsibility that refers to the future instead of the past, arguing that we must operate according to a precautionary approach if we want to avoid irreversible mistakes (see Muniesa and Lenglet (Chapter 10) and Von Schomberg (Chapter 3) for more on precaution, and Grinbaum and Groves (Chapter 7) and Owen *et al.* (Chapter 2) for the need for a future orientation in responsibility). This, however, does not seem the way of the world today, where to a great extent market success or failure are used as markers of ethical purity, innovation touted as the savior of the global economy and "anyway if we don't do it here they will do it in China".[2]

As Grinbaum and Groves note in Chapter 7, the problem seems to lie in the simple fact that innovators cannot predict or control how their developments will be used, as novel applications may well be discovered. Legislation and restriction do not seem to be viable approaches. We may be able to stipulate that, for example, software can only be used for the advancement of humankind, or that innovations must only be used for their intended purposes, but these are subjective requests and can we really guarantee any of these wishes? I personally do not believe that we can, so we must try to instill responsible behavior into what Beck calls "a system of organized irresponsibility"[3] in the hope of lessening the risk of what Muniesa and Lenglet describe in Chapter 10 as "aggregate consequences."

Having said this, if we want to instill responsibility into a process with a lot of actors, we may well conclude that decision-makers hold the key. They play the pivotal role in directing the process and should be the most reflexive and conscious of their role within the larger society. They come in many shapes and sizes throughout the process though, and we want to address these playmakers at each crucial developmental point, in order to socialize them into thinking and behaving responsibly.

All of this leads to the next question, who are the decision makers and how do we gain access to them? A few come to mind, such as regulators, entrepreneurs, scientists, funding bodies, educators, and politicians (in that they make decisions on behalf of the public). The question is how can we act to socialize or incentivize them into behaving responsibly? How should we find a suitable communication channel to reach out to them?

Decision-makers are not the only important players in this process. We also need to forge a new cultural framework of responsible innovation, so that it becomes common sense to question the innovation process, its objectives and outcomes, so that it is the general public who demand a responsible approach. The strategy that I will outline below and followed by the Bassetti Foundation aims at what Cristina Grasseni describes as "instilling a sensitivity for this argument in policy and opinion makers as well as the general public, independently of disciplines, creeds, or methods."[4]

---

[2] Quote from 23andMe CEO Anne Wojcicki www.fondazionebassetti.org/en/focus/2012/05/architectures_for_life_with_23.html.
[3] http://ajw.asahi.com/article/0311disaster/opinion/AJ201107063167 interview with Ulrich Beck.
[4] Cristina Grasseni was Scientific Director of the Bassetti Foundation from 2006 to 2011.

Building Capacity for Responsible Innovation:
Awareness and Engagement

Any process of responsible innovation that advocates reflection and deliberation (Sykes and Nacnaghten, Chapter 5) needs to be reflexive and deliberative itself. The Bassetti Foundation in Milan first addressed the issue of how to define and promote responsible innovation with a seminal workshop in Alz on 30 January, 1999.[5] Since then the main body of thought of the Foundation has revolved around its web site, which hosts a full 14 years of reflections, workshops, interviews, reviews, news, events, and online publications on the subject.[6] Almost a decade and a half of research and policy work has contributed the idea that innovation does not simply mean novelty, but rather "something previously improbable, now made real."[7] Furthermore, innovation forges new links between knowledge and power that bring into existence previously unknown objects, relations, or situations. Innovation thus does not coincide with invention (which is often science and capital intensive), but with the ability to transform lifestyles. In particular, *Poiesis*-intensive innovation refers to the cultural aspects of work practices, such as beauty and taste, logistics and design. In other words, innovation is not an individual creative act, but a social process that permeates politics and institutions and, in turn, depends on them. A praxis approach to responsible innovation is favored by the Bassetti Foundation in the belief that *responsibility must lie within the innovation process.* Responsibility lies in the day-to-day operating practices of all actors involved, as much as in the reflexive deliberation of decision-makers.

The Foundation is particularly interested in publics and how they can participate in decision-making through innovative forms of collective deliberation (see also Sykes and Macnaghten, Chapter 5). They sponsored the first Italian survey on public participation in the governance of the environmental hazards of techno/scientific innovation[8] and successfully promoted the inclusion of a participatory clause in the Lombard Regional Statute regarding policy-making in similar matters, such as the introduction of GM crops.[9]

Nevertheless, capacity building that involves wider audiences includes the engagement of "quick-and-dirty" means of communication such as blogging. I personally contribute to the Bassetti web site, but have a broader project to create discussion and promote the idea of responsible innovation, and this is why I choose to blog. There are many blogs dedicated to Responsible Innovation and related topics, Jack Stilgoe's Responsible Innovation[10] and Richard Jones' Soft Machines[11] to name just two. Another approach however that aims at sensitizing a wider public is to write on broader interest blogs.

---

[5] www.fondazionebassetti.org/it/pagine/2009/02/workshop_sulla_fondazione_gian.html.

[6] See for instance the interviews with Bruno Latour, Sophie Houdart, Thomas Murray, Peter Galison, Vincent Lepinay, and so on www.fondazionebassetti.org/en/events/.

[7] The Foundation uses the line "Realization of the improbable" to define innovation.

[8] www.fondazionebassetti.org/en/pages/2008/07/public_participation_and_the_g.html.

[9] www.fondazionebassetti.org/it/focus/2007/07/la_responsabilita_politica_del.html.

[10] http://jackstilgoe.wordpress.com/.

[11] www.softmachines.org/wordpress/.

A series of articles on a technology blog or an innovation blog brings the argument to a new and wider audience in a way that a dedicated blog might not. The obvious question is whether critical thinking can be nurtured using these means and to how great an extent?

My job entails doing just this, and I see positive returns for my current project. Posting regularly on a single technology blog[12] has meant that in some way I have been able to influence the entire content of the blog, and continuity of style and issue has generated a follower base. On average, an article is read by more than 3000 individuals in the first three months of publication, and that number is constantly growing, as is the geographic distribution of comments received. All of this brings people into contact with the concept of Responsible Innovation and its related sites and publications, and seems to target at least a section of our "market" with precision. Triangulation is the key to expanding readership and I would argue that this mode must extend to all forms of communication if they are to be at their most efficient.

Blogging can play some part in promoting debate around this issue, but there are obviously many other avenues to follow in terms of communication, particularly with a view to sensitizing decision-makers. If we are to take Richard Owen's evolving definition of responsibility as "a commitment of care for the future through collective stewardship of science and innovation in the present"[13], one imperative must be to involve the public in decision-making processes (see Chapter 5 for a critique of dialogue and debate on science technology and innovation). This obviously requires an opening up on the part of both the public (the aim described above) and those working toward innovation, as well as achieving a shared understanding between all parties involved. This requires a public that is willing and able to converse about science, innovation and ethics, and push politicians and regulators into action. For this they need to have the cultural baggage necessary for an informed debate, which given much of the subject matter involved and the effect of political interference in the reporting process may be no easy objective. Different "constitutional moments" in governing science and technology have already been reviewed (Jasanoff, 2011) as oscillating between public participation in the definition of societal values, and the professionalization of ethical deliberation. Would more openness in the process mean that greater public accountability might lead to greater responsibility?

On this argument Mario Biagioli[14] believes that the patent system currently works against any opening up of research processes today. The involvement of profit-based organizations in research (including universities) means that the process has become more secretive than ever (see Chapter 13 for further discussion). If the argument holds that responsibility might come through openness, we are definitely going in the wrong direction.

Less Stick and More Carrot: Building Capacity through Education

If we agree with the Union of Concerned Scientists that education is the key to responsible thinking then we must think about how to further disseminate the argument into schools and universities. Business schools, engineering faculties, the natural sciences,

---

[12] www.technologybloggers.org.

[13] www.youtube.com/watch?v=n-LPuvF187w&feature=player_embedded.

[14] www.fondazionebassetti.org/en/focus/2012/02/intellectual_property_and_resp.html.

computing are all skills that enter into the innovation process. Students attending "innovation" courses may be offered a course in "responsible innovation," but in some ways this reiterates the same dilemma: is it possible to pre-package "courses in ethics and responsibility" in blanket fashion? Is it a skill in professional deliberation that we wish to instill, or a greater awareness of the histories, cultures, and normative frameworks that have led and regularly lead to the ethical conundrums of an "irresponsible" innovation? The content of such educational courses must be carefully considered in this regard.

One of the biggest problems faced by an organization such as the Bassetti Foundation is deciding upon and following a fixed strategy. The very elusive nature of innovation means that its "responsibilization" is an equally elusive task. I would agree that the four dimensions of responsible innovation as outlined by Owen *et al.* in Chapter 2 are valid goals and should be embedded in the innovation process. Education and communication remain key factors. Much ground has been covered since the initial framework of "public understanding" of science (Chapter 5) and I believe that the Bassetti Foundation's insistent murmur on the necessity of coupling "responsibility" and "innovation" in frontier research and policy-making has contributed to establishing "responsible innovation" as a key word in current debates and developments.[15]

Many institutions have more recently latched on to the idea of responsible innovation. Universities such as Exeter and Ecoles des Mines (Chapter 10) have dedicated initiatives, and there are many centers in the US with interests spanning the issues around Responsible Innovation (such as the Hastings Center and the Arizona State University Center for Nanotechnology in Society, etc). The Netherlands is coming to the fore in governmental investment with its ambitious Responsible Innovation project and conference.

Hopefully, the many organizations presently working in this field will achieve a higher impact by networking and sharing their different skills, contacts, and frameworks. Two heads are always better than one, and after all, reversing 23andMe CEO Anne Wojcicki's defensive argument, if we want them to do it in China, we'd better start here.

Acknowledgments

I would like to thank Cristina Grasseni and Francesco Samore' for their input and David Guston and Richard Owen for their comments upon previous drafts.

References

Jasanoff, S. (2011), Constitutional moments in governing science and technology *Science and Engineering Ethics* **17** (4), 621–638.

H. Jonas (1984) *The Imperative of Responsibility: In Search of an Ethics for the Technological Age*, University of Chicago Press, Chicago.

---

[15] As well as a distinguished lecture series in Milan, FGB has sponsored students as well as academic workshops and conference panels, such as the 2006 Cerisy Colloque *L'anthropologie historique de la raison scientifique* led by Bruno Latour and Philippe Descola; the 2008 workshop *The Challenges of Innovation: Insights from STS, the Social Sciences, and Bioethics* at The Hastings Center for Bioethics, the 2010 EASST (European Association for the Study of Science and Technology) conference held in Trent (where Cristina Grasseni and Giuseppe Pellegrini co-convened the panel *Practicing responsibilities*), the 2012 Conference of the European Association of Social Anthropologists, with a panel on *Who is Responsible?* The FGB publications are available both as printed books and as open access digital pamphlets.

Name Index

Arendt, Hannah, 121,125, 132
Auden, W.H., 135

Bainbridge, William, 248
Bassetti, Piero, 269
Beck, Ulrich, 270
Bentham, Jeremy, 122
Biagioli, Mario, 272
Bradley,F.H., 120

Callon, Michel, 32, 101
Collingridge, David, 33, 35, 79, 145,
   149
Carson, Rachel, 31, 86
Chesborough, Henry, 10
Chilvers, Jason, 95, 100

Drexler, Eric, 244, 253
Doubleday, Robert, 99

Goodin, Robert E, 127
Grasseni, Cristina, 270
Gregory, Jane, 95
Grove-White, Robin, 91

Hacking, Ian, 124
Hart, H.L.A., 120–121

Leonard, Dorothy, 5
Lowe, Judah, 137

Jaspers, Karl, 133
Jonas, Hans, 31, 36, 127, 129, 270

Jones, Richard, 41, 71, 98, 271
Joy, Bill, 246, 260

Kearnes, Matthew, 98

Merton, Robert C., 187
Musil, Robert, 130, 140

Nordmann, Alfred, 124, 133

Pielke, Roger, 96, 99

Richardson, Henry, 122
Roco, Mihail, 167,169, 245, 248,
   250–251
Rothwell, Roy, 10

Santor, Eric, 55
Shakespeare, William, 114, 135
Shelley, Mary, 137–8, 190
Stirling, Andy, 95, 103
Sunstein, Cass, 79

Thorpe, Charles, 95
Tillich, Paul, 140

Von Hippel, Eric, 14–15
Von Schomberg, Rene, 37

Warner, Michael, 99
Weber, Max, 122, 127
Wynne, Brian, 95, 99

Responsible Innovation, First Edition. Edited by Richard Owen, John Bessant and Maggy Heintz.
© 2013 John Wiley & Sons, Ltd. Published 2013 by John Wiley & Sons, Ltd.

Subject Index

Accountability – see responsibility
Altzheimer's Society, 36
Anticipation, 29, 38, 65, 76, 109
    cultural narratives of, 137
    prediction and, 111
Aravind Eye Clinic, 15

Beacons for Public Engagement, 94
Body scanners, 62
Bottom of the Pyramid, 11, 15
    Grameen Shakti, 19
Boundary work, 246, 249, 253

Care, 29, 35, 37,132
    duty of, 32, 132, 154
Choice architecture, 79
Codes of conduct, 28, 30, 40, 67, 131,
    147, 151, 166, 168
Collaborative assurance, 40, 179
Contractarianism, 127
Contractual liability structures, 153
Corporate social responsibility, 186, 191
Corrigibility, 35, 145
Cumulative incrementalism, 179

Danish Board of Technology, 87
Deliberation (see also Dialogue), 29, 35,
    38, 41, 71, 85, 146, 211, 219, 232
Democracy, 35, 44, 64, 95,191
Design, 70, 177
    safety by, 110, 131
    values-sensitive or based, 37, 75
Development risk defense, 126, 153
Dilemma of control, 33, 62, 79, 145

Enactors, 176, 244, 260
Environmental Liability Directive, 152
Ethical review, 212
Ethics, 61, 64, 70, 75, 103, 136
    ICT, 203, 205
    Speculative, 114
ETICA (Ethical Issues of Emerging ICT
    Applications), 199
European Committee for
    Standardization, 69
Experiment Earth Public Dialogues on
    Geoengineering, 223
Externalities, 150, 187

Finance, 185
Financial instruments, 191
Foresight, 38, 51, 63, 65, 122, 204
    limits of, 126, 131, 210
FRRIICT (Framework for Responsible
    Research and Innovation in ICT),
    199, 208

Geoengineering, 42, 149, 155, 219
    Integrated Assessment of
        Geoengineering Proposals project
        (IAGP), 224
GM (genetically modified) foods and
    crops, 60, 90, 232, 235, 271
GM nation debate, 92
Governance
    adaptive, 143
    anticipatory, 29, 38, 65, 110, 171
    codes of conduct – see codes of
        conduct

Responsible Innovation, First Edition. Edited by Richard Owen, John Bessant and Maggy Heintz.
© 2013 John Wiley & Sons, Ltd. Published 2013 by John Wiley & Sons, Ltd.

Governance (*continued*)
  de facto, 169, 179, 258
  deliberation, dialogue and, 99, 101, 104
  geoengineering and, 230
  ICT and, 212
  of intent, 28, 34
  labeling, 157
  by the market, 27, 53, 58, 150
  regulation – see Regulation
  soft intervention and, 173
  standards and certification, 69

House of Lords report on science and society, 89
Hype, 241

Information and Communications Technologies (ICT), 69–70, 78, 199
  emerging, examples of, 204
Informed consent, 208
Innovation
  as a process, 3
  contemporary trends in, 9
  definition of, 80, 202
  dilemma of control, 33, 62, 79, 145
  disruptive, 9
  dual use, 116, 143
  dynamic capability and, 4, 18
  emergent properties of, 21
  finance, examples of, 186
  governance, see Governance
  incremental and radical, 4, 17
  International Risk Governance Council, 146
  irresponsible, 30, 37, 60
  Lock-in, 33, 35
  modulation of (see also responsiveness), 39, 41, 70, 174
  open, 10
    Connect + Develop, 10
    crowd sourcing, 12, 105
    employee involvement in, 16
    recombinant, 13
  opening up, 16–17, 35

pace of, 159, 185
path dependence, 33, 35
product, process, position, paradigm, 4
promises of, 177, 222
purposes and motivations of, 28, 34, 41, 71, 102, 105, 147, 260
right impacts of, 28, 37, 44, 54, 56, 131
social contract and, 30
stage gating, 42, 149
strategic management of, 4
strategy, 4
suggestion schemes and, 16
uncertainty and, 28, 32–3, 36, 143, 153, 242
user-led, 11, 14
visions, 204, 241
Insurance, 153
Intellectual Property, 14, 201

Kaizen, 16, 18
Knowledge
  assessment, 70
  flow, 10, 159
  limits to, 80, 128, 153, 231
  regulation and, 155
  responsibility and, 32–3, 80, 123
  spaghetti, 9, 30
  technology transfer and, 256
  uncertainty and, 123, 153

Liability – see responsibility
Lock – in (technological), 33, 35
Luddites, 85
Lund Declaration, 58, 64

Meeting of Minds project, 90
Midstream modulation, 41, 70, 174
Monsanto, 45, 60, 91, 235
Moral
  division of labour, 178
  hazard, 229
  luck, 28, 34, 122, 138
  overload, 77
  rules, 188

Nano Risk Framework, 173
Nanotechnology, 41, 71, 89–90, 97–8,
    112, 145, 154, 166, 175, 241
Narratives, 135, 139, 221, 243, 246
National Consensus Conference on Plant
    Biotechnology, 90
New product committees (in finance),
    192
Non-disclosure, 258
Novelty, politics of, 112

Passarola, 52
Patient Record System, 61, 76
Power, 37, 85, 103, 127, 234, 269
Precaution, 63, 66, 129,144, 155, 190
Predictability, 30, 38, 55, 211
Privacy, 61, 69, 70, 75, 201, 206, 210
    'by design', 77
Procter and Gamble, 10
    Connect + Develop, 10
Product
    financial, 185, 192
    labeling, 157
    Liability Directive, 152
    safety, 151
Public concerns on science and
    technology, 102
Public dialogue
    claims for, 97
    good practice guidelines, 100
    impact on policy, 70, 97, 104
    models of, 88, 220
        honest broker model of, 96
        issue advocate model, 96
        knowledge deficit model, 220
        upstream model, 29, 96, 97, 103,
            221, 247
    motivations for, 38, 94, 160, 220
    professionalization of, 100
    public understanding of science,
        87–9, 220
    uninvited, 98, 220

Rathenau Institute, 71, 88, 176
REACH, 156
Reasonable foreseeability, 34, 124, 154

Reflection, 29, 38, 41, 174
    Reflexive capital, 38
Regulation, 28, 31
    adaptation of, 154
    data before market, 32, 53, 67
    equivalence, 156
    finance, in 187
    frameworks, 145
    General Food, 152
    instruments of, 150
    limitations of, 32–3
    objectives of, 151
    products of, 151
    process, 158
    rationale for, 150
    self -, 149, 154
Research
    funding agencies, 169, 178, 216
    integrity, 31
Responsible development, 39, 166, 250
Responsible innovation
    care and, 35, 37
    deliberation and, 35, 38, 70
    capacity, education and, 44, 215, 271
    definitions of, 36, 39, 63, 82
    dimensions of, 29, 38, 65, 187, 225
    discourses of, 166
    dynamics of, 165
    emergent features of, 44
    examples of, 40
    expectations and, 149
    finance and, 185
    ICT and, 199
    framework for, 27, 63, 203
    governance – see governance
    historical foundations and cognates,
        39, 165
    integration and, 41, 172
    legislative initiatives and, 168
    meta-responsibility as, 201, 214
    motivations and, 38, 135, 226, 234
    multi-level dynamics of, 165
    perceptions of, 208
    policy and, 39, 51, 56, 167, 213
    political and economic dimensions of,
        37, 216

Responsible innovation (*continued*)
  purposes and, 35, 38, 135, 187
  reflection and, 38
  responsiveness and, 35, 38, 235
  soft interventions and, 173
  stage gating and, 42
  transparency and, 78
  umbrella term as, 178
  universities and, 257
  values and, 35, 54, 75, 188
  virtues of, 134
  vision of, 51
Responsibility
  accountability and, 33, 36, 69, 120, 131, 147, 151, 189, 230
  capacity and, 32, 44–5, 123
  care and, 35, 130
  collective, co-responsibility, 30, 46, 59, 68, 70, 127
  conditions for, 200
  consequentialism and, 32, 36, 59, 121–2, 189
  deontological, 53, 120
  dimensions of, 29–30, 35, 81, 147, 187, 200
  emotion and, 129
  etymology of, 121, 147, 200
  gap and innovation, 31
  human rights and, 36, 56
  imputability, 120
  indeterminacy and, 121
  knowledge and, 32–3, 80, 123
  liability, 32, 36, 120, 123, 148, 151, 190
  moral luck and, 28, 34
  moral overload and, 77
  obligation and, 147
  parental, 130
  political, 132
  precaution and, 129
  responsiveness, 35, 70
  reciprocal and non reciprocal, 36, 126
  role and professional, 81, 121, 178, 200, 229
  social ascription as, 200
  subject and object, 81, 200, 215

  trauma and, 128
  vulnerability and, 127, 130
Responsiveness, 29, 35, 38–9, 41, 44, 70, 90, 211, 235
Risk, 29, 144, 152
  adaptive governance and, 145
  assessment, 31, 41, 54, 64, 150, 158
    limits of, 41, 116, 146
  lifecycle, across, 157
    register, 41, 149
  society, 146, 189

SAPPHO, 10
Sarbanes– Oxley Act, 190
Science,
  and technology studies (STS), 241
  autonomy of, 28, 46, 101, 229
Sciencewise, 92–4
Shared value, 19
Silent Spring, 86
Small Talk, 89
Smart metering, 62, 70, 75
Socially responsible investment, 186
Societal challenges, 30, 58, 102, 171
Sociology of expectations, 242
Socio-technical integration, 41, 172, 173
Solar radiation management, 42, 149, 222
  SPICE project, 42, 45, 224
Stage gating, 42, 149, 224
Stakeholders, 14, 38, 43, 60, 65, 67, 146, 176, 191, 216
Standards, labeling and certification, 69, 150, 173, 245
Sustainability, 17, 30, 37, 64, 77
Synthetic biology, 34, 65, 103, 110, 113, 149

Technology assessment, 29, 38, 62, 65, 87, 172, 207, 241
  Constructive, 40, 175
  Real time, 160, 171, 246
Technology forcing, 153
Technology push, 60
Technology readiness levels, 209

Trust, 102, 147
Tyranny of urgency, 159

Uncertain World report, 91
UK Royal Commission on
    Environmental Pollution, 156
US Presidential Commission for the
    Study of Bioethical Issues (PCSBI),
    111

US National Nanotechnology Initiative,
    39, 166, 168, 246, 250

Values, 30, 35, 37, 41, 56, 89, 175
    sensitive design, 37, 75
Voluntary reporting schemes, 154

World Wildlife Fund, 37